Divine Sophia

Divine Sophia

THE WISDOM WRITINGS
OF VLADIMIR SOLOVYOV

Judith Deutsch Kornblatt

INCLUDING ANNOTATED TRANSLATIONS
BY BORIS JAKIM, JUDITH KORNBLATT,
AND LAURY MAGNUS

Cornell University Press   *Ithaca and London*

First published 2009 by Cornell University Press
First printing, Cornell Paperbacks, 2009

Library of Congress Cataloging-in-Publication Data
Solovyov, Vladimir Sergeyevich, 1853–1900.
   [Selections. English. 2009]
   Divine Sophia : the wisdom writings of Vladimir Solovyov /
[edited and annotated by] Judith Deutsch Kornblatt.
      p. cm.
   Includes bibliographical references and index.
   ISBN 978-0-8014-4729-7 (cloth)—
   ISBN 978-0-8014-7479-8 (pbk.)
   1. Wisdom—Religious aspects.   2. Religion—Philosophy.   3. Solovyov, Vladimir
Sergeyevich, 1853–1900—Criticism and interpretation.   I. Kornblatt, Judith Deutsch.   II. Title.
   B4262.A5K67 2009
   231.'6—dc22   2008027724

Cloth printing   10   9   8   7   6   5   4   3   2   1
Paperback printing   10   9   8   7   6   5   4   3   2   1

To my family

Contents

Preface

Divine Sophia: The Wisdom Writings of Vladimir Solovyov examines the ancient/modern figure of Divine Wisdom, aka Sophia and the Eternal Feminine, through an analysis of the writings of the late-nineteenth-century Russian poet and philosopher Vladimir Sergeevich Solovyov (1853–1900). Solovyov's own visions and his later "re-visions" of the Divine Sophia in written form are the culmination of varied verbal as well as visual references to Sophia in the Western tradition beginning in the Bible and Greek philosophy but continuing into the nineteenth century in European romanticism's cult of the eternal feminine. The "Wisdom writings" collected here in turn influenced several generations of poets and philosophers in the pre- and postrevolutionary period in Russia and abroad. Sophia's impact on Russian culture cannot be underplayed, and her appearance in Solovyov's life and work must take its place in the history of Wisdom.

The book is written for a mixed audience and should appeal to a variety of readers both within and outside Russian studies, from those interested in intellectual history, literature, and religious philosophy to spiritual adventurers exploring Sophiology, mysticism, and manifestations of the feminine Divine. Specialists as well as lay readers should find the book useful, for it gathers for the first time in one place a series of otherwise scattered but nonetheless thematically linked texts. Not only is the audience mixed, but, following Solovyov's own lead, so is the genre of this book. The first half is a monograph on Sophia and Solovyov, and the second half presents extensively annotated translations of the texts that underpin the analysis of the first part. In some cases, these translations appear for the very first time in English, and in others they are revised from previously published translations that have appeared in small print runs by Boris Jakim, Laury Magnus, and me.

Recognizing the different needs of various readers, part 1 of the book, "Who Is Solovyov and What Is Sophia?" presents background both on Solovyov and the issues that surrounded him in Russia at the end of the nineteenth century and on the history of Sophia in religion, philosophy, and literature as it was bequeathed to him. The notes explain references to philosophy, history, and geography for those less acquainted with the background and also point toward other studies in both Russian and English for those wishing to explore the subject in more depth.

In part 2, reading guides to each of the annotated translations focus on contextualization and interpretation intended for the beginner and expert alike, while footnotes lead the curious investigator to further sources. By the end of the book, readers will have been introduced to an important cultural phenomenon in modern Russia and will have seen how it developed in its multiple images through the intuition and expression of a major figure in Russian intellectual and artistic life: the odd but immensely popular Solovyov. He, in turn, will be shown to represent and re-present through his diverse texts a complicated but fascinating tradition of Divine Wisdom in the Western world.

I owe many debts for the research and writing of this book. I thank the Institute for Research in the Humanities at the University of Wisconsin, as well as the Wisconsin Alumni Research Foundation (WARF) and the Graduate School for the time and resources I needed to accomplish this project. The latter has provided me with funding for many graduate students through the years, all of whom contributed in some way to my work. For their contributions both large and small, I acknowledge Ann Belyaev, Chad Boutin, Alexandra Evans, Nina Familiant, Anna Guigauri, Ben Jens, Rachel Kilbourn, Leo Livak, Cathy McKenna, Melissa Miller, Betsy Mulet, Naomi Olson, David Polet, Amy Singleton, Dima Spasov, Matt Walker, and Xania Walter.

My teachers in Russian Orthodoxy and religious philosophy along the way also deserve credit, although they share no blame for any wrongheaded interpretations I might have hit upon. They include Richard Gustafson, Paul Valliere, and the late Father John Meyendorff. Father Michael Meerson also contributed many years ago by his introduction to me of the *Sophia* manuscript, and Andrei Kozyrev helped me immensely with his erudition about Solovyov and his tips on negotiating the archives in Moscow. Gary Rosenshield, Patricia Rosenmeyer, Laura McClure, and James McKeown all helped with Greek and Latin references. Patricia Hunt opened up the world of wisdom icons to me, and the librarians at the University of Louisville made available to me the wonderful photo archive of Sophia icons belonging to Donald Fiene. Thank you also to Rabbi Kenneth Katz for his insightful comments on a penultimate draft, to Michael Fox for his wisdom on the Wisdom of the ancient Near East, to my supportive readers and editors at Cornell University Press (especially John Ackerman), and to Lori Hubbard and Jane Roberts for their ongoing support of my research needs. For the latter needs and much,

much more, I extend my loving friendship to Jean Hennessey, who has seen me through several books and lots of angst. I would also not have arrived here without the support of Susan Bernstein, who listens to me endlessly around the track, and who introduced me to the reading room of the British Museum, where Solovyov saw Sophia beneath its gold and azure dome.

And finally, what goes without saying must nonetheless be said: Thank you, Jacob and Louisa, and forgive me for the many distracted meals, the aborted rides here or there, and my frequent answer to your calls that "I can't help with your homework now. I'm doing my own." The help they needed often fell to Marc, to whom I owe it all: Jacob and Louisa, this book, and just about the whole of my wonderful life.

For the final finally: may my parents be proud.

Editorial Method

Note on pronouns: As the following pages will make abundantly clear, Sophia can be male, female, or both at once. "It" would seem the best pronoun to use consistently, if not for the feminine gender of the term for "wisdom" in Greek, Hebrew, and Russian and the consequent strong pull toward personification of Sophia as a woman. Indeed, in some cases "she" is the Eternal Feminine, and despite the abstract nature of that appellation, a neuter pronoun would seem rather bizarre. And indeed, Divine Wisdom is also "he" in a number of contexts. When plausible, this book uses the awkward she/he/it formulation but concedes to the more natural "she" or, less often, "he" when necessary for sense or readability.

Note on translation/transliteration: Solovyov had a standard classical education for his day, including knowledge of Greek and Latin, French, German, and English. He also studied Hebrew during his adult life and was proud to show off his ability in this less familiar language. Translations are provided for non-English terms within the text if Solovyov's own text does not make the meaning of the foreign words clear. Transliteration of Russian words follows the modified Library of Congress system, although names familiar to an educated English-speaking audience are transliterated as usually printed or as most easily pronounced: Dostoevsky rather than Dostoevskii, Tolstoy rather than Tolstoi, Solovyov rather than Solov'ëv.

Note on notes: Notes to part 1 and to the individual translations, as well as the translator's own explanatory notes, appear as regular footnotes. In the translations, notes that Solovyov himself included are indicated with symbols rather than numbers. Source notes for each of the translations are provided at the end of the book. When the text or notes quote from a Solovyov work translated later in the book, the quotation is followed by the reference in the original and the page in part 2.

Permissions

PART I

Revised and expanded version of the entry "Solov'ev" from *Dictionary of Literary Biography: Russian Writers of the Silver Age*, 1st edition by Judith E. Kalb (Editor), J. Alexander Ogden (Editor), I.G. Vishnevetskii (Editor). 2004. Reprinted with permission of Gale, a division of Thomson Learning: www.thomsonrights.com. Fax 800 730-2215.

Mosaic of Christ as Holy Wisdom in Hagia Sophia reprinted with permission of Directmedia Publishing GmbH.

Page from the Divine Liturgy of St. John Chrysostom from the *Orthodox Prayer Book*, 3rd edition (South Canaan, PA: St. Tikhon's Press, 1975), p. 211. Reprinted with permission of St. Tikhon's Press.

Fresco of the Novgorod-Sophia image in the northern apse of the Cathedral of the Dormition in the Moscow Kremlin reprinted from E. S. Smirnova, ed., *Uspenskii sobor moskovskogo kremlia: materialy i issledovaniia* (Moscow: Nauka, 1985). Reprinted with permission of Nauka RAN.

Diagram of the Kabbalistic *sefirot* depicted as Adam Kadmon from Charles Ponce, *Kabbalah* (Wheaton, IL: Theosophical Publishing House, 1973). Reprinted with permission of Quest Books, imprint of the Theosophical Publishing House (www.questbooks.net).

Automatic writing by Solovyov reprinted with permission of the Russian State Archive of Literature and Art (RGALI).

PART 2

Revised versions of Solovyov's *Poems of Sophia* and *The White Lily* reprinted with permission of the Variable Press.

Diagrams from *The Sophia* and "Fragments," published in V. S. Solov'ev, *PSS*, 2: 93, 129, 164, 172, and 178, reprinted with permission of Nauka RAN.

Revised versions of Solovyov's *Lectures on Divine Humanity* reprinted with permission of Lindisfarne Press.

Revised version of *Three Encounters* from *The Silver Age: Russian Literature and Culture 1881–1921*, 2 (1999), reprinted with permission of Charles Schlacks.

PART I

Who Is Solovyov and What Is Sophia?

Regaining consciousness, I saw only the bright sunlight, a strip of blue sky, and bending over me in that light, and against the sky, the image of a beautiful woman. . . . It was as though my entire existence—all my thoughts, feelings, and desires—had melted and flowed together into a single, endless, sweet, bright, and dispassionate sensation. A single wondrous image was motionlessly reflected in that sensation, as in a pure mirror, and I felt and knew that in that one was all.

VLADIMIR SOLOVYOV, "At the Dawn of Misty Youth"

Introduction: Visions and Re-Visions of Sophia

My tsaritsa appeared to me
Today, wrapped all in azure.—
My heart beat with a sweet delight,
And in the rays of approaching day
My soul shone with a quiet light.
While smoldering in the distance
Rose the fierce flame of earthly fire.

    Vladimir Solovyov, "U tsaritsy moei est' vysokii dvorets"

In January 1878, in the cold, gray Russian capital of St. Petersburg, the young philosopher Vladimir Sergeevich Solovyov delivered the first of his twelve *Lectures on Divine Humanity* (*Chteniia o bogochelovechestve*, 1878–80). Notables in attendance at his lectures included the writers Fedor Dostoevsky and Lev Tolstoy, as well as Konstantin Pobedonostsev, who was then tutor to the tsarevich and soon-to-be lay head of the Russian Orthodox Church. For this audience of intellectuals and imperial officials, Solovyov propounded a vast metaphysics, a cosmology, and a history of religion that were based on his extensive reading in classical and Western philosophy. Such a public event in itself is noteworthy, and the fiery-eyed Solovyov's appearance on the Petersburg scene indeed produced notices in many of the local papers. Even more significant, however, was the impact of the words of this precocious thinker—academic philosopher, poet, and public gadfly—on the next century of readers at home and abroad. The Silver Age poets Blok, Bely, Ivanov, and Kuzmin[1] and the Sophiologists Florensky and Bulgakov,[2] not to a mention a new generation of post-Soviet readers, are all indebted to the sometimes odd, often audacious, and always provocative ideas of Vladimir Solovyov.

---

1. The principal Symbolist poets of the so-called second generation who saw themselves as heirs to Solovyov include V. I. Ivanov (1866–1949); Andrei Belyi (pseudonym of B. N. Bugaev, 1880–1934); A. A. Blok (1880–1921); and a somewhat lesser poet, Solovyov's nephew, S. M. Solovyov (1895–1942). The early poetry of Mikhail Kuzmin (1875–1936) is also considered Symbolist, although his later work is more often labeled Acmeist. Like Solovyov, he traveled to Egypt and wrote an important cycle called "Sophia."

2. P. A. Florensky (1882–1943) directly acknowledged his debt to Solovyov and even affected the long-haired demeanor of his mentor. He remained in Russia after the Bolshevik Revolution and insisted on continuing to wear his priest's cassock. Florensky wrote his later works from prison camp in Siberia. S. N. Bulgakov (1871–1944) was expelled from the Soviet Union in 1922 and went to Prague and then Paris, where he helped found l'Institut de Théologie Orthodoxe Saint-Serge that propagated many of Solovyov's ideas in the West. During his final years, Bulgakov's Sophiology led to accusations of heresy by many in the Orthodox establishment, but his publications in French and English helped spread the teaching through the West.

Perhaps unbeknownst to many of his new acolytes but never far from the consciousness of his later "heirs," Solovyov's views grew equally from scholarly readings *and* from intimate visitations by the Divine Wisdom, or Sophia.[3] In *Three Encounters* (*Tri svidaniia*, 1898), a narrative poem written twenty years after the *Lectures*, Solovyov claims to have had three personal visions of a woman with azure eyes and a radiant aura, who nodded and spoke directly to him: once in a Moscow church, once in the Reading Room of the British Museum in London, and finally, less than two years before his *Lectures*, after he had awakened from a night of troubled sleep on the desert sands outside Cairo. Solovyov's visions, if indeed they occurred—or rather, in whatever sense we can understand them to have occurred—arose in his own consciousness from his own intimate experiences, unique to him. That they occurred there and then, however, and as they did, depended equally on the more general circumstances of a creative intellectual in late imperial Russia and on a millennia-old tradition of Divine Wisdom in Western culture as a whole.

This book examines one man's attempt to articulate one type of mystical intuition in one cultural context. Yet that one man had a profound impact as both accumulator and propagator of cultural imagery at an intellectually, as well as creatively, turbulent time in Russia and Europe. Solovyov's influence on the next generation of Russian intellectuals of all stripes cannot be understated. The Russian poets, writers, theologians, and philosophers who were forced into exile by the Bolshevik Revolution brought Solovyovian ideas to their new homes, new academies, new presses, and new international contacts in Prague, Berlin, Paris, and other capitals around the world. According to Sergei Bulgakov, writing in 1905, "To understand, master, and absorb Solovyov is the first and ensuing task set before contemporary Russian thought" (Bulgakov, "Po povodu" 367). Six years later, Bulgakov returned to Solovyov's legacy: "Thanks to the multifaceted nature of his philosophy, the name of Solovyov unites people from a variety of spiritual pasts and presents—philosophers and poets, sociologists and natural scientists, Marxists and decadents, priests and laymen, the right and the left. Every person finds *his own* road to him, receives answers to *his own* questions, distinguishes his or her favorite motif within the sonorous chord" (Bulgakov, "Priroda v filosofii Vl. Solov'eva" i; emphasis in original). And according to the Symbolist theoretician and poet, Viacheslav Ivanov, Vladimir Solovyov was "the true *educator* of our religious aspirations, a lyricist of Orpheus, the bearer of the principle of creative order." Nonetheless, "ten years after his death, we are engaged in neither the continuation nor the perfection of his task, but again only in its search" (Ivanov, "O Znachenii Vl. Solov'eva" 34; emphasis in original).

---

3. Michel Grabar agrees with the importance of the mystical visions for Solovyov's philosophy: "Si, par la rigueur de ses ouvrages philosophiques, Solov'ëv est en droit d'être considéré comme le précurseur théorique majeur de la philosophie religieuse du tournant du vingtième siècle, on ne doit cependant pas penser que son oeuvre sort toute armée de sa culture philosophique. Il y a dans la genèse de l'oeuvre de Solov'ëv une racine érotique et mystique qu'il serait fâcheux de passer sous silence" (147).

Solovyov's writings, what I call his verbal "re-visions" of the personal visions he claimed to have had in his youth, spurred his heirs in both Sophiology and modernist poetry to adopt the figure of Sophia for their descriptions of the interaction—or "economy," to use Bulgakov's term—of the divine and human worlds. Religious philosophers such as Fathers Florensky and Bulgakov devoted a large part of their theological writings to Sophia.[4] Ivanov based many of his theories of art and the symbol on Solovyov's abstract discussions of Sophia as a mediator and unifier.[5]

Ivanov's fellow Symbolists, Andrei Bely and Alexander Blok, as well as Solovyov's own nephew, Sergei Solovyov, all turned to Sophia for inspiration in their poetry, and in the name of Sophia they created a short-lived love triangle among Blok, Bely, and Blok's wife, Liubov' Mendeleeva. Blok's first book of verse, *Verses on a Beautiful Lady* (*Stikhi o prekrasnoi dame,* 1904), draws directly on the figure of the "beautiful" Sophia. Likewise, Bely's first collection, *Gold in Azure* (*Zoloto v lazuri,* 1904), takes its title from the colors most frequently associated by Solovyov with his visions of Divine Wisdom. The Symbolist revision of Solovyov's re-visions proved more abstract than Solovyov's multivalent expressions of Sophia and soon became debased in images such as Blok's famous "Stranger" (*Neznakomka,* 1906). That Blok's beautiful woman in the latter poem turns out to be a prostitute suggests the Symbolists' disillusionment at their inability to create a bridge from mundane reality to the spiritual world of Beauty. It does not disprove Sophia's own ability to do so.

Later twentieth-century Russian writers also took up the figure of Sophia, adopting and adapting her for their own aesthetic and spiritual reasons. Perhaps the most extreme example is the mystical novel/revelation/treatise, *The Rose of the World* (*Roza mira,* publ. 1989, 1991), by Daniil Andreev. And through the medium of Sergei Bulgakov, Solovyov's Sophia also became known to a visionary as far-flung as the Trappist monk Thomas Merton (1915–68), who claims to have seen her in a dream in 1958 in his Kentucky monastery in the guise of a young Jewish girl named "Proverb" (Groberg, "Sweet Yielding Consent of Sophia"). With the advent of *glasnost'* and the later collapse of the Soviet Union, Solovyov's own visions became widely

---

4. See Florensky's "Letter Ten: Sophia," in *The Pillar and Ground of the Truth* and virtually all of Bulgakov's writings, including his *Philosophy of Economy* (*Filosofiia khoziastva*). A succinct discussion of Sophia by Bulgakov can be found in *Sophia the Wisdom of God: An Outline of Sophiology.* See also the works of many of Solovyov's other "heirs," including N. A. Berdiaev (1874–1948) and S. L. Frank (1877–1950).

5. See for example, Ivanov's "Thoughts on Symbolism": "If art in general is one of the most powerful means of human union, then it is possible to say about symbolist art that the principle of activity is union par excellence, union in the direct and deepest meaning of that word. In truth, it not only unites, it weds. Two elements are wed by a third and higher element. The symbol, this third element is like the rainbow, blazing between the verbal ray and the dewdrops of the soul that reflects the ray. . . . And Jacob's ladder rises from each work of truly symbolist art.

"Symbolism weds consciousnesses in such a way that together they give birth 'in beauty'" (Ivanov, "Mysli o Simvolizme,"149).

known among the Russian intelligentsia, and his works have gone through multiple republications in the past twenty years.

Approaching an answer to the question of "Who is Solovyov?" posed in this first half of the book, we might begin by a comparison with a contemporary figure closer to the American tradition but unique within it, just as Solovyov was within his: the psychologist and philosopher William James. Solovyov, who died in 1900, could not have read about visions and mystical experience in James's influential *Varieties of Religious Experience*, for the latter was not published until 1902 and not translated into Russian until 1910. But the American philosopher was already well known in Solovyov's day for his writings on psychology, many of them published in the journal *Problems of Philosophy and Psychology* (*Voprosy Filosofii i Psikhologii*), of which Solovyov was one of the original founders in 1889. In addition, James had personally met Nikolai Grot, a close friend of Solovyov and the head of the Moscow Psychological Society and editor of its journal. The amiable meeting took place in Paris in August 1889, at the Congress of Physiological Psychology in Paris. Grot brought back his interest in James to his Moscow colleagues, Solovyov among them. As the editors of the collection *William James in Russian Culture* assess,

> James arrived in Russia originally at a propitious moment. The social and political turmoil of the 1890s and early 1900s was matched by ferment in the country's intellectual, artistic, and spiritual life. It is hardly news by now that the period 1890–1910 was a time of brilliant cultural productivity there. It was also an era of renewed activity in philosophy, when resurgent idealism energetically challenged the positivist cult of scientific facts. . . . James's psychology went against the grain for some, while others saw its author as the pioneer of a third way between positivism and idealism. (Grossman and Rischlin 2–3)

Solovyov's challenge to positivism, not to mention his mystical visions, preceded rather than followed the promulgation of James's writings in Europe and Russia. Indeed, James's involvement with the London Society for Psychical Research postdated Solovyov's investigation of the psychic scene in the English capital by some ten years. If not influence, however, we can certainly talk of an intellectual and perhaps even spiritual affinity and of a similar mixture of intellectual skepticism and visceral fascination with the irrational in both thinkers, Russian and American.

James called himself a "piecemeal supernaturalist." "If one should make a division of all thinkers into naturalists and supernaturalists," he writes in the postscript to his *Varieties of Religious Experience*,

> I should undoubtedly have to go, along with most philosophers, into the supernaturalist branch. But there is a crasser and a more refined supernaturalism, and it is to the refined division that most philosophers at the present day belong. If not regular transcendental idealists, they at least obey the Kantian direction enough to bar out ideal entities from interfering causally in the course of phenomenal

events. Refined supernaturalism is universalistic supernaturalism; for the "crasser" variety "piecemeal" supernaturalism would perhaps be the better name. It went with that older theology which to-day is supposed to reign only among uneducated people, or to be found among the few belated professors of the dualisms which Kant is thought to have displaced. It admits miracles and providential leadings, and finds no intellectual difficulty in mixing the ideal and the real worlds together by interpolating influences from the ideal region among the forces that causally determine the real world's details. (409–10)

Had James known Solovyov, he would no doubt have included the Russian in his short list of contemporary "piecemeal supernaturalists." The Russian visionary's multiple expressions of a figure he identified as Sophia live side-by-side with a loud belly laugh, his serious academic writings, and a bold public persona. Solovyov's visions of Sophia, like James's writings on the spirit, remain fully grounded in the mundane world of reality. Solovyov's various re-visions of Sophia in written form make full use of all aspects of that material world, including the variety of verbal genres with which we articulate our thoughts, feelings, and beliefs; the sometimes crude humor that accompanies those feelings; and the visual and aural stimuli that excite our senses as well as our spirits. He wrote continually about Sophia throughout his career not only because he sought the one appropriate but elusive verbalization of his visual experience, but also because he knew that Divine Wisdom is not only one, but many; not only his, but all. Both individual and universal, Sophia is the bridge between opposites, and more: the transfigurer of them both.

But what, really, *is* Sophia, if she—or as we will see, sometimes he or it—is so many things at once? Prior to *Lectures on Divine Humanity*, Solovyov wrote several untitled poems inspired by his visions[6] and completed most of, but never published, a manuscript in French that features a character named Sophie.[7] Solovyov introduces Sophia by that name publicly for the first time, however, only in lecture 7 of his popular presentations:

In the divine organism of Christ, the acting, unifying principle, the principle that expresses the unity of that which absolutely is, is obviously the Word, or Logos. The second kind of unity, *the produced unity, is called Sophia* in Christian theosophy. If we distinguish in the Absolute in general between the Absolute as such (that which absolutely is) and its content, essence, or idea, we will find the former directly expressed in the Logos and the latter directly expressed in Sophia, which is thus the *expressed or actualized idea*. And just as an existent

6. In these poems, translated below, Solovyov refers to the beautiful figure of his "dreams" as *tsaritsa* (empress) or *boginia* (goddess), not specifically as Sophia or Wisdom, but the identity is obvious.

7. This manuscript, as a whole entitled *The Sophia*, contains both dialogic and monologic segments. It remained unfinished, and was not published for another one hundred years, despite the fact that Solovyov called it the basis of all of his future work. Except for small segments, the translation into English in part 2 is the first.

being is distinct from its own idea but is at the same time one with it, so the *Logos, too, is distinct from Sophia but is inwardly united with her.* (SS 3:115; emphasis added; see page 176)[8]

In an earlier section of this lecture, Solovyov asserts that we can speak of the Absolute as both a "divine" and "universal organism" that is at once the most universal and the most individual of all organisms, for it is the All. "Multiplicity reduced to unity," he tells us, "is wholeness." And "the universality of an entity stands in direct relation to its individuality: the more universal it is, the more individual it will be. Therefore, the absolutely universal entity will be an absolutely individual entity" (SS 3:113, 114). He calls the individual entity, or the actualized expression of the absolutely existent God, by the name Christ. But just as the Absolute, which is one, can be looked at in two ways, as universal (the Absolute) or as individual (Christ), we see in the quotation above that Christ, too, can be looked at in two ways. Christ is both Logos and Sophia. These are not two different names for Christ, nor are they two different, discrete manifestations. Insofar as Christ is the "acting, unifying principle," he is the Word. But insofar as he is, at the same time, that which is produced by the action, he is Sophia. The reader should not be concerned if this explanation does not satisfy. Having introduced Sophia to his Russian colleagues at this lecture in 1878, Solovyov spent most of the rest of his career trying to articulate her in a variety of different genres and discourses.[9] The content of her definition, as we will have a chance to explore in the second half of this book, is as multivalent as the forms. We should not be convinced, for example, that Sophia is always passive, despite the straightforwardness of the declaration on unity in the quotation above. Sometimes she is quite an active person . . . or principle . . . or energy. It is not at all obvious who or what she is nor how and why she is.[10] Still, we cannot lay all the blame for the confusion on the proliferation of Solovyov's own pronouncements. By the time of Solovyov's alleged first vision as a child in the middle of the nineteenth century, Sophia had already had a long and contradictory history in Western and Russian culture. It is this history that part 1 of this book explores.

8. Wherever possible, quotations from Solovyov in the text are from *Polnoe sobranie sochinenii* (*PSS*), of which three volumes have appeared to date. Other citations refer to *Sobranie sochinenii V.S. Solov'eva* (*SS*), the second edition of Solovyov's collected works edited by S. M. Solovyov and E. L. Radlov, reproduced by the publisher Zhizn' s Bogom in Brussels with two additional volumes; *Pis'ma Vladimira Sergeevicha Solov'eva* (*Pis'ma*), also appended to the Brussels edition; and *Stikhotvoreniia i shutochnye p'esy* (*Stikhotvoreniia*), edited by Z. Mints and included in the Biblioteka poeta series. Translations are my own and/or refer to translated texts in the second part of this book where appropriate.

9. "One of the most fascinating features of Solov'ëv's writings is found in his unwavering search for a way to express this sophianic intuition" (de Courten 208).

10. Copelston, who has done much to popularize Russian religious philosophy, although sometimes ignoring its nuances, agrees: "We cannot find one single consistent use of the word Sophia, or Wisdom, even in the writings of Solovyev, who is credited with being the first Russian philosopher to develop the subject" (*Russian Religious Philosophy* 82).

Solovyov elaborates on his definition of Sophia immediately after his first mention in *Lectures* by calling her "God's body, the matter of Divinity," explaining in a footnote that "I use such words as *body* and *matter* in the most general sense, as relative categories. I am not connecting them with those particular representations that can be applied to our material world but are absolutely inapplicable to Divinity" (*SS* 3:115; see page 176). Nonetheless, he has now associated Sophia with both the divine world and the natural, or produced, one. She is both an "idea" that "God has before Him in His work of creation" and the actualization of that idea (*SS* 3:115; see page 177).[11]

Later in *Lectures*, Solovyov is even more explicit about the paradox, calling Sophia both the eternal body of God and the eternal soul of the world. As such, she *is bogochelovechestvo* (*SS* 3:127; see page 184), that is, the name for the very concept he is introducing into Russian culture through his *Lectures on Divine Humanity*: the real interaction of God and humanity that is variously translated as Godmanhood, Divine-Humanity, or the Humanity of God.[12] He suggests other definitions for Sophia as well, associating her simultaneously with both the divine or ideal and the created worlds: "the principle (or beginning) of humanity," "the ideal or normal" human being, "perfect humanity," the realization of the divine principle, the image and likeness of the divine principle, archetypal humankind, one and all, the real form of Divinity, all-one humankind, and the mediator between the multiplicity of living entities and the absolute unity of Divinity (*SS* 3:140–41; see page 188). In fact, Sophia's definition is both too much and too little determined in this work, as it remains throughout his oeuvre. We cannot begin to know who or what she is until we analyze each of the definitions in context, until we parse her contradictions and multiple articulations. Is she divine as well as created? Is she the same as the World Soul, its reverse face, its pre-fallen form, or something else entirely? Is she the same in poetry and in prose, in philosophy and in farce? All these questions are important for an understanding of modern Russia, for Solovyov bequeathed his Sophia to the next generation of Russian writers and thinkers, and they, in turn, embedded her firmly in Russian culture of the twentieth century. Even the Marxist-Leninist materialism of the Soviet period did not uproot

11. This definition of Wisdom as primal idea of God derives from Proverbs 8:22–23: "The Lord created me at the beginning of his way,/ at the start of his works of old./ In primeval days I was formed,/ at the start, at the world's origin." English quotations from Proverbs will rely on the comprehensive translations of Michael Fox. Variations and possible mistranslations of these verses will be discussed below.

12. Many have pointed out that the traditional translation of "Godmanhood" is too static, not to mention too gendered to convey the full meaning of *bogochelovechestvo*, for Solovyov understood divine-human interaction as a continuing process of creation and salvation for all of humankind and, indeed, for all the natural world. "Divine Humanity" puts, perhaps, too much emphasis on one side of the equation, the "Humanity of God" too much on the other. The best discussion of the term is found in Valliere 11–15. Valliere favors the "Humanity of God" and takes as his surprising ally Roland Barth: "Since God in His deity is human, [theological] culture must occupy itself neither with God in Himself nor with man in himself but with the man-encountering God and the God-encountering man and with their dialogue and history, in which their communion takes place and comes to fulfillment" (55).

her entirely, and her branches continue to grow now, over a century after Solovyov's death. What is more, Solovyov's Sophia is herself a bequest from any
number of intellectual and religious traditions that made their way into Russia
before his birth and found there a convergence with other, more native aspects
of Russian culture. Solovyov's own visions—or rather, his attempts at an articulation in verbal form of what is otherwise an ineffable mystical experience—in
many ways can be seen as the watershed moment for the multiple manifestations of Wisdom in modern culture.

In its first part, this book examines the rich historical and cultural bequest
to Solovyov in Russia in the second half of the nineteenth century. We will see
that no one tradition fully explains the poet-philosopher's discussions of Divine Wisdom, but each contributes vocabulary, terminology, and authenticity
to Solovyov's varied attempts to articulate his visions in verbal form. The second part of the book analyzes each of Solovyov's Sophianic works in turn,
presenting translations of all the important texts in which she occurs for readers to experience his expressions of Divine Wisdom themselves. Extensive
notes point the specialist reader back to the original and to other scholarship
in the areas of Russian intellectual history, religious philosophy, and the history and philosophy of religion in general. The reading guides to each selection
are designed for all readers, lay and expert alike, who are interested not only in
Solovyov and Russia but in questions of mysticism, the Eternal Feminine, and
the Spirit. Many notes to the translations help readers with little knowledge of
Russia and Russian to place the texts presented against a broader background.
This book for the first time presents Solovyov's Sophia as a whole, allowing us
to enter more deeply into the life and works of this major visionary, philosopher, poet, and public intellectual. It explains Solovyov's influence on modern
Russian culture[13] and shows how his Sophia does or, in some instances, does
not fit into the historical tradition of Divine Wisdom.

Justifying his introduction into *Lectures* of a new name—Sophia—with its
complex of determinations, Solovyov reminds his audience that the figure
has long ago been identified by Solomon in the apocryphal book The Wisdom
of Solomon, and again as a personified Wisdom through the Hebrew term
Hokhmah in the canonical book of Proverbs (Prov. 8 and 9). Furthermore, she,
or in this case, he, is identified with Christ by Paul in First Corinthians: "Christ
the Power of God, and the Wisdom of God" (1 Cor. 1:23–31).[14] Does this appeal to biblical authority or authorities explain Sophia to his readers or only
further confuse? Is she/he an azure-eyed female person, an attribute of God, or

---

13. Solovyov's interests—and influence—extended far beyond Sophia, and his impact in
law, ethics, civil rights, and other areas was equally strong. Those subjects are beyond the scope
of this book.

14. See also Luke for less abstract associations between the quality of wisdom and Jesus:
Luke 2:40: "And the child grew, and waxed strong in spirit, filled with wisdom"; and 2:52: "And
Jesus increased in wisdom and stature, and in favor with God and man."

a coequal in creation? On several occasions, Solovyov had to defend himself against accusations of bringing a fourth, female hypostasis into the Trinity[15] and had to differentiate her from several close acquaintances named, perhaps not coincidentally, Sophia. The Sophias include his older friend, Sophia Tolstaia, his contemporaries Sophia Khitrovo and Sophia Martynova, and one self-proclaimed "Sophia," Anna Shmidt. The latter offered herself as partner to Solovyov: she as Divine Wisdom incarnate, he as Logos.[16] Ultimately, Solovyov's multifaceted Sophia is his own: a verbal incarnation of his personal visions. They are clearly informed by a host of earlier religious and literary traditions, including the biblical ones he cites here, as well as by Neoplatonism, early Christian Gnosticism, Russian and Byzantine iconography and liturgy, the Jewish Kabbalah, various medieval and later Protestant mystical seers, and the romantic cult of the Eternal Feminine. However, he takes these traditions, which confirmed and possibly in some cases induced his own mystical visions, and then remembers/reviews/re-creates Sophia anew in a series of different genres (poetry, prose, drama), discourses (philosophy, fiction), and modes (humorous, serious), all of which he bestows on the next generation of Russian and European readers.

As we will see, Solovyov's audacious combination of humor and mysticism, of sexuality and sacred vision, of fiction and spiritual truth, all raise fascinating questions about who or what Divine Wisdom is. The modern Russian fascination with her as a manifestation of the Eternal Feminine further questions her gender, for in many ways "she" appears in Byzantine iconography as male (Christ the Wisdom of God), and the Kabbalistic use of the term *Hokhmah* on which she is partly based, despite the grammatical feminine gender of that noun, is also male. Solovyov plays with the interaction of spirit and matter in Sophia, just as he plays with the interaction of gender and with the tension between religious philosophy and literary genres. And as Solovyov himself participated in many of the various intellectual debates, artistic movements, and social questions of the late imperial period in Russia and in modern Europe as a whole, Sophia also partakes in all these contexts. Before examining them, we turn first to a biographical survey of Solovyov's life and works so that we might understand his unique perspective on the traditions he absorbed and the contemporary issues in which he was engaged.[17]

---

15. See, for example, the preface to the third edition of his poetry, where Solovyov declares with ironically inflated rhetoric: "These [the poems "Das Ewig-Weibliche" and *Three Encounters*] might give occasion for some to accuse me of a pernicious heresy" (SS 12:4).

16. See S. Solov'ev, *Zhizn' i tvorcheskaia evoliutsiia*, 399–401; *Vladimir Solovyov*, trans. Gibson, 513–15; also see Bulgakov, "Vladimir Solov'ev i Anna Shmidt" 71–114; Kravchenko, "Religiozno-misticheskie otkroveniia A. N. Shmidt v kontekste problem 'russkogo dukhovnogo vozrozhdeniia' i 'novogo religioznogo soznaniia,'" in *Mistitsizm* 156–77; and Kravchenko, *Vestniki* 183–93.

17. The following biography is adapted and expanded from the author's entry on Solovyov in the *Dictionary of Literary Biography* 593:377–86.

THE "LIFE DRAMA" OF SOLOVYOV

> In *The Life Drama of Plato*, Solovyov describes the creative work of the Greek
> philosopher as a tragedy whose main hero turns out to be himself. There is a
> hidden resemblance between the fate of Plato and the fate of his Russian student.
>
> KONSTANTIN MOCHUL'SKII, *Vladimir Solov'ev: Zhizn' i uchenie*

> He was a mystic, a poet, a prankster . . . , a commentator, and along with all that,
> in deep harmony with all that, he was a first-class scholar and tireless thinker.
>
> V. V. ROZANOV, "Pamiati Vl. Solov'eva"

Vladimir Sergeevich Solovyov (also transliterated as Solov'ev, Solovёv, Soloviev, Solowjew, Solov'jov, Solovieff, and Solovioff)[18], was born into a large,
comfortable family of Moscow intellectuals in January of 1853. His mother,
Poliksena Vladimirovna, was by all accounts an extremely pious noblewoman
and a distant relation to Grigorii Skovoroda, the famous Ukrainian poet and
religious philosopher.[19] She was a powerful master of the household, kept the
many Solovyov siblings on speaking terms, and maintained a constant correspondence with Solovyov throughout her life. Solovyov's father, Sergei
Mikhailovich, was professor, dean, and then rector of Moscow University and
acclaimed historian and author of the multivolume *History of Russia from
Ancient Times (Istoriia Rossii s drevneishikh vremen,* 1851–79). Despite the
fact that an academic career moved Sergei Mikhailovich away from the Church
(his own father was an Orthodox priest) and no doubt under the influence of
Poliksena Vladimirovna, the family largely continued its traditional practices.
Sergei Mikhailovich reputedly would attend the Italian opera on Saturday
night and the Divine Liturgy the next morning. His son Volodia, as his family
called him, was thus exposed to Orthodox ritual and doctrine as well as to a
secular worldview as a child, and he returned to the Church as an adult, albeit
in a way transformed by the social and philosophical debates of his day.

Solovyov grew up at a time when German idealist philosophy, first discussed widely in Russia in the 1830s, had already become entrenched in the
university where his father taught. An equally important influence, stemming
from the same source, was the continuing Slavophile-Westernizer debate begun in the 1830s, including the question of nationalism and the mission of the
Russian people that had first taken root in the romantic period.[20] The writers

18. In the Signature Book at the British Museum, Solovyov signed "Solovioff Vladimir" for
library ticket #5284 on July 14, 1875 (Central Archives British Museum). Unfortunately, the
record of which books he requested at the library no longer exists.

19. G. S. Skovoroda (1722–94) wrote religious and philosophical discourses, Platonic-style
dialogues, poems, musical compositions, and translations.

20. Much has been written about the philosophical disagreements between the Slavophiles
and Westernizers in the first half of the nineteenth century. Both loosely affiliated groups had their
origins in the study of the German Idealists—Hegel, Schelling, Fichte—and both sought answers
to what has been referred to as the "accursed question": Whither Russia? The former group
looked to traditional Russian values for its answer, including a rebirth of interest in Russian

Kireevsky, Khomiakov, Chaadaev, and Belinsky all played a role in Solovyov's intellectual heritage.[21] Furthermore, like his older friend and confidant, Dostoevsky, Solovyov was as aware of current events as of theoretical debates.[22] Alexander II's "Great Reforms" in the 1860s,[23] the ensuing social and economic instability, a series of difficult and sometimes humiliating wars, an increasing threat from Turkey that ultimately led to war in the Balkans and aroused "Pan-Slavic" nationalism, and the related revolutionary movements of the sixties and seventies all affected the young religious philosopher's understanding of the meaning of Orthodox Russia. More generally, it enhanced his sense of the responsibility of humans toward one another and of humanity toward the rest of the created world.

Solovyov first entered the Faculty of History and Philology at Moscow University in 1869, probably with strong encouragement from his historian father. Like many young people in the 1860s, however, Solovyov fell under the sway of positivism and utilitarianism and quickly transferred to the more "materialist" Faculty of Physics and Mathematics. The decision proved to be a mistake, for after nearly three years of course work, Solovyov petitioned to withdraw from his studies. At the same time, he applied to take examinations for the degree of *kandidat* back in the Faculty of History and Philology, and, as a mark of both his talent and his audacity, he received his degree in June of 1873 without completing any classes as an official student of that faculty. A year and a half later he defended his master's thesis, "The Crisis of Western Philosophy (Against the Positivists)" ("Krizis zapadnoi filosofii [protiv pozitivistov]," 1874), which, despite his earlier materialist interests, aimed to prove that modern philosophy had reached its end point and that humanity required a new synthesis based on religious principles to continue its teleological path.

Solovyov completed the thesis while pursuing an unusual project for a young man of that skeptical day. In the summer of 1873, Vladimir wrote to his cousin Katia—one of many with whom he admitted to being serially infatuated—with the news that he would soon reside at the monasteries of Sergiev Posad, about

---

Orthodoxy, while the latter looked to the West as a model for Russia's future. For a short introduction, see Jakim and Bird 7–25. For more detailed discussion, see the standard studies by Walicki cited in the bibliography.

21. A. S. Khomiakov (1804–60) and I. V. Kireevskii (1806–56) were the principal theoreticians of Slavophilism in the 1830s. Both opposed what they considered the Westernism of P. Ia. Chaadaev (1794–1856), as expressed in the latter's famous Philosophical Letters. Despite their negative assessment, they too developed some of Chaadaev's more nationalist ideas. V. G. Belinskii (1811–48), often cited as the primary Westernizer, was an influential literary and social critic of the 1830s and 1840s.

22. See Kostalevsky for a discussion of the unlikely friendship and sharing of ideas between the famous novelist and much younger Solovyov.

23. Alexander II, tsar from 1855 until his assassination in 1881, instituted a series of reforms of the judiciary system, the schools, the military, and local and municipal governance; revised censorship practices; and, perhaps most famously, abolished serfdom in 1861. These reforms, although necessary for the modernization of Russia in the context of Europe in the second half of the nineteenth century, proved immensely destabilizing and served as backdrop for the growing revolutionary movement in the late imperial period.

forty miles from Moscow (*Pis'ma* 3:91). In the fall of that year, he indeed moved the short distance from his parents' home in order to audit courses at the Moscow Theological Academy.[24] It is generally considered that Solovyov was attracted to the academy because of his growing spiritual, even mystical consciousness, but his continuing interest in Western philosophy may also have played a role; the extremely conservative secular university had provided him only limited access to primary philosophical texts, many of which were readily available in Sergiev Posad. The theological training available at the academy, as well as the exposure to mysticism prevalent among the monks at Sergiev Posad may have been, initially, of secondary importance.

Solovyov's early biographer, S. M. Luk'ianov, cites a letter from Pavel Floren-sky, who became a professor at the academy in the early twentieth century: "It seems to me that Solovyov entered the academy simply for theology and church history. But then, having come across the idea of Sophia, as it already existed in his soul, he left the academy and theology entirely and occupied himself solely with Sophia. Or at least that is my guess. It would be very interesting to verify it" (Luk'ianov, *O Vl. S. Solov'eve v ego molodye gody* 1:344 n. 662).[25]

Whatever the primary reasons for Solovyov's interest in the Theological Academy, whether as cause or effect, we know that it coincided with a turn toward mystical speculation. Having taught less than a year as docent at Moscow University and at the V. I. Ger'e (Vladimir Guerrier) Higher Courses for Women, Solovyov in 1875 applied for permission to travel to London, where it would be possible to study "Indian, Gnostic, and medieval philosophy," as he wrote in his formal request for a leave, as well as to participate in the English occult scene (see Luk'ianov, *O Vl. S. Solov'eve v ego molodye gody* 3/1:64). Some believe that the trip abroad was precipitated by an unsuccessful proposal of marriage to one of his students, Elizaveta Polivanova, but there is little evidence for this supposition.[26]

Once in London, Solovyov sought out the active spiritualist community, much as William James had done on his trips to England in the following decades. We have strong evidence that the young and somewhat wild-looking

24. The Moscow Theological Academy (*Moskovskaia dukhovnaia akademiia i seminariia*) was founded in 1685 and moved to the Trinity-Sergei Monastery in Sergiev Posad (renamed Zagorsk during the Soviet period) two years after the burning of Moscow in 1812. It is currently the seat of the Russian Patriarchate.

25. Luk'ianov's biography is still the most thorough of all works on Solovyov's life, although it covers only the years until 1875. It is divided into three parts, with the first published in volume 1, the second and the first section of part 3 published in the second volume, and the last half of the third part published in volume 3. The third part will be cited as 3/1 (published in volume 2, and 3/2 (published in volume 3).

26. A number of biographers remark on this failed affair, although others focus more on Solovyov's estrangement from earthly concerns. The biographer who sees the most passion in Solovyov's life is Konstantin Mochul'skii. Olga Matich makes a strong case as well for Solo-vyov's libido, citing erotic verse as well as a letter of 1897 in which Solovyov writes that he broke the biblical commandment against adultery (see Matich 79–80 and 292 nn. 50–52).

Russian attended a number of séances in London and indulged in bouts of automatic writing, during which spirits (principally Sophia herself) spoke to him through his own pen. His long hair, heavy brows, lean form, and increasing disregard for his outward appearance must have struck an unusual chord in formal, even if occult-leaning Victorian England. His command of English, as well as a variety of other European languages, must also have made a strong impression on his hosts. In addition to social activities, Solovyov was seen immersed in Kabbalistic and occult texts at the British Museum, where, he claims, he experienced his second mystical vision of what he came to call the "Divine Sophia," or "Premudrost'" and "Bozhestvennaia Sofiia" in Russian. According to the poem *Three Encounters*, Solovyov had first seen Sophia during a church service while contemplating his childish infatuation with a young girl. As the royal doors of the iconostasis opened, he was suddenly overwhelmed by "Azure around me, azure within my soul." In London in 1875, again according to the poem, the face of Sophia appeared to the young mystic, as before infused with golden azure, and ordered him to seek her in Egypt. His third vision of Sophia occurred in the Sahara, where he had gone, according to a letter to his mother of 25 November, on his way to the Thebaid, "a wild and uncivilized place" west of Cairo made famous by the desert fathers of the Church. Two days later, he wrote, "My trip to the Thebaid that I wrote about in my last letter turned out to be impossible. Having gone only twenty versts [twelve miles] from Cairo, I was almost killed by Bedouins who mistook me in the night for the devil. I had to spend the night on the bare earth, and consequently was forced to return home" (*Pis'ma* 2:18–19). Solovyov makes no mention of a vision in this letter and instead asks his parents to send two hundred rubles, since he had run out of money for his lodging. Besides the poem, and his other re-visions, then, we have little external evidence for a mystical vision. We do know that he made friends with the Russian expatriate community in Cairo, frequented the spiritualist community there, and invited his childhood friend Dmitrii Tsertelev (1852–1911) to join him in Egypt and to partake in the psychic scene (*Pis'ma* 2:230).

Returning to Russia from Egypt in the winter of 1876, Solovyov stopped in Italy and France, where he established contacts that were to prove useful to him later in the 1880s when he would find it difficult to publish at home. Here he also completed much of a manuscript in French—part fictional dialogue between "Sophie" and an unnamed "Philosophe," part metaphysical tract—which he called "a work of mystical-theosophical-philosophical-theurgical-political content and dialogical form" (letter to mother, March 4, 1876, *Pis'ma* 2:23). Despite the fact that Solovyov refers to what he tentatively titled *The Sophia* as "the basis of all my future endeavors" (letter to father, May 16/28, 1875; *Pis'ma* 2:28), the unusual and still unfinished work was not published in its original French until more than seventy-five years after the philosopher's death, and not published in Russian translation until 1991–96. Until very recently, neither biographers nor scholars of Solovyov had more than a very limited knowledge of this important work.[27]

Following his search for Sophia in Europe and the Middle East, Solovyov returned to teach in Moscow but unexpectedly resigned from his teaching positions in 1877 and moved to St. Petersburg both to teach and to work toward his doctoral degree. Convincing evidence suggests that the hasty resignation was caused by a desire to spare his father embarrassment, for in a political struggle within Moscow University the latter stood on the opposite side from the conservative leaders who were at the time the young Solovyov's closest friends.

Solovyov made his first public appearance in St. Petersburg with a lecture titled "Three Powers" ("Tri sily," 1877), expressing his response to Russia's recent declaration of war on Turkey. The lecture had a markedly conservative agenda, close to the Slavophile belief in Russia's divinely inspired historical mission. In it he criticizes the blind, monolithic power of the East as well as the fragmented power of the West; the former destroys the freedom of the individual, while the latter leads to unchecked egoism and anarchy. Solovyov argues that hope for the future resides only with a third people, the Slavs, whose national character has the power to integrate the two other geographic, political, and metaphysical extremes and, from the integration, to create a new, organic whole, veering neither toward moribund totality nor to a mere collection of unrelated, competing, and ultimately meaningless parts.

"Three Powers" is an early formulation of Solovyov's central concept of *vseedinstvo* (translatable as "the unity of all things," pan-oneness, multiplicity in unity, or "the whole of things")[28], in which wholeness appears as the organic interrelatedness of limitless interpenetrating parts. Here the Slavic world plays the part of integrator, but the role easily passes in his later writing to a series of other "third powers." These provide the energy that allows for the interpenetration of opposites and their resultant transfiguration into a new, vibrant, interactive vseedinstvo. In all cases, the third power motivates a new whole, in which the individual elements remain, using the Christological terminology that Solovyov preferred, "undivided, yet unmerged."[29] Sophia is one of those third powers.

Soon after delivering "Three Powers," Solovyov left St. Petersburg to participate in the war effort in the Balkans but returned after only a month and a

27. S. M. Solovyov discusses the manuscript and reproduces fragments of it (*Zhizn' i tvorcheskaia evoliutsiia*, 129–46; *Vladimir Solovyov*, trans. Gibson, 138–61). See also the discussion in Losev, *Vladimir Solov'ev i ego vremia*, 183–227, which is based only on the fragments from S. M. Solovyov. Notes by and conversations with the Russian translator of the manuscript, A. Kozyrev, have been invaluable for my own analysis. Others who have written effectively on Solovyov's *The Sophia* include Helleman, de Courten, Kochetkova, Kravchenko, and Daigin.

28. See Valliere 120–27 for the latter, very thoughtful translation.

29. "Undivided, yet unmerged" defines the relationship of the two natures of Christ confirmed by the Christological council at Chalcedon. Solovyov uses the term extensively throughout his oeuvre to describe "true" relationships.

half, having never fired the gun he had acquired to fight for the pan-Slavic cause. He returned to a ministry job more suited to his bookish temperament. In the same year, a substantial but unfinished work titled "The Philosophical Principles of Integral Knowledge" ("Filosofskie nachala tsel'nogo znaniia," 1877) appeared in the *Journal of the Ministry of National Enlightenment* (*Zhurnal Ministerstva Narodnogo Prosveshcheniia*). This work, indebted to Slavophile ideas about the organic rather than abstractly logical nature of knowledge, contains many of the ideas on wholeness articulated in "Three Powers," as well as some word-for-word translations from his unpublished *The Sophia* manuscript. It was appended to his doctoral dissertation when the latter was published in 1880.

Also in 1877, Solovyov met and fell in love with Sophia Petrovna Khitrovo (née Bakhmeteva) through her aunt, Countess Sophia Andreevna Tolstaia, widow of the poet A. K. Tolstoy. As far as we know for certain, Solovyov's romantic feelings for Khitrovo were never consummated, but they also never abated, and this Sophia, "the unique love of Solovyov's entire life" (S. Solov'ev, *Zhizn'i tvorcheskaia evoliutsiia* 210; *Vladimir Solovyov*, trans. Gibson, 249), sat at the side of his bed as he died. Despite her married status and her rejection of at least one proposal by Solovyov, Khitrovo opened up her estate, Pustyn'ka, to her admirer, and it, along with the A. K. Tolstoy home in Krasnyi Rog, became the closest thing to a permanent residence that the adult philosopher-poet would ever have.

Summering at Pustyn'ka, Solovyov indulged in literary as well as philosophical pursuits, and he produced much of his well-received poetry there. Some of that poetry is lyrical, but other verses are ironic and farcical, in the manner of Koz'ma Prutkov, the fictional poet created by A. K. Tolstoy and his coauthors the Zhemchuzhnikov brothers.[30] Solovyov was famous for his irreverent epigrams, as in the ditty mocking his friend, Afanasii Fet:[31] "There lived a poet / Known to all / Who, growing old/Became a dolt" (*Stikhotvoreniia* 149), or in an attempt at his own epitaph: "Vladimir Solovyov lies on this spot; / Once a thinker, now his body is rot" (*SS* 12:124).[32] Some of the poetry makes fun of his own most precious beliefs, including his long narrative poem, *Three Encounters*, perhaps not coincidentally also written at Pustyn'ka. Solovyov called the latter work "humorous verses"

---

30. A. K. Tolstoy (1817–75) and Aleksei, Aleksandr, and Vladimir Zhemchuzhnikov together created the fictitious poet Koz'ma Prutkov and published their parodies in the 1860s and 1870s mainly in the journal *The Contemporary* (*Sovremennik*). See Solovyov's entries on Prutkov and on Zhemchuzhnikov in the Brokgauz and Efron *Encyclopedic Dictionary* (*Entsiklopedicheskii slovar'*; *SS* 10:520–23 and 505–6) and his longer article of 1895 on Tolstoy, "Poeziia gr. A. K. Tolstogo" (*SS* 7:135–58). Solovyov also wrote the introduction to an edition of A. K. Tolstoy's novel *The Vampire* (*Upyr'*; *SS* 9:375–79) that includes an important definition of the fantastic, cited by Tzvetan Todorov in his famous study *The Fantastic* 25–26.

31. A. A. Fet (1820–92) was a friend of the family of Solovyov's maternal grandmother, Ekaterina Fedorovna Brzhesskaia, and knew Solovyov from the latter's early years.

32. In the original, the latter ditty much more cleverly rhymes "on this spot" (*na meste etom*) with "became a skeleton" (*stal skeletom*).

that, nonetheless, express "the most significant moments of my life up until today" (see page 272). Solovyov's play-in verse, *The White Lily* (*Belaia liliia*), written at Pustyn'ka in 1878–80 and describing a hapless search for Sophia, also fits into the category of self-mocking works.

From January through March of 1878, Solovyov solidified his precocious fame with the series of twelve public lectures in St. Petersburg already cited, apparently originally intended to raise money for the Red Cross and for the restoration of the cathedral Hagia Sophia in Constantinople.[33] Using a mixture of Hegelian and trinitarian terminology, Solovyov here articulates his central concept of bogochelovechestvo, the ongoing, historical process of the interaction between humanity and divinity. It is the latter speculation that brought Solovyov close to Dostoevsky; the two philosopher-writers journeyed together to the popular pilgrimage monastery of Optina Pustyn' in the summer of 1878, shortly after the death of Dostoevsky's young son, Alyosha.[34] The two first became friends in early 1873, when the novelist was already fifty-one and the philosopher-poet only twenty.[35]

Solovyov lost his imposing but beloved father in 1879, the year before he was able to defend his doctoral dissertation, "Critique of Abstract Principles" (Kritika otvlechennykh nachal, 1880), that he had been writing and publishing pieces of for the previous three years. This work continues his master's thesis claim "against the positivists," but condemns *all* abstract philosophical thinking as inadequate, calling it "negative," and proposing instead positive principles, which can be either "traditional" or "mystical" in origin.[36] He continued to lecture as private docent through the fall of 1880 and hoped, unsuccessfully, to be accepted for a faculty position in the Philosophy Department of either Moscow or St. Petersburg University. According to the scholar Konstantin Mochul'skii, Solovyov's failure to secure for himself a stable life in academia was for the best: "Solovyov was not created for solitary work in his study; he had the temperament of a preacher and a fighter. He was too fantastical, eccentric, and restless to be satisfied with the writing of philosophical tracts. His was to be a homeless, difficult, and insecure life, a stubborn and to all visible signs a hopeless fight, and in this lay his calling" (Mochul'skii 122).

33. There is much more on the Church of Hagia Sophia (Ἁγια Σοφία), or Divine Wisdom, in the following pages. For over one thousand years it served as the seat of the Patriarchate of Constantinople.

34. Optina Pustyn' is a monastery in the Kaluga region, about 250 kilometers from Moscow. In the nineteenth century it became known as the spiritual heart of Russia and served as home to many influential elders. Father Zosima in Dostoevsky's *Brothers Karamazov* is based on one of those elders.

35. Some speculate that Solovyov served as the model for Alyosha in *Brothers Karamazov*. Others say that he inspired the character of Ivan. For more on the relationship between Solovyov and Dostoevsky, see Kostalevsky. In contrast, Solovyov's relationship with Tolstoy—who also attended the lectures—was more antagonistic, although the two collaborated on a letter concerning the defense of the Jews, published in England by Solovyov and undersigned by Tolstoy, among other leading intellectuals (*Pis'ma* 2:160–61).

36. See *SS* 2:13–14, and Valliere's discussion on 119, 167.

Indeed, Solovyov spent his life traveling, often penniless, living off the largesse of friends, and tirelessly championing his philosophical, theological, and activist causes.

Solovyov's work of the late 1870s begins to reveal signs of a move away from Slavophilism and from the conservative friends of his university years. All observers recognized the change by March of 1881, following the assassination of Tsar Alexander II. At a public lecture, Solovyov called on Alexander III to show Christian forgiveness toward his father's assassins and to commute their death penalties to Siberian exile.[37] Although Solovyov was never officially barred from teaching because of the controversial lecture, he voluntarily withdrew and committed himself, for the rest of his life, to preaching what he called "Christian politics."[38] He soon severed ties with conservative publications, and by the late 1880s had established a long collaboration instead with the liberal journal the *European Herald* (*Vestnik Evropy*).[39]

Despite his popularity, Solovyov consistently provoked criticism from Russians of all schools. For Slavophiles, he focused too much on the West; for Westernizers and liberals, he was an irrational mystic; for Orthodox clergy, he was a freethinker who flirted with Catholicism; for Tolstoyans, he supported Orthodox doctrine; for Dostoevky's reactionary acolytes, he was too sympathetic to Jews. In an article on the Slavophiles written in 1889, Solovyov ironically points to the number of conflicting labels attached to him by the press: Catholic, Protestant, rationalist, mystic, nihilist, Old Believer, and, finally, Jew.[40]

The 1880s were, indeed, a decade of strong and often controversial stands for Solovyov. He published in French when censorship would not allow publication at home, as with the work *La Russie et l'église universelle* (*Russia and the Universal Church*, 1889; translated into Russian as *Rossiia i vselenskaia tserkov'*, 1911; see selections at page 192). Major projects in the 1880s for Solovyov included *Three Speeches in Memory of Dostoevsky* (*Tri rechi v pamiat' Dostoevskogo*, 1881–83), in which Solovyov praises his recently deceased friend but subtly condemns the latter's xenophobia and antisemitism; *Jewry and the Christian Question* (*Evreistvo i khristianskii vopros*, 1884), in which Solovyov accuses Russians of unchristian behavior toward the Jews, a people that mutually

37. "The current moment," writes Solovyov, "presents an unprecedented occasion for the government to justify in deed its pretensions as the highest leader of the people. Today the murderers of the tsar are being judged, and most certainly will be condemned to death. The tsar can forgive them, and if he truly feels his connection to the people, he must forgive them" (*Pis'ma* 4:246).

38. See Gaut; Schrooyen, "Vladimir Solov'ëv"; Walicki, *Legal Philosophies*, chap. 3.

39. In the late 1880s, Solovyov also began to publish extensively in *Voprosy filosofii i psikhologii*, of which he was a founding member. He published in a number of other centrist and liberal journals and abroad when censorship made it impossible to publish at home. For a list of journals and newspapers that printed Solovyov's *publitsistika*, see Schrooyen, "Vladimir Solov'ëv" 149–56.

40. SS 5:266. See Valliere 203: "Soloviev believed in Israel and also in Orthodoxy. He was a liberal and also a theocrat; a humanist and also a dogmatist. These unusual linkages account for the enormous power of his thought."

chose and was chosen by God, and posits the supposed prophetic element of Judaism as the third power necessary for the rejuvenation of both Eastern (the kingly element) and Western (the priestly element) Christianity; and the many polemical essays collected in two volumes of *The National Question in Russia* (*Natsional'nyi vopros v Rossii*; published separately between 1883 and 1888 and 1888 and 1891). *The Spiritual Foundations of Life* (*Dukhovnye osnovy zhizni*, 1882–84) and *The History and Future of Theocracy* (*Istoriia i budushchnost' teokratii*, 1885–87) further develop his work begun in the 1870s, with a focus on the realization of a theocratic ideal here on earth. It is in these hybrid works and in *La Russie et l'église universelle* that he brings back to his nonfictional writing the idea of Sophia as a reconciler of heaven and earth, as well as the theology and social activism of his earlier publications. The future theocracy, he contends, can be established only after the unification of the churches. It will exhibit the spiritual and material integration that he ascribed in earlier works to the Jews and will be based on the principles of "Christian politics." As Solovyov writes in the preface to *The History and Future of Theocracy*, his purpose is to "justify the faith of our fathers by raising it to a new level of rational consciousness, to show that this ancient faith, freed of local exclusivity and national egoism, corresponds to the eternal and universal truth." [41]

Solovyov also returned more than once to Europe in the 1880s, including a trip to Zagreb in June of 1886, at which time he met with Josip Juraj Strossmayer, Catholic bishop of Bosnia and Sirmium. Strossmayer had become interested in Solovyov after publication of the latter's *The Great Controversy and Christian Politics* (*Velikii spor i khristianskaia politika*, 1883), a work that praises the Catholic Church. Solovyov remained close to Bishop Strossmayer throughout his life, causing many Orthodox observers to accuse Solovyov of betrayal of his native Russian Church. More likely, the friendship between Catholic priest and lay Orthodox philosopher was based on Solovyov's firm desire to bring about the ultimate reunion of the churches. Speculation continues to this day about Solovyov's possible conversion to Catholicism, but we know that he received his final communion from an Orthodox priest. As one of his followers, Semyon Frank, has written, "From the age of thirty to the end of his life Solovyov was conscious of himself as a member of the one indivisible universal 'Orthodox-Catholic' Church, though his interpretation of it underwent a change. But formally and canonically he always regarded himself as belonging to the Russian Orthodox Church, and, if his last confession be taken into account, such he remained to the end, even from the purely ecclesiastical point of view" (Frank 252).

41. SS 4:243. See Valliere 3: "This engagement reflected an interest in philosophy not just as a specialized academic pursuit but in the most basic sense of the word: the quest for *Sophia*, for wisdom, for insight into the meaning of life. Challenged and also energized by modernity, the Russian school [of which Solovyov is a prime representative] sought to reconstruct the Orthodox theological tradition, to move beyond patristic Orthodoxy to a philosophic Orthodoxy for new times."

According to most biographers, during the last decade of his life the philosopher repudiated his idealism of the 1880s and abandoned hope for the establishment of a collective Kingdom of Heaven on earth. In actuality, however, the eighties also had seen much more practical than utopian ideals. And his writings on beauty, art, and love that dominate the 1890s, as well as his own poetry, show that Solovyov did not so much abandon his hope for a future society based on universalist Christian ideals as seek out new ways to express his vision. His articulation of an aesthetic theory in "Beauty in Nature" ("Krasota v prirode," 1889) and "The General Meaning of Art" ("Obshchii smysl iskusstva," 1890), combined with a renewed interest in natural science, suggests an attempt to look to individual expression rather than to social institutions for the establishment of the future Good. In "The Meaning of Love" ("Smysl liubvi," 1892–94), a text read ardently by the later Symbolist poets who claimed Solovyov as spiritual father, the philosopher investigates the complexity of human individuality, including human sexuality. For Solovyov, the attractions of the body are not profane but rather participate in bogochelovechestvo, and they are the best means to free humans from the separation of egoism. A child who results from marital love, then, is not only, or even principally, the biological result of reproduction but also proof of the divine-human process, for only in erotic love do two people understand each other both spiritually *and* materially. Their union transforms nature or, rather, transfigures it through the incarnation of the spirit.

"The Meaning of Love" was written under the influence of a supposedly "deeply mystical love" for another woman named Sophia: Sophia Mikhailovna Martynova, whom Solovyov met at the end of 1891 and to whom he wrote a number of love poems (see S. Solov'ev, *Zhizn' i tvorcheskaia evoliutsiia,* 307–12; *Vladimir Solovyov*, Gibson trans. 383–90; Losev, *Vladimir Solov'ev i ego vremia* 83–87). In a letter to Martynova of 1892, Solovyov writes of a change he has noticed in his female friend: "For the time being this change—the loss of your iridescent radiance or marks of the Divine Sophia—only affects your conversation and your face, which is already half a tragedy. When it spreads to the whole body, then that will be the end of everything. Only one attribute will remain—that of being the smartest and most original of all women (that is, peasant ladies and mothers). No one can take that away from you, but it means very, very little, and, in the other world, absolutely nothing." He goes on to say that the Madonna (he calls her *"ci-devant* Sophia and Madonna") had flown from her and left instead a matronly dame (*matrona*). He presents her with two humorous acrostic poems called by a common peasant name: "Matryona," which rhymes with but seems equally far from both Madonna and matron (*Pis'ma* 4:150–52).

The continuing correspondence between the two proves that Martynova had a sense of humor about Solovyov's assessment, itself probably tongue-in-cheek, and that his disillusionment at not finding the Divine Sophia in this earthly one had little negative effect on their relationship. In the same letter, Solovyov promises to send Martynova a copy of the humorous playlet "Solovyov in the

Thebaid," written for him by his friend F. L. Sollogub. As we saw, Solovyov was on his way from Cairo to the Thebaid when he allegedly had his third vision of Sophia. This play-in-verse about the devil's temptation of Solovyov in the desert—complete with a Sphinx unable to shake the painful memory of Oedipus's triumph, a self-absorbed Queen of Sheba past her prime, and a secret meeting of Russian Freemasons brought in to build a new temple—shows the continuing influence on Solovyov and his friends of Koz'ma Prutkov and the fictional poet's sarcastic and farcical verse.[42] Bad puns, endless rhymes, and absurdist antics link Solovyov's search for Sophia in this play with the earthiness of his own bald humor. The offer to send a copy to Martynova, as indicated above, again shows Solovyov's willingness to mix earthly humor and divine love, as well as laughter and metaphysics. Apparently, Sophia can be manifest in many forms.

In the fall of 1894, Solovyov moved temporarily to Finland, where he worked on his major volume on ethics, *The Justification of the Good* (*Opravdanie dobra*, 1894–98), and where he completed a series of poems inspired by what he called his last love, Lake Saimaa (actually a vast system of lakes that cover the eastern side of Finland). The Symbolists in the next decade were greatly impressed by the lyricism of these poems and read the lake as yet another incarnation of the Divine Sophia.

During the final decade of his life, Solovyov also turned to literary criticism and wrote a series of articles on many of the major Slavic writers of the nineteenth century, including Pushkin, Tiutchev, Lermontov, and the Polish poet Mickiewicz.[43] Many years earlier, Solovyov had begun his first attempt at what he called "real poetry" with a translation of a poem ascribed to Plato,[44] and in the 1890s he returned to the life and work of the Greek philosopher as well. His friend Afanasii Fet had urged Solovyov to "do his patriotic duty" and "give Plato to Russian literature," and the philosopher thus embarked on a major translation project from the original Greek with his brother Mikhail (*SS* 12:360). In addition, in 1898 Solovyov completed *The Life Drama of Plato* (*Zhiznennaia drama Platona*), in which he speculates on the tragic curve of Plato's life

---

42. This unfinished but hilarious short play by Solovyov's friend, the painter and amateur poet Count Fedor Lvovich Sollogub (1848–90), was given by N. V. Davydov to S. M. Luk'ianov and printed by the latter in his biography of Solovyov (3/1:283–307). According to Davydov, "Sollogub's ironic portrayal of Solovyov's battle with the devil not only didn't distress the philosopher, but, on the contrary, brought him even closer to Sollogub. The latter, in contrast to Vladimir Sergeevich, while not believing in the spiritual side of 'Spiritualism,' willingly attended spiritualist séances and made friends with both professional mediums and dilettantes. He was interested in the technical side of the matter, with the way in which these individuals produce this or that manifestation. Solovyov, on the contrary, acknowledging the charlatantism and deceit of the mediums, nonetheless never doubted in the possibility of the real manifestation of intercourse between the spiritual world and our own, and himself experienced such a manifestation more than once" (cited in Luk'ianov 2:308).

43. Aleksandr Pushkin (1799–1837), often called the father of Russian literature, inspired several works by Solovyov. Fedor Tiutchev (1803–73), Mikhail Lermontov (1814–41), and Adam Mickiewicz (1798–1855) also appear in a number of essays.

44. See *SS* 12:57 and epigraph at page 34 for translation.

and in particular on the Greek philosopher's relationship with Socrates. According to Solovyov, Plato fell into "pessimistic idealism" after the death of his teacher, but he underwent an erotic crisis that brought back the mediating memory of Socrates and returned him to faith in love as a connecting link between the ideal world and this one. Ultimately, though, Solovyov condemns Plato for failing to understand the significance of his own erotic daemon: "If Socrates brought philosophy down from heaven and put it in the hands of people, then his greatest student raised it high over his head and from that height dropped it onto the earth, into the dirt and garbage of the street" (*SS* 9:240).

Nietzsche also disappointed Solovyov. "The Idea of the Superman" ("Ideia sverkhcheloveka," 1899) praises the popular German as a talented thinker but accuses him of perverting the true Godman (*Bogochelovek*) into a man-god (*chelovekobog*). Here Solovyov identifies three fashionable but "dangerous" ideas of the time: economic materialism, associated with Marx; abstract moralism, associated with Lev Tolstoy; and the demonism of the "superman," associated with Nietzsche, which he considers, nonetheless, "the most interesting of the three" (*SS* 9:266). In a similar vein, Solovyov also attacks the first generation of Symbolist poets for their faddish interest in Nietzscheanism. Ironically, of course, the Symbolists were among Solovyov's most ardent followers.[45]

Solovyov's interest in the history of philosophy never abated throughout his life, and in 1891 he was asked to be the philosophy editor of the important multivolume *Encyclopaedic Dictionary* (*Entsiklopedicheskii slovar'*, 1891–1907), edited by F. A. Brokgaus and I. A. Efron. Before his death in 1900, Solovyov wrote dozens of articles for the encyclopedia on ancient and modern philosophers and on such philosophical topics as beauty, reason, nature, mysticism, and evil (see *SS* 10:227–523 and 12:547–620). Unfortunately he died before he was able to pen the entries after the middle of the letter *s*.

Solovyov continued his peripatetic existence during the last decade of his life, visiting Sweden, Scotland, and France, even returning to Egypt in March of 1898, perhaps in search of the vision he had had there almost twenty-three years previously. In a repeat of his earlier journey, he ran out of money and was therefore unable to make a planned trip to Palestine. Nonetheless, he returned to Moscow refreshed and again spent the summer at Pustyn'ka. It is after this return trip to Egypt that Solovyov wrote *Three Encounters*, describing all three of his earlier visions.

Along with his visions/re-visions of Sophia, perhaps the most profound legacy that Solovyov left to the next generation of the romantically minded Silver Age poets and biographers is his last major work, *Three Conversations*

---

45. The Symbolist movement in Russia is often divided into two generations. Members of the first, which included the poets Bal'mont, Sologub, Briusov, and Gippius, are sometimes referred to as Decadents. Solovyov wrote extremely critical reviews of three collections of Symbolist poetry of this first generation (*SS* 7:159–70). The second generation included the poets Blok, Belyi, Ivanov, and Solovyov's nephew, Sergei Solovyov. These latter poets, as we saw, openly acknowledged their debt to Solovyov for, among other things, his image of Sophia.

(*Tri razgovora*, 1899–1900).[46] In this text, written in the form of three drawing-room dialogues,[47] Solovyov polemicizes with Tolstoy on the questions of nonresistance to evil, the meaning of human progress, and the truth of revelation. Its form and its content are equally important, for Solovyov uses the occasion of the polemic to critique what he saw as Tolstoy's monolithic and declarative philosophy, parading as fiction, and to substitute a more multivalent fictional voice, here inscribed in philosophy.[48] Solovyov concludes his work with a short story, titled "A Short Tale of the Antichrist" ("Kratkaia povest' ob antikhriste"), in which he uses fiction to urge his readers toward an active struggle against evil. The story of an evil emperor who promises peace in exchange for freedom clearly draws on Dostoevsky's Grand Inquisitor and serves as one of Solovyov's many predictions about the terror to come in the twentieth century. Indeed, many people read the poem "Panmongolism," the opening lines of which Solovyov uses as an epigraph to the short story, as a prediction of the coming Russo-Japanese War. The poem was written in 1894 but not published until 1905, five years after its author's death.

As if ignoring his real interest in current affairs (including a prescient sense of ecological disaster, a topic ignored by Marxists and Nietzscheans alike), memoirs that refer to Solovyov often describe him as wandering in a kind of daze, seemingly unaware of the world around him. According to Evgenii Trubetskoi, Solovyov was "so nearsighted that *he did not see what others saw*" ("Lichnost' V. S. Solov'eva" 70; emphasis in original). The Symbolist poet Aleksandr Blok called him a "knightly monk" ("Rytsar'—monakh" in Averin and Bazanova 329–34). Those eyewitnesses who chose to emphasize Solovyov's odd, otherworldly behavior produced an interpretation of him that valued his mysticism over his equally important social ethics, his utopian theocratic vision over his practical politics. Solovyov himself did not divide the contradictory aspects of his personality, including his sometimes crude sense of humor, from his philosophical outlook or his activist interests any more than he separated his poetry from his philosophy. He often quoted his own and others' verses in his essays and suffused even his humorous works with important, if sometimes hidden, discussions of vseedinstvo, bogochelovechestvo, and, of course, Sophia.

46. The emphasis in this book on Solovyov's Sophianic works, and here on *Three Conversations*, does not mean to deny the very significant influence of Solovyov's other works on the next generation(s) of liberal philosophers, who focused more on his social Christianity or his ethics.

47. The number "three" is clearly not accidental throughout his work. It appears in "Three Powers" in the seventies; "Three Speeches in Memory of Dostoevsky" and the poem "Three Deeds" in the eighties; *Three Conversations* and "Three Encounters" in the nineties; and "Three Characteristics" in 1900, in the last months of his life. Three is multiplicity that can unite into unity, for it is beyond mere dualism. The first two elements in a Solovyovian triad do not merely supersede each other, nor do they cancel each other out or even merely merge. Instead, the third element unites them in such a way that they retain their identities but in a new, transfigured whole. Ivanov later calls this union a "wedding." As Solovyov wrote in the preface to *Three Conversations* about the three viewpoints personified in the coming dialogues: "The highest unconditional truth does not exclude or negate the preliminary [two] conditions of its appearance, but justifies, gives meaning to, and sanctifies them" (*SS* 10:87).

48. For more on this polemic, see Kornblatt, "The Truth of the Word."

Solovyov died at the home of his good friend Sergei Trubetskoi on July 31, 1900 (some sources say August 1). He complained of pains throughout his body, and the doctors found an extreme case of malnutrition and exhaustion, as well as sclerosis of the arteries and cirrhosis of the liver. Solovyov's diet was marked by lack of protein and missed meals, and he was known to utterly disregard his own needs in favor of those of others. Solovyov prayed continually in his last days and asked to confess and receive communion from an Orthodox priest on July 18, after which he grew increasingly weaker. At one point he turned to Trubetskoi's wife, Ekaterina Ivanovna, and said, "Do not let me fall asleep, force me to pray for the Jewish people. I must pray for them,"[49] and he began to recite a psalm in the original Hebrew. He died surrounded by friends but with neither a family nor a home of his own.

POSITIVISM AND SPIRITUALISM / FEMINISM AND PANSOPHISM

> Pan Sophius? Was he a Pole?
>
> SOLOVYOV, *Three Conversations*

> You don't know Jules Landau, *le fameux Jules Landau, le clairvoyant?* He also is half-witted, but your sister's fate depends on him.
>
> LEV TOLSTOY, *Anna Karenina*

Whether or not we recognize Solovyov as an eccentric knightly monk in Blok's neoromantic terms, we cannot ignore the fact that he was what Russians call an *original*: a vegetarian in a land of meat-filled pastries and cutlets, a Slavophile who rejected Russian nationalism, and a scholar willing to give up a stable university career to speak out against the tsar. Nonetheless, he was also firmly rooted in the Russia of his day, and his articulations of Sophia are informed by, or sometimes reactions against, contemporary issues. We would do wrong to dismiss Solovyov's visions as purely personal pathology—or ecstasy, depending on our perspective.[50] To the contrary, we cannot help but see them embedded in the context in which he lived.

Various related political or social theories that penetrated Russia in the second half of the nineteenth century serve as the most important historical context for Solovyov's work. At the risk of oversimplifying what was in fact

---

49. Trubetskoi, Sergei. "Smert' V. Solov'eva. 31 iiulia 1900g.," *Vestnik Evropy* 9 (1900), reprinted in Averin and Bazanova 294.

50. According to Solovyov himself, "the ability to have Visions is always connected to some kind of pecularities in the organization or function of the nervous system. Nonetheless, we must distinguish the hallucinations of the insane from Visions as such, that is, from those in which the entire anomaly of the subject is exhausted by his visionary propensities, unaccompanied by any other pathological manifestations" (*SS* 12:556).

a complex of competing ideas from France, England, and Germany, I will focus here mainly on positivism, using a small *p* and not drawing distinctions between it and empiricism, utilitarianism, or materialism, as most Russians of the time did not. What links these movements is the elevation of sense experience over other ways of knowing, whether intuition, revelation, or reason, and a reliance on what was understood to be concrete and thus "true" scientific evidence. The figure most closely associated with positivism is the French thinker Auguste Comte, about whom Solovyov wrote in at least three places: first in an appendix to *The Crisis of Western Philosophy (Against the Positivists)* that he titled "The Theory of Auguste Comte about the Three Phases of the Rational Development of Humanity" ("Teoriia Ogiusta Konta o trekh fazisakh v umstvennom razvitii chelovechestva," 1874); then in an entry titled "Comte" ("Kont") in the Brokgaus-Efron *Encyclopedic Dictionary*; and finally in a public lecture in 1898 titled "The Idea of Humanity in Auguste Comte" ("Ideia chelovechestva u Avgusta Konta"; see selection on page 213) (*PSS* 1:37–138; *SS* 10:380–409; *SS* 9:172–93). Although in his last years Solovyov came to focus quite positively on Comte's idea of the Great Being (*Grand Être*) as somehow related to Sophia, he at first criticized the French philosopher's extreme immanentism, his rejection of all ideas of transcendence, and his belief in positive science as the sole means to create a happy society.[51]

The most important Russian activist in the positivist vein was N. G. Chernyshevsky (1828–89), about whom Solovyov also wrote several times, again with both negative and positive assessments, most significantly in his essay on aesthetics, "First Step toward a Positive Aesthetics" ("Pervyi shag k polozhitel'noi estetiki," 1894; *SS* 7:69–77). Chernyshevsky was a radical journalist as well as a literary critic, in the mode of the earlier activist Vissarion Belinsky. In his master's essay, "The Aesthetic Relations of Art to Reality" ("Esteticheskie otnosheniia iskusstva k deistvitel'nosti," 1855), Chernyshevsky claims that science is always superior to art and that the latter should serve the forces of historical change. He became known as the conscience of the "generation of the sixties," whose early but still most famous literary portrayal is Bazarov in Ivan Turgenev's *Fathers and Sons* (*Ottsy i deti,* 1862). In Bazarov's utilitarian view, "A decent chemist is twenty times more useful than any poet." He continues, "And as regards the age—why should I depend on it? Let it rather depend on me. No, my friend, it's all that lack of discipline, shallowness! And what about those mysterious relations between a man and a woman? We physiologists understand all that. You just study the anatomy of the eye: where does that enigmatic gaze come from that you talk about? It's all romanticism, nonsense, rubbish, artifice. Let's go have a look at that beetle." Pavel Petrovich, Turgenev's representative of the idealist "generation of the forties" in the novel, says of Bazarov, "He doesn't believe in principles, but he believes in frogs" (Turge-

---

51. For more on Comte and Solovyov, see de Courten 193–206; Shakhmatov 50–67; Rotsinskii 67–89.

nev, trans. Katz, 20, 26, 19). "Principles" for the older Pavel Petrovich mean largely the abstract ideals of the German idealist philosophy. Known as an astute observer of his time, Turgenev thus points out the weaknesses and strengths of both the romantic idealism of the forties *and* the newly popular positivism of the sixties.

Solovyov's philosophical critique of positivism, like Turgenev's fictional one, was not a mere negation.[52] In fact, the religious philosopher assimilated and transformed much of positivism's focus on the material world, just as he was able to see in Chernyshevsky's theory of art the "first step toward a positive aesthetics" that erred neither in its withdrawal from society into "art for art's sake," nor in a devaluation of art as a mere tool for change. Indeed, positivism came to form part of Solovyov's synthetic understanding of reality that was neither purely abstract or rational nor purely empirical.[53]

We might see Solovyov's articulation of Divine Wisdom as a reaction against the prevailing positivist attitudes of the day. Most crucially, however, we need to understand it not as a mere negation but rather as an *incorporation* of materialism, as the union of Solovyov's intangible intuition of ideal reality and the "facts" of the modern world. It is this role of mediation that most marks Sophia. For Solovyov, the world is not binary or dualistic but profoundly triadic. Sophia is the third, uniting or completing side of a triad, not simply equivalent to the other two but a transfiguring force that makes of the union a new whole, undivided, yet unmerged.

Placing Solovyov's interest in Sophia in the context of Chernyshevsky's positivist writings in particular proves important for a related issue as well. Chernyshevsky is perhaps best known in the West not for his political activism but for his novel *What Is to Be Done?* (*Chto delat'?*, 1863). This tendentious work proved immensely influential for several generations of revolutionaries in Russia. Translated into both English and Yiddish, the novel also accompanied the Russian Jewish immigrants who formed the core of the American labor movement and progressive social politics from the 1880s.[54] Written as a radical response to *Fathers and Sons*, *What Is to Be Done?* introduces a collection of "new" men and women who preach positivism, reject patriarchal tsarist society, and instead support socialist ideas in the workplace and open relations in marriage and sex.

---

52. "The main objective of Solov'jov's critique was not simply to deny positivism but to learn from it and to build a new metaphysics free from the limitations and inconsistencies of preceding theories. . . . Solov'jov's encounter with positivism resulted in his clear awareness of the gap between *phenomena* and *noumena*, between inner and outer experience, and his determination to bridge it. . . . Solov'jov's critique of positivism became the real origin of his philosophy" (Kochetkova, *Vladimir Solov'jov's Theory of Divine Humanity*, xviii, 37).

53. See Valliere 140–41.

54. For this fascinating chapter in Russian Jewish and American history, see Steven Cassedy.

What Is to Be Done? became a sort of bible for the socialist movement in Russia, as well as for the women's movement that had an early and powerful genesis in Russia at the end of the nineteenth century. According to the historian Richard Stites, "Chernyshevsky's teaching, reduced to its essentials, is this: men must cease being the clients of prostitutes and thus eliminate the market; women must help the victims by giving them work. Any feminist from 1860 right up to the Revolution could have said (and did say) the same thing" (Stites 93). In one of the best examples of art influencing life, the heroine of the novel, Vera Pavlova, inspired countless women to break from stifling marriages, seek an education, and develop careers and lives of their own.

We might see Solovyov's stint as lecturer at Vladimir Ger'e's "Higher Courses for Women" as a sign of his personal contact with, and sympathy for, the women's movement of his day. Ger'e, a history professor, opened his school for women in 1872 with the help of Solovyov's father, the rector of Moscow University, although without permission to use the university's name.[55] Against the background of the prerevolutionary feminist movement, however, with its often unsophisticated association with radical politics, it is no accident that Solovyov's Sophia is as much androgynous as female. Her oxymoronic—or rather, inclusive—gender is in part a reaction to what seemed to be the reductive politics of socialism, but it also grows from an Orthodox emphasis on mystical wholeness over rational hierarchy. Both positivism and feminism informed Solovyov's Sophia but as integration rather than mere negation.

It is this suprarational, supramaterial Sophia that attracted so many artists, poets, and religious philosophers at the turn of the century. As the scholar Maria Carlson has written about this turbulent time, "In the face of a fragmenting world marching inexorably toward world war and revolution, the Russian creative intelligentsia sought to structure an ultimate synthesis of culture in which art was identified with religion, and aesthetic theory was transformed into a metaphysical worldview" (Carlson, *No Religion Higher Than Truth* 7). In contrast to the radical intelligentsia represented by Chernyshevsky and his following, those in the Russian educated elite who can be called the "creative intelligentsia" sought not to liberate the downtrodden women around them but to transform everyone through art, mysticism, and the Divine Feminine.[56] These include, of course, the Sophiologists and Symbolist poets who saw Solovyov as their inspiration. But by the turn of the twentieth century, political Russian feminism had become equated for many with the increasingly violent revolutionary movement. In popular parlance, *revoliutsionerka, feministka,* and *prostitutka* had become synonymous. According to their critics, the socialists debased femininity by viewing the women's question through models of crude materialism. Sophiology, however, purportedly

---

55. For more on the school, see Stites 81–82.

56. As we will see below, many of them were attracted to the "relatively chaotic, feminine, intuitive Theosophy of Mme Blavatsky and Mrs. Besant" (Carlson, *No Religion Higher Than Truth* 34).

sought to raise women, and all of material creation, into divine speculation. Sophia for Solovyov did not divide humans into the poles of male and female, rich and poor, Russian and foreign. Rather, she united and transformed opposites in universal humanity.

For many in Solovyov's day, the influx of the Western ideas of positivism, utilitarianism, materialism, and socialism, combined with a growing crisis in the Russian Orthodox Church,[57] pushed them away from traditional religion. Darwinism seemed to have put a nail in the coffin of belief, but it failed to provide a substitute. As Nietzsche once remarked, "[W]hen skepticism mates with longing, mysticism is born" (Nietzsche 14:14).[58] By mysticism, Nietzsche more accurately meant the occult, or a syncretic mixture of all sorts of esoteric systems, as were found in Europe and Russia in the 1870 and 1880s, together with poorly digested Eastern and quasi-Eastern religions. If anything, spiritualism of various sorts competed with positivism for the hearts and souls of Russians as the imperial regime disintegrated around them. The end of the nineteenth century was largely a syncretic time, when a collection of eclectic ideas occupied the elite and masses alike. Tolstoy captures the mood in *Anna Karenina*, when Petersburg high society becomes enraptured by the Parisian clairvoyant/charlatan Landau:

> What? You don't know Jules Landau, *le fameux Jules Landau, le clairvoyant*? He also is half-witted, but your sister's fate depends on him. See what comes of living in the provinces: you know nothing! Landau, you see, was a *commis* in Paris and went to see a doctor. He fell asleep in the doctor's waiting-room, and while asleep began giving advice to all the patients, and very strange advice too. Afterwards, the wife of Yury Meledinsky—the invalid, you know—heard of that Landau, and took him to see her husband. He is treating her husband. No good has been done in my opinion, for he is still just as weak, but they believe in him and take him about with them. So they brought him to Russia. Here everyone rushed at him, and he began treating everybody. He cured the Countess Bezzubova, and she took such a fancy to him that she adopted him. (Tolstoy, *Anna Karenina* pt. 7, ch. 20, 661–62)

Fascination with the occult that rolled through Europe and America in the last half of the nineteenth century was fed by all sorts of charlatans (Solovyov calls them cranks, or *chudodei*, in *Three Encounters*), but it proved nonetheless highly attractive for many otherwise "scientifically minded" and university-trained intellectuals. Indeed, the end of the nineteenth century in Russia and the West can be compared to the wake of the Renaissance in Western Europe, when "Hermetism, Neoplatonism, and Kabbalism became so thoroughly mingled with the alchemistic, speculative, and mystical trends of thought sweeping Europe, that it is no longer easy to trace individual strands of influence" (Weeks 49). Apostles of the new positive science did not shy away from the inexplicable but tried to use

57. See the excellent collection of essays in Nichols and Stavrou.
58. Quoted also in Buber xiv.

scientific method to prove its reality. Like chemistry in the Renaissance, technology, including the newly invented camera, promised the answer to all riddles. "Scientists" descended on séances en masse to photograph spirits. Describing visitors to the home of the curious Eddy brothers, who acted as self-professed mediums in Vermont in the 1870s, the *New York Tribune* journalist and former barrister Henry Steel Olcott wrote of the diversity of those drawn to manifestations of the "other world":

> They are a motley crew, in sooth. Ladies and gentlemen; editors, lawyers, divines and ex-divines; inventors, architects, farmers; pedlers [sic] of magnetic salves and mysterious nostrums; long-haired men and short-haired women; the "crowing hens" of Fowler, and the cackling cocks, their fitting mates; women with an idea, and plenty of men and women without any to speak of; people of sense and people of nonsense; sickly dreamers who prate of "interiors" and "conditions" and "spheres" as intelligently as a learned pig or a chattering magpie; clairvoyants and "healers," real and bogus; phrenologists, who read bumps without feeling them, under "spirit direction"; mediums for tipping, rapping, and every imaginable form of modern phenomena; "apostles" with one and two arms; people from the most distant and widely-separated localities; nice, clever people whom one is glad to meet and sorry to part from; and people who shed a magnetism as disagreeable as dirty water or the perfume of the *Fetis-Americanus*. They come and go, singly and otherwise; some after a day's stay, convinced that they have been cheated, but the vast majority astounded and perplexed beyond expression by what their eyes have seen and their ears heard. (58–61)[59]

The eclectic nature of this gathering points to a major characteristic of Solovyov's time. The plethora of believers in the occult both marked a surfeit of faith and gave rise to a dearth of it. Everything was being questioned. As Janet Oppenheim declares in her study of psychical research in England, the destination of investigators and psychics traveling from both America and Russia, "If they turned to spiritualism and psychical research as refuge from bleak mechanism, emptiness, and despair, they did so as part of a widespread effort in this period to believe in *something*. Their concerns and aspirations placed them—far from the lunatic fringe of their society—squarely amidst the cultural, intellectual, and emotional moods of the era" (Oppenheim 4). And as Deborah Blum explains about the atmosphere in which William James, the American "ghost hunter" and founder of pragmatism, lived, "The era was one of intense moral imbalance—religion apparently under siege from science, technology seemingly

---

59. Solovyov knew of the Eddy brothers from an article by N. P. Vagner in 1875, published in *Russkii Vestnik*. Solovyov parodies the article in his playlet "Evenings in Cairo," written by him and his friend Dmitrii Tsertelev in 1875 in Cairo. See Luk'ianov 2:247–55. For a translation of the play into English, with introduction, see Kornblatt, "Spirits, Spiritualism, and the Spirit."

rewriting the laws of reality. Finding some balance, a way to make sense of existence in the changing world, seemed to him an imperative" (8).

A skeptical Olcott went to the Eddys' farm in Vermont in 1874 together with a carpenter, an architect, two illustrators, and instruments to detect fraud. Ultimately won over, he became convinced of the authenticity of the full-form materialization of spirits he observed, measured, and photographed. He then wrote his pro-spiritism book, *People from the Other World*, but only after having met another seeker of psychic truth at the farm, the famous (or notorious) Russian, Mme Hélène Blavatsky.[60] Together, the two went on to found the Theosophical Society, based on a syncretic mixture of Eastern religious mysticism, decadent secularism, and personal charisma. Its adherents included many of Solovyov's contemporaries and most of his intellectual heirs. As Carlson has written, "Like their European contemporaries, the Russians were intrigued by spiritualism, table turning, fortune-telling, magic, and mysticism of every stamp." She cites Solovyov and his brother Vsevolod, the poets Bal'mont and Minskii-Vilenkin, Merezhkovskii and his wife, Gippius, Bely, and many others who were touched in their day by Theosophy (3, 8).[61] Theosophy and Spiritualism were the two largest organized groups in Russia at the end of the nineteenth century, the latter having had as one of its most ardent promoters the inspiration for some of Solovyov's own works: the writer A. K. Tolstoy. It seems that in Solovyov's day an international following of artists and writers flocked to séances, manifestations, and other exhibits of parapsychic events. They did not necessarily distinguish between mystical experience—a nonrational revelation that can take place within the norms of a traditional religion—and the occult—an esoteric "science," a knowing and freeing of the hidden truth supposedly available only to a select few.[62]

According to Carlson, "from the Theosophical point of view, an enlightened individual could lay out the Tarot on Tuesday night, participate in sectarian ecstasy on Wednesday, speak to his Theosophical circle on Thursday, and receive the Eucharist on Sunday with no violence done to his inner convictions. Theosophy as a system catered to the eclectic spirit of the age" (30). This syncretic period, as we saw, also harbored the rise of the revolutionary movement and the women's movement out of positivist, materialist, and utilitarian ideas, and it coincided almost exactly with the life of Vladimir Solovyov. As a witness

---

60. Helena Blavatsky (1831–91), née Elena von Hahn, traveled throughout the world until her immigration to New York in 1873, where she apparently surprised people by her psychic abilities. She traveled to India in the late seventies, and by the mid-eighties the Theosophical Society that she founded with Olcott had international membership. Her notoriously scandalous behavior was met with equal parts of enthusiasm and skepticism.

61. Konstantin Bal'mont (1867–1942), N. M. Minskii-Vilenkin (1855–1937), Dmitrii Merezhkovskii (1865–1941), Zinaida Gippius (1869–1945).

62. For a good articulation of the distinction between the occultist and the mystic, see Carlson, *No Religion Higher Than Truth* 11–12.

of his age, he could not avoid the cultural currents of his day; his Sophia had a rich soil in which to grow.

In his biography of the post-Renaissance mystic seer Jacob Boehme, Andrew Weeks called the synthetic interests of that earlier time "Pansophism":

> The hope of a reconciled Christendom was nourished by the widespread movement toward a universal synthesis of beliefs and ideas—a synthesis invoked by the term *Pansophia*. The quest for this all-encompassing, "pansophic," wisdom presupposed the erstwhile perceived harmony of diverse notions which— from our distant vantage—appear to be divided between forward- looking theories and retrograde superstitions. *Pansophia* could entail philosophy as well as religion, esotericism, and even science. In Boehme's age, the longed-for concordance of knowledge and belief carried forward traditions of Renaissance Platonism and Hermetic magic, crossbreeding them with certain trends of the Reformation and of the new exact sciences. (Weeks 48)

It can be no coincidence that Solovyov gives the name Pansophius to the monk who serves as spiritual mentor and Solovyov's closest mouthpiece in his influential work *Three Conversations*. The monk who narrates the "Short Tale of the Antichrist" in that work should be read as nothing other than a parodic comment on Solovyov's own synthesis of beliefs in all- or pan-unity and Sophia: Pan-Soph-ius. As we complete this section on the historical context of Solovyov's visions, we need to look briefly at this late work, which spoke so poignantly to Solovyov's contemporaries as they struggled with the prevailing ideas of their time. *Three Conversations* reflects all the current issues at play in Solovyov's day, from the women's question (the dialogues take place in the salon of an educated "Lady" who facilitates the drawing room conversation) to imported ideas of social reform to the purpose of war and patriotism. Although the work does not mention Sophia directly, she is present in the "wise" words of Pansophius that close the wide-ranging conversations.

Yet Solovyov's Pan-sophia/sophius differs from the sometimes random syncretic impulse at the end of the Renaissance that Weeks describes, as well as from the occult teachings of Mme Blavatsky and Theosophy. In the difference, we can begin to see Solovyov's special contribution to his heirs with his own visions and re-visions of Sophia. First of all, Solovyov's visions are not a mere jumble of symbols.[63] He, in fact, insisted on placing his intuition of Sophia in a historical context and cited sources without confusing them. At the same time, as we saw, Solovyov's mystical vision was not a simple and opposite reaction to positivist tendencies or political feminism. His Sophia is not purely ideal any more than she is purely material. Instead, she is, or somehow affects, the interpenetration of opposites, transforming them through her own third agency into

---

63. Solovyov severely criticized Blavatsky's *Isis Unveiled*: "In my whole life I have never read a more obscure and disjointed book" (*Pis'ma* 4:290–91 and *SS* 6:394–398). See also "Retsenziia na knigu E. P. Blavatskoi: *The Key to Theosophy*," in *SS* 6:291.

a new whole. As in Christ, in whom the two opposing natures of human and divine are believed to coexist mutually but independently, in Solovyov's vseedinstvo (all-oneness) the multiple elements (*vse*, or all) retain their integrity while creating a new whole (*edinstvo*, or oneness/wholeness). In this way, Solovyov's Pansophius *is* truly wise, as he is truly good and truly beautiful.

A reading of *Three Conversations* reminds us of Solovyov's proclivity for threes, with the third being a mediating force that somehow transfigures the first two opposing elements. We saw this in his first public lecture "Three Powers," in which Russia is the third power that unites the East and the West to form a new whole. We saw it with the prophetic role of the Jews that will reconcile the kingly and priestly elements of the Eastern and Western churches to manifest itself as the eternally existing, true, "Universal" Church. Both love and art are such third transfiguring forces in Solovyov's aesthetic and "erotic" articles of the early 1890s, and Socrates is this "tertium quid" in his writing on Plato (*SS* 9:198). Sophia, however, is the most consistent of these mediators, "interpenetrators," or "mystical transfigurers."

Although it is obvious from its preface that *Three Conversations* is a fierce polemic with Lev Tolstoy, whom he derisively calls a "Hole-Worshipper" (*SS* 10:84), Solovyov claims that his work also has a "positive" goal: "to present the question of the struggle against evil and the meaning of history from three different points of view" (*SS* 10:87). As he continues in the preface, Conversation One features the words of the General, representing the "everyday religious" point of view of the past; Conversation Two focuses on the Politician, who expresses the "cultural progressive" ideas of the present. We then expect a third point of view that reconciles the preceding two: "The third, 'unconditionally religious,' which still stands to reveal its deciding significance in the future," is shown in the third conversation in the combined arguments of Mr. Z. and in Pansophius's story. It is principally the story "A Short Tale of the Antichrist," or rather, the interplay between the written story and its oral conclusion (since, Mr. Z. tells us, Pansophius died before he could complete the manuscript), that reconciles the earlier views and makes of them not a simple binary pair but a triadic process of interaction and interpenetration. What the story tells us is that we can arrive at the "highest unconditional truth" that "does not exclude nor does it negate the preparatory conditions of its appearance, but rather justifies, interprets, and sanctifies them," only through the interaction of the discussants and, finally, the reconciling power of Pansophius's vision of the future.[64]

As we conclude this section, we can see that Sophia helped Solovyov in his efforts to approach contemporary issues with the triadic ideals of bogochelovechestvo and vseedinstvo, the project of divine humanity and the "whole of things." His goal was the full reconciliation of the divine and the human—or spirit and matter, male and female—not through a motley, syncretic

---

64. *SS* 10: 87. For a more complete analysis, see Kornblatt, "Soloviev on Salvation."

accumulation of beliefs or a crude dualism that privileged either the material world or the world of spirits, but through a triadic and ultimately mystical operation of faith. Sophia provided him with the third element to effect this interpenetration.

WISDOM'S BEQUEST: SOPHIA THROUGH THE AGES

> You gaze at the stars, you, my bright star,
> O, if I were but the sky, to hold you
> In broad embraces, and with a myriad of eyes
> To feast upon you in wordless radiance.
>
> SOLOVYOV'S 1874 translation of a poem ascribed to Plato

Sophia's entrance into Russian culture took many paths, and the image that was bequeathed to Solovyov had many forms. Wisdom is a she and a he, foreign and familiar, at once highly esoteric and yet infused in everyday life through Russian folk and religious culture. This section looks at many of the traditions that took a religious or mystical form, or what could be called theosophic mysticism,[65] as well as at philosophical and literary articulations of the related ideas of the Eternal Feminine and the World Soul. Sources known to Solovyov at the time of his visions and his later re-visions include Hebrew and Christian scriptures, Platonic and Neoplatonic writers, patristic texts, Orthodox ritual and practice, Gnosticism, Kabbalah, medieval and early modern mysticism (including the writings of Jakob Boehme), and the tradition of the Eternal Feminine in Western literature. If Solovyov *did* see Sophia, he certainly had plenty of prior traditions in Western culture with which to compare his own vision(s) and from which to borrow explanations, descriptions, and authority. This section takes a largely chronological approach to those traditions, at the same time suggesting when in Solovyov's intellectual development a given explanation might have held the greatest sway. As we will see, however, Solovyov refers to almost all the Sophianic traditions examined here as early as his twenties, suggesting at least a cursory acquaintance with them as he began his writing career and thus the ability to pick and choose from their vocabularies of Wisdom as he sought the best articulation of his own intuitions. In no case do I claim that Solovyov was a Kabbalist, a Gnostic, a Neoplatonist, a Boehmian, a Mariologist, or a Christian heretic. He was instead an original thinker raised in the Russian Orthodox tradition at a time of tremendous political and social change in Russia, who traveled and read widely in a search of "the verbal form," as he says about *Three Conversations*, that would serve as "the simplest expression for that which I wanted to say" (*SS* 10:83).

---

65. See David's use of this term in relationship to Boehme in "The Influence of Jacob Boehme on Russian Religious Thought."

Wisdom in Hebrew Scriptures

> And I was near him, growing up,
> And I was his delight day by day,
> Frolicking before him at all times,
> Frolicking in his habitable world.
> And my delight is in mankind.
>
>   (Proverbs 8:30–31)

> Wisdom has built her house,
> set up her pillars seven.
>
>   (Proverbs 9:1)

As we saw earlier, Solovyov connects his Sophia to Hebrew scriptures as early as his *Lectures* in the 1870s, where he uses the Hebrew word for wisdom (*hokhmah*) in Cyrillic transliteration (Хохма): "There is an entire book in the Old Testament ascribed to Solomon that carries the title Sophia. This book is not canonical, but, as is well known, in the canonical book 'Proverbs' we find the development of the idea of Sophia (under the corresponding Hebrew name 'Khokhma')" (*SS* 3:115). *Hokhmah* is a feminine noun that appears as a personified figure in a handful of late biblical texts, most notably in Proverbs (a collection of sayings by ancient sages, compiled sometime before the second century BCE) and in the apocryphal Book of Wisdom (37–41 CE), also called the Wisdom of Solomon because of Solomon's alleged authorship of the earlier book. It is this figure of Wisdom, or Sophia as translated in the Greek Septuagint version of the Bible, that forms the biblical basis of all later discussions of Divine Wisdom. Sophia is of course not the only feminine divine figure to emerge in the ancient Middle East; there are also the Canaanite Asherah and Phoenician Astarte, the Sumerian Inanna, Ishtar of the Babylonians, and the Egyptian Isis, to name only a few.[66] But Wisdom/Hokhmah is never fully personified in the five books of the Torah, the earliest texts of Hebrew scriptures and those that form the core of Judaism's religious teachings. Only in historically later books of the Bible, like Proverbs, does she take on the female form of her possible predecessor goddesses from the surrounding peoples.

Even in the later biblical texts where she *is* personified, she is nonetheless ambiguous: at once a creation of God, coeternal with God, an intermediary between God and the created world, and a wise and powerful woman. In the Book of Job, "God understands the way to her and he alone knows where she dwells" (Job 28:23). In Proverbs:

> The Lord created me at the beginning of his way,
> At the start of his works of old.
> In primeval days I was formed,

---

66. See Matthews, Reuther, and Schüssler Fiorenza for feminist readings of the development of a female goddess as Wisdom.

At the start, at the world's origin.
When there were yet no deeps I was born,
When there were yet no springs, sources of water.
Before the mountains were set down,
Before the hills I was born,
Ere he made the earth and the ground,
The land's first lumps of soil.
When he established the heavens, there was I,
When he inscribed a circle on the face of the deep,
When he secured the clouds on high,
When he strengthened the founts of the deep,
When he marked the bounds of the sea,
That the waters transgress not his command,
When he firmed up the foundations of the earth.
And I was near him, growing up,
And I was his delight day by day,
Frolicking before him at all times,
Frolicking in his habitable world.
And my delight is in mankind.

(Proverbs 8:22–32)

Wisdom has built her house,
Set up her pillars seven,
Slaughtered her cattle,
mixed her wine,
set her table.
Having sent forth her maids, she cries
At the tops of the city heights:
"Whoever is callow—let him come over here!
Whoever is senseless—to him I'll say:
'Come, dine on my food;
drink of the wine I have mixed.
Abandon the callowness and live;
Walk in the path of understanding.

(Proverbs 9:1–6)

Proverbs in turn served as an inspiration for a number of later apocryphal texts,[67] the most important being, as already mentioned, the Book of Wisdom:

And whatsoever is secret and manifest I learned to know,
For Wisdom the contriver [artificer/artist] of all taught me.

(Wisdom 7:21; Reider 115)

For she is a vapour [breath] of the power of God,
And a pure emanation of the glory of the Almighty.
Therefore nothing defiled creeps into her.
For she is a reflection of eternal light,

67. See Fox 24–27.

And a spotless mirror of the working of God,
And an image of his goodness.
But she being one can do all,
And abiding in herself makes all things new,
And generation by generation passing into holy souls,
Makes them friends of God and prophets.
For nothing does God love save him that dwells with wisdom.
For she is fairer than the sun,
And above all order of the stars;
Being compared with light she is found superior.
                    (Wisdom 7:25–27; Reider 117)[68]

Sophia is thus many states, activities, and persons at once, even in these related texts. The term used for wisdom is a noun that requires feminine pronouns and verbal forms, as though Hokhmah refers to a woman who somehow was "with" God in the "beginning," who can build a house and invite guests, yet who is an abstract metaphor: the "brightness of everlasting light" itself. Hebrew has no capital letters, further playing on the ambiguity of Hokhmah as a proper name. We read that she is a mirror of God's power and the image of his goodness and can enter into human souls to transform them into God's friends. Even further complicating the figure of Wisdom is the fact that several of the terms in the original Hebrew text of Proverbs are in fact ambiguous and have been variously translated through the centuries. In particular, in the phrase above "And I was near him, growing up," "growing up" is in fact a noun in Hebrew that has also been translated as child, ward, nursling, artisan, workman, and artist. The latter translations have clearly affected the understanding of Wisdom as a cocreator and/or a model for our own creation. In addition, she is the delight and joy of God, and similarly delights in humanity. It is not absolutely clear from these references, obviously, who or what she is. As the biblical scholar Michael Fox argues about Hokhmah in Proverbs, "Lady Wisdom is a strange being, a personification of a mental power who claims to have preceded creation and to exist in a daughter-like relationship to God. She transcends mundane reality and human minds, individually and collectively, yet is active in the busiest spheres of human existence. She is not simply a symbol of ordinary human wisdom, yet she is in some way identified with it" (352). Despite the possibility of comparison to other ancient goddesses as suggested above, and regardless of her attraction to many contemporary feminist readers as a female God, female side of God, or female consort with God (she is referred to as his wife or "friend" as well as daughter),[69] in Proverbs she is what Fox calls a "mythos," or "narrative trope that serves as an explanatory paradigm in areas where literal discourse must be supplemented by poetic imagination" (352). Further, "Lady

---

68. For other noncanonical personifications, see the Book of Sirach (Ecclesiasticus) 1 and the Qumran wisdom texts.
69. See Matthews; Johnson.

Wisdom is indeed godlike, but that is a literary disguise. . . . Wisdom's role in relation to God is intellectual and aesthetic" (354, 355).

Fox's analysis of Wisdom as a literary disguise is indeed helpful for the present discussion, for "her" appearance in Russia came largely in literary and iconographic form. Yes, she is a woman but a woman as metaphor, a woman who "stands for" many different and sometimes contradictory things and one who has poetic as well as explanatory or discursive power. Her image as mirror is particularly striking ("And a spotless mirror of the working of God," Wisdom 7, 26): and is associated with her by Boehme as well as by Solovyov later. The mirror reproduces or, more literally, re-visions the quality of another, uniting viewer and viewed. Wisdom for Solovyov unites and transforms through vision and through light, which itself makes vision possible, whether directly or in a mirror. This uniting and enabling quality of light is perhaps the reason he was attracted to the poem he ascribed to Plato used as the epigraph to this section. "You" and "I" in the poem become one as the speaker transforms into a star to embrace his beloved star "with a myriad of eyes."

In Proverbs, Wisdom's message, to the extent that we can determine one, takes more than one literary form and requires our literary and aesthetic sense to interpret. The book itself is composed of at least two types of writing: "lectures" (mostly "sayings" in the form of adages, admonitions, aphorism, apothegms, epigrams, precepts, or proverbs) and "personification interludes" (Fox, 14–15 and 44–47). The lessons teach wisdom, and the interludes describe Wisdom as a person and have her speak. Thus, what we learn from Proverbs is a paradox: Wisdom is both teacher and what is taught. She is both the content and the vehicle, both the house and the inhabitant, both the builder/creator and the creation that is built. It is this paradox that drives the complexity of Solovyov's own Sophia.

Despite the apparent concreteness of Wisdom's female personification in Proverbs and the apocryphal texts that emphasize her personhood, she did not continue to develop as such in postbiblical Judaism, just as she did not exist as such in the earlier biblical texts. What does occur in the Talmud and elsewhere is another feminine term: *Shekhinah.* Shekhinah first appeared in the popular second-century translation of the Torah into Aramaic by Onkelos that became the basis of much later Jewish commentary (much like the Septuagint translation did for Christian exegesis). There the term Shekhinah helps the translator cope with passages that imply too anthropomorphic a reading of God, who sometimes rests, angers, leads, descends, and speaks. In the Hebrew Bible we can find multiple variations on the root *sh-kh-n,* meaning to dwell. When the letter "mem" is added as prefix, the root becomes a "mishkan," the term for the sanctuary or dwelling place of God. Adding instead a "hay" to the end of the three-letter root, the word changes to represent that which dwelled, or the manifestation of God: Shekhinah. In the postbiblical era, then, the translator can claim that it is not God who dwells, but His Shekhinah.

The Shekhinah becomes extremely important in the Talmudic period in the fourth to sixth centuries and even more so in medieval mysticism. In the latter, she has a familial relationship with Hokhmah, a fact—or rather a confusion—that Solovyov exploits even later, as we will see in the selection from *Russia and the Universal Church*. Before discussing the mystical tradition of Kabbalah that develops these particular manifestations of the Divine, however, we must take a look at Wisdom in the later Greek world. Hellenic culture paralleled the stages of Jewish writings on Wisdom discussed above and in some cases intersected with them. Plato is an obvious starting point, as he was for Solovyov himself, but we must also look at Wisdom in the Neoplatonists and in the writing of the "middle Platonist," Philo of Alexandria, a late Hellenic Jew who sought to combine Platonic thought with Hebrew scripture. Philo is particularly important in the development of the idea of Divine Wisdom, for he served as a basis for the interpretation of Sophia in several New Testament passages by important patristic authors. As Philo attempted to reconcile the Wisdom of Proverbs with that of Greek philosophy, he turned away from her/its concrete female associations in the later biblical texts and paved the way for her/its/his identity with the abstract, male Logos.

Greek Wisdom, Love, and the Soul of the World

> If Eros is the positive and substantive union of two natures—divine and mortal—divided in the universe and united in man only in an external way, then what can be his true and definitive task if not to make that mortal nature into an immortal one?
>
> SOLOVYOV, *The Life Drama of Plato*

> To the motions of the soul answer the motions of the universe, and by the study of these the individual is restored to his original nature.
>
> PLATO, *Timaeus*

> Thus may the divine spirit of wisdom not lightly shift His dwelling and be gone, but long, long abide with us.
>
> PHILO, "On the Giants"

Afanasii Fet's suggestion to Solovyov to "give Plato to Russian literature" (*SS* 12:360) led to the 1899 publication of translations of seven of Plato's dialogues with introductions to each, as well as an introductory essay of what was to be the first of several volumes (*SS* 12:360–480). A year earlier, Solovyov had already turned his attention to Plato in a lengthy essay he titled *The Life Drama of Plato*,[70] in which he identifies Eros as a mediating figure

---

70. Kochetkova translates the work as the *Existential Drama of Plato*, because "Solov'jov indicates the existential sources of Plato's idealism": "either truth does not exist at all (and thus life is meaningless), or it is transcendental. In this situation, Plato reached a conclusion about the existence of the world of ideas, of truth and the good as such, transcendental to the imperfect material world" (Kochetkova, *Vladimir Solov'jov's Theory of Divine Humanity*, xx–xxi). See also Kochetkova, *The Search for Authentic Spirituality*, 65–67.

between the divine and material worlds. Eros in this text in fact operates in much the same way as light mediates between spirit (often also figured as light) and matter in other essays on love and beauty: "In this unmerged, yet undivided union of matter and light, both preserve their own nature, but neither one nor the other is visible in its separateness. What is visible is only light-bearing matter and incarnated light—illuminated coal and petrified rainbow ("Beauty in Nature," *SS* 6:40).

As we have seen, Solovyov had already associated Plato with the transfiguring power of both light and love. In 1874 he published what he called his first attempt at real poetry (*nastoiashchie stikhi*), the translation of a poem allegedly written by the ancient Greek thinker:

> You gaze at the stars, you, my bright star,
> O, if I were but the sky, to hold you
> In broad embraces, and with a myriad of eyes
> To feast upon you in wordless radiance.
> (*SS* 12:57 and *Stikhotvoreniia* 180)

In this poem, love causes the speaker to transform from an observer of light to an emitter of light—the star-filled sky—so that he can shine with the "wordless radiance" that is the primary quality of the "you" of the poem: "my bright star." From a "myriad of eyes," his vision of light thus transfigures him into light. For Solovyov, this poem is an example of Plato's erotic period, when Socrates' best student discovered love as a mediating force between his world of ideas and the crude matter around him. In his life drama, Plato presumably fell into dualistic pessimism immediately after Socrates' death. He could see "no connection between the perfect fullness of the gods' ideas and the hopeless wilderness of mortal life. There was, indeed, no rational connection. But something irrational happened. An intermediate force between gods and mortals appeared—neither a god nor a human, but some powerful daemonic and heroic being. His name was Eros, and his task was to build a bridge between heaven and earth, and between those two and the underworld" (*SS* 9:226). Solovyov thus writes of love as a mediating force that can bridge alienating dualism and create a new whole, as he says, "in beauty" (*SS* 9:228). Love allows the "I" and the "you" of the poem Solovyov ascribed to Plato to embrace, allowing a new whole: the radiant night sky, itself an interpenetration of light and dark.

Interestingly, but typical for many of Solovyov's transfigured wholes, the two opposing elements and the third power that allows for their union are paradoxically both united and distinct. Sometimes their qualities, descriptions, and even designations seem to overlap; thus light in this poem is both a third power connecting two other states and a metaphor for one of the two: the star for which the "I" yearns. Furthermore, the "I" and the "you" are confused even before the union in the night sky, for who is it who "gazes" in the first line? The star or the viewer? The resulting union also defies reason.

Like the beautiful diamond of the quotation from "Beauty in Nature" above, it is at once "illuminated coal and petrified rainbow."

Perhaps the best way to understand this ongoing, nonrational process is to see the third element, or mediator—whether the daemon Eros, immaterial light, or Sophia—not as a thing, being, or even a state, but as a force or action that enables the potential for wholeness to emerge from the interaction of two opposing beings, things, or states. Solovyov uses the term *podvig* (heroic feat) for this activity; a word that typically refers to the action of saints and martyrs. The third member of the triad makes possible the interpenetration and transformation of the first two. Eros as the catalyst for potentiality is clear in the following passage from *The Life Drama of Plato*: "Love, in the sense of erotic pathos, always has *corporeality* as its subject. But corporeality that is worthy of love, that is beautiful and immortal, does not grow on its own from the earth nor fall ready-made from the sky. It is acquired through a spiritual-physical and divine-human feat [*bogo-chelovecheskim podvigom*]" (SS 9:234). Here Solovyov connects his reading of Plato's philosophy to his own philosophy of divine humanity (bogochelovechestvo). Recognizing the potential for transfiguration, Eros affects a union between two beings and through its divine-human podvig affects divine humanity.

Solovyov discusses love most extensively in his long essay from the early 1890s, also heavily indebted to Plato, "The Meaning of Love." In numerous passages, love, meaning principally the psycho-physical (or spiritual-material) attraction of sexual love, sounds quite a bit like Sophia:

> The meaning and value of love, as a feeling, consists in the fact that it causes us truly, with all our being, to recognize in *another* that unconditional, central significance that, due to egoism, we sense only in ourselves. Love is important not as one of our feelings, but as the transference of all of our life's interest out of ourselves and into another, as the relocation of the very center of our personal lives. This is true of all love, but of sexual love in particular. (SS 7:21–22)

> True love is that which not only affirms in subjective feeling the unconditional significance of human individuality in another as well as in oneself, but also justifies that unconditional significance in reality, truly delivering us from the inescapability of death and filling our life with unconditional content. (SS 7:32)

> In sexual love that is truly understood and truly manifest, this divine essence receives the means for its final and ultimate incarnation in the individual life of a human being, the means for the deepest and at the same time the most external, actual, perceptible union with it. From here shine those rays of unearthly divinity, that current of unearthly joy that accompanies even incomplete love and that makes it—even the incomplete love—into the greatest delight of people and gods—*hominom divomque voluptas* [Latin: the desire of men and gods].[71] (SS 7:46)

---

71. From Lucretius, "On the Nature of Things."

Despite their similar abilities to create joy and to transfigure ("When Eros enters into an earthly being, he immediately transfigures him; the one in love feels within himself a new and endless power, he receives a new, great gift" [SS 9:227]), Sophia and Plato's erotic love are not exactly synonymous in Solovyov. Rather, Eros is but one of the metaphors used in the modern poet-philosopher's many re-visions, and a contradictory one at that. Love, after all, is itself intangible, nonmaterial, and ultimately nonrational. Perhaps because the author of *The Life Drama of Plato* ultimately saw Plato's drama as a tragedy, he did not draw a direct link between his own vision of Wisdom and Plato's "pontifex."[72] Reading what he considered Plato's last works, in which the great philosopher of irrational love and author of the masterpieces *Symposium* and *Phaedrus* submits fully to crude earthly law, Solovyov believed that Plato proved too weak to take up the legacy of Socrates, the original lover of wisdom (see SS 9:240). Plato's tragedy was his inability to make use of the interpenetrating Wisdom—Sophia—that had been handed to him by his mentor. Despite his brush with Eros, the world remained for him dualistic.

Still, Plato's legacy to Solovyov was powerful, both directly and through the Neoplatonic thinkers who followed on Plato's heels and elaborated—or sometimes mystified—his metaphysics and cosmology. References to the Neoplatonists and creative use of their philosophical or mystical vocabulary pepper Solovyov's poetry as well as his philosophy. The Greek thinkers of the decades surrounding the turn of the Common Era indeed play a special role for Solovyov, for they represent the transitional period between the idealism of ancient Greece and the nascent Christian world. Their Logos is the abstract, transcendental Word of Greek philosophy at the same time as it moves toward the personal immanence of divinity brought into the world through the Jews. Therefore, Solovyov does not blame his Greek mentor for failing to see the integration of spirit and matter, undivided, yet unmerged: "The impotence and fall of the 'divine' Plato were important because they clearly underline and clarify the inability of man to fulfill his calling, i.e., to become a real *superman* by the power of mind, genius, and will alone. They clarify the need for a real, substantive *Godman*" (SS 9:241). Plato's failure thus leaves the way open for the next historical period in Solovyov's oft-repeated scheme: the integration of the Hellenic and Jewish worlds, leading to the birth of Christianity in the figure of Jesus Christ.

Solovyov knew of the Greek Neoplatonists as well as of the Jewish writer Philo of Alexandria early in his career. He wrote of them in his sixth lecture on Divine Humanity, just before the lecture in which he introduced Logos and

---

72. "This is not a god, but the natural and supreme priest of divinity, i.e., *a mediator* [posrednik]—a maker of bridges. The younger brother and heir of Greece—the Roman nation—explains the identity of these concepts with a single word: "pontifex," meaning both priest and bridge-builder" (SS 9:226).

Sophia as two kinds of unity within the Absolute: "Logos, too, is distinct from Sophia but is inwardly united with her" (*SS* 3:115; see page 176): "Since one of these divine elements (the absolute personhood of God) was preeminently revealed to the genius of the Jewish nation while the other (the absolute idea of Divinity) was especially perceived by the genius of Hellenism, it is clear why the synthesis of these two elements (a synthesis that is necessary for the complete knowledge of God) would occur when and where the Jewish and Greek nationalities collided" (*SS* 3:80).

The Neoplatonist Plotinus, who lived in the second century CE, distinguished three principal hypostases in the Absolute: the One, Mind, and Soul. Solovyvov seemed particularly influenced by Plotinus's cosmology as early as *The Sophia* (see page 140), but by the end of the 1890s and his encyclopedia articles on Plotinus, Porphyry, and Proclus (*SS* 10:479–87), the visionary of Sophia recognized his differences as well as similarities with them. According to this later Solovyov, the Neoplatonists find no role for social, political, or historical works and seek escape upward, away from the physical world. Solovyov, instead, seeks to transfigure reality, often through social activity, rather than escape it. Furthermore, the Neoplatonic divine emanations proceed from the Absolute down through the hypostases, diminishing in power as they move toward the created world. Solovyov's Sophia, unlike Plotinus's, is not weaker as she looks toward humanity. Instead, she creates a union between humanity and divinity, sacralizing the former without diminishing the latter.

Because of his Jewish origins and his Greek education, the earlier writer Philo of Alexandria (c. 25 BCE–45 CE) represented for Solovyov an even better bridge between Hellenic idealism and the reality of the Christian God-man. As he wrote in *Lectures*: "Philo, as we know, developed the doctrine of the Logos (the word, or reason) as the 'expresser' of the divine universal essence and the mediator between the one God and all that exists" (*SS* 3:80–81). It is thus from Philo that Solovyov probably derived the intimate relationship between Logos and Sophia:

> It has been aptly said that in Philo's God-idea the First Cause of the metaphysicians has been blended with the Lord of the Bible. . . . The two aspects of perfection were united in the concept of the Divine Logos, the Word and Wisdom of the Supreme Being, who also is represented as being simultaneously abstract and personal. He is, on the one side, the sum of the divine thoughts (the ideas) and the force of the deity, on the other side God's first-born son (after Proverbs 8, 22), who executes the volition of his father (hence the prominence of this idea in Christian dogma), and his deputy in the character of head of the angels. This many-faced entity is the connecting link between the Inaccessible and creation; it embodies God's presence in the world." (Lewy 11)

Philo's Sophia/Logos became particularly influential for the early Greek fathers of the Christian church, who, like the Hellenistic Jewish thinker, needed to relate the philosophical tradition of the gentiles with the Jewish one of Jesus' first disciples. We will see below how Wisdom—now depersonalized and defeminized—became an attractive model for Logos in the early church. Solovyov's own Sophia could then look back through the patristic writings to Philo and through Philo back both to Plato and the original Hebrew texts that the Russian visionary so loved. Although no Sophia was exactly his, each of the traditions he studied provided him with material from which to choose the closest approximation to the Wisdom that he personally "saw."

Before moving to the early Christian understanding of Sophia, an area of particular interest to Solovyov as he sought to justify in modern terms the "faith of our fathers" (SS 4:243), we need to parse another seeming contradiction in Solovyov's articulations of Wisdom: the relationship of Sophia to the World Soul (Mirovaia dusha or Dusha mira). This relationship is often misunderstood and requires some exploration here.

In his encyclopedia article "The World Soul" written at the end of his career (SS 10:246–47), Solovyov acknowledges Plato as the originator of the concept and traces its development through the philosopher's successors up to the nineteenth century. This drily academic rather than poetic or metaphorical definition implies that Plato's World Soul does not encompass all the properties, abilities, and/or tasks of Divine Wisdom. For one, it/she lives in nature as a "living being." Despite the fact that earlier in his career Solovyov sometimes uses the terms "World Soul," "Soul of the World," and "Sophia" interchangeably, in the article the first two designations refer to only part of the visionary's intuition about Sophia, the intermediary and transfigurer of heaven and earth. The World Soul as Solovyov looks back on her is a "living being, possessing desires, ideas, and emotions," herself an idea but more closely allied to the created world than the Absolute. This encyclopedia entry suggests that the World Soul is, in a sense, an earthly, rather than divine Sophia.

In "The Meaning of Love," Solovyov explains the irrational interpenetration of opposites in love as created (or reborn—he uses the term pererozhde-nie) through a dual process of ascending and descending love. The third, transforming element thus has two faces, upward and downward:

> The subject of true love is not simple, but dual. In the first place, we love the ideal being (ideal not as an abstraction, but in the sense that it belongs to another, higher realm of existence), which we must bring into our own ideal world. And, second, we love that natural human being who provides the living, personal material for that realization, and who, through it, is idealized, not in the sense of our subjective imagination, but rather by its real, objective transformation or rebirth. Thus, true love is inextricably both *ascending* and *descending* (*amor ascendens* and *amor descendens*, or those two Aphrodites that Plato so clearly discerned, but poorly distinguished—Ἀφροδίτη Οὐρανία and Ἀφροδίτη Πάνδημος [Greek: Aphrodite Uranis and Aphrodite Pandomos]. (SS 7:46)

Plato's two Aphrodites, one who ascends from the created world to heaven and the other who descends in the opposite direction, open the way for a bifurcation not only of love (philo-), but of wisdom (-sophy) with which it is united. To cope with this duality, Solovyov connects Plato's bidirectional Eros to the manifestation of at least one aspect of Sophia: the World Soul. In *The Life Drama of Plato*, Solovyov writes of the dialogue *Timeaus* as representative of Plato's erotic period: "There is no longer any mention of the unconditional opposition between two worlds and two lives. Only a relative opposition between the principles that form the universe remains. In the *Timeaus*, a central place belongs to the *World Soul* that connects ideal and real being. The *World Soul* is another name for Eros" (*SS* 9:238).

Solovyov's association between Sophia and what one scholar calls her "doublet," the World Soul, is not consistent throughout his oeuvre.[73] Solovyov first mentions the World Soul in *The Sophia*, where he claims that Soul exists as the third element of the classical triad—from Plotinus—of Spirit (or One), Mind, and Soul and thus plays a vital role in the development of the universe. The cosmology of Neoplatonism seems to have preoccupied the philosopher during this period of his stay in England and Egypt, and the World Soul, or Plato's Cosmic or Universal Soul, is a natural outgrowth of that interest. But is Soul equal to Wisdom? In the third dialogue of *The Sophia*, Sophie instructs the Philosophe about the structure of reality and the relationship between individuals and the cosmic whole, but she does not make a direct association between herself as Wisdom and the third element of the cosmic triad:

> There are as many particular souls as there are ideas, but all of these souls are only parts and elements of the World Soul. In other words, they are objective and material in relation to the World Soul—they form the body of the Soul—while the bodily elements strictly speaking, that is the direct products of the material principle, form the external or material body of the great organism.
>
> Mind is Spirit entered into the ideal process; Soul is Spirit entered into the real process. Mind is the first complete appearance of the absolute first principle (as the principle of ideal unity); Soul is its second complete appearance (as the principle of real unity). But we saw that the absolute principle does not lose itself when it becomes manifest; it remains in and of itself, always separated from its manifestations. Thus, we have three divine hypostases: Spirit, Mind, and Soul. (*PSS* 2:110–111; see page 139)

Where is Wisdom in this triad? Solovyov makes the connection in *Lectures on Divine Humanity* just two years later, when he calls the World Soul "the principle of humanity," "the ideal or normal human," which is the "unity, to

---

73. De Courten writes: "From the outset of his career, this experience urged him to investigate the topic of Sophia and its doublet, World Soul" (207, 209). Solovyov was not even consistent with the capitalization of World Soul and did not always imply that it/she is a discrete person.

which we give the mystical name Sophia" (*SS* 3:121; see page 180). Sophia is thus the "universally human organism as the eternal body of God and the eternal soul of the world" (*SS* 3:127; see page 184). Here Sophia is identical to the World Soul, which itself is identical to the clearly paradoxical body of God. As in the fuller passage from *Lectures* cited at the beginning of this study, the World Soul/Sophia is passive, in partnership with the active Logos. It/she is "pure striving, at first not knowing toward what it strives."[74] And what does it/she strive for? The same goal as the divine principle: "Thus, here the divine principle strives toward the same thing as the World Soul—toward the incarnation of the divine idea or toward the divinization (theosis) of all that exists through the introduction of it in the form of the absolute organism" (*SS* 3:145). World Soul, like Sophia, is here the power that allows for both incarnation and transfiguration, thus creating a new whole from the opposition of spirit and matter.

Despite the above identification of Sophia, the World Soul, and the body of God, *Lectures* also suggests a differentiation. "Insofar as it receives the divine Logos into itself and is determined by the divine Logos, the World Soul is humanity, the divine humanity of Christ, the body of Christ, Sophia." But the World Soul "has in itself the principle of independent action, or will, that is, the capacity to initiate in itself an inner striving. In other words, the World Soul can itself choose the object of its life-striving" (*SS* 3:140, 141; see page 189). "The World Soul can separate the relative center of its life from the absolute center of divine life; it can assert itself outside God. But thereby the World Soul necessarily loses its central position, falls out of the all—one center of divine being—and ends up at the multiple periphery of creation, losing its freedom and power over this creation." The result is evil, and the fruit of evil is then suffering.[75] "All of creation is thus made subject to the vanity and bondage of corruption not willingly but by the will of that which has subjugated it: by the will of the World Soul, as the one free principle of natural life" (*SS* 3:142; see page 190). By an assertion of her/its own will, the World Soul thus pulls free of God and is opposed to the divine world. In this formulation, she no longer appears identical to the Divine Sophia.

We have already seen that Solovyov recognizes two Aphrodites in Plato, suggesting that Eros splits in two, depending on the direction of its action. And Eros is another name for World Soul. Soul in Neoplatonic thought is the "principle of real multiplicity" and thus the hypostasis most closely connected to our fragmented world. It is itself divided into two: the upper and the lower soul. Solovyov adopts this vocabulary and tells us that the lower soul is called nature (*SS* 10:481). The World Soul at this point in *Lectures* is far indeed from Divine Wisdom.

---

74. *The Sophia* also associates Soul with "blind desire." See page 138.

75. Here Solovyov draws not only on Neoplatonic imagery but also on the more vivid cosmology of Gnosticism, also developed in the early centuries of the Common Era. We will examine this legacy in a later section.

The confusion only becomes greater. Does the existence of the World Soul mean that Sophia is split in two, into a divine and an earthly wisdom? Or does the World Soul mean that Sophia is not half and half but one plus one, both fully created and fully divine? But would this not be Jesus Christ, the Godman? In *Lectures on Divine Humanity*, Solovyov calls Sophia the "body of God" (*SS* 3:115; see page 176). In *La Russie et l'église universelle*, however, Sophia herself has a body, which Solovyov explains by reintroducing the World Soul. Here the Soul of the World is called the "corporeality of Wisdom" (*SS* 11:310). Where Sophia had been the intermediary above, the World Soul becomes it below.

This chain of reasoning does not prove that Solovyov's World Soul is only a kind of creaturely Sophia, in opposition to a somehow better, untainted divine one, untouched by evil, just as earlier articulations did not prove that Sophia and the World Soul are one. Solovyov's own evocations of the Soul of the World are too contradictory for that simple conclusion. Perhaps, indeed, Sophia remains whole, not bifurcated. Despite, or perhaps because of, her wholeness, she or it can focus her attention in two directions, manifesting herself as the World Soul when she moves upward from earth toward her divine self and as Divine Wisdom when she moves toward humanity and the world. Her bidirectional gaze thus increases rather than diminishes her scope. Indeed, in *Lectures*, even the two worlds, natural and divine, are not opposed: "Thus, these two worlds are distinguished not by essence, but only by position" (*SS* 3:132–133).

Solovyov's Sophia is free (SS 3:140; see page 188) because she is at the same time both one and the other. Unlike the Neoplatonists' World Soul, she does not diminish in strength or divinity as she moves toward humanity. Instead, she strengthens humanity by her participation with it in the process of Divine Humanity. In her role in the deification of flesh, she is, as Philo suggests, quite a bit like God-the-Son/the Logos/Christ.

At least one scholar of Solovyov explains the difference between the World Soul and Sophia in the *Lectures* as a result of a mere change in vocabulary, not definition. If Neoplatonic terminology dominated his earlier expression in *The Sophia*, he here adopts the language of the church fathers. Instead of the triad of Spirit-Mind-Soul that comprises the divine and cosmic organism, Solovyov speaks in his *Lectures* of the Christian Trinity of God the Father, Logos the Son, and Holy Spirit. But where is Sophia? She becomes the metaphysical body of the entire Trinity and the energy that binds the three hypostases together. She is at once beyond the Trinity and integral to it.[76] And where is the World Soul? According to Kochetkova, "The core of Sophia is that She is a transcendental archetype of the Cosmos, contained with the

---

76. "Solov'jov's analysis of the Trinity is important for us here because, firstly, it places Sophia beyond the Trinity as such, and secondly, it shows that the inner dynamics of the triune Absolute necessarily leads to the idea of Sophia" (Kochetkova, *Solov'jov's Theory of Divine Humanity*, 155).

Divine; when this archetype is embodied, incarnated, then She appears as Cosmic soul" (134). Cosmic or World Soul can then "assert itself outside of God" (*SS* 3:142); it can fall. Kochetkova reconciles Sophia and the willful, desiring, and fallen Soul by seeing an evolutionary process of the "transcendental archetype of the Cosmos" from Divine Wisdom to World Soul. The latter then longs to return to the Divine; that return takes place in human history in the process of bogochelovechestvo.

Unfortunately, this evolutionary scheme only partly explains the multiplicity of designations for Sophia throughout Solovyov's oeuvre, even within *Lectures* itself. Instead, we have Sophia as sometimes identical to the World Soul and sometimes in opposition to it, as Divinity is opposed to fallen matter. Instead of a clear development of the meaning of Sophia, we see Solovyov work his way back and forth through a variety of traditions and vocabularies as he seeks an ever-closer approximation for the articulation of his own visions. Sophia changes throughout Solovyov's oeuvre—indeed, even within a single work—not because of an evolution of Sophia or a unidirectional development of Solovyov's own thoughts on her, but because Solovyov casts about in different traditions for her best expression. Sometimes one tradition works better than others, but never does one provide the entire explanation. We can recognize Plato when Solovyov focuses on Eros, we see Philo in his connection between Logos and Sophia, and we see the Neoplatonists in his attempt to place her as World Soul in the triad of Spirit-Mind-Soul. We have already seen her as the Hokhmah of Hebrew scriptures, and in the following sections we will see her in the Gnostic Agia Sophia as separate from Sophia Prouneikos, as Kabbalah's Shekhinah, and, closer to Solovyov's own home, as Moist Mother Earth and the Divine Wisdom of Russian iconography.

Wisdom in Christian Scriptures, Patristics, and Orthodox Liturgy

> Christ the Power of God, and the Wisdom of God
>> 1 Corinthians 1: 24

> Wisdom! Attend!
>> DIVINE LITURGY OF ST. JOHN CHRYSOSTOM

The term "wisdom" occurs at least twenty times in the books of the New Testament, and the Book of Luke refers specifically to the "wisdom of Solomon" (11:31), pointing directly to Proverbs and/or the Book of Wisdom. The classic New Testament citation for Divine Wisdom, however, is found in First Corinthians 1:24: "But unto them which are called, both Jews and Greeks, Christ the power of God, and the wisdom of God." In this letter to the newly christianized Greeks of Corinth, Paul uses the term "wisdom," referring to who or what existed in the "beginning of His way" (Proverbs 8:22), as a synonym for Christ. Christ is wisdom, just as He is light and love in other New Testament passages. Although there is some controversy in New Testament scholarship about what wisdom meant to Paul as well as to the Corinthians when this letter was written (see Horsley 224–39), it was clear to all the earliest Christian interpreters that wisdom here is *not* a feminine hypostasis as she was in Proverbs. She, he, or it is an attribute of God and a name for Christ the Logos, an abstraction that has as much to do with the Greek philosophy practiced in pagan Corinth as metaphors for "her" in Hebrew scriptures to which Paul allegedly refers.[77] Philo and the Neoplatonists had prepared the way for Wisdom-Logos.

Paul's association of wisdom with Christ had a strong influence in the first several centuries on the fathers of the church, to whom all later theologians refer.[78] Many of these Christian writers and preachers—including Origen, Methodius, Epiphanius of Salamis, Gregory of Nyssa, Arius and Athanasius, Sophronius, and John of Damascus—presuppose both the identity of Sophia and Logos/Christ and thus the mutually divine and created nature of the two (Schiplinger 58–59).[79] Christ *is* Sophia, or Wisdom, just as He is Love.

The naming of the central cathedral of Hagia Sophia (Holy Wisdom) in Constantinople no doubt stems from the reference to Christ as wisdom in First Corinthians and the interpretation given to the passage by the church fathers.[80] One strong indication of the association can be found in a ninth-century mosaic identified as Christ as Holy Wisdom, found in the narthex of Hagia Sophia. This mosaic shows Christ on a throne, flanked by two medallions, one of a woman and one of an angel. An emperor bows at Christ's feet. The location of the mosaic over the main entrance suggests it is a depiction of the church's patron saint, in this case St. Sophia. She/He/It is Christ enthroned. The emperor has been identified as Leo VI (886–912), who must have commissioned this particular iconographic arrangement: "Thus above the entrance of the greatest church in the Empire the Basileus depicted his heavenly ruler, Christ-Holy-Wisdom, with himself kneeling at his Master's feet receiving the investiture of Wisdom" (A. Grabar, *Byzantine Painting* 97).

Wisdom first appears in Orthodox liturgy around the ninth century, at about the same time as the creation of the mosaic in Hagia Sophia. There, too, Sophia seems to be associated only with Christ. In the Divine Liturgy and at

77. Some scholars concerned about the Orthodoxy of Sophia are adamant about the single association of her with Christ. According to Metropolitan Antonii, "There is no doubt that the Fathers of the Church understood Divine Wisdom as the Incarnated Word—Jesus Christ . . . and that Byzantium remained unconditionally faithful to the tradition for a millennium" (61). Georges Florovsky enumerates the various patristic identifications of "Sophia-Wisdom" with Christ in "The Hagia Sophia Churches" 132.

78. "Greek philosophy and the writings of Philo had begun to blur the distinctions between Sophia (the Idea of the ideas) and the Logos, and some Old Testament texts also placed God's Word and God's Wisdom in close proximity to one another (Ps 33,6; Is 55, 11; Wisd. 9,1). The Corinthians passage further contributed to identifying Sophia with the Logos among some Church Fathers and the theologians" (Schiplinger 44).

79. Origen of Alexandria (185–254 CE); Methodius of Olympus (?–c. 311 CE); Epiphanius of Salamis (310–403 CE); Gregory of Nyssa (?–c. 385 CE); Arius (250–336 CE); Athanasius (296–373 CE); Sophronius (fifth century); John of Damascus (676–749 CE).

80. Florovsky, "Hagia Sophia" 132, and "O pochitanii Sofii" 485.

Mosaic of Christ as Holy Wisdom, from the narthex of Hagia Sophia, Constantinople.

Блаже́нни миротво́рцы, я́кѡ ті́и сы́нове Бо́жїи нареку́тсѧ.

Блаже́нни изгна́ни пра́вды ра́ди, я́кѡ тѣ́хъ є́сть ца́рство небе́сное.

Блаже́нни єстѐ, єгда̀ поно́сѧтъ ва́мъ, и изжену́тъ, и реку́тъ всѧ́къ ѕо́лъ глаго́лъ на вы̀ лжу́ще Менѐ ра́ди.

Їере́й: Го́споду помо́лимсѧ.

Ли́къ: Го́споди, поми́луй.

Ра́дуйтесѧ и весел**и́**тесѧ, я́кѡ мзда̀ ва́ша мно́га на небесѣ́хъ.

Вхо́дъ съ Ева́нгелїемъ.

Їере́й: Прему́дрость, про́сти.

Ли́къ: Прїиди́те, поклони́мсѧ и припаде́мъ ко Хрісту̀. Спаси́ ны̀, Сы́не Бо́жїй, воскресы́й изъ ме́ртвыхъ, пою́щыѧ Тѝ: аллилу́їа.

Аще же бу́дній день:

Во свѧты́хъ ди́венъ сы́й, пою́щыѧ Тѝ: аллилу́їа.

"Wisdom Attend," from the Divine Liturgy of John Chrysostom.

matins and vespers, the call "Wisdom! Attend!" or simply "Wisdom" precedes each reading of scriptures and introduces the Great Entrance of the priest that leads up to the Eucharist.[81] The term "wisdom" alerts the participants to an important segment of the service to come, a segment directly related to Christ at the time of the Gospel reading and, especially, when the elements of communion are carried through the church and back to the altar for consecration. At each of these times, the doors of the iconostasis are opened, revealing the sacred space behind. Again, there seems to be no suggestion of a feminine hypostasis in this call, and wisdom remains an abstract quality, common to both Christ and, to a lesser extent, the human worshippers.

Mother Moist Earth and Russian Images of Divine Wisdom

> Sophia the Wisdom of God incomprehensibly sometimes resembles Christ and sometimes the Mother of God. At the same time, there is never complete identity either with Him or with Her, for it is obvious that if it were Christ, it could not be the Mother of God, and if it were the Mother of God, it could not be Christ.
>
> SOLOVYOV, "The Idea of Humanity in Auguste Comte"

Despite the lack of feminine personification in early uses of Sophia in Byzantine liturgical practice, the pull of female imagery proved compelling in Russian Orthodox pious practice. To understand this attraction, we must take a detour to Mary as Mother of God. The detour is justified, particularly in Russia, where Proverbs 9 ("Wisdom has built her house") was and continues to be read at Great Vespers of the Feast of the Dormition, one of the most important Marian festivals in the Orthodox calendar.

In the morning service for the day commemorating the Birth of Our Most Holy Lady the *Theotokos* (September 8 in the Orthodox calendar), the Orthodox festal liturgy declares, "Today the death that came to man through eating of the tree, is made of no effect through the Cross. For the curse of our mother Eve that fell on all mankind is destroyed by the fruit of the pure Mother of God, whom all the powers of heaven magnify" (*Festal Menaion* 125). The *Theotokos* (literally "Bearer of God"), or *Bogoroditsa* in Russian (literally God-birther), is here depicted as a fruit-bearing tree, compared to the tree of Paradise associated with the beginning of humankind. Thus even at the celebration of Mary as an infant on the liturgical anniversary of her birth, Orthodox liturgy marks her fertility. This baby who is destined to become mother undoes the tragedy begun when Eve ate the fruit of the tree of the knowledge of good and evil, for that first fruit brought death; the fruit of the Bogoroditsa brings life. It does not matter that the metaphor is not exact.

---

81. See, however, Mateos: "A notre avis, il n'est que l'équivalent de πρόσχωμεν (soyons attentifs), c.-à-d. un rappel de l'attention." The term "attend" is more ancient in the liturgy (84). See also Taft 405.

The Mother of God is not the new Eve, although her son will be the new Adam. Instead, through this metaphor so central to Orthodoxy, Mary becomes the fruit-bearing/life-birthing tree of Paradise itself.

The emphasis on fecundity and birth implied in this metaphor for Mary is ancient and common to both the Eastern and Western churches. Indeed, the term for "Bearer of God" formed the basis of a major fifth-century heresy, long before the division of the churches into Western Catholic and Eastern Orthodox and served to shape Christological doctrine from that time on. At the Third Ecumenical Council held in Ephesus in 431, the gathered bishops anathemized Nestorius, an eloquent monk from one of the monasteries of the Thebaid in Egypt whom Emperor Theodosius II had named Patriarch of Constantinople in 428.[82] Nestorius's alleged impiety consisted of repeated criticism of the term the "Bearer of God." In his writings on the two natures of Christ—the subject of an earlier controversy surrounding Arius—Nestorius was understood to assert that the human and the divine were only artificially joined, not integrally united (undivided, yet unmerged) in the Son of God. And Nestorius's attack on the term *Theotokos* thus implied that Mary was mother of only one of those natures, the human one (Pelikan, *The Emergence of the Catholic Tradition* 1:242). She might be *Christotokos*, Bearer of Christ, but not Theotokos, the Mother of God. With the anathematizing of Nestorius and rejection of his criticism of the term in the middle of the fifth century, Theotokos became the chief title ascribed to the "Blessed and glorious Lady, the Birth-giver of God and ever-Virgin Mary."

For both the Catholic and the Eastern Orthodox Church, Mary is both Virgin and Mother, as the Third Ecumenical Council determined, and it would be wrong to imply that her maternal role belongs exclusively to the Eastern branch. Yet observers are often struck by the repeated emphasis on fertility and motherhood in the Orthodox liturgy and especially in the Russian pious tradition. The Russian Orthodox Church refers to her repeatedly as "the Holy Birth-giver of God," Bogoroditsa, much less frequently as Virgin, *Devitsa* or *Prepodeva*. At the risk of oversimplifying, we can say that if the miracle of a virgin conception is repeatedly emphasized in the Western Catholic tradition, the fecundity of the birth is celebrated in the East.[83]

Of the twelve great feasts of the Orthodox Christian year, almost half are devoted to the Mother of God: the Birth of the Theotokos (8 September), the Entry of the Theotokos into the Temple (21 November), the Meeting of Our

82. Monasteries in the desert surrounding the upper Nile valley were home to thousands of monks in the first five centuries of the Common Era. As we saw, this was presumably the destination for Solovyov's trip into the desert that provoked his third vision of Sophia.

83. Interestingly, the relationship between miracle and physical reality is reversed in ritual practice commemorating the other end of Jesus' life. Although the belief that Christ was fully man and fully God is shared, the Western Church often places emphasis on the physical suffering of the Passion, while the Orthodox Church focuses on the miracle of resurrection. The central icon of an Orthodox church tends to be Christ the Pantocrator, and the crucifix is often conspicuous by its absence. See Ware 227–28.

Lord (2 February; the Western "Presentation" or "Purification," sometimes seen as a feast of the Lord), the Annunciation (25 March), and the Dormition of the Theotokos (15 August; the Western "Assumption"). Furthermore, Mary is one of the most metaphorically productive of all the images of the Orthodox liturgy. In the liturgy of her feast days, she is called variously the burning bush, the rod of Aaron, Jacob's ladder, a throne, abode, temple or palace, the source of life, a living Heaven, a table of the bread of life, a fertile mountain, the tent of Abraham, a divine jar or vessel of manna, a furnace moist with dew, a living and plentiful fount, fertile ground, and fruit. Many if not all of these metaphors suggest, again, fertility. They involve the cooking, serving, and storing of food; she is, notably, a divine jar of manna, the food miraculously provided by God to sustain the Israelites in the desert. And like the barren desert that brings forth food for the hungry, the Mother of God is a bare rod that sprouts leaves and a rocky mountain that becomes fertile. She is also the tent of Abraham, filled with food to offer the angels to whom the patriarch extends his hospitality in Genesis 18. All these metaphors suggest the fecundity of Mary in the Orthodox tradition and indicate her adaptability and even organicity in the popular imagination.

The association of the Mother of God with birth in the early and Byzantine church proved especially resonant in the Slavic land of Rus' in the tenth century, when Christianity was adopted by the young and still fragile Kievan state. According to Nikolai Berdiaev, one of Solovyov's followers in the twentieth century, the "fundamental category [in Russian culture] is motherhood" (Berdyaev, *The Russian Idea* 6). Here, of course, we are in danger of arguing both historically backward and forward, for Berdiaev's assertion of the maternal nature of Russia in part stems from his own interest in Solovyov's Sophia. Nonetheless, he is not the only modern thinker to explore the possibility that the Orthodox interest in Mary as mother might have found so-to-speak fertile ground in early Russia, dating back as far as Kievan Rus', because of the latter's own local proclivity toward maternity as a divinely powerful category. George Fedotov, emigré professor of church history in both Paris and the United States and author of multiple volumes on Russian and Orthodox tradition, claims in *The Russian Religious Mind*:

> In Mother Earth, who remains the core of Russian religion, converge the most secret and deep religious feelings of the folk. Beneath the beautiful veil of grass and flowers, the people venerate with awe the black moist depths, the source of all fertilizing powers, the nourishing breast of nature, and their own last resting place. The very epithet of the earth in the folk songs, "Mother Earth, the Humid," known also in the Iranian mythology, alludes to the womb rather than to the face of the Earth. It means that not beauty but fertility is the supreme virtue of the earth, although the Russian is by no means insensible to the loveliness of its surface. Earth is the Russian "Eternal womanhood," not the celestial image of it: mother, not virgin; fertile, not pure; and black, for the best Russian soil is black. (3:12–13)

Some scholars suggest that even modern peasant traditions in Russia reflect ancient pagan worship of goddesses, such as that of Zhiva (from the verb *zhit'*, "to live") by the Elbe Slavs or Mokosh (see Hubbs 13, 19–20). Evidence on painted vessels and embroidery suggests a cult of fertility that predates Christianity and confirms the emphasis on female power in the pagan tribes who were baptized only in the tenth century. According to Joanna Hubbs in *Mother Russia: The Feminine Myth in Russian Culture*, "In the peasant tradition, however, all things are borne by the earth and derive from her fertility. The soil is the great *baba* (woman), the giant Matrioshka who enfolds the historical Mother Russia. The soil is sacred: The peasants implore 'Mother Moist Earth' for aid in their lives. She seems to need no mate. She is self- moistened, self-inseminated. . . . Man was her son rather than her master" (xii–xiv, 54).

Hubbs's last comment on self-insemination is significant and bears on our later discussion of the particular type of "eternal Womanhood," in Fedotov's terms, or "Ewig-Weibliche" in Goethe's, into which the Russian Sophia also feeds. Not only is this cultural figure a sexualized, moist mother rather than a pristine virgin, but she is also more than a she. Mother Moist Earth (*mat' syra zemlia*) is androgynous, consuming both male and female reproductive processes as she produces and nourishes her offspring.[84]

Against this background of sensual worship of the ancient androgynous earth mother came the official conversion of Russia to Christianity by the baptism of Prince Vladimir and his subjects in 988 CE. Although Vladimir's choice of Eastern Christianity likely stemmed from a desire to ally himself politically and economically with the powerful Byzantine Empire to his south and west, tradition passes down that his attraction to Orthodoxy was precisely a result of the sensuality of Orthodox worship.[85] Under the year 987, the Russian Chronicles report that Vladimir sent his emissaries around the world to discover the best faith. In Constantinople they met with the Byzantine emperor, who

> sent a message to the patriarch to inform him that a Russian delegation had arrived to examine the Greek faith, and directed him to prepare the church and the clergy, and to array himself in his sacerdotal robes, so that the Russians might behold the glory of the God of the Greeks. When the patriarch received

---

84. According to Fedotov: "There is no Russian parallel to Athena, or any other Virgin Goddess, and it seems that neither purity nor beauty was essential to the Russian worship of Sacred Womanhood. . . . Mother Earth is shapeless and faceless. The beauty to which the Russian is so sensitive is not embodied primarily in the woman. Beauty dwells in nature. And the beauty of nature for the Russian is the embracing, the enveloping, rather than the contemplated. Man is lost in nature, unwilling to master her. Hence it follows that the greatest religious temptation for a Russian will be pantheism of a sensual (hylozoistic) kind. Sacred matter rather than spirit is the object of veneration. . . . Sensual mysticism, however, is a necessary complement to the social discipline of the *rod*" (20).

85. Hubbs also emphasizes the role of the earlier conversion of Vladimir's grandmother, Olga. She uses this to reinforce her assertion of a strong feminine myth in Russian culture (88–89).

these commands, he bade the clergy assemble, and they performed the customary rites. They burned incense, and the choirs sang hymns. The emperor accompanied the Russians to the church, and placed them in a wide space, calling their attention to the beauty of the edifice, the chanting, and the offices of the archpriest and the ministry of the deacons, while he explained to them the worship of his God. (S. Zenkovsky 67)

The Byzantine emperor's ploy must have worked, for "the Russians were astonished, and in their wonder praised the Greek ceremonial." The emissaries returned to Vladimir to report that as they stood in Hagia Sophia in Constantinople, "We knew not whether we were in heaven or on earth. For on earth there is no such splendor or such beauty, and we are at a loss how to describe it. We know only that god dwells there among men, and their service is fairer than the ceremonies of other nations" (67). The sensual aspects of the Orthodox ritual—the incense, the hymns, the "wide space" with its icons and mosaics—in the beautifully decorated cathedral attracted these seekers from Rus', brought up as they were on the sensuality of their local earth worship.

Whatever the geopolitical or aesthetic-mystical reasons for the mass baptism, Christianity came abruptly to Rus' in the tenth century. The Eastern Slavic tribes of the area had already entrenched sacred beliefs and rituals, many apparently centering on female deities, in particular an all-encompassing Mother Moist Earth. News of Christ and Mary could only have been imperfectly grafted onto this existing pantheistic religious system, and it is only natural that Mary as the fertile mother of God would be adapted by the local culture with its emphasis on fertility.

Although it might seem obvious that Russians would associate wisdom with Mary,[86] concrete manifestations of the association did not develop for several centuries. The tendency to conflate Mary with Sophia was perhaps most marked in the cathedrals dedicated to Sophia in Kiev and Novgorod that over time came to commemorate their founding on days associated with the Mother of God: Kiev on the Feast of the Birth of the Most Holy Lady and Novgorod on the Feast of the Assumption. The historical reasons for these commemorations are complex and uniquely Russian; they did not occur significantly elsewhere in the Byzantine Empire (see Florovskii, "O Pochitanii Sofii" 487). We need to look more carefully at the specifically Russian iconographic tradition, however, to see the development of Sophia as a personified figure, associated with both Christ and Mary but also decidedly distinct from them, and to speculate on the visual images of Sophia that existed in churches

---

86. In the wide-ranging *Sophia-Maria,* Schiplinger argues that Mary is the incarnated Sophia. In his view, the process of dividing the two and associating Sophia with Christ began with Philo, thereby anticipating a development that continued into Christianity and climaxed with the church fathers (35). From this point of view, we might see the medieval association with Mary as a return to the earliest understanding of Wisdom. Unfortunately, some of Schiplinger's conclusions, while provocative, remain unprovable.

into the second half of the nineteenth century, when Solovyov would have been exposed to them.

As background, we must remember that the symbolism of icons of the Divine Sophia is far from standardized and is decidedly ambiguous.[87] Florovsky asserts that "in Byzantine art we never had any canonized scheme for the representation of Divine Wisdom."[88] Although wisdom icons are often wrongly confused with those depicting St. Sophia, martyred during the reign of Hadrian (117–38 CE), images of wisdom remain the most abstract of all holy pictures,[89] for the Divine Sophia never existed as a real being. Even the gender of Sophia in Russian icons is ambiguous, as in different centuries and locations the personified figure is sometimes associated with Christ or Mary or depicted as an androgynous angel with "feminized" features otherwise attributed to Gabriel.[90] Multiple depictions of Christ sometimes appear on a single wisdom icon, and those icons in turn are often associated with images of other figures and events, including the Transfiguration with its "wisdom star,"[91] icons depicting the Mother of God, and the Holy Trinity, partly because of common eucharistic symbolism. (Wisdom in Proverbs 9 invites "whoever is callow" to "Come, dine on my food; / drink of the wine I have mixed.") The situation becomes increasingly complex as Western images of Mary are more and more conflated in the later Muscovite period with the traditional Orthodox symbolism of Christ-Wisdom (see Florovskii, "O pochitanii Sofii").

As we saw, the very first wisdom images in Byzantine worship were most probably associated with New Testament passages about Christ as wisdom, especially those from Paul in First Corinthians. Indeed, before the twelfth century few icons of Sophia had any female associations at all. As the icons developed over time, however, wisdom became increasingly personified as a female figure, as she clearly is in the Hebrew verses from Proverbs. Yet at least one popular icon based on Proverbs that depicts a building with seven pillars

87. For a fuller discussion, see Kornblatt, "Visions of Icons and Reading Rooms."

88. Florovsky, "The Hagia Sophia Churches" 135. See also Ammann; Averintsev; Balčarek; Grabar, "Iconographie"; Hunt, "Hesychasm and the Iconography of Divine Wisdom" and "The Novgorod Sophia Icon"; Lebedintsev; Lifshits; Meyendorff, "L'iconographie de la Sagesse Divine" and "Wisdom-Sophia."

89. As Fiene states, "Quite probably no other icon type was (or is) so abstract and allegorical in its content" (450).

90. Multiple gender refractions in the image of Sophia occurred in Western medieval culture as well. As Barbara Newman asserts, "No earlier development was lost: side by side we continue to see the christological understanding of Wisdom, the sapiential liturgy of the Virgin, the allegory of Philosophia and the seven arts, the epiphanies of Nature and other fictive goddesses." "In the late-mediaeval devotion directed explicitly toward Wisdom, the figure of Christ-Sophia becomes fully androgynous, with the genders no longer alternating but coexisting" (29, 30). A comparative analysis of Western and Eastern visions of Sophia will need to wait for another study.

91. On the wisdom star in icons of the Transfiguration, see Hunt, "Hesychasm and the Iconography of Divine Wisdom." I thank Dr. Hunt for her invaluable help in deciphering this icon and its many forms.

The Novgorod-Sophia Icon. Print on board, from author's collection.

("Wisdom has built her house. She has set up her seven pillars," Proverbs 9:1) also includes an inscription from Corinthians: "Power and Wisdom of God" (Meyendorff, "Wisdom-Sophia" 394).

"Wisdom has built her house" icons, known throughout eastern Europe, were complemented by a uniquely Russian type of wisdom icon—the Novgorod Sophia or Sophia-Angel, developed in the Novgorod region in the fifteenth and sixteenth centuries and subsequently brought to Moscow.

In this type of icon, all images of Christ come together: Christ-Wisdom or Sophia, Christ Emmanuel on a medallion on Mary's chest, and Christ on High (Balčarek 604). In icons, frescoes, and other images that follow this pattern, Sophia appears as a feminine-looking angel seated on an altarlike throne, the latter usually with seven legs or placed on top of seven steps. The number seven refers to the passage from Proverbs, as well as to the seven Ecumenical Councils, and in later versions with stronger Western influence, to the seven virtues. Although angels are androgynous and Christ is male, because of the feminine facial features and the reference to Proverbs, this Sophia seems decidedly female.[92] Solovyov surely understood Sophia in this icon as a woman, for in a late article he described the icon in detail as "a unique female figure in royal dress, sitting on a throne" (SS 9:187; see page 225). The angel's wings are fiery red, and her/its face is red or pink as well. The Sophia figure wears a crown and holds a staff in one hand and a rolled scroll in the other. The angel is flanked by the Mother of God, usually with a medallion of the Christ child on her chest, and by John the Baptist. Thus this section of the icon is a kind of intercession icon that usually has central place on the iconostasis, with Christ in the middle, Mary to his right, and John the Baptist to the left. In this Wisdom image, the Sophia figure replaces Christ, with an aureole of blue or azure surrounding her/him/it. Above the winged Sophia sits Christ making the traditional gesture of blessing with His right hand, and above Him floats a light blue cloud with six seraphim and cherubim or six smaller angels. Between them on this cloud often stands another altar or Prepared Throne, usually with a cross or a lance and sometimes with the Bible open to John 1:1 ("In the beginning was the Word, and the Word was with God, and the Word was God"). Some later seventeenth-century versions replace the altar with the enthroned Lord of Hosts.[93]

It is almost certain that Solovyov knew the Novgorod-Sophia icon as a child. Sophia images were located in churches that might very well have been visited by Solovyov's family, including the main Cathedral of the Dormition

---

92. Fiene, however, states, "Because the face and braided hair recall the angel Gabriel, it is not out of place to use the masculine pronoun. Often the face is described as 'virginal'" (459). Fiene's article contains a fuller description of the icon, along with a picture, as does the article by Balčarek.

93. For a critique of this icon, see Florovskii, "O pochitanii Sofii." For a critique of Florovskii's critique, see Hunt, "The Novgorod Sophia Icon."

Fresco of the Novgorod-Sophia image, from the northern apse of the Cathedral of the Dormition, Kremlin, Moscow.

in the Moscow Kremlin.[94] In addition, the Novgorod-Sophia image was the church icon of the Church of the Dormition of the Holy Trinity Monastery in Sergiev Posad (Lifshits 145), which Solovyov visited during his time at the Theological Academy in the early 1870s, shortly before his trip to London. This icon, with its image of Wisdom as a royal, feminine-looking angel, with

94. Balčarek reports that "an icon of Sophia of the Novgorodian type (from 1540–1560) was kept in the sanctuary of the main Cathedral of the Dormition [Assumption] in the Moscow Kremlin (now in the Museum of the Moscow Kremlin, No. 480)." Furthermore, "other similar icons were in the sanctuary: e.g. the icon from Pavel Korin's collection (Moscow School, second half of the 16th century) was in the upper part of the sanctuary." He continues: "Other examples are from fresco images: this type of Sophia is in the eastern upper part of the façade of the Dormition Cathedral in the Moscow Kremlin where frescoes were painted by imperial icon painters under the direction of Simon Ušakov in the early 17th century. Above the apse, on the external wall of the same cathedral, in [one of] the three arches, there [is an image of] . . . Sophia of the Novgorodian type (on the upper part of the prothesis). There is a similarly placed example of the Novgorodian Sophia in the prothesis apse at the top of the eastern sanctuary of the Cathedral of the Archangel in the Moscow Kremlin, from the 16th century" (607).

its gold and azure color scheme and its bright heavenly bodies, would make a strong impression on any young viewer as "Wisdom!" is called out and the royal doors of the iconostasis open to reveal the otherwise hidden holy area around the altar.

Wisdom and Folly in Gnosticism and Kabbalah

An-Soph, Jah, Soph-Jah
SOLOVYOV, Notebooks

We wed white lily with rose,
With scarlet rose.
We unearth the eternal truth
Of the furtive dream of the seer.
SOLOVYOV, "Song of the Ophites"

What is the gaiety of Divine Wisdom, and why does she find her highest sense of joy in the sons of man?
SOLOVYOV, Russia and the Universal Church

For I recognize
The White Lily in you.
SOLOVYOV, The White Lily

As we have seen, Hebrew scriptures, the New Testament, Orthodox liturgy, Byzantine art, and Russian iconography all contributed to the complex of ideas and symbols of wisdom that we call Russian intellectual and material culture of the second half of the nineteenth century. As in all cases of influence, no one source need predominate.[95] Rather, Solovyov's voluminous reading led him to a wealth of descriptions that resonated with his unique personal experience. The philosopher and poet was an *original*, who sought in religious and literary traditions the best expression for his own essentially ineffable visions of Sophia, sometimes mixing imagery and terminology from several different traditions in a single text.

As the grandson of a priest and a regular parishioner, Solovyov probably knew the religious traditions described in the last section better than many of his contemporaries. Other, less orthodox, points of entry for Sophia also existed, however, and in some cases may have been even more powerful for Solovyov. These influences include the theosophic mysticism of Kabbalah that

---

95. As Slesinski cautions, "Solovyov . . . already enjoyed an intuition of Holy Sophia or Divine Wisdom at the root of all creation when he undertook his serious study of Gnostic and kabbalistic sources at the British Museum. He may well have been searching for indications to guide his own speculations, but it does not follow that these sources were the principal, let alone leading, determinants in the subsequent articulation of his thought. Assessing their overall importance for the development of the Solovyean synthesis thus remains problematic" (Slesinski, "Toward an understanding of V.S. Solovyov's 'Gnosticism'" 81–82).

came into Russia first in the eighteenth century, as well as echoes of Hellenistic and Christian Gnosticism that survived in various forms in Eastern Christianity and were revived by post-Renaissance mystics, by the eighteenth- and nineteenth-century Masons, and in the writings of European romantics. Our tour of Sophia through the ages must thus take us into these less canonical areas as well.

Both Gnostic and Kabbalistic terms are present in a prayer found in Solovyov's early notebooks from London, inspired by his reading in the British Museum library.[96]

Prayer of the Revelation of the Great Secret
In the name of the Father and of the Son and
of the Holy Spirit An-Soph, Jah, Soph-Jah

By the unutterable, awesome, and omnipotent Name, I call upon gods, demons, humans, and all that lives. Gather into one the rays of your power, bar the source of your desire, and participate in the communion of my prayer: May we capture the pure dove of Zion, may we find the priceless pearl of Ophir, and may the roses unite with lilies in the Sharon valley.

Most holy Divine Sophia, essential image of beauty and sweetness of the transcendent God, the light body of eternity, the soul of worlds and the one empress [*tsaritsa*] of souls, I beseech you by the unutterable depths and grace of your first son, the beloved Jesus Christ: Descend into the prison of the soul, fill our darkness with your radiance, melt our spirit's shackles with your fire of love, grant us light and will, appear to us in visible and concrete form, incarnate yourself in us and in the world, restoring the fullness of the ages. Then may the depths confine themselves to their boundaries, and may God be all in all. (*SS* 12:148–49)

Although we find Kabbalistic terms in the title of the prayer ("An-Soph"), not to mention standard references to Jewish tradition (such as the use of "Name" as a name of God, and evocation of Zion, Ophir, and Sharon, all places named in Hebrew scriptures), we will look first at possible Gnostic sources for Solovyov's writing, which refer more directly to Neoplatonic as well as early Christian elements discussed in earlier sections.

Gnosticism arose in the first few centuries of the Common Era and is sometimes interpreted as a form of early Christianity. In fact, Gnosticism is not really a religion at all but a philosophy in which special knowledge (gnosis) rather than faith reigns supreme.[97] There have been many studies of the esoteric

---

96. Solovyov writes in *Three Encounters*, "I would receive, picked out by powers unknown, / All books on her that I could ever read" (see below). The prayer was discovered in Solovyov's notebooks by his nephew Sergei and first published by him in "Ideia tserkvi v poezii Vladimira Solov'eva" (74). Sergei Bulgakov reprinted it in "Vladimir Solov'ev i Anna Shmidt" (74).

97. See Carlson, "Gnostic Elements" 54: "Gnosticism is a religious-philosophical system that holds that the concept of *knowledge* is superior to the concept of *faith* (the foundation of the traditional religion). Gnosticism is thus a religious *philosophy*, but not a religion; as such, it

teachings of Gnosticism, especially since the discovery of a large cache of ancient manuscripts in 1945, and there is neither space nor need to reproduce
them here.[98] Before the discovery at Nag Hammadi in Upper Egypt, Gnosticism was known largely through a handful of incomplete texts and the words
of the church fathers who condemned them. With the translation of the thir-
teen found codices, representing over fifty-five texts, we have a much more
complete view of a complex, often splintered and contradictory mythology,
theodicy, and soteriology involving births and battles between multiple actors
before the creation of time and space. The arcane names in this precosmic
drama seem an amalgamation of Eastern religions, ancient philosophy, and
biblical terms. Furthermore, Gnosticism is no single teaching, having quickly
broken into several branches, the best known voiced in the writings of Mani
and the Manicheans and of Valentinus and the Valentinians. Solovyov wrote
encyclopedia entries on both of these schools in the late 1890s (*SS* 10:416–21
and 285–90; see also the more general entry on Gnosticism, 10:323–28).

In the broadest strokes, Gnostic teachings reveal a Neoplatonic emanationist or genetic mythology, where the evil inherent in lowly matter is diametri-
cally opposed to a fully perfect, immobile, and immutable higher sphere. Our
human quest is to escape the material world through acquisition of special
knowledge and thus reenter the Divine. This "anti-cosmic" dualism[99] rests on
the uneasy recognition that the creator of the world can in no way be identical
to the absolute, unknown, and transcendent Godhead, the One or Monad,
sometimes called Father, whose domain is the divine Pleroma. As with the
Neoplatonists, whose teachings were interspersed by the Gnostics with early
Christian and Hebrew texts, the Godhead let forth emanations that developed
into a host of intermediate powers, or aeons. One aeon is called Primal Man:
not humanity as we know it but a precosmic, eternal, and divine principle. In
most Gnostic writings, another of those emanations bears the name Sophia, or
Akhamoth, the latter a probable corruption of the Hebrew Hokhmah, or its
plural form, *Hokhmot*. All the emanations projected by the One come in pairs,
or syzygies, who couple to conceive the next lower set of emanations.[100]

---

would have a certain appeal to thinkers of mystic inclinations who were raised in a historically
positivistic age, as was Soloviev."

98. For the best studies, see Jonas and Pagels. Cioran argues strongly for the influence of
Gnosticism on Solovyov (*Vladimir Solov'ev and the Knighthood of the Divine Sophia*, 17–21),
as do Paul Allen (122ff.) and Kochetkova (164). The late Donald C. Gillis began a project
on "Gnosis and Cabala in the Early Works of Vladimir Solov'ev," and I am thankful to Maria
Carlson for the use of his short unpublished manuscript. A concise case for Gnostic influence in
Solovyov is made by Carlson in "Gnostic Elements" (49–67). Slesinski, however, critiques both
Cioran and Carlson in "Toward an Understanding of V. S. Solovyov's 'Gnosticism'" (77–88).

99. Rudolph 60; cited in Slesinski, *Toward an Understanding*, 79.

100. Solovyov uses the term "syzygy" in "The Meaning of Love" and includes the following
note, perhaps to evade the censors: "From Gk. *sizigiia*—union. I am obliged to introduce this
new expression, since I can find no other, better one in existing terminology. I note that the
Gnostics used the word syzygy in a different meaning and that, in general, the use of a given
term by heretics does not make the term itself heretical" (*SS* 7:57).

What is most important for us here is the crucial role that Sophia plays in Gnosticism's cosmogony. Inexplicably, she decides that she would like to conceive *without* a partner, in the way of the Father, who simply "brought forth" the first syzygy. Not being the Father, she is able to produce from her efforts only an unformed "abortion" that threatens to destabilize the divine harmony. The One quickly produces another syzygy—Christ and the Holy Spirit—that takes Sophia's misshapen offspring out of the Pleroma into another realm, called the Ogdoad. This realm of exile begins to replicate the downward movement of the emanations in the Pleroma, and out of it appears Prime Matter, also called the Demiurge or, sometimes, the Soul of the Universe. This Demiurge is our own "lesser" God, the Creator, who is beset by all the evils, passions, pride, and insecurities that mark the abortion as a whole. From him originates the cosmic order in the form of seven planets and, eventually, human beings. This is the material universe from which we all, apparently, wish to escape.

To explain Sophia's presence both above and below, or within and without, the Gnostics draw on the Platonic concept of an ascending and descending Eros, as well as on the Neoplatonists' divine triad of One-Mind-Soul as it differs from the lower World Soul. Thus, Gnosticism speaks of two different Sophias: divine and earthly, the latter often called Prouneikos, the Whore. It is also possible that this Gnostic duplication of Sophia is based on the occasional use of the plural form for "wisdoms" in Proverbs (1:20; 9:1; 14:1; 24:7) or, even more likely, on an association between Wisdom and Folly in that same seminal wisdom text (Good 65–67). Exactly parallel to Wisdom as she stands by her seven-pillared house, lays her table, and invites her guests in Proverbs 9: 1–6, Folly also calls her guests to a banquet in Proverbs 9: 13–18:

> The foolish woman is boisterous—
> Callowness itself! She knows nothing at all.
> She sits at the door of her house,
> On a chair at the city heights,
> Calling to those who pass by,
> Who are going straight ahead.
> "Whoever is callow, let him come over here!
> Whoever is senseless—to him I'll say:
> 'Stolen water is sweet,
> secret food a delight.' "
> But he knows not that ghosts are there,
> That her guests are in the depths of Sheol.

It is not too far from this duplication of Wisdom and Folly to arrive at two Sophias: one, though willful, still fully of the divine Pleroma, and the other one fallen, a whore immersed in flesh and matter. Gnosticism divides sharply between the two, although even the lower Sophia carries the divine spark that she relays to humanity. Thanks to this spark, the proper knowledge/gnosis will allow our possible ascent back to the One.

Solovyov's early knowledge of Gnostic mythology is uncontestable. His elaborate cosmogony in *The Sophia*, with its references to seven planets and a cosmic battle between the Demiurge and Satan, recalls Gnostic mythology quite closely.

> Cosmic Mind is not passive: *mens agitat molem* [Latin: mind moves mass]. In order to give it a name that is consecrated by Christian Gnosticism, I will call it the Demiurge.
>
> Satan and the Demiurge are not independent substances; they are two opposite actualities of the [Soul, which, as potential unity, remains their common substance. The Soul is the Demiurge as much as it is Satan, but it also is distinct from both of them. The best term to express the substantial identity and the actual division is *generation*. Thus we can say that Satan and the Demiurge are engendered by the Soul; they are its sons.]
>
> Now, let us pass on from the sphere of principles to the sphere of elements. (*PSS* 2: 124; brackets in original; see page 146)

At this point in the French manuscript, Solovyov includes the following list in Russian, although he crossed it out with a different pen, probably at a later time. He names seven planets, associating some of them with Satan, the Demiurge, or Sophia.

> x Saturn—Satan
> *xx Jupiter—Demiurge*
> *xxx Venus—Sophia*
> *x Mars*
> *xx Mercury*
> *Sun (Apollo)*
> xxx Moon (Earth?) *(PSS 2:124; see pages 146–47)*

This section of *The Sophia* is filled with crossed-out material, incomplete thoughts, and samples of automatic writing. Yet we cannot dismiss all the contradictions and ambiguities of this and surrounding passages on the basis of Solovyov's disturbed fantasy alone. Many of his passages come directly from the imagery of the Gnostic sources he might have seen in the British Museum during his 1875 stay in London[101] or even in texts that had

---

101. Unfortunately, the request slips from the Reading Room were destroyed in the early 1900s, so we can not confirm exactly which books Solovyov read. Carlson claims that "most of the information on gnosticism available to Soloviev would still have come from the works of the early heresiologists: Irenaeus, Tertullian, Hippolytus, and Clement of Alexandria. . . . Additional gnostic themes and elements are found in the writings of the mystical theologians most admired by Soloviev: Origen, Saint Maximus the Confessor, and Dionysius the Pseudo-Areopagite

been available to him in the Theological Academy, where he had spent the previous year. His bibliographies to the encyclopedia articles on Gnostic topics cite texts in various languages, including an 1871 Russian translation of *Pistis Sophia*.[102] There is no doubt that Solovyov had read at least some Gnostic works by the mid-seventies, and it is not difficult to see why many have labeled the prayer that opens this section—also probably written in the British Museum—a "Gnostic incantation." The opposition in the prayer of fetters and freedom, of dark and light, of descent and ascent recalls Gnostic dualistic imagery quite directly. Gnostic texts often speak of our world as a "prison"; in the prayer the supplicant asks Sophia to descend into our prison for a moment in order to infuse our darkness with light. Even more, the references to pearls and to roses and lilies in the prayer recall similar imagery in Gnostic texts. They are developed extensively by Solovyov in a poem of the mid- to late seventies called "Song of the Ophites," referring to the Egyptian Gnostic sect that left the Coptic-language text *Pistis Sophia* (see Solovyov's encyclopedia article at *SS* 10:327).[103] The snake was their symbol; thus the coils to which Solovyov refers in the poem below.

SONG OF THE OPHITES

White lily with rose,
With scarlet rose we wed.
We unearth the eternal truth
Of the furtive dream of the seer.

Utter the visionary word!
Throw quickly your pearl in the cup!
Bind our dove
With the new coils of the ancient snake.

The hurting heart does not hurt . . .
Should it fear Prometheus' fire?
The pure dove is free
In the fiery coils of the powerful snake.

(whose works incorporated or discussed various Neoplatonic and gnostic elements and who placed special emphasis on the doctrine of *theosis*, or the deification of man). Soloviev, who studied at the Moscow Spiritual Academy as well as at Moscow University, would have been familiar with this body of literature" ("Gnostic Elements" 51).

102. "All of these works are rather old. From the new investigators of Gnosticism, we should name Hilgenfeld and especially Harnack (*Zur Quellenkritik der Gesch. D. Gn.* and others). In Russian there is the remarkable work by Prot. A. M. Ivantsov-Platonov: *Heresies and Schisms of the First Three Centuries*, dedicated in large part to Gnosticism. Unfortunately, it ends after the first volume (the investigation of sources)" (*SS* 10: 327–28).

103. The text of *Pistis Sophia* includes a dialogue between Jesus and Mary Magdalene, inspiring some to include her as one of the disciples and even to suggest a special marriage relationship between the two.

> Sing of the scarlet storm.
> We find peace in the scarlet storm.
> White lily with rose
> With scarlet rose we wed. (1878; *SS* 12:14)[104]

This poem refers to the pearl, the dove, and the flowers also mentioned in the incantation, in which the speaker prays: "May we capture the pure dove of Zion, may we find the priceless pearl of Ophir, and may the roses unite with lilies in the Sharon valley." The white lily may be the Divine Sophia of Gnosticism and the scarlet rose, the earthly creation. Their union is thus a binding of heaven (dove) and earth (snake). The result is an oxymoronic peaceful storm.

Solovyov chose the "Song of the Ophites" as the concluding lines of his humorous play *The White Lily*, also written toward the end of the 1870s but not published until 1893. It is particularly characteristic that Solovyov would take what on its own is a very serious statement about Sophia, the dove of Zion, and place it in a farce. As suggested in the notes to the play's translation (see page 248), it is possible that Solovyov took so long to publish his play because he was not fully satisfied with the seemingly haphazard blend of Eastern and Western symbolism in the play or with the particular combination of humor and seriousness. In refutation of the latter explanation, however, we must acknowledge that he continued throughout his life to write humorous verse, up to and including his important Sophia *poema, Three Encounters,* often poking fun at himself. More likely, Solovyov found through these particular verbal re-visions that Gnosticism did not provide him with an adequate articulation of his vision, and he continued to cast about for more versions of Sophia. Even Carlson, who sees a very close tie between Solovyov's Sophia and those of Gnosticism, admits that "in Soloviev's later works, the more sensational and clearly 'mythological' gnostic elements disappear, some replaced by more traditional Christian vocabulary" ("Gnostic Elements" 61). Indeed, Solovyov might have found some key tenets of Gnosticism incompatible with his core Trinitarian rather than dualistic beliefs. As Slesinski reminds us, Solovyov "does not subscribe to a dualistic view of creation whereby spirit is good and matter is bad. Nor is his teaching emanationist. Furthermore, his quest for integral knowledge is one of true synthetic vision and is not at all syncretic" ("Toward an Understanding" 86). Even more important, the Gnostic Sophia, whether upper or lower, is always a troublemaker. The Divine, or Agia, Sophia is jealous of her Father and usurps his reproductive role in the upper realm; Sophia Prouneikos wreaks havoc below. Solovyov's Sophia might laugh, but her laughter elevates rather than destroys us. Despite Solovyov's obvious use of Gnostic vocabulary in these early texts, he continued his search for an adequate re-vision of his vision(s) of Sophia.

---

104. Mints dates the poem to the beginning of May 1876, making it roughly contemporaneous with the early Sophia lyrics translated below. See *Stikhotvoreniia* 64.

Returning to the Sophia prayer found in Solovyov's London notebook, we can identify obvious Kabbalistic as well as Gnostic vocabulary, suggesting that Solovyov himself wrote the incantation or, at least, compiled it from a variety of sources. As we saw, the entry begins: "In the name of the Father and Son and Holy Spirit" and continues, using Latin letters: "An-Soph, Jah, Soph-Jah."[105] "An-Soph" seems to refer to the transcendent, unknowable Godhead of Kabbalah: *Ein-Sof*, which is mentioned twice by Solovyov in the 1876 French work *La Sophia* and transliterated into Russian by Solovyov sometimes as "èn-sof" [эн-соф].[106] "Ein-Sof" or "Ain-Sof" (אין-סוף) literally means "there is no end" in Hebrew, and it is the boundless, eternal, groundless ground of All. "Jah" is one of the many biblical names of God, the discussion, arrangement, and interpretation of which form the core of speculative Kabbalah.[107] Perhaps not surprisingly for our discussion, it is the name usually associated with the *sefirah* (pl. *sefirot*), or divine manifestation, of Hokhmah. Solovyov, then, in a technique reminiscent of the wordplay of Kabbalah, derives "Sophia" from the union of "Soph," meaning end, and "Jah," or God. "Soph-Jah" corresponds to the Holy Spirit in the first line of the prayer's invocation, and Solovyov thus makes the end of God into the third divine hypostasis. As seen in all of Solovyov, the third principle is a bridge or connector, and in this case the intermediary unites God and humanity, as the subsequent prayer makes clear. "Descend into the prison of the soul," he pleads, and "fill our darkness with your radiance" (*SS* 12:149). Soph-Jah thus moves God from transcendence to immanence: the end of God is man. We can conclude, then, that this manuscript is not simply a Gnostic imitation but instead demonstrates Solovyov's understanding of Kabbalistic vocabulary, method, and, most important, theology. The *sefirot* beginning with Hokhmah are the connecting links between an eternal Godhead and humanity. Solovyov was seen in the British Museum reading texts of the Kabbalah,[108] and this prayer demonstrates that he commanded more than a cursory knowledge of it by the time of his alleged second and third visions.

105. This second line was not printed in the first publication of the prayer by S. M. Solov'ev in "Ideia tserkvi" but was added in the sixth edition of Solov'ev's poetry. See commentary by Luk'ianov 2:146.

106. The reference to Kabbalah in this invocation was recognized by Luk'ianov and subsequent scholars, including Dmitrii Stremooukhoff, but never fully analyzed. For references to Solov'ev's use of Kabbalah see Stremooukhoff 50–51, 83, 201–4, 306–7, 343n, 365n; Losev, *Vl. Solov'ev* 67–77; Klum 20, 32, 255–57; and the works dedicated to this topic by Burmistrov. Most recently, see the unpublished dissertation "Kabbalah in Russian Religious Philosophy," where Daigin refutes Burmistrov and carefully explicates all uses of Kabbalistic terminology and concepts in Solovyov's writing.

107. See the works of Gershom G. Scholem, as the foremost scholar of Kabbalah, as well as those of Moshe Idel. Idel, who has specifically studied gender and eroticism in Kabbalah, challenges some of Scholem's assumptions in *Kabbalah: New Perspectives*.

108. A Russian acquaintance in London claims to have seen Solovyov poring over the bizarre illustrations from a book on Kabbalah and to have heard him declare, "It is very interesting; in every line of this book there is more life than in all of European scholarship. I am very happy and content to have found this edition" (Ianzhul 481–82).

It seems likely that Kabbalah attracted Solovyov because of its understanding of these very tangible relations between God and man. Although Solovyov initially studied Eastern philosophy as avidly as he did Jewish theology, he quickly rejected Buddhism for its idealization of Nirvana, or "nothingness," as opposed to human reality (SS 3:45, 48; 11:320).[109] Gnosticism, despite its influence on him as described above, draws Solovyov's wrath for its teaching, as he says, that the world cannot be saved (mir ne spasaetsia, SS 10:325). And, as we saw, he borrowed ideas from Platonic idealism but also turned from it because of its dualism and ultimate rejection of the world of man (SS 11:321). Both Buddhism and Platonic philosophy, Solovyov claims, are only stages on the path toward true revelation. The mystical vocabulary of Kabbalah culminates in—rather than descends to—humanity and provides Solovyov with yet more possibilities in his attempt to articulate his own revealed Sophia.

The Zohar is perhaps the best-known Kabbalistic text and the one that Solovyov may have studied in Latin translation in London. It is largely an exegesis on the first five books of the Hebrew Bible, supposedly written in the second century by Rav Shim'on ben Yohai. In truth, it is a thirteenth-century text written by the Spanish Kabbalist Moses b. Shem Tov de Leon and, as was common practice, ascribed to an earlier sage. After a lengthy prologue, the Zohar opens with a frequently verse-by-verse interpretation of the book of Genesis. The first selection describes the birth of the sefirot in a manner similar to most Kabbalistic teachings: Ein-Sof, or Keter, who is the first sefirah here considered coeternal with Ein-Sof, allows for the existence of Hokhmah.[110] Hokhmah, despite the feminine gender of the noun, is the Father, and couples with the next sefirah, Binah, who is Mother. The two then unite to give birth to the following seven sefirot. Together, the ten sefirot are sometimes diagrammed as representing various limbs of the human body, with the suggestion that the right-hand members are masculine, the left, feminine. The lower sefirot also form a sexual union; Tiferet (male), or Beauty, unites through Yesod (represented as the male sexual organ) with Shekhinah, also called Malkhut or King/Queendom (female), which is the closest sefirah to humanity and is the first to have direct dealings with us.

Therefore, in Kabbalah it is not Hokhmah but Shekhinah who becomes the female partner to the masculine mystic and to all of humankind. Her main appellative in the Zohar is in fact "Female." She is the closest stage to the human world, and entrance into the divine realm must be made through her "gates."[111]

---

109. For an analysis of Solovyov's attitude toward Eastern mysticism, see Sutton, 161–78.

110. Later Lurianic Kabbalah refers to this process as a contraction unto itself. Although the Zohar rarely uses the names of the sefirot, the terms it chooses for the ten manifestations of God correspond to the traditional ones, and medieval commentators on the Zohar inserted them with no difficulty. For a table of correspondence, see The Zohar, trans. Sperling, Simon, and Levertoff 1:385.

111. "The emphasis placed on the female principle in the symbolism of the last Sefirah heightens the mythical language of these descriptions. Appearing from above as 'the end of

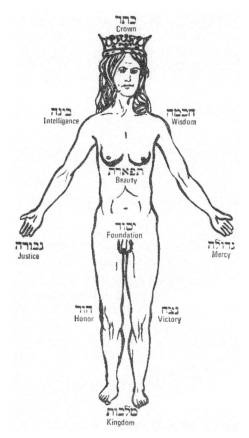

בתר
Crown

בינה
Intelligence

חכמה
Wisdom

תפארת
Beauty

יסוד
Foundation

גבורה
Justice

חסד
Mercy

הוד
Honor

נצח
Victory

מלכות
Kingdom

The Kabbalistic *sefirot* depicted as the androgynous Adam Kadmon.

Kabbalah describes sexual relations between the sefirot modeled on male-female relations on earth and reinforces a traditional Jewish focus on marital relations. Under the Kabbalah, by contrast with many other mystical systems, sex is seen as giving life, not death, and one way of uniting with Shekhinah is for a male Jew to have intercourse with his wife on the Sabbath.[112]

Without denying major discrepancies between Jewish mysticism and Christian Trinitarian dogma, Solovyov found in Kabbalah confirmation of his mystical vision of an erotic yet androgynous divine ideal within the Godhead. He understood Kabbalah's sefirot as multiple hypostases of the one living God, who act like humans and are acted upon by mortal men and women.

---

thought,' the last *Sefirah* is for man the door or gate through which he can begin the ascent up the ladder of perception of the Divine Mystery" (Scholem, *Kabbalah* 112).

112. See Idel, "Metaphores et pratiques sexuelles" 336–38, 344, 347.

For him, they were expressions of his own connection to the divine world through Sophia.

Solovyov's knowledge of Kabbalah is easily documented. We do not know what he might have read at the Theological Academy, but while in the British Museum he was seen studying a volume which was likely Knorr de Rosenroth's Latin translation of the Zohar.[113] In 1896 Solovyov wrote a scholarly introduction to "Kabbalah: Mystical Philosophy of the Jews" by David Ginzburg, and later, drawing on German and French sources, he contributed the entry on Kabbalah to the Brokgaus-Efron Encyclopedic Dictionary (*SS* 12:332–34 and 10:339–43). By this time Solovyov had learned Hebrew well enough to read the Bible in the original and had committed himself to the study of the Talmud and Jewish medieval philosophy (see Gets 165–68).

For both Kabbalah and Solovyov, the intimate connection between God and humanity is more than metaphor. According to Kabbalistic texts, our earthly actions affect the balance of power within the divine world.[114] Proper fulfillment of the laws of the Torah increases the flow of divine light from the Godhead, called the *shefa*, and the makeup of the divine structure is therefore governed by human beings (see Dan 221). For Solovyov, social action—that is, our engagement here on earth—intimately affects the Kingdom of God. He condemns philosophers who withdraw from the social arena (*SS* 11:240, 318), criticizes his own church for its worldly apathy (*SS* 11:175), and praises the Jews precisely for their orientation toward the world of man and the activism that brings them closer to the Kingdom of Heaven. As he writes in *Russia and the Universal Church*, "[The Jews] alone understood true redemption . . . in the sanctification and renaissance of the entire human essence and all of its being by the way of living moral and religious activism, in faith and deeds, in prayer, in work and charity" (*SS* 11:322).

As Solovyov argues, the union of flesh and spirit takes place along the lines of sexual intercourse. Wisdom finds man and rejoices in the union (*SS* 11:306); Earth and heaven unite to create man (*SS* 11:306); the Soul and the Word unite in gladness (*SS* 11:307).[115] The feminine gender in Solovyov, therefore, does not represent evil or corruption of the flesh, as it does in Gnosticism and the philosophy of Philo, for example.[116] Rather, Solovyov insists on the sexually androgynous or outwardly feminine aspect of his Divine Sophia and elevates

---

113. Christian Knorr von Rosenroth (1636–1689), the son of a Protestant minister from Germany, developed an interest in Kabbalah, probably through the writings of Boehme (see below), and produced the first Latin translation of the Zohar, called *Kabbalah Denudata* (*The Kabbalah Unveiled*, 1677 and 1684). The two volumes of this massive work were available for Solovyov to study at the British Museum in the 1870s.

114. "Thus, man is conceived of as an active factor able to interact with the dynamic Divinity. Kabbalistic anthropology and theosophy, then, are both similar and complementary perceptions" (Idel, *Kabbalah: New Perspectives*, 166).

115. See also Solovyov's discussion in "The Meaning of Love" (*SS* 7:45).

116. See Meeks 176; Baer 40–44.

erotic love to the role of divine mediator.[117] Sexual love leads humanity toward the image and likeness of God, which is androgynous. Androgyny for Solovyov is the highest of five paths of love:

> "The Eternal God created man, He created him in His image and likeness: husband and wife created He them" [Gen. 1:27; Solovyov's own paraphrase]. This means that the image and likeness of God, that which is open to renewal, refers not to a half, and not to only one gender, but to the whole human being, that is, to the positive union of masculine and feminine principles—true androgyny—without external confusion of forms, which would be ugliness, and without internal division of personality and life, which would be imperfection and the principle of death. (SS 9:234)

Solovyov takes his image of androgyny from Plato's *Symposium*, but he may have found confirmation for his own intuition of its centrality in the Zohar, which explains: "Any image that does not embrace male and female is not a high and true image," and "A human being is only called Adam when male and female are as one" (Zohar I:55b).[118] For both Kabbalah and Solovyov, the ideal is bisexual, not asexual. Our visionary's "Soph-Jah" is this erotic, male/female manifestation—drawn from Plato's world and the Gnostic Sophia but also from Kabbalah's mystical interrelationship of the male Hokhmah and decidedly female Shekhinah. This divine indwelling—the female presence of God from Hebrew scriptures now united with male Wisdom—connects heaven and earth in joy. As we saw in Proverbs, "I was his delight day by day, / frolicking before him at all times, / frolicking in his habitable world. / And my delight is in mankind" (Proverbs 8:30–32).

Solovyov's Sophia goes by many names. In the prayer reproduced above, she is dove of Zion, pearl of Ophir, image of beauty and sweetness, bright body of eternity, soul of worlds, empress of all souls. Regardless of this multiplicity of appellations, her role is theologically, psychologically, and socially focused: "[A]ppear to us in visible and concrete form, incarnate yourself in us and in the world, restoring the fullness of the ages. Then may the depths confine themselves to their boundaries, and may God be all in all."

Christian Mystics and the Jungfrau of Jakob Boehme

> The only substantial individuals in this context turn out to be Paracelsus, Boehme, and Swedenborg, so the field remains wide open for me.
>
> SOLOVYOV, letter to Sophia Tolstaia, April 27, 1877

---

117. "Eros is not a god, but something divine, halfway between eternal and mortal nature, a powerful demon who unites heaven and earth" ("Tvorenie Platona," SS 12:391). See also Kornblatt, "The Transfiguration of Plato."

118. *Zohar: The Book of Enlightenment*, trans. Matt 55–56. Scholem considers the introduction of a female aspect of God in Shekhinah "one of the most important and lasting innovations of Kabbalism." Scholem, *Major Trends* 229.

So far we have seen a number of obvious antecedents to the Sophia of Solovyov's day: biblical texts and their interpretation/interpolation in liturgical and iconographic settings, Greek and Jewish Platonism and Neoplatonism, as well as the mystical traditions of Gnosticism and Kabbalah. Other mystics through the ages felt these same influences and in turn bequeathed their own visions of Sophia to Solovyov. The most influential of these was Jacob Boehme (1575–1624), a German shoemaker from Silesia who has been called the "Father of Western Sophiology" (Schiplinger 189). His first vision was of a pure, mystical light—not specifically in female form—that suffused him with a sense of bliss. Boehme went on to have several more visions of what he understood to be the true structure of the universe and to write a number of treatises that were increasingly influenced by other visionaries, by alchemy and astrology, and by his readings in Kabbalah.[119] The proper name Sophia appears only in later writings, but he speaks repeatedly throughout his life of Divine Wisdom (*himmlische Weisheit*) and the Heavenly Maiden (*himmlische Jungfrau*). We will recognize the Sophia of earlier traditions—and later of Solovyov—in Boehme's words:

> Wisdom is God's revelation and the Holy Spirit's corporeality; the body of the Holy Trinity.

> She is a being of wonder without number or end and has no beginning.

> As the soul is in the body and reveals itself in the flesh's essence . . . God's wisdom is the outspoken being by which the power and Spirit of God . . . reveals itself in form. She bears . . . but she is not the divine principle. [She is] the mother in which the Father works. And therefore I call Her a virgin because She is the chastity and purity of God and brings no desire behind Herself . . . but Her inclination goes before Her with the revelation of the Divinity.

> She is the dwelling place of the Spirit of God.

> She is a mirror of the divinity, for each mirror is silent, and bears no likeness except the likeness it receives. Thus the Virgin wisdom is a mirror of divinity in which the Spirit of God beholds itself . . . and in Her the Spirit of God saw all the forms of creatures.

> At the same time she is like the eye that sees.[120]

Like the Ein-Sof of Kabbalah, Boehme's *Ungrund*, or abyss, is the absolute primordial ground of all existence. The Ungrund unfolds in creation through a mirror. Sophia, whom no tongue or person can describe (Boehme 9), aids this process, strikingly like the activity of the sefirot that unfold from Ein-Sof. The explicit addition of reflection imagery comes directly from the Wisdom of

---

119. Boehme's writings include "The Aurora," "Concerning the Three Principles of Divine Essence," "Of the Incarnation of Jesus Christ," and "The Way of Christ." For more on Boehme, see Koyré and Weeks. For Boehme in Russia, see Berdiaev, "Iz etiudov o Ia. Beme," in English as *Studies Concerning Jacob Boehme* at http://www.berdyaev.com; David, "The Influence of Jacob Boehme on Russian Religious Thought"; and Tschiževskij.

120. Cited by Erb in the introduction to Boehme 9–10.

Solomon 7:26: "For she is the brightness of the everlasting light, the unspotted mirror of the power of God, and the image of his goodness," but Boehme may also have developed the image from other medieval and renaissance sources. Solovyov, too, repeats the association of Sophia and mirrors in several of his poems, emphasizing the role of sight and light in his visions and re-visions. As in the translation from Plato's poem examined above, Sophia is both the eye and the image, the seer and the seen.

Before Solovyov, Boehme's writings had influenced the Sophianic and other philosophical works of later Christian mystics including George Gichtel, Gottfried Arnold, Lady Jane Leade, John Pordage, Louis-Claude de Saint Martin, Franz Baader, and Christoph Oetinger. Boehme also apparently influenced the philosophical writings of Hegel, Fichte, and Schelling.[121]

We do not know when Solovyov first read Boehme, although it is likely that he knew of the mystic while still at the university. Russian Freemasonry had shown a great interest in Boehme, and the members of the Society of Wisdom Lovers (*Liubomudry*) collected his works secretly in the 1820s.[122] More directly, Solovyov most likely encountered Boehme through his professor of philosophy at Moscow University, Pamfil Iurkevich, who was immersed in the ideas of theosophic mysticism. In addition, the memory of Professor Fedor Golubinskii, himself strongly influenced by Boehme, was preserved at the Moscow Theological Academy. Later, when he spent time on the estate of the late A. K. Tolstoy, Solovyov could have again come in contact with a library of Boehme's writings.

In his collection of treatises called *The Way to Christ*, written in the last four years of his life, Boehme includes a section with the following extended heading:

A Little Prayer, or Conversation in the internal ground of man, between the poor wounded soul and the noble Virgin Sophia, as between the spirit of Christ in the new birth and the soul; how much joy there is in the heaven of the new, regenerated man; how graciously the noble Sophia presents Herself to Her bridegroom the soul when the soul enters repentance, and how the soul acts when the Virgin

121. Johann Georg Gichtel (1638–1710) and Gottfried Arnold (1666–1714) were both directly inspired by Boehme. Indeed, Gichtel published the first edition of Boehme's collected works. John Pordage (1607–81) and Jane Leade (1624–1704) both had visions and popularized the work of Boehme in England. Louis-Claude de Saint Martin (1743–1803) was the first mystic to translate Boehme's works into French. Christoph Oetinger (1702–82) and Franz Baader (1765–1841) brought his work into the eighteenth and nineteenth centuries. Oetinger also translated Swedenborg. Georg Wilhelm Friedrich Hegel (1770–1831), F. W. J. von Schelling (1775–1854), and J. G. Fichte (1762–1814) were the most influential German Idealist philosophers of the late eighteenth and nineteenth centuries.

122. The Society of Wisdom Lovers (*Obshchestvo liubomudriia*) met secretly in Moscow between about 1823 and 1825. The *Liubomudry*—an archaic word for "philosophers"—studied German metaphysics, concentrating on the transcendental philosophy of Schelling. They disbanded after the failed Decembrist uprising of aristocrats and intellectuals in 1825, but some of their members later became important Slavophile thinkers.

Sophia is revealed to it. The gates of the paradisiacal rose garden no one but the children of Christ who have experienced this may understand. (56–62)

It is possible, although by no means certain, that this short dialogue served as a source for Solovyov's dialogue between himself as "Philosophe" and Sophie, set in Egypt after his third vision. In Boehme's conversation, Sophia speaks directly to the soul as bride to bridegroom. Solovyov has Sophia speak with the philosopher in *The Sophia* not *to*, but *of* the soul, and in a decidedly more aggressive and mocking tone (see page 120). Nonetheless, in both cases, Sophia both instructs and consoles the male interlocutor using the images of light and love, thus leading him to the Kingdom of God. We will encounter some of the imagery of Boehme's Sophianic dialogue again in a poem by A. K. Tolstoy, chosen by Solovyov to end lecture 7 of his *Lectures on Divine Humanity* and discussed in a later section. In Boehme: "But the noble Sophia draws Herself near to the soul's being and kisses it in a friendly manner and tinctures the dark fire of the soul with Her love beams and penetrates the soul with Her loving kiss" (Boehme 57). For A. K. Tolstoy, the "dark glance" of the speaker brightens when he experiences the love that beats even in the "stone heart of the mountains" (see page 179). Solovyov also writes of this soothing love in his poem of Sophia, "My Empress Has a Lofty Palace":

> And bathed in light, she bends down over him
> Like youthful spring over somber winter
> And, full of quiet tenderness,
> Covers him with her radiant veil.
>
> And the dark powers are stricken to the ground.
> His whole being burns with a pure flame,
> And with eternal love in her azure eyes
> She softly tells her beloved: . . ."
> (*SS* 12: 12–13; see page 106)

"She" here is an empress clothed in light who lives in a palace with seven pillars and a garden of roses and lilies. The biblical and Gnostic references to Wisdom are inescapable, as are the hints of Boehme's loving Sophia.

We know for certain that Solovyov was reading Boehme the year after he began working on *The Sophia*. In April of 1877, Solovyov wrote to Sophia Tolstaia about the library research he was undertaking in St. Petersburg at that time:

I haven't found anything special in the library yet.

There is a lot of corroboration for my own ideas among the mystics, but no new light on the subject. Furthermore, they almost all have an extremely subjective and, well, dithering [*sliuniavyi*] character. I found three specialists on Sophia: Georg Gichtel, Gottfried Arnold, and John Pordage.

All three had a personal experience almost exactly like mine, and that is the most interesting fact. But all three are rather weak precisely in theosophy. They follow Boehme, but do not rise to his level. I think that Sophia came to them more because of their naiveté than anything else. As a result, the only substantial individuals in this context turn out to be Paracelsus, Boehme, and Swedenborg, so the field remains wide open for me. (*Pis'ma*, 2: 200)

This letter is a stunning indication of Solovyov's sense of the reality of his own vision(s). It is interesting that he chooses to use the word "field" (*pole*), meaning both a physical and intellectual expanse. His Sophia exists both in space (with colors, sounds, and human language) and in the history of thought. This field reaches into the future; his re-visions later in his career take a part in filling the historical space.

As late as March of 1900, only months before his death, Solovyov still referred to Boehme and his disciples as precursors to his own visions. In a letter to Anna Shmidt, the woman who proposed herself as the incarnation of Sophia, he wrote, "Having read your letter with the greatest of attention, I was pleased to see how closely you have come to the truth of the question of greatest importance, placed at the very essence of Christianity, but not yet distinctly presented in ecclesiastic or general philosophical consciousness. However, individual theosophists do speak about this side of Christianity (especially Jacob Boehme and his followers: Gichtel, Pordage, Saint-Martin, Baader)" (*Pis'ma* 4: 8).

There is a major difference between Boehme's Sophia and that of Solovyov, however. Although influenced by Kabbalah, Boehme's Wisdom shares none of the erotic imagery of the Kabbalistic sefirot. She is thus devoid of many of the important aspects of Solovyov's vision, aspects that may have come more directly from either Kabbalah or the Russian religious tradition: the mystical androgyny, the eroticism and fertility, the paradoxical union. Boehme's Sophia is close to the Virgin Mary in her Western Christian mode of purity. This virginal Sophia comes to influence Russian iconography only *after* the original Sophia icons in Russia and complicates her legacy from Byzantine images of Christ with a Western image of the Virgin Mary. As we have seen, Solovyov's Divine Wisdom and the re-vision of her/him bequeathed to later Russian culture are both pure and erotic, both female and male.

As we saw, Solovyov found little inspiration in most of Boehme's followers in Sophiology, yet he called one, the eighteenth-century mystic Emanuel Swedenborg, "the most remarkable (after Jakob Boehme) theosophist of modern times" (*SS* 10: 487). Swedenborg, who had no training in mystical or theological texts, claimed to have had a vision of a seated man wrapped in a radiant aura, emerging from a dense fog. The vision was clearly masculine and identified itself as "God, the Lord, the Creator and Redeemer," not Sophia. Like Solovyov's alleged second vision of Sophia, however, this light-emitting figure appeared to Swedenborg in London, and his theosophic writings are clearly infused with the Sophia of Boehme. Nonetheless, as Solovyov wrote to Sophia Tolstaia, "the field remains wide open for me" (*Pis'ma* 2: 200).

The Eternal Feminine of Goethe, Dante, and Cervantes[123]

> Do you remember the roses over white foam,
> A purple reflection in azure waves?
> Do you remember the image of a beautiful form,
> Your confusion, and trembling, and dread?
>
> SOLOVYOV, "Das Ewig-Weibliche"

> Das Ewig-Weibliche zieht uns hinan.
>
> GOETHE, *Faust*

Solovyov turned to re-visionaries of Sophia in the area of literature as well as religion and theosophy but found them as well only partially adequate. It is under the influence of this poetic bequest that the Russian visionary attaches yet another title to his vision: the Eternal Feminine, or, in Goethe's famous phrase, *das Ewig-Weibliche.*

In 1874 Solovyov had written to his friend Dmitrii Tsertelev about Goethe's evocation: "I completely agree with your remarks concerning *das Ewig-weibliche*, although, on the other hand, you must recognize the sad truth that this Ewig-weibliche nonetheless and by some fatal necessity *zieht uns an* [draws us/ attracts us] with an irresistible strength, regardless of its apparent insubstantiality" (*Pis'ma* 2:224, cited in *PSS* 2:335–36; Solovyov's capitalization). Goethe's original use of the phrase appears in the very last lines of the rather disjointed and fantastical second part of *Faust*. It is spoken up high in the mountains by the "Chorus Mysticus," originally called the "Chorus in excelsis":

> Alles Vergängliche
> Ist nur ein Gleichnis;
> Das Unzulängliche,
> Hier wird's Ereignis;
> Das Unbeschreibliche,
> Hier ist's getan;
> Das Ewig-Weibliche
> Zieht uns hinan.

> [All that is changeable
> Is only an image;
> The inaccessible
> Here will be manifest;

---

123. Johann Wolfgang von Goethe (1748–1832); Dante Alighieri (1265–1321); Miguel de Cervantes (1547–1616).

The indescribable
Here is complete;
The Eternal Feminine
Draws us upward.][124]

Solovyov translates these same lines in full, but inaccurately, in *The Sophia*. Rather than reproducing the last line as "Draws us upward" from Goethe's *Zieht uns hinan*, Solovyov incorrectly writes to Tsertelev that the Eternal Feminine "draws us on" or even "draws us in" (*zieht uns an*). Solovyov also ends his translated quotation in *The Sophia* incorrectly, with the Russian verb *vlech'* (to draw, drag, or attract). The change from "up" to "in," whether misremembered or intentional, has the effect of deemphasizing the heavenward direction of Goethe's text. Solovyov's vision of the Eternal Feminine is not merely transcendent but effectively operating on earth.[125] She does not take us away from life but instead infuses our present material life with her special aura.

That Solovyov associates this Eternal Feminine with Sophia is obvious early in his career. When he complained to Tsertelev while still in Moscow in 1874 that the Eternal Feminine pulled him with a fatal necessity, he referred, it would seem, to his imminent plans to travel to London and seek out references to Sophia in the British Museum. In April of 1877, Solovyov wrote a letter to Sophia Tolstaia complaining that he had had to leave off his work on the Divine Sophia, here probably referring to his *Sophia* manuscript: "I stopped in at my brother's and found various papers for me from the Ministry. It's good that I didn't remain in Moscow; it seems that my post is not a sinecure. Oh well, *un métier comme un autre* [French, a job like any other], but *die göttliche* Sophia must take a back seat" (*Pis'ma* 2:199). Solovyov's use of the German for "divine" points his Sophia directly back to the high seriousness of Goethe's Ewig-Weibliche, drawing him toward her. On the other hand, Solovyov's cavalier reference to the transfer of attention from Sophia to his day job reinfuses humor into his own re-vision of the Eternal Feminine.

In the same period as Solovyov's letter to Tolstaia, the poet's friend Count Fedor Lvovich Sollogub (1848–90) wrote his farcical play *Solovyov in the Thebaid,* based on Solovyov's trip to Egypt. Like *Faust*, the play begins with a prologue in heaven, but instead of presenting an otherworldly discussion among God, Mephistopheles, and three archangels, Sollogub's prologue "takes place in heaven of course, and therefore the public is not in a position to see it. At the end of the prologue the curtain rises" (Luk'ianov, *O Vl. S. Solov'eve* 3/1:283). In this satire, Solovyov's göttliche Sophia remains hidden

---

124. This translation is my own but informed by the introduction to the Luke translation (*Faust: Part Two* lxxviii). Luke's translation reads: "All that must disappear / Is but a parable;/ What lay beyond us, here / All is made visible;/ Here deeds have understood / Words they were darkened by; / Eternal Womanhood/ Draws us on high" (239).
125. Kravchenko suggests that this and the use of the phrase *zieht uns an* in the earlier letter might be a "Freudian" misprint on Solovyov's part (*Vestniki russkogo mistitsizm* 116).

from both the visionary and his readers/viewers. She is an "un-vision" and appears, as we will discuss in a later section, only in the humor of the play.

Despite these mocking associations, Solovyov did not forget his partial legacy from Goethe throughout his career. In 1890 he refers again to the final lines of the *Faust: Part Two*, criticizing his predecessor precisely for the merely transcendent, and thus fantastic, nature of das Ewig-Weibliche. In "The General Meaning of Art," he writes:

> To see that even the greatest works of poetry realize the meaning of spiritual life only through its *reflection* off nonideal human reality, we can take Goethe's *Faust*. The positive meaning of this lyrical-epic tragedy is openly revealed only in the last scene of the second part, where it is abstractly summarized in the concluding chorus: *Alles Vergängliche ist nur ein Gleichniss* etc. But where then is the direct, organic connection between this apotheosis and the other parts of the tragedy? The heavenly powers and "das Ewig Weibliche" appear from above, and thus from without, rather than revealing themselves from within the content itself. The idea of the last scene is present throughout all of *Faust*, but it simply reflects off the action—part real, part fantastic—of which the whole tragedy consists. Just as a ray of light plays on a diamond, creating pleasure in the viewer but without in any way changing the material basis of the stone, so here the spiritual light of the absolute ideal, refracted through the imagination of the artist, illuminates the darkness of human reality, but in no way changes its essence. (*SS* 6:89–90)

In this passage we see clearly the ways in which Goethe's formulation proves inadequate for Solovyov in his quest for a suitable articulation of his own Divine Sophia. *Faust*'s Eternal Feminine, no matter how real it may be in itself, fails to transfigure nature. The greatest ideal is not shown in itself but only as a reflection off the hard surface of material reality, having no ultimate effect on the content or essence of that reality. Solovyov continues in the passage:

> Let us suppose that in a complex poetic work a mightier poet than Goethe or Shakespeare was able to present us with an artistic, i.e., correct and concrete depiction of true, spiritual life, of the life that should be, that completely realizes the absolute ideal. Nonetheless, even that miracle of art, hitherto unattained by a single poet, would be merely a magnificent mirage in an arid desert amidst actual reality. It would irritate, rather than quench our thirst. In its final task, real art must incarnate the absolute ideal not in imagination alone, but in deed itself. It must spiritualize and transubstantiate our real life. (*SS* 6:90)

For Solovyov, Goethe's Ewig-Weibliche fails to do what his own Sophia apparently can: inspire the interpenetration of spirit and matter, resulting in the incarnation of the former and the transfiguration of the latter.[126]

---

126. Wachtel also examines this passage from "The General Meaning of Art," but, I believe, misreads Solovyov as an extreme dualist (63–64).

In "The Meaning of Love," Solovyov writes again of the Eternal Feminine. Here he does not mention Goethe or use the German term. Instead, he employs vocabulary closer to his own theosophical formulation, associating femininity with God's "other," the universe:

> For God, His *other* (that is, the universe) has had for eternity the image of perfect femininity. He wants not only that that image be for Him but that it be realized and incarnated for every individual being who is capable of uniting with it. The Eternal Feminine itself strives toward that realization and incarnation. The Eternal Feminine is not only an inactive image in the mind of God, but a living, spiritual being who possesses the full totality of powers and actions. The entire world and historical process is the process of its realization and incarnation in the great multiplicity of forms and degrees. (*SS* 7:46)

Here, the Eternal Feminine sounds more like Wisdom in Proverbs; Solovyov's ideal feminine is an active principle that strives for the incarnation of spirit and the transfiguration of matter, not the abstract and ultimately ineffective Ewig-Weibliche of romantic poetry.

Perhaps most characteristically, in 1898 Solovyov wrote a humorous poem that points directly back to Goethe in its German title—"Das Ewig-Weibliche"—but treats the feminine ideal with a combination of laughter and seriousness. The "I" of the poem, presumably Solovyov on his beloved Lake Saimaa in Finland, is pursued by annoying, self-satisfied demons. These demons apparently are the same dispersers of evil who once cowered before Aphrodite on other shores ("Where Amathous and Pafos stood"). In pagan times, however, the Greek goddess of love proved unable to resist the corruption of the flesh that the demons offered. Solovyov warns the demons who now stalk him that they will not succeed in the same way with the Eternal Feminine, the "unearthly beauty" that accompanies him today. He censures his pursuers as follows:

DAS EWIG-WEIBLICHE
(A word of admonition to sea demons)

Sea demons took a liking to me,
And scour about in search of my tracks;
They caught me anon on the Finnish shore,
I'm in the Archipelago—and there they are back.

It's clear that the demons want my death,
As is fitting and proper for such beasts.
God speed, my demons! But believe my word,
I'll not surrender myself to your feast.

Better instead you should attend to my word,—
A kind word I reveal to you:
To return to God's fold, dear demons,
Depends alone on you.

'Do you remember how, by this sea,
Where Amathous and Pafos once were,[127]
You once came to feel
Your first ever-bewildering woe?

Do you remember the roses over white foam,
A purple reflection in azure waves?
Do you remember the image of a beautiful form,
Your confusion, and trembling, and dread?

Demons, you did not fear that beauty
In its first power for long;
Your wild malice was tamed for a moment,
But beauty could not conquer it for good.

O crafty demons, you soon found
Your secret way into that splendor,
And in the beautiful image you sowed
Your hellish seed of corruption and death.

Know then: the imperishable body
Of the eternal feminine today comes to earth.
Heaven is flooded by the watery abyss
In the new goddess's unfading light.

In all ways that the earthly Aphrodite is beautiful,
The joy of homes, and woods, and seas,—
The unearthly beauty will replace it,
But purer, stronger, with more fullness and life.

Don't seek in vain to approach her!
Smart demons, why make such a fuss?
You can't delay or subdue
That for which nature pines and awaits.

Proud demons, you all are men,—
There's no honor in fighting a woman.
Well, if for no other reason than this,
Dear demons, surrender up now!
      (SS 12:71–73; *Stikhotvoreniia* 120–22)

In this poem, Divine Beauty comes to earth in the colors Solovyov has associated repeatedly with Sophia: the red and white of roses and lilies,[128] the purple of her royal clothing, the azure of the very atmosphere around her ("Do you remember the roses over white foam, / A purple reflection in azure waves?"). Furthermore,

---

127. Amathous (or Amathus) and Pafos were ancient cities on the island of Cyprus, known for their association with Aphrodite, the Greek goddess of love.
128. As we saw, Solovyov borrows the red and white flowers from Gnosticism. The images became part of alchemical vocabulary, as well, from whence Goethe borrows them. Speaking of his father's work in the "Black Laboratory," he states, "Thus in tepid immersion he would wed / The Lily to the Lion bold and red" (*Faust: Part One* 34).

her appearance is marked by the interpenetration of sky and earth ("Heaven is flooded by the watery abyss") in a grand reversal of creation, when "God made the firmament and separated the waters which were under the firmament from the waters which were above the firmament. And it was so" (Genesis 1:7). This Divine Sophia, with her paradoxical "imperishable body" and "unfading light," will reverse the demon's actions and transfigure rather than debase nature, making earthly beauty "purer, stronger." Although the poem draws its title from Goethe's creation, it does not end with an escape *hinan,* up into the mountains and away from the material world. Instead, Solovyov's Eternal Feminine remains on earth, transforming it "with more fullness and life."

To strengthen the earthiness of his image, Solovyov ends with a humorous stanza, reminding the demons that they are men and thus should give up their fight in the interest of preserving their honor. Better to concede than lose to a woman, he taunts them.

Solovyov critiques another famous poet for a less than concrete divine feminine as well. In a footnote to the passage cited above from "The General Meaning of Art," Solovyov refers to the third part of Dante's *Divine Comedy,* where "paradise is depicted in a way that might be true, but is not in any case sufficiently alive and concrete—an essential flaw that cannot be redeemed even with the most melodious verses" (*SS* 6: 90). Solovyov had made an attempt four years earlier to translate some of Dante's "melodious verses" from the *Vita Nuova,* which he dedicated to his brother Mikhail and sent to Sophia Khitrovo in 1886. The sonnet, from chapter 15 of Dante's love poem, must have attracted Solovyov because of its typical address of a beloved "you," its references to light and joy ("O radost' svetlaia" in his Russian translation), and its repeated emphasis on sight, vision, and glances (*Pis'ma* 2:196; *Stikhotvoreniia* 194). Although Solovyov never wrote about Dante in a sustained manner, he does mention the Italian poet in a number of works, including *The Great Controversy and Christian Politics* and *La Russie et l'église universelle.* And other scholars have seen "Dantesque motifs in Solovyov's poetry" (Davidson 71).[129] Like Goethe's romantic Feminine, however, Dante's medieval love proved too abstract for Solovyov, as we saw in the quotation above about Dante's *Paradise.* Solovyov calls this kind of love a "falsely incarnated ideal" (*SS* 7:28). As he wrote in "The Meaning of Love," discussing medieval chivalry:

> Don Quixote's disenchantment marked the height of knighthood in the new Europe. It operates in us even to this day. Yet idealization of the beloved, having stopped serving as the source of mad exploits, no longer inspires them. It turns out to be merely a decoy, forcing us to desire possession of the physical and

129. See Davidson 53–71 for a discussion of references to Dante and Petrarch in Solovyov's work. Davidson correctly observes that the Symbolists tended to read Dante through Solovyov but tended to "present a composite, syncretic figure in their poetry," blurring the distinction between Sophia and the Virgin Mary (65–66). See also Florovsky, "Vladimir Soloviev and Dante" 152–60); and Helleman, *Sophia, Mary and Beatrice.*

mundane, and disappearing as soon as this goal—the opposite of ideal—is reached. The light of love serves no one as the ray directing us to a lost paradise. We look at it as on the fantastic illumination of the brief beloved "prologue in heaven" [from the opening of *Faust: Part One*]. Nature in its time entirely extinguishes such light as completely unnecessary for the future earthly production. In fact, that light is extinguished by the weakness and unconsciousness of our love, distorting the true order of things. (*SS* 7:29)

As we have seen, Solovyov's Sophia often is female and is sometimes depicted in the image of the Virgin Mary, of Mother Earth, and, in the case of comparisons with Goethe and Dante, with an idealized Eternal Feminine. But she is never solely female, just as she is never solely divine or solely earthly, solely abstract or solely material, solely ideal or solely debased. Instead, her truest manifestation is at once incarnated and transfigured into a new whole, both male and female. She is the androgynous angel on Divine Sophia icons, enthroned above the seven pillars of God's proverbial Wisdom, surrounded by the Mother of God and the Precursor of Jesus, and protected from above by Christ on High. Dante's, Cervantes's, and Goethe's versions of the idealized feminine are unable to interpenetrate and thus transform reality into its truest form. Solovyov might recognize earlier traditions, and he might mine their prose and poetry for approximate terminology, but as we have seen, no one Sophianic ancestor proves capable of fully expressing his visions on its own. Solovyov's poetic and philosophical re-visions—combining imagery and vocabulary from all the traditions we have examined—are themselves approximations, an effort to express what is ultimately ineffable, to write what is inexpressible.

SOLOVYOV AS SELF-CONSCIOUS HEIR

> Kabbalah and Neoplatonism.
> Boehme and Swedenborg.
> Schelling and me.
> SOLOVYOV, 1875 notebooks[130]

That Solovyov understood himself within a historical line of mystics, or those who have "known" the Absolute as he defines it, is obvious from a jotting in his early notebooks that serves as epigraph to this section. The section continues with a comparison between law and the Old Testament; Gospels and the New Testament; and on the third line, corresponding to "Schelling and me," freedom and Eternal Testament (*PSS* 2:177; see page 172) Thus, not

---

130. The editors of *PSS* date this jotting fairly reliably to 1875 from a reference in automatic writing to the suicide of Solovyov's friend P. A. Bibikov, on November 14, 1875 (*PSS* 2: 354).

only does Solovyov understand his own intuition of Sophia within an ancient and enduring tradition, but he sees his responsibility to articulate that intuition in a third, or eternal, testament of freedom, to participate in the creation of a teaching that would supersede even the holy scriptures in the Old and New Testaments. How can we accept Solovyov's claims of direct lineage from the Jewish Kabbalah, from the millennia-old teachings of the Neoplatonists, from Swedenborg, Boehme, and Friedrich Schelling as more than naïve boasting? And how can we go on to explain his interest in mysticism throughout his twenty-five-year writing career, during which his early poems evoking the appearance of Sophia are followed up with discursive analyses in his philosophy and then with humorous renditions in play, story, and poem? If it was only youthful hubris, why return so often, in so many genres and discourses, once he had established himself as a major figure in Russian letters? One question that must lie behind all the others is whether or not Solovyov actually experienced visions of Sophia. This, of course, is impossible to determine. Indeed, we cannot analyze the intuition itself but only the articulation of it. We are thus at once fortunate and confounded that Solovyov left so many different attempts at that articulation.

We might begin by asking what Solovyov wrote explicitly about mysticism and visions in his academic prose. When doing so, we need always to keep in mind the historical circumstances of his statements and that they are all made at some remove from the alleged visions themselves. Quite late in his career, Solovyov provides a definition of visions in an entry in the *Encyclopedic Dictionary*. "In the strict sense," he writes, they "are involuntary visual images and pictures, received while awake, that produce a more or less complete impression of objective reality, but which do not have any external material substance." Visions differ from ordinary fantasies, he continues, both because of their clarity and concreteness and also in that they cannot be induced in any way. Visions, rather, "arise and are maintained regardless of a subject's own conscious acts, and therefore seem to him like external reality." Relying on his scientific background, as well as on the contemporary fad to seek out scientific explanations for psychic events, Solovyov connects the ability to see visions with certain "specifics in the organization of the nervous system," yet he categorically rejects the equation of them with the deranged hallucinations of the insane. They are real. Nonetheless, despite their reality, the visions are cut off from the visionary's ordinary surroundings "as though they carry around themselves a special environment, distinguished at once from our internal psychic world and from the realm of material phenomena" (*SS* 12:556). If Solovyov's poetic re-visions are to be trusted as at least an approximate expression of his own visions, we find that the environment is highly developed: "The room all fills with azure and with gold." Each of his visions occurs in a clearly delineated physical space—church, library, desert—yet transports the visionary momentarily out of that space:

The altar door's agap . . . But where're the celebrants?
And where's the crowd that milled around in prayer?
My flood of passions—drained all of a sudden,
As azure fills my soul, and fills the air.

(*SS* 12:81; see page xxx)

Visions, of course, are only one form of mystical experience, and Solovyov's late, academic explanation only partly explains his own visual and other experiences, which were broad and multivalent, like Sophia herself/itself. Solovyov also claims to have heard voices at various times throughout his life,[131] and he kept a journal of his dreams in the 1880s, assuming that they held some hidden, mystical meaning.[132] Throughout the three decades of his writing career, Solovyov experimented with yet another popular form of intercourse with the spiritual world: automatic writing. In this type of psychical practice, the medium or psychic lightly holds a writing implement (sometimes attached to a wooden board, or planchette) and allows her/his hand to roam about a paper as the pen, pencil, or chalk traces letters, words, or even whole sentences. According to the Symbolist writer Georgii Chulkov, Solovyov's automatic writing is the "key to understanding his poetry, especially those poems like *Three Encounters* and "Das Ewig-Weibliche" (123). We find the following example of automatic writing in French in his notebooks of 1875, presumably in the words of Sophia herself, identified by the name "Sophie":

Sophie. Mange un peu plus aujourd'hui. Je ne veux pas, que tu t'épuises. Mon chéri, nous voulons te préparer pour la grande mission, que tu dois remplir. Médite toujours sur les principes. Ne donne pas un accès aux pensées de désespoir, mais chasses aussi l'orgueil et l'ambition.

[Sophie. Eat a little more today. I don't want to see you waste away. My dear, we want to prepare you for the grand mission that you must fulfill. Always meditate on the principles. Do not give over to thoughts of despair, but also chase away pride and ambition.] (*PSS* 2:177; see page 172)

Here Sophie talks directly and intimately—if not particularly profoundly—to the philosopher through his own pen, showing her concern for his physical as well as emotional well-being.[133] Chulkov cites similar examples, written in either a flowery Latin script or with a wavering Russian hand, as though the author was in a trance and did not look at the paper:

Sophie. What is it my dear? How do you feel now? My dear I love you. Sophie.

---

131. See Nosov 207; cited in Davidson 652.

132. For some examples, see S. M. Solovyov, *Zhizn' i tvorcheskaia evoliutsiia*, 207–8; *Vladimir Solovyov*, trans. Gibson, 244–46.

133. For more on Solovyov's experiments in automatic writing and how it fits into the spiritual atmosphere of the late nineteenth century as well as into his articulations of Sophia, see Kornblatt, "Who Is Sophia and Why Is She Writing in My Manuscript?"

Sample of Solovyov's automatic writing with channeling from Sophia in French and Russian.

Sophie. I will be delighted to get news from you. My dear how I love you. I can't live without you. Soon soon [sic] we will be together. Don't be sad everything will be good. Sophie. (124)

The philosopher-poet's enduring interest in his own and others' mystical experiences is evident in his contribution of another entry to the *Encyclopedic Dictionary*, this one titled "Mysticism" (*Mistika, Mistitsizm*). He begins with mention of the Greek term τὰ μυστιχά τὰ, which referred originally only to the cults of Demeter and Dionysus. Defining the term in a figurative sense, however, Solovyov divides mysticism (*mistika*) into "real or experiential mysticism" (including clairvoyance, divination, and various kinds of materialization, dematerialization, or manipulation of objects over a distance), and "a special kind of religious-philosophical cognitive activity" (*SS* 10:243–44). It is the latter that interests him most and into which his own mystical experiences fall. As he writes:

Beyond the ordinary means of knowing truth—experience, pure contemplation, tradition, and authority—the majority of religious and metaphysical minds have always admitted the possibility of an unmediated relationship between the knowing subject and the absolute object of knowledge, the essence of all, or the Divine. If such a relationship is recognized as the single or, at least, most faithful and worthy means to know and realize the truth, and all other means are more or less rejected as base and unsatisfactory, then we recognize an exclusive manner of cognition that is called mysticism [*mistitsizm*]. If, regardless of the extremity of this manner, the internal relationship of the human spirit with the Absolute is recognized as an essential basis for true knowledge, then teachings arise that are defined as *mystical theology, mystical philosophy* or *theosophy*, depending on the preponderance of religious or philosophical elements in them. (*SS* 10: 244)

Having defined mysticism (he uses the word *mistitsizm* here, rather than *mistika*) as a special means of religious, philosophical, or theosophical knowing, Solovyov provides examples of individuals and teachings that demonstrate mystical cognition. Among others, he lists: the Upanishada, the secret teachings of Lao-tse, Heraclitus, the Pythagorians, Empedocles, Plato, Philo, the Egyptian-Hellenistic books of Hermes Trismegistus, the Neoplatonists and Gnostics, Origen, Dionysius the Pseudo-Areopagite, the Philokalia (or *Dobrotoliubie* in its Russian translation), Gregory Palamas, Maximus the Confessor, the Victorines and followers of Saint Bonaventure, and St. Theresa. He mentions Kabbalah among the Jews and Sufism among the Muslims of Persia, as well as Paracelsus, Boehme, Gichtel, Pordage, Saint Martin, and Swedenborg.[134] This list of mystics is broad-ranging, both geographically and historically, and those included differ as much as they resemble each other. What they all share for Solovyov is a consciousness of experience beyond the rational and, in many cases, a specific reference to Wisdom/Sophia as embodying or expressing that experience.

Solovyov's distinction between mistika (practical mysticism) and mistitsizm (mystical knowledge) differs in this late formulation from a much earlier one in the opening chapter of the unfinished *Philosophical Principles of Integral Knowledge*: "On the Law of Historical Development."[135] It is this work, written shortly after his trip to London and Cairo in search of Sophia, that incorporates some passages from the unpublished *Sophia* manuscript. Here he uses *mistika* rather than *mistitsizm*, calling the former the "creative relationship of human emotion to the transcendent world." He clarifies the distinction in a footnote: "We must strictly distinguish between mistika and mistitsizm: the first is the direct, unmediated relationship of our spirit to the transcendent world. The second then is our mind's reflection on that relationship, and forms a special branch of philosophy, about which we will speak later. Mistika and mistitsizm are related to each other as are, for example, empire [*émpiriia*] and empiricism [*émpirizm*]" (*PSS* 2:195).

What is common in the two definitions, from quite early and then late in his career, is the seriousness with which Solovyov takes mystical experience as

---

134. Many of these names or movements, especially those from the Western traditions, have been cited previously in this book. Others, like the Upanishada from Hindu scriptures, the writings of the ancient Chinese philosopher Lao-tse, and Islamic Sufi practices demonstrate the breadth, although not necessarily the depth, of Solovyov's knowledge of non-Western traditions.

135. Kravchenko also tries to distinguish the terms in *Mistitsizm v Russkoi filosofskoi mysli* 6–10.

a way in which the human individual can relate to the Absolute or Divine. The definitions differ, however, in the types of interaction that connect the created being with the transcendent: the early writings talk of an emotional relationship, the later of a cognitive one. We find that these differing terms— "feeling" (*chuvstvo*) and "cognitive activity" (*poznavatel'naia deiatel'nost'*) or "thought" (*mysli*)—are in fact not so distinct when we examine the role of mistika in Solovyov's abstract scheme for the "all-human organism." This is illustrated in the following table, also from *Philosophical Principles of Integral Knowledge* (*PSS* 2:196):

	I SPHERE OF CREATIVITY	II SPHERE OF KNOWLEDGE	III SPHERE OF PRACTICAL ACTIVITY
	Subjective basis: FEELING	Subjective basis: THOUGHT	Subjective basis: WILL
	Objective principle: BEAUTY	Objective principle: TRUTH	Objective principle: GENERAL GOOD
1. ABSOLUTE LEVEL	Mysticism	Theology	Spiritual society (Church)
2. FORMAL LEVEL	Fine Arts	Abstract Philosophy	Political society (Government)
3. MATERIAL LEVEL	Technical Arts	Positive Science	Economic society (*zemstvo*)

Solovyov here divides objective reality into the three classical objective principles of good, truth, and beauty, with beauty taking the primary position (see second row). He associates each realm with a subjective human activity; feeling, associated with beauty, appears to take precedence over thought and will. Mysticism (mistika) in the scheme is placed in the primary, left-hand column of feeling and beauty, in the sphere of creativity rather than the sphere of knowledge, where thought and truth fall. In fact, mysticism is the highest, or absolute, level of all the creative endeavors (above the fine and technical arts), which, in turn, are the highest spheres of activity. As such, mistika is superior both to creative art below it in the sphere of creativity and to theology to the right on the absolute level. The mystic, then, interacts with the world in the same way as the artist but more so (more beautifully), and in the same way as the theologian or philosopher but, again, more so (more absolutely). The mystic's realm is not mere emotion, but neither is it mere cognition. As this table indicates, the movement of reality runs both upward and leftward toward mysticism. Mysticism, then, is the best, truest, and most beautiful interaction with absolute reality that is possible for human beings. In the 1890s, Solovyov apparently took a more cautious approach to the meaning of mystical experience, calling it an exclusive form of cognition. But as he began his philosophical and poetic career in the 1870s, he granted it the highest significance; he saw those visions as elements of an eternal testament. He clearly believed that his visions granted him special interaction with the Absolute, the Divine, the Ein-Sof of the Kabbalists, and the Ungrund of his predecessor Boehme. For him, his visions of Sophia belonged to the highest form of mystical reality, which is the highest form of reality itself. His task became how to articulate the vision, to write it as a translation for others, and ultimately to transfigure others with the light that had shone through him. His writings, whether poetic, fictional, or philosophical, are all re-visions of his original vision of absolute truth, goodness, and beauty, aimed at making his readers view or re-view as well.

How to Write a Vision?

And my dark glance brightened,
And the unseen world became visible,
And since that time my ear hears
What others cannot catch,
And I came down from the mountain heights,
Fully penetrated by her rays.

    A. K. TOLSTOY, "Menia, vo mrake i v pyli"

The most common phenomenon revealing man's metaphysical character is the phenomenon of laughter. It is known that man alone possesses this faculty. Animals sometimes cry, but they never laugh; even the slightest of smiles is impossible for them. If one were to ask me to define man by a sign as characteristic as it is apparent, I would call him "the being that laughs."

    SOLOVYOV, *The Sophia*

The schema from *Philosophical Principles of Integral Knowledge* reproduced above reminds us of the close connection Solovyov draws between mysticism and artistic creation. His intuition of Sophia as a mediator that can connect the human and the divine spheres, as a "third element" that transfigures the resulting union, is part and parcel of his creative sensibility. Indeed, Sophia becomes the subject of human creativity in his poems, the vehicle for that creativity in poetic form, and the goal of that creativity/transfiguration all at once. Poetry *is* Sophia in its incarnating and transfiguring ability.

If we return now to Solovyov's first introduction of the name Sophia into his writing, we see that he concludes his seventh part of *Lectures on Divine Humanity* by associating the human ability to create poetry with Sophia's role as uniter of "clear" heaven and "muffled" earth. I quote the passage in full, for it, like Solovyov's whole oeuvre, combines philosophic discourse with poetry, in this case a not completely accurate selection from the poem "Me, in the murk and dust" by his literary mentor, A. K. Tolstoy:

And man, who belongs to both worlds, can and must touch the divine world by an act of mental contemplation. And though living in the world of conflict and muffled disquiet, he enters into relations with the clear images from the kingdom of glory and eternal beauty. This positive, although incomplete, knowledge of or penetration into the reality of the divine world is particularly characteristic of poetic creation. Every true poet must necessarily penetrate "into the fatherland of flame and word,"[136] in order to take from there the primal images of his creation and, together with them, that internal lucidity that is called inspiration and through which we, in our natural reality, can find the sounds and colors for the incarnation of ideal types, as one of our poets says—

> And my dark glance brightened,
> And the unseen world became visible,
> And since that time my ear hears
> What others cannot catch,
> And I came down from the mountain heights,
> Fully penetrated by her rays,
> And on the agitated dale
> I gaze with new eyes
> And I hear as incessant talk
> Rings everywhere,
> As the stone heart of the mountains
> Beats with love in the dark depths;
> And slow clouds curl
> With love in the sky-blue firmament,
> And under the bark of trees
> The living juice in the leaves
> Rises up with love as a singing stream.
> And I understood with a prophetic heart
> That all that is born from the Word,
> Pouring out the rays of love,
> Thirsts to return to him again.
> And every stream of life,
> Submissive to the law of love,
> Rushes irrepressibly to God's loins
> With all the strength of being.
> And sound and light are everywhere,
> And there is only one principle for all the worlds,
> And there is nothing in nature
> That would not breathe with love.

(SS 3: 118–19; see page 179)

---

136. This phrase is the fourth line of "Menia, vo mrake i v pyli." In *Lectures*, Solovyov omits the first four lines of the poem, which read: "Me, in the world of murk / Who 'til now was possessed of fetters / The wings of love raised me / Into the fatherland of flame and word." Instead of the murky darkness of the full poem, Solovyov begins his citation with light: "I prosvetlet moi temnyi vzor," which translates literally: "And lighted up / through my dark glance."

This short passage and the poem that completes it raise multiple questions. What does it mean for Solovyov to touch or penetrate the reality of the divine world? How does Sophia do that, whether in poetry or philosophy?[137] Or is poetry the only way to penetrate reality? Then how do we understand all his attempts to explain Sophia in philosophical prose? On a different level, who precisely is the "she" who brings down her rays? How does "she" relate to the Word from which all is born? What are her "rays" and the "internal lucidity" that she represents/provokes? And most of all, what is our role as humans in the "incarnation" of this "penetration," this touching, this experience of lucidity?

As always, Solovyov does not directly answer the questions he implicitly raises. His method is associative, even in some of his more rational philosophical texts. As we will see in part 2, Solovyov repeatedly and in various genres and modes associates Sophia with light, suggesting that she/it is the embodiment of immaterial but nonetheless beautiful spirit that transfigures our natural world. Even in this passage of poetry and prose, poetry seems to be but one of her/its modes, not the only one. Love is clearly another ("As the stone heart of the mountains/ Beats with love"), as are light ("And I came down from the mountain heights, / Fully penetrated by her rays") and aesthetic beauty in various media, including music ("The living juice in the leaves / Rises up with love as a singing stream" and "the sounds and colors for the incarnation of ideal types").

Solovyov does not seem to separate Sophia's invocation in poetry from her description in prose, just as he does not separate her various modes of union. In verse, however, she is both the message *and* the bearer of the message or, in the imagery from Proverbs, both the house builder and the house itself, where God's Shekhinah dwells with humanity. If a poem penetrates the fatherland to bring back primal images of creation, then not only is it about Sophia, but it acts like Sophia itself. Like Sophia, the poem is a third, uniting and transfiguring element.

Sophia has yet another guise in which she appears throughout Solovyov's writing: laughter. Two years before his *Lectures*, Solovyov stated, "Among the many characteristic peculiarities of human nature, only one belongs uniquely to man and constitutes his unequivocal distinction from other living beings. This characteristic is not sociability, as Aristotle determined when he said that man is a social animal. . . . The characteristic peculiarity of man is found in the fact that only he has the ability to laugh. This ability is extremely important, and lies at the very essence of human nature. I therefore define man as a *laughing animal*."[138]

---

137. "Il y a chez le Solov'ëv de cette époque une volonté très claire de montrer que le lieu de la mètaphysique n'est pas seulement le traité philosophique, dont la logique est celle des sciences positives contre laquelle il est parti en guerre dans sa *Crise de la philosophie occidentale* (1874), mais aussi l'art et la poésie" (M. Grabar 148).

138. Solov'ev, "Lektsiia ot 14 ianvaria 1875 g.," *SS* 12:526. The editors of the Brussels reprint, quoting from M. Filippov's study of Solovyov, point to an error in Solovyov's interpretation of Aristotle, who spoke of man not as a "social" but as a "political" animal (*SS* 12:526).

In *Lectures*, Solovyov asserts that human nature participates in Divinity, always striving to interact with God (e.g., *SS* 3:19, 25, 32). Yet he claims that we should look first for the Divine not above but within: "Before one can *know* [the unconditional content] as a reality *outside himself*, one must *recognize* it as an idea *within himself*" (*SS* 3:26). Humanity itself is the "uniting link between the divine and natural worlds" (*SS* 3:121; see page 180). Thus, we forever participate with both the created world and God. This "real, mutual interaction of God and man," Solovyov calls, as we saw, the "*bogochelovecheskii* [divinely human/god-manly] process" (*SS* 3:36). Where can we find this process at work? If the divine is within human nature as well as above it, then laughter, which lies at the core of human nature, must also bring us in active contact with the divine.

Solovyov again wrote on the connection between laughter and true humanity in "Principes de la doctrine universelle," the first monologic section of *The Sophia*: "In any profound examination, the most common phenomenon revealing man's metaphysical character is the phenomenon of laughter. It is known that man alone possesses this faculty. Animals sometimes cry, but they never laugh; even the slightest of smiles is impossible for them. If one were to ask me to define man by a sign as characteristic as it is apparent, I would call him 'the being that laughs'" (*PSS* 2:12; see page 117).

Sophia, as the "all-human organism, as the eternal body of God and eternal soul of the world" (*SS* 3:127), must therefore ride the ultimate laugh. As the soul of the laughing animal, Sophia brings humor to the body of God as well, transfiguring matter and embodying the divine. Considering the close association in these passages of laughter, Sophia, and poetry—all through the medium of "the being that laughs" and the "internal lucidity" of poetic inspiration—we should no longer be surprised that Solovyov sometimes chose humorous verse genres in which to depict his beloved tsaritsa.

Solovyov's own laugh was one of his most distinguishing characteristics. "When he laughed, his loud infectious laughter 'with unexpected, outrageous, and hiccup-like high notes' would drown out all other voices," wrote his friend Evgenii Trubetskoi.[139] The scholar Mochul'skii remarked, "He possessed a great sense of humor and a frenzied, almost tormented passion for humorous verse, parodies, and puns; he loved even the most inept play on words, senseless buffoonery, coarse, even obscene anecdotes. Gaiety would descend upon him in elemental fits, like a kind of epilepsy" (25).

What makes Solovyov's laughter all the more interesting is that it often turned upon the poet-philosopher himself. Volodia is the hapless narrator of *Three Encounters* who wanders into the desert in top hat and frock coat in search of Sophia (*SS* 12:80–86; see page 270). Solovyov is the title character of the unpublished farce by his friend Fedor Sollogub, *Solovyov in the Thebaid*, a

---

139. Trubetskoi,, "Lichnost' V. S. Solov'eva" 70. Originally in *Sbornik pervyi* 45–77. Internal quotation from Velichko 142.

ridiculous rhymed romp that the philosopher delights in sending around to his friends. He is the author of his own deprecating epitaph, as we saw: "Vladimir Solovyov lies on this spot; / Once a thinker, now his body is rot." And although he is probably closest to the questing character of Mortemir in *The White Lily*, the poet/playwright also has the bumbling characters of Chaldean, Instrument, and Sorval finally recognize Sophia in their own flighty girlfriends, Galactea, Alconda, and Terbinda. The recognition comes only after the White Lily/Sophia appears to Mortimir above the grave of a common bear and announces the absurdity: "I was in the bear, now the bear's in me" (see page 259). Solovyov seems to have wanted his audience to laugh at his quest for Divine Wisdom.

Solovyov's association of wisdom with laughter, joy, and delight is not unique. He could very well have adopted the idea from the very passages from Proverbs that he cites, and from Philo, Kabbalah, Boehme, and many other sources that look back to the biblical figure of Wisdom. In *Russia and the Universal Church*, Solovyov writes, "Wisdom revealed to us the meaning of her activity; she constructs the universe (she was an artist). She will now tell us as well the meaning of her possession:—Rejoicing before Him always, rejoicing in His world, and my joy was with the sons of man" (*SS* 11:289).

In this passage, Solovyov includes a transliteration into Cyrillic of the Hebrew text of Proverbs and his own translation of Proverbs 8:30–31:

> And I was near him, growing up,
> And I was his delight day by day,
> Frolicking before him at all times,
> Frolicking in his habitable world.
> And my delight is in mankind.

About this passage, the scholar of ancient wisdom literature, Michael Fox, writes in a section titled "Wisdom is Fun": "God set the example by taking delight (ša'ă šu'im) in young Wisdom's play, at the very time he was busy creating the world. Wisdom's only function during creation seems to have been to give God pleasure." Furthermore, and probably also of interest to Solovyov, this primordial sense of fun is inherently associated with art, poetry, and creative activity itself: "God is the supreme and quintessential artist (note that *hokhmah* includes artistry), and he feels the joy of the creative act, just as he savored the goodness of his handiwork in Gen 1." Wisdom herself embodies this fun: "While commentators have recognized Wisdom's pride, few have remarked on her *exuberance*. She delights in all aspects of her life: her history, the privilege of being present during creation and watching the divine artistry at first hand, her playfulness as the work proceeded, her delight in humanity" (Fox 294).

Sophia for Solovyov allows and indeed *is* the process of creation, a process accompanied by joy and laughter, no matter how serious the task.

CONCLUSION: SOPHIA AS DIVINELY HUMAN MEDIATOR

Light from darkness! The visages of your roses
Could not rise up
Above the black soil
If their dark root
Did not pierce, immersed,
Into the dusky womb.
> SOLOVYOV, "My soshlis' s toboi nedarom"

As we consider the legacy that Solovyov left his philosophical and literary heirs, we must remember his role as synthesizer and propagator of earlier traditions, in particular his justification of the "faith of our fathers" (*SS* 4:243), which helped bring in the modern period in Orthodox theology. Paul Valliere claims that the theology of the "Russian school," of which Solovyov was an originator, "grew out of the need to relate the Orthodox faith to what is usually called a modern or free society, that is to say, a society consisting of relatively autonomous, unharmonized spheres of activity operating outside the tutelage of church or state. The Russians were the first eastern Christian people to wrestle with the problem of Orthodoxy and modernity because a society of the modern type began to develop in Russia earlier than in other Orthodox lands" (2). Valliere further quotes Father Alexander Schmemann's definition of this "theological task": "Orthodox theology must keep its patristic foundation, but it must also go 'beyond' the Fathers if it is to respond to a new situation created by centuries of philosophical development. And in this new synthesis or reconstruction, the western philosophical tradition (source and mother of the Russian 'religious philosophy' of the nineteenth and twentieth centuries) rather than the Hellenic, must supply theology with its conceptual framework. An attempt is thus made to 'transpose' theology into a new 'key,' and this transposition is considered as the specific task and vocation of Russian theology" (Schmemann 178).

Solovyov was truly at the crossroads of several intellectual and cultural currents. He looked both backward to tradition and forward to modernism and spoke the languages of philosophy, theology, and artistic creativity with ease. All those cultural endeavors came together in his intuition and then in various articulations of the Divine Sophia in poetry and prose.

Ultimately there can be no single definition of Sophia, only a pastiche of possibilities put into historical, literary, and theological context. If we ask, as we did in the introduction, whether Wisdom is divine or created, we can only answer that she/he/it is both, depending on your perspective. From the human perspective, she is the divine body of God. From the divine perspective, insofar as we can estimate it, she is ideal humanity, its soul or concentration. Because of her participation above as below, she is both subject and object, one and many, divine and human, spirit and matter. Yet, of course, she is neither, for she is not merely a person but a relationship, the principle or energy or potential that can conjoin. She does not exist in either a sacred or a natural world, but mediates dynamically between the two.

Is she the same for Solovyov, as well as for his readers, in all genres and discourses? Yes and no. Each of Solovyov's re-visions brings out a different aspect: her association with poetry as a divinely human activity; her role in bogochelovechestvo and ultimately the deification of humanity; her identity as laughter, whether ridiculous, parodic, or spiritually joyful. Like an icon, she is a window into the spiritual world but also a door. According to Solovyov's follower in Sophiology, Father Florensky:

> An icon remembers its prototype. Thus, in one beholder, it will awaken in the bright clarities of his conscious mind a spiritual vision that matches directly the bright clarities of the icon; and the beholder's vision will be comparably clear and conscious. But in another person, the icon will stir the dreams that lie deeper in the subconscious, awakening a perception of the spiritual that not only affirms that such seeing is possible but also brings the thing seen into immediately felt experience. Thus, at the highest flourishing of their prayer, the ancient ascetics found that their icons were not simply windows through which they could behold the holy countenances depicted on them but were also doorways through which these countenances actually entered the empirical world. The saints came down from the icons to appear before those praying to them. (*Iconostasis* 71–72)

Like an icon, Sophia brings heaven to earth and in the interaction of the opposites creates a new whole: a poetic, often joyful, light-infused creation. She is the mediator and the element that causes us to see reality from more than one perspective at once. Whether a conjoining principle, a personal mystical vision, or the union of believers in the united and transfigured church, she is a tension, the energy that binds and transforms through the binding itself. She alters reality, making it better, truer, and more beautiful. With her interaction, spirit is incarnated and matter divinized. She can have many names, faces, and functions, because she, who is the "true reason for creation and its goal" (*SS* 11:298), is no one thing. Sophia not only links but fully participates in two opposites and in the new creation their relationhip produces.

And thus we have at best approached an answer to the second question posed in the title to part 1: What is Sophia? Can we also answer, at least in part, the first question: Who is Solovyov? As already stated, he was an *original*, incomparable in his age yet fully a part of it. In her book *Erotic Utopia: The Decadent Imagination in Russia's Fin de Siècle,* Olga Matich explains him with the popular fin de siècle metaphor of "the palimpsest, a figure of overwriting and cultural layering": "Situated generationally between the positivist 1860s and the symbolist early 1900s, his utopian project represents an amalgam of paradoxical ideas borrowed from a variety of mystical, scientific, and aesthetic traditions and sensibilities. . . . The anecdote of Solov'ev wearing a European top hat in the Egyptian desert in search of Sophia or the desert fathers certainly presents an eccentric physical and cultural palimpsest" (59).

Matich points to examples of Solovyov's obscene verse and his apparent cultivation of the "twin myths" of his virginity and his self-castration, suggesting a typically decadent desire to shock (78–79). But Solovyov was not a typical decadent. His social activity and engaged writings contrasted sharply to the morbid ennui of the end of the century, and his philosophy was more than a mere hybridization of eclectic traditions. This book looks principally at his Wisdom texts, but Solovyov made an impact on Russian culture with his activist *publitsistika*, his legal philosophy, his literary criticism, and much, much more. Indeed, A. F. Losev asks not "Who is Solovyov?" but "Who was Solovyov Not?" (Losev, *Vladimir Solov'ev i ego vremnia* 486–88). The task of this great visionary, poet, and philosopher was nothing less than the integration of heaven and earth and the true transfiguration of nature through the incarnation of spirit. He saw the possibility for integration everywhere and called it by many names, the most striking and pervasive of which, as we have seen, is Sophia. He lived Sophia through his poetry and prose and through his laughter, scholarship, and loving friendships.

An analysis of two of the pseudonyms occasionally used by Solovyov reminds us of both the poet's earthy humor and the seriousness with which he took his own role as a mediating force in the world of ideas. The pseudonym "Prince Hope of the Heliotropes" (Kniaz' Èsper Geliotropov) elevates the playful intellectual to royal status, but the surname brings him down to the world of common flora. A heliotrope is a purple (royal?) flower with its roots firmly planted in the soil and its face ever reaching toward the sun (heliotropic). Èsper may come from the French *j'espére*—"I hope"—or, equally evocative, from the Greek for evening star. We are reminded of Solovyov's translation from Plato's poem, in which the "I" of the poem hopes to be transformed into the evening sky, to embrace the star, "you," that is his lover. Another pseudonym, "the Marquis of Tulips" (Narkiz Tiul'panov), similarly plays on an elevation to royal status united with the created world of earthly flowers. Narkiz may be a corruption of the French "marquis," or, again, a corruption of the Greek name Narcissus, itself a flower and the source of philosophical (if solipsistic) contemplation. To a Russian ear, Narkiz also conjures up an exotic Tatar or other Central Asian name, combining both the chaotic East and the classical West, a uniting role he ascribes to his homeland of Russia in the lecture "Three Powers" as early as 1877. Not accidentally, both heliotropes and tulips are commonly associated with one of Solovyov's prime mediators, love. What could be more appropriate for the daemonic poet-philosopher, whose own surname itself conjures up the nightingale (*solovei*), whose song inspires both poetry and love?[140]

---

140. I thank Nina Familiant, Andrew Reynolds, and Anna Tumarkin for their helpful suggestions about these names. For a list of Solovyov's various pseudonyms, see Masanov 4:447.

I conclude with Solovyov's 1894 poem "Emanuel" ("Immanuel'"). The short lyric is not explicitly about Sophia, but it brings into proximity the philosopher's belief in the transfiguring power of poetic expression; his interest in the prophetic power of Judaism with its immanent but mystical God; the Word, or Logos; recurrent images of azure and light; and, most of all, the "you" of his early Sophianic poetry, who rules "with an all-joyful mystery." In eternal, universal joy, "you" brings the God of the distant heavens and supernatural world into the "turbid flood of life's alarm," just as Sophia appears to the speaker of *Three Encounters* in London amid "myriads of people [who] push and scurry by, / Beneath the thunderous breath of fiery motors." The poem's title means "God is with us" in ancient Hebrew. In a bit of Kabbalistic wordplay, Solovyov turns that expression into a compound proper noun in Russian to conclude the first stanza: "And in quietude was born With-us-is-God" (I v tishine rodilsia S-nami-Bog). Humanity and the Divine unite in silent birth, for God, says Solovyov, is ever with us:

> That night had receded into the murk of times,
> As the earth, fatigued by malice and alarm,
> Had gone to sleep in heaven's arms,
> And in the quietude was born With-us-is-God.
>
> And much today no longer can be done:
> Tsars glance no more into the sky,
> And shepherds do not listen in the wilderness
> As Angels speak among themselves of God.
>
> But what was revealed that night endures,
> It cannot be destroyed by time,
> And the Word again was born inside your soul,
> The one born in a manger years ago.
>
> Yes! With us is God,—not up above the azure vault,
> Not out beyond the edge of countless worlds,
> Not in evil fire and not in stormy breath,
> And not in the drowsy memory of ages.
>
> He is *here, now*,—among the casual bustle,
> In the turbid flood of life's alarm.
> You rule with an all-joyful mystery:
> Evil is impotent; we—eternal; God—with us!
>   (SS 12:34)

Did Solovyov have a mystical vision of Sophia, whatever or whoever she is? Whether or not he did, he spent a lifetime re-visioning its meaning. Exploring his intuitions of the triad of Good, Truth, and Beauty through the lens of

---

For an analysis of the significance of the pseudonym Heliotrope in particular, see Schrooyen, "Professional Intellectual" 114–17.

Divine Wisdom as she/he/it appeared to mystics and philosophers through the ages, Solovyov produced poems and prose, plays and polemics throughout a quarter century of his creative career. In the end, we can know quite a bit and very little: Sophia weds us to the azure and gold that exists both within and beyond us. As Solovyov expresses in his own familiar Orthodox Christian idiom, "You rule with an all-joyful mystery: / Evil is impotent; we—eternal; God—with us!"

PART II

The Wisdom Writings of Solovyov

Annotated Translations

1 Early Sophianic Poems

Reading Guide

Poetry both begins and ends the second part of this book, in which we present annotated translations of Solovyov's Wisdom texts. The bookends should not imply that Solovyov confined his forays into verse to the extremes of his writing career but rather that poetry embraces and indeed suffuses all of his work. Many of his philosophical and critical texts incorporate poems—both his own and those of his favorite poets—and many of his poems, especially the Sophianic poems, address issues that he also explored in prose. As we saw in part 1, Solovyov tried to explain Sophia through the special language of poetry, just as he associated her with the "divinely human" activity of laughter.

Solovyov wrote the following three short poems in 1875, probably soon after his alleged third vision of Sophia in the desert outside Cairo. The young academic had left his teaching positions in Moscow in the spring of 1875 to pursue research into mystical texts in London and then claimed to have followed Sophia's directions to Egypt for his final meeting. The third poem refers specifically to a vision or dream that the speaker saw as "a strange child" and then to a recent vision when "I see you now not in a dream, / Your speech is clear to me."

It seems important to begin our collection of Solovyov's Sophia texts with these poems because they provide more than biographical evidence of real encounters with Divine Wisdom. Visions, after all, can never be fully proven, and the written articulations of them are always at some remove from the experience itself. The persistence of imagery, however, helps paint a verbal picture of the elements with which Solovyov chooses to begin his re-visions, and many of the references in these three poems recur throughout the next two decades of his writing career. All share similar imagery of an empress or goddess with golden curls, azure eyes, and a rosy visage who appears at dawn to the male visionary and embraces him in a veil of light. The metaphor of reflection is present in the second poem, where "a silvery stream catches the reflection / Of her curls and brow in its transparent waters," and then in the third, where "My homeland's reflection in ethereal rays" can be seen in "the light of your azure eyes." In these poems, Sophia's eyes both reflect and emit light. Even more, the light-emitting vision transfigures the viewer so that he, too, shines and, in the third poem, becomes the mystical reconciliation of opposites: "In free bondage and in living death, / I am the sanctuary, I am the sacrifice and priest. / Tormented by bliss, I stand before you." In all of Solovyov, Sophia unites opposites, transforming both into a new whole.

The poems that evoke a beautiful and royal female Sophia run counter to the traditional Christian understanding of Wisdom as the male Christ (1 Cor. 1:23–31). As is patently clear in the second poem—"My empress has a lofty palace / With seven golden pillars"—Solovyov bases his image of royal beauty not on the New Testament text but on Proverbs: "Wisdom has built her house, / set up her pillars seven." As argued in part 1, this image comes not only directly from the biblical verses but also from Russian icons of Sophia that depict seven-columned palaces and/or thrones with seven legs or placed atop seven steps. The Sophia of Proverbs and the Wisdom of Solomon is a personified woman who at times is divine and at times fully human. Solovyov's Sophia, too, is both heavenly and human or, more abstractly, allows for material human nature to shine like the divine.

Solovyov's personification of a feminine principle in these and later poems, as well as in his subsequent discussion of her in his philosophy, drew criticism that he was trying to insert her into the Divine Trinity as a fourth, female hypostasis. In the author's preface to the third edition of his poetry, only months before his death, Solovyov felt compelled to defend at least two of his poems from the accusation of heresy. His defense recognizes ultimately that Sophia is an embodiment of Beauty, which itself is the mother of Truth and Goodness. She does indeed participate in divine reality, even if not as a hypostasis herself. As he wrote:

> Two works require more serious reservations: "Das Ewig-weibliche (an admonition to sea demons)" and "Three Encounters." They could give reason to accuse me of fatal heresy. Do we not have here the insertion of a feminine principle into Divinity itself? Without entering into an analysis of the core of the theosophical question, but in order not to lead the reader into temptation and to protect myself from idle reproach, I must attest the following: 1) The transfer of fleshly animal-human relations into the sphere of the superhuman is the greatest *abomination* and the cause of the most extreme forms of destruction (the Flood, Sodom and Gemorrah, "the satanic depths" of the final days);[1] 2) the worship of

---

1. Gen. 7:11; Gen. 19:24; Rev. 2:24.

female nature in and of itself, that is, of the principle of ambiguity and indifference, which is susceptible to lies and evil no less than to truth and good, is the greatest *insanity* and the main reason for the softening and weakening of society that rules today; 3) this stupidity and abomination has nothing in common with the true worship of the eternal feminine as that which grasps the power of Divinity from all ages, that incorporates the real fullness of Goodness and Truth, and, through them, the incorruptible radiance of Beauty.

But the more perfect and closer the revelation of actual beauty that cloaks Divinity and Him with the power that leads us to deliverance from suffering and death, the more delicate the line that divides it from its false likeness,—from that deceptive and powerless beauty that only perpetuates the kingdom of suffering and death. Woman, clothed in the sun,[2] is already tormented by childbirth: she must reveal the truth, must give birth to the Word, and here the ancient serpent gathers its last strengths against her and wants to drown her in poisonous streams of comely lies, of plausible deceits. This is all foretold, as is the end: in the end Eternal Beauty will be fruitful, and from her will emerge the salvation of the world, when her false likenesses will disappear like the sea foam that gave birth to the common Aphrodite. My poetry does not serve *this latter* with a single one of its words, and this is the single inalienable worth to which I can and must admit. (*SS* 12:4)

Despite the inflated and, I suggest, tongue-in-cheek tone of this declaration, or perhaps because of it, Solovyov does indeed elevate his Sophia to the grandest of statures. She inspires a worship that "grasps the power of Divinity from all ages, that incorporates the real fullness of Goodness and Truth, and, through them, the incorruptible radiance of Beauty." Those who confuse this divine consort with mere earthly beauty express only "abomination," "insanity," and "stupidity." Yet Solovyov's Eternal Beauty promises to save the world precisely through the all-too-earthly act of birth. The contrast between the overwrought rhetoric and the imagery of the "common Aphrodite" gives rise, I suggest, to an earthy laugh. Although "Das Ewig-weibliche" describes the emergence of salvific beauty like Aphrodite from the waves ("Do you remember the roses above white foam, / A purple reflection in azure waves?"), the poet addresses his poem to simple sea demons and ends with a the following colloquial admonishment:

2. See Rev. 12: 1: "And a great portent appeared in heaven, a woman clothed with the sun, with the moon under her feet, and on her head a crown of twelve stars; she was with child and she cried out in her pangs of birth, in anguish for delivery." Solovyov uses this image again in *Three Conversations* at the end of "A Short Tale of the Antichrist." After the victory of the Antichrist in Jerusalem, the final representatives of the Orthodox, Catholic, and Protestant churches escape to the desert: "Thus, the union of the churches was accomplished in the dark of night, on a high and solitary place. But the night darkness was suddenly illuminated by a bright splendor, and a great sign appeared in the sky: a woman, clothed in the sun, the moon under her feet, and on her head a crown of twelve stars" (*SS* 10:218). The apparition, perhaps like Solovyov's own visions of Sophia, leads the new disciples toward Sinai.

Proud demons, you all are men,—
There's no honor in fighting a woman.
Well, if for no other reason than this,
Dear demons, surrender up now!
(SS 12:73)

The earthly Aphrodite comes from the same realm of red roses and white lilies as the Divine Sophia; she emerges from the same reflection of royal purple and azure. In fact, the physical beauty of the Finnish coast—where Solovyov sets "Das Ewig-weibliche"—or of the coast of Cypress, where the Greeks worshipped Aphrodite, allows for the emergence of the "imperishable body" of the eternal feminine. Heaven "floods with the watery abyss." For Solovyov, Sophia/Aphrodite unites Revelation with Genesis, the woman clothed in sun with Noah's deluge. Perhaps she carries her worshippers even further back, before—or outside—time, when God said, "Let there be light" and "let there be a firmament in the midst of the waters, and let it separate the waters from the waters. And God made the firmament and separated the waters which were under the firmament from the waters which were above the firmament. And it was so. And God called the firmament Heaven."

Solovyov wrote many more poems with the imagery of light that is evoked in the three poems translated here, and he continued throughout his writing career to evoke the reality of Sophia with the colors azure and gold, with reference to dreams and jewels, to the mysterious glow of the Finnish landscape, and to the incomprehensible interpenetration of the divine and the material. The following sample stanzas come from poems written as early as March 1875 and as late as 1895, long after the visions of Sophia that may have appeared to Solovyov in his childhood and youth.

As the heavenly glory is reflected
    In the pure azure of the quieted seas,
So in the light of the free spirit's passion
    To us eternal good appears.
        (1875; SS 12:88, and *Stikhotvoreniia* 60)

I see your emerald eyes,
A bright vision stands before me.
In these waking dreams, unwakable,
A new wave carried me away.
        (1892; SS 12:16, and *Stikhotvoreniia* 94)

And amid those flowers, and in eternal summer,
Enveloped in azure silver,
How beautiful you are, and in the starry light
How free and pure is love!
        (1892; SS 12:21, and *Stikhotvoreniia* 95)

Lands of jaded clouds are already silvered
   By the moon's hidden rays.
One moment more, and its countenance will shine
   Over us in azure.
      (1891; *SS* 12:29, and *Stikhotvoreniia* 82)

   Azure eye
Through gloomily threatening clouds . . .
   Stepping deeply
Through the desert's sprinkling snow,
   Toward the mysterious goal
   I go alone.
      (1895; *SS* 12:45–46, and *Stikhotvoreniia* 110)

The three following poems—all from the time of the third vision—are chosen for their direct reference to a Sophia figure, imaged in the azure and gold light of the Russian holy icon.

Early Poems

"My tsaritsa appeared to me"

My tsaritsa appeared to me
Today, wrapped all in azure.—
My heart beat with a sweet delight,
And in the rays of approaching day
My soul shone with a quiet light.
While smoldering in the distance
Rose the fierce flame of earthly fire.
                    (1875, Cairo)

Translated by Judith Deutsch Kornblatt

"My empress has a lofty palace"

My empress has a lofty palace
With seven golden pillars.
My empress has a seven-pointed crown
With countless precious stones.

In my empress's green garden
Fair roses and lilies bloom[3]

---

3. Roses and lilies point to Gnostic influence on this poem, and the image will be repeated, most notably the play *The White Lily*. There the White Lily clearly represents Sophia. See also the poem "Song of the Ophites," a slight variation of which is included as the last stanza of the play and which begins: "We wed the white lily / With the rose, the scarlet rose. / We seek out eternal truth / With a secret prophetic dream" (*SS* 12:14; see page 262).

And a silvery stream catches the reflection
Of her curls and brow in its transparent waters.

But my empress does not hear what that stream whispers.
She does not so much as glance at the flowers.
Sorrow beclouds the light of her azure eyes.[4]
And all her reverie is full of grief.

She sees: far off in a midnight land
Amidst the freezing mists and blizzards,
Her beloved, whom she has forsaken, is perishing
In solitary combat with the evil powers of darkness.

She throws aside her diamond crown,
Abandons the golden palace, and arriving,
An unexpected guest, at her faithless beloved's door,
She knocks upon it, her hand full of grace.

And bathed in light, she bends down over him
Like youthful spring over somber winter
And, full of quiet tenderness,
Covers him with her radiant veil.[5]

And the dark powers are stricken to the ground.
His whole being burns with a pure flame,
And with eternal love in her azure eyes
She softly tells her beloved: "I know

Your resolve is more inconstant than sea waves;
You vowed to keep fidelity to me. You have
Betrayed your vow—but could your betrayal really have caused
My heart to change?"

(Between the end of November 1875 and
March 6, 1876, Cairo)

Translated by Boris Jakim and Laury Magnus

---

4. To the extent that I have been able to determine, the Sophia icons do not have azure eyes, although the color azure figures prominently in them. It is a typical color associated with Christ in iconography and often the color of the aureole surrounding the angel in the Novgorodian Sophia icon. Furthermore, wisdom icons are often associated with the so-called wisdom star, used also in many icons of the Transfiguration. This symbol can look like an eye that both emits and absorbs light. And the round aureoles behind the Sophia-angel and Christ the Pantocrator on the icon themselves resemble eyes peering out at the reader and/or in which the viewer can see herself/himself reflected.

5. As we have seen, light and radiance are among the most pervasive images surrounding Sophia in Solovyov's work. The veil here also reminds the reader of the protective veil of the Mother of God and of Pokrov, the holiday on October 1 dedicated to Mary in the Orthodox festal cycle (but not one of the twelve "Great Feasts"). The feast, called *Hagia Skepe* in Greek, was introduced into Russia in the twelfth century. The Pokrov icon in part resembles the Sophia-Novgorod image, with Mary in the middle, flanked by apostles and prophets and standing under her veil, held aloft in a semicircle by two angels. Above and behind them rise the five cupolas and two towers of a church, recollective of the seven domes or pillars of Wisdom's "house."

"Near, far off, not here, not there"

Near, far off, not here, not there,[6]
In realms of mystic reveries,
In a world invisible to mortal eyes,
In a world neither of laughter nor of tears,[7]

There it was, goddess, that I first
Recognized you one misty night.
A strange child was I,
And strange dreams did I see.[8]

It was in an alien guise that you appeared
To me. Your voice sounded obscure.
And as the obscure creation of a childish dream[9]
I long considered you.

Now you appear to me once more
With a caress of unexpected love.
I see you now not in a dream,
Your speech is clear to me.

I, who had been deafened in an alien world
By the roar of incoherent speech,
Suddenly heard in your salutation
The word of my homeland.

The voice of my homeland in your magic speech,
In the light of your azure eyes,
My homeland's reflection in ethereal rays.
In the golden color of your marvelous curls.

Everything by which my heart and mind live,
Everything trembling here within my breast,
All powers of feeling, will, and thought
That are mine I've given into your hands.

---

6. The opening line of this poem echoes a line in a popular folk song of the type called a *ko-liada*, usually sung on Christmas Eve, and one that also refers cryptically to a house on seven columns: "Not near, not far,—/ On seven columns (*Ni blizko, ni daleko,—/ Na semi stolbakh*). It clearly associates Wisdom/Sophia with the folkloric space that is neither here nor there. For a complete translation of the folk song, see Reeder 86–87. The original of the folk song was first published in Shein 305–6. We cannot know for certain whether Solovyov knew this song, but, coincidentally, it was first collected by an N. F. Solovyov, as explained in a note at the end of Shein's volume. My thanks to Ben Jens and Margaret Beissinger for tracking down this reference.

7. Here is another example of how the Sophianic visions take place in a liminal time and space or a place that is all places at once.

8. Solovyov here refers to the vision that he will describe more fully in *Three Encounters*. See page 266.

9. The dialogue "Sophie" opens with a claim that "a vague dream led me to the banks of the Nile" (see page 120). That dream is described by Solovyov as his vision of the face of Sophia in the British Museum, which instructed him to seek her in Egypt. (See page 268). Solovyov frequently associates dreams with Sophia.

That morose despot, the cold ego,
Sensing its death, trembles.
As soon as it sees you approaching from afar
It grows silent, pallid, and then flees.

Let it perish, arrogant fugitive!
In free bondage and in living death,
I am the sanctuary, I am the sacrifice and priest.
Tormented by bliss, I stand before you.[10]
(Between the end of November 1875
and March 6, 1876, Cairo)

Translated by Boris Jakim and Laury Magnus

---

10. Oxymorons are common in Solovyov's Wisdom writings. Here free bondage, living death, the sacrifice and the priest, and the torment of bliss all accompany the encounters of Sophia. Like the liminal space of the visions, the emotional quality suggests all states experienced at once.

2 *The Sophia*

A "Mystical-Theosophical-Philosophical-Theurgical-Political" Dialogue

Reading Guide

In a letter from London in September 1875, Solovyov assured his parents, "I am trying to return to Russia before July, if only I can manage to finish the work that is occupying me, and that I should publish in English. I have found a suitable translator" (*Pis'ma* 2:11). Solovyvov never completed the French manuscript that was later found by his nephew, Sergei Solovyov, in a folio titled *The Sophia*, nor, as far as we know, did the author have any of it translated into English. Leaving London abruptly for Egypt rather than Russia and only then traveling home via Italy, Solovyov wrote again about this work in March 1876: "I'll stay for a month in Sorrento, Italy, where in the quiet of solitude I will finish writing a kind of work of mystical-theosophical-philosophical-theurgic-political content, in a dialogic form" (*Pis'ma* 2:23). In May of 1876 he wrote to his father, "As for my essay, I absolutely must publish it, since it will be the basis of all my future endeavors, and I can do nothing without referring to it" (*Pis'ma* 2:28). The "work of mystical-theosophical-philosophical-theurgic-political content" was clearly more—or less—than an ordinary essay. What is preserved of the manuscript includes several chapters of differing length and completeness, filled with notes to himself, snippets of barely decipherable automatic writing, and Gnostic and other mystical terminology and incorporating a substantial dialogue between "Sophie" and a "philosophe." The dialogue is preserved in several parts but devolves toward the end into monologic prose.

At one point, Solovyov apparently understood the mixed-genre work as the first step toward his dissertation, but he later realized that this rather unusual expression of his comprehensive and original philosophy was not appropriate for a defense. According to A. P. Kozyrev, one of the first scholars to seriously analyze the full manuscript, and following Solovyov's own pronouncement in the letter to his father referred to above, *The Sophia* indeed was crucial to the philosopher's development. In both the dialogic and monologic chapters that comprise the unfinished work, Solovyov "in essence plans out all the basic themes of his subsequent creative path: about the Absolute as an all-one being and about its triadic definition; about the 'meaning of love'; his philosophy of history; and the eschatological fate of the world" (*PSS* 2:313). In fact, whole sections of *The Sophia* appear verbatim in *The Philosophical Principles of Integral Knowledge* (1877), and other ideas are worked out more fully in *Lectures on Divine Humanity*, "The Meaning of Love" (1892–94) and other works.[1]

The short monologic chapter from *The Sophia* that is translated below as "On Man's Metaphysical Need" defines man as a metaphysical being who has a connection to both the ideal and the real, or physical, world. One mark of man's metaphysical nature is what Solovyov deems to be his unique ability to laugh. Solovyov identifies the second mark of the metaphysical nature of human life as art and poetry. Although there is no direct reference to Sophia in this one chapter, the connection of laughter and poetry runs throughout Solovyov's works on Wisdom. As we have seen in the first half of this book, humor and laughter were extremely important to Solovyov and were intimately connected to poetry. His humorous plays in verse that evoke Sophia and his final re-vision of Sophia in *Three Encounters* all suggest a connection among Wisdom, his own creative inspiration, and his sense of humor.

Following "On Man's Metaphysical Need," we include here a complete English translation of Solovyov's dialogues featuring Sophia. The choice of dialogue form by Solovyov does more than evoke the father of philosophy, Plato. By giving Sophia a voice, he begins the process of personifying the figure of Wisdom throughout his work. This personification accompanies his association of Sophia with artistic creation. Indeed, he first called the entire work *Sophie,* instead of the more abstract *The Sophia*, but crossed out that title above the monologic chapters, reserving the personal name only for the dialogues (and their ultimate devolution back into a monologue by Sophie) that follow. With the French proper name for the latter, then, he suggests an intimate conversation or a fictional discourse, in contrast to the "serious" philosophical genre of the rest of the manuscript. Sophia remains part—perhaps the unifying part—of all of his generic experiment. She will appear in his fiction, his drama, his humorous ditties, and his serious lyrics, as well as throughout his philosophy.

---

1. As mentioned in part 1, Losev's second study of Solovyov, *Vladimir Solov'ev i ego vremia*, includes an excellent synopsis of what he sees as the ten different manifestations of Sophia in Solovyov's work, including *The Sophia*, but he bases his analysis only on the sections translated into Russian by Sergei Solovyov rather than on a review of the entire manuscript. When discussing *The Sophia*, Losev is largely concerned with Solovyov's tendency toward pantheism, and he calls the manuscript "a philosophical delirium" (195). Despite this seemingly negative assessment, Losev claims that "this delirious ruckus is very valuable for a historian of philosophy" (196), and he continues with a concise and invaluable analysis.

It is in the dialogues and through the dialogic form that Solovyov presents the clearest explanation of how Sophia can partake of both the divine and human worlds. In a discussion of why we can know the essence of things, or "being-in-itself," Sophia unites the seemingly contradictory philosophical schools of idealism and empiricism, telling the Philosopher that he should neither radically separate nor carelessly confuse inner truth with outer appearance:

> *Sophie*: Do you know me? Do you know with whom you are speaking?
>
> *Philosopher*: As if I could not know you!
>
> *Sophie*: You no doubt know me as a phenomenon, that is, insofar as I exist *for you* or in my external manifestation. You cannot know me as I am *in myself*, that is, my thoughts and intimate feelings as they are in me and for me. You know them only when they manifest themselves outwardly in the expression of my eyes, in my words and my gestures. These are only external phenomena and yet . . .
>
> *Philosopher*: And yet, when I look into the deep azure of your eyes, when I hear the music of your voice,[2] is it outward phenomena of sight and sound that I perceive? My God! I know your thoughts and feelings, and, by your thoughts and feelings, I know your inner being.
>
> *Sophie*: And this is the way that all beings know each other. (*PSS* 2:80–83; see page 123)

Sophia is both ideal or divine Wisdom *and* the manifestation of wisdom in the material world, where she is known through sensual phenomena. Furthermore, she can be known in the real world by the effect that she has on her interlocutor. She affects him, even transforms him, so that he comes to know her both really *and* ideally. Although Solovyov couches this discussion of epistemology in Kantian terms—phenomenon, intelligible character, being-in-itself—he could just as easily have made reference to Gregory Palamas, the "theologian of Hesychasm."[3] Hesychasm is sometimes understood as a mystical method to know God centered on repetition of the "Jesus Prayer" and made popular through the *Philokalia*, a collection of writings by church fathers. It is, however, also a sophisticated theology—both verbal and iconographic—that expresses much of the distinction of Orthodoxy, clarified in the writings of Gregory Palamas.[4] Two aspects of hesychast teaching are particularly important for Solovyov's writings on Sophia: the distinction

---

2. In his poetry, as we saw in the last section, Solovyov consistently associates Sophia with the colors azure and gold: "My tsaritsa appeared to me / Today, wrapped all in azure"; "In the light of your azure eyes"; "Suffused throughout with golden azure." In *Three Encounters*, he also mentions her ringing laugh, or the ringing of bells that accompanies her appearance (see page 271).

3. See Meyendorff, *St. Gregory Palamas* 75 for this title, and the chapters on "The Theology of Hesychasm" and "A Christian Existentialism" (108–29) for a clear explanation of Hesychasm. See also Lossky 217–35 for a discussion of the "Divine Light" of Hesychasm; and Pelikan 2:254–270 on "The Mystic as New Theologian."

4. "Gregory Palamas identified the three basic themes of Eastern Christian spirituality—theology as apophaticism, revelation as light, and salvation as deification" (Pelikan 2:264).

between God's essence and his energies and Palamas's central focus on the light of the Transfiguration. The latter connection to Sophia is obvious in all of Solovyov's re-visions. The former is evident in this discussion of *knowing* Sophia not in her essence but, essentially, through her energies, her outward manifestations and effect on others.

Knowing the essence through the energies does not mean confusing the material or sensual with the metaphysical or spiritual. Just as Christians say that we can know Christ as human and God, to use Solovyov's favorite theological trope, "undivided, yet unmerged," so can we know divine and earthly Wisdom. Sophie instructs the Philosopher:

> When you act, you do not lose your proper being, you do not pass into that action, but, rather, are the master of it; you retain the independent power to act. The agent, or that which manifests itself, always retains something more than the manifestation; it can never transform all of its being into the manifestation or the phenomenon. And not only the absolute being, but even the inner or subjective manifestations of any being can never pass as such into the immediate consciousness of another. When I communicate my thoughts or my feelings to you, it is only their objective content that you know. Or, to put it better, in manifesting thoughts and feelings through external phenomena, I evoke in you corresponding thoughts or feelings, but not the act itself of thinking, or the subjective state I found myself in when I had those thoughts or feelings. (*PSS* 2:84–87; see page 125)

She continues:

> When you act, when you manifest yourself, do you cease to be what you are? Do you leave your state as psychic agent and, in manifesting yourself materially, do you become matter? In producing objective phenomena, do you lose your subjective being? So? Do you really think that the absolute substance is less powerful than you are? When it realizes itself, the substance does not lose its absolute state, but rather acquires a relative state. Without ceasing to be infinite, it becomes definite as well; and that is true infinity, the true absolute. You comprehend that, by its very definition, the absolute principle cannot be deprived of anything, cannot lack anything in itself. If it were only infinite and absolute, then it would lack relativity and finitude; it would be imperfect. Thus, in order to be that which it is, it must also be the opposite of itself, or, it must be the union of itself and of its opposite. In order to be truly absolute and infinite, it must also be the principle of relativity and finitude. (*PSS* 2:90–93; see page 128)

In order to press his point, Solovyov has Sophie speak in a decidedly condescending tone to the Philosopher, indicating her superiority over the merely human being who seeks her advice but also lending her a personality, itself a human trait. In some cases her retorts become almost humorous in their sarcasm. "A naive fantasy," she calls the Philosopher-cum-Solovyov's trip to Egypt. "Would you like me to become just as ridiculous as the rest of you?" she asks, calling the Philosopher and his ilk "poor children." Yet her insults themselves have a childish character, lending the dialogue a tone of play as much as of serious philosophical discourse.

The first large section of dialogic fragments, which Solovyov titled "Sophie. First Triad. First Principles," consists of three dialogues: "The Absolute Principle as Unity (The Principle of Monism)," "The Absolute Principle as Duality (The Principle of Dualism)," and an untitled third dialogue. It opens in the middle of a conversation between a figure identified as Sophie and a Philosopher, apparently taking place somewhere in Egypt. This location, in the ancient cradle of civilization, suggests the primal nature of the instruction to be given and connects this manifestation of Sophia to the poems written around the time of Solovyov's alleged third vision of her. The resumption of a dialogue in medias res again suggests an intimate conversation rather than logical philosophical discourse, thus further humanizing Wisdom and allowing the reader to experience the theatrical or fictional representation of a drawing-room conversation. Solovyov echoes this technique at the end of his career in his *Three Conversations*, where he refuses to name any character Sophia but clearly suffuses the lengthy discussion with "wise" talk, culminating in the short story by "Pan*soph*ius."

Solovyov begins the First Triad with Sophie's explication of the metaphor of the fruit of a living tree. She offers the image to the Philosopher as a visual explanation for the "universal religion" she professes. The tree itself has its roots in early Christianity but now sprouts mostly the withered branches of the divided Christian denominations that henceforth developed. The dying nature of those branches belies the vigor of the original trunk, however, for the wisdom that Wisdom preaches derives directly from the Tree of Knowledge. Its living fruit, the universal religion, carries the original seed of truth offered to humankind. Sophie proceeds to teach the Philosopher about the Absolute principle and the true and necessary interaction of spiritual and concrete reality, for universal religion, she says, does not eternally divide the holy from profane but finds always one in the other. In keeping with his later works, Solovyov maintains through Sophie that creation is a necessary accomplishment of the Absolute but in no way limits or diminishes the latter. All of reality is the union of itself and its opposite and presupposes an interaction between the most universal and the most individual.

In the third of the dialogues from this first part, Solovyov expresses what will become a leitmotif throughout his work: that the most universal is in fact the most individual of all beings, just as the most individual of all beings, or the being that exhibits the most individuality, is also the most universal. This paradox makes sense when we remember that Solovyov focuses always on the relationship between opposites, not on their distinction. The larger the number of individual parts, the greater the number of possible interactions, relationships, and combinations. The larger the number of interactions, the closer the entity comes to the all. On earth, humans are the manifestation of this principle, but Christ, he says, is the example in the divine realm. Solovyov will include some of the statements of this principle almost word for word in his *Lectures*, delivered a year or so after the writing of this manuscript.

Sophie mentions her partner/doublet/reverse/extension/prodigy, the World Soul, for the first time in this section. She/it is presented as parallel to the universal Mind and interdependent on it. As Solovyov writes in the margin: "The Mind receives its reality from the Soul, as the Soul receives its form or its ideality from the Mind." Both are related to Spirit: "Mind is Spirit entered into the ideal process; Soul is Spirit entered into the real process."

The second large dialogic section, titled in the manuscript "Second Dialogue. The Cosmic and Historical Process," rather than the expected "Second Triad," continues the conversation between Sophie and the Philosopher. Sophie is somewhat less sarcastic and condescending toward the Philosopher in this fragment than she had been in the first, and the remarks of the two characters become longer and less interactive, until Solovyov abandons the dialogue form altogether. Sophie, or perhaps now Solovyov himself, goes on to explain the emergence of the Demiurge and the cosmic battle with Satan in Gnostic terms. It is in this context that the World Soul emerges as a major force. The World Soul is the possibility of being, and as long as it allies itself with the Absolute, it is the principle of love. When it separates itself, however, it becomes the model of dissension and enmity. Nonetheless, even as the soul of the material world, it maintains its connection to the Spirit. The World Soul remains ever one with Sophia, and we are not lost from Wisdom.

> The Soul is a principle of unity and love insofar as it is passive and submits to the ideal and spiritual world. But in rising up against them and in separating itself out, in becoming egotistical, it becomes the principle of separate and exclusive being, of division, of hatred and struggle. In actuality as well as in possibility (*in potentia*), it preserves its divine origin.
>
> The Soul as a principle of division, of egoism, of hatred and struggle, in a word, as principle (or prince) of this world, or of this age, is Satan, the devil. The Soul is Satan—here is Wisdom. It is the principle of cosmic existence and the principle of our own partial and egotistical existence; it is our actual soul. (*PSS* 2:123; see page 145)

The third section, "Morality and Politics," has no dialogic aspects whatsoever, but in its discussion of the universal religion it seems to follow more closely from the dialogues than the other prose chapters. It ends with an elaboration of a note found also in the margin of the first dialogue, listing divisions of the Universal Church. Each of the divisions finds itself in a relationship with the order above and below, and Solovyov calls this relationship "love." Using the model of physical love, Solovyov sees these relationships in a gendered way, ascribing masculine and feminine attributes to alternating levels. He will later develop his image of ascending and descending love, using Platonic terms, in "The Meaning of Love." Here the discussion remains cryptic and only loosely related to the title "Morality and Politics."

The synopsis of sections presented above should make abundantly clear that there is no easy way to read and understand this multigenred manuscript. Even the briefest of segments in automatic writing suggest that parts of the work were written in an altered state of some kind.[5] Yet the frequent marginal comments to himself and the presence of markings in pencil and different-color inks also show that Solovyov went back to edit the manuscript more than once. Despite the caution of some scholars that we should not place too much credence in this early, incomplete manuscript,[6] we cannot help feeling that Solovyov believed he was relaying to his reader the truth about the structure of the divine, cosmic, and human worlds—through both the form and content of *The Sophia*.

Because Solovyov never completed this work for publication, the manuscript that he left includes a number of crossed-out sections, as well as additions and notes to himself in the margins. Some of the marginal comments that Solovyov penned appear to be unrelated notes to himself, and some are examples of his automatic writing, perhaps channeling Sophia. Straight brackets in the text indicate sections that Solovyov crossed out but remain legible, or they provide translations of foreign words where appropriate. Wavy brackets indicate text marked off as such by Solovyov. Angle brackets in the text indicate undecipherable words. Unless otherwise noted, this translation accepts the interpolated words and phrases surmised by Kozyrev in the Russian translation of the manuscript published in volume two of *PSS*. Following Kozyrev, I also assume that Solovyov wrote the monologic essays *before* the dialogues and that they should be read in that order. Under the constraints of space, this translation includes only the first chapter of the first of those essays.[7] Finally, this translation tries to standardize Solovyov's erratic capitalization.

The Sophia[8]

"On Man's Metaphysical Need"

It is obvious that the universal and ultimate goal of all human activity is the well-being of man, that is to say, the fullest possible satisfaction of all of his natural human needs. In this regard, humans do not differ in any way from all other animate beings; all aim equally to satisfy their natural needs, all aspire to well-being. The only difference between humans and the other animals is in the special character of those needs, the satisfaction of which constitute his or its respective well-being. In effect, man is not content simply with those pleasures that satisfy his physical appetites and which he has in

5. See part 1 for discussion of Solovyov's interest in spiritualism and his attendance at séances in London and Cairo around the time of the writing of *The Sophia*. For a lengthier study of Solovyov and spiritualism, and particularly his interest in automatic writing, see Kornblatt, "Who Is Sophia and Why Is She Writing in My Manuscript?"

6. Slesinski 31 and Losev, *Strast' k dialektike* 207–26.

7. Jonathan Seiling is currently translating the entire *Sophia* manuscript.

8. Solovyov's manuscript has the French name "Sophie" crossed out under the title, followed by the subtitle "Principles of the Universal Doctrine." The first section, "On Man's Metaphysical Need," begins as "Part One, First Chapter."

common with beasts. To be happy, he must also satisfy a need that belongs exclusively to him: the need to act morally and to know the truth. To act morally means to act according to general and universal principles, and not under the influence of animal instincts. To know the truth means to know things in their universality and totality, and not according to their surface reality, which is always only partial and transient. Stating this supreme need as a fact says nothing of its historical origin or genesis. We are not currently concerned with whether or not there was a time when it did not exist, and when man lived the life of a brute. It is sufficient to know that it exists now, and that without it a human would not be human.[9]

When speaking of the needs to act morally and to know the truth, I consider the two as a single unit, for they are identical in their essential character. In a beast, a single animal life is formed from both the subjective side—its animal appetites, and the objective side—the sensual perception of external objects that serve to satisfy those appetites. Its essential character—exterior as well as interior—is completely subjugated to the given physical reality. The same is the case with man as a spiritual being (être spirituel). The subjective or moral side, which consists of aspirations toward general and universal goals, and the objective or intellectual side, which consists of knowing universal truths by which the supreme goals are determined, form a single spiritual life. The essential character of that life is meant to transcend nature as it is given, to transcend superficial reality, both within external objects and within the subject himself. Neither the universal goals of moral activity nor the universal truths of knowledge are given in the apparent or contingent nature of things. Thus, man's moral need and his intellectual need unite into one single need: to elevate himself above apparent reality, to affirm himself as a being superior to that nature that is contingently given. This spiritual need has previously been called a *metaphysical need*, and I will retain this term as sufficiently expressive. Considering the fact that this metaphysical need, together with the intellectual and moral activity that it produces, forms the distinctive character or the special essence of man, the latter can well be defined as a metaphysical being (être métaphysique), a designation which, as we will shortly see, is strictly true in another sense as well.

The metaphysical nature of man directly produces all the religious and philosophical systems that aim to give to human intelligence the universal truths that it seeks and to human activity its principles and supreme norms. Thanks to these systems, man affirms himself in metaphysical realms and <exp>lores his place in them. But this same quality of metaphysical being manifests itself also in other phenomena of human nature, phenomena that at first glance seem to have no relationship with the metaphysical, and which are regarded by the vulgar as completely natural and ordinary, but which have always caught the attention of the greatest philosophers. After all, it is well known that the difference between superficial and profound minds

9. Solovyov ignores this rejection of diachronic analysis in much of his later work, including this manuscript, and, indeed, he is often at pains to reconcile his cosmological and historical scheme with the recently popular ideas of Darwin.

consists principally in the fact that the former unreflectively pass over issues that are for the latter an object of admiration and a problem to resolve.

After careful examination, the most common of the phenomena that reveal man's metaphysical character is the phenomenon of *laughter*. It is known that only man possesses this faculty; although animals sometimes cry, they never laugh. Even the slightest of smiles is impossible for them. And if one were to demand a definition of man based on a sign both characteristic and apparent, I would name him "the being that laughs" (*l'être qui rit*).[10] We will soon see that this designation returns us to the preceding definition of man as a metaphysical being.

An animal, completely absorbed in given reality, cannot put itself in a critical or negative position toward that reality, and it is for this reason that it cannot laugh. Laughter supposes a state of freedom; a slave does not laugh. The world of phenomena and the various states of its sensual consciousness are an animal's entire world; it cannot disengage from that world, it is preoccupied in it and it is for this reason that the animal is so serious. Man can be frivolous, he can laugh, and this is the proof of his natural freedom. But it is obvious that man can only be free of the exterior necessity of the phenomenal world because he does not belong completely to it, because he is not exclusively a physical being. He can only be free of the world because he belongs to another one. Thus, human laughter, which proves man's natural freedom, proves as well his status as a metaphysical being. In natural laughter, in the laughter of an infant or a young girl, man's metaphysical freedom manifests itself unself-consciously. It acquires consciousness of self only in the thoughtful laugh of a thinking man.[11] Such a person has a clear knowledge of another, ideal world, which he contrasts to the apparent reality that comprises the total reality for a beast or for a bestial human. Such a person sees the contrast and makes fun of the false reality; he laughs. How could he possibly laugh if he actually believed in this miserable reality? He laughs, rather, because he knows quite well that true reality belongs to that other world, to the ideal world, of which this one is only a deformed shadow.[12] He feels himself free in this world only because he is a citizen of another; it is only in his quality as a metaphysical being that he can make fun of his physical being. The same, truly human laughter is produced in us by the great satirical poets and comics, and by the great humorists. Let no one tell me that a satire that mocks the contemporary reality of a certain epoch or society does not have as its ideal transcendent reality, but simply the same phenomenal reality, only of a different epoch or society. The latter is true only of a type of superficial satire that attacks the surface of evil, without reaching toward its

10. See also Solovyov's January 14, 1875, lecture at the Higher Women's Courses of V. I. Ger'e, reconstructed from the notes of a student in *SS* 12:526.

11. Solovyov's male-centered paradigm here and elsewhere, is, of course, typical of his time.

12. Solovyov will modify this rather strict dualism in later writings, most of which celebrate the natural, created world. Nature, he believes, is in a constant tension of spiritualization, just as the spiritual world always strives toward embodiment. He refers here to Plato's allegory of the cave in *The Republic*, a work he dismisses later in his life for its pessimism (see *SS* 9:236).

roots. True satire presents us not with such and such partial phenomena, but with the human state itself. It mocks our entire apparent reality and man himself, insofar as he subordinates himself to that reality. And if that state of misery were our definitive state, if that contemptible reality were the sole reality, one would do well to commit suicide. Instead, we defy it and laugh. It is not our fatherland; what can it do to us?

Another phenomenon of human life that reveals its metaphysical character is that of *art* and *poetry*. What is the true subject of art? In ancient times, when man had control over things, but not over the idea of things, he defined art as the imitation of nature. But it is evident that if art were only that, it could have no independent value, and one could say, along with a certain writer,[13] that an apple that can be eaten is worth much more than a painted apple. But the fact is that works of art produce in us an absolutely special impression that is still more powerful, or even much more powerful than the impression produced by the corresponding reality. This would not be possible if the work of art were a mere reproduction of that reality. Art does not copy individual phenomena; it is not photography.[14] All works of art must have a general and universal character, but, on the other hand, they must not be pure generalities; nothing is more inimical to art than abstractions. Art and poetry take as their subject matter concrete realities and individualities, but individualities that are universal or typical. And this intimate union of the individual and the universal in works of art was recognized as the specific character of art, whereas in our apparent world, individuals are not universal and universals are not individual. Thus, although the world of art is materially the same as our real world, formally it is different, and if there is a relationship of imitation between the two, it must be said that our apparent reality is the one that is the bad copy, a parody of the ideal world, whose distinct images present themselves to us in inspired works by artists and poets. And if a man can produce these images, and if others can understand them immediately, this proves that that ideal reality, that metaphysical reality, is the proper territory for man. It proves that man is a metaphysical being.

In speaking of man's metaphysical being insofar as it manifests itself in laughter and in the fine arts, I am not at all sure that I will be understood by the majority of my listeners. In our insane and serious age, divine genius has

13. Solovyov refers here to the master's dissertation of N. G. Chernyshevsky, "The Aesthetic Relationships of Art to Reality" ("Esteticheskie otnosheniia iskusstva k deistvitel'nosti," 1853). He could not mention the radical writer Chernyshevsky by name, since any reference would surely have been censored at the time. In the nineties, Solovyov devoted the essay "A First Step toward a Positive Aesthetics" ("Pervyi shag k polozhitel'noi estetike"; SS 7:69–77) to Chernyshevsky's dissertation, and he found much in it to praise.

14. Photography was first developed during Solovyov's lifetime, and the 1870s saw a popular proliferation of photography studies, especially in England and France, where this essay was written. Solovyov remained interested throughout his lifetime in advances in science and technology as he explored the worlds of religion and art. Photography became an important part of the Society for Psychical Research, in an attempt to bring "scientific proof" to the world of spiritualism. Only later in the twentieth century did photography take its current place as an art form rather than a tool of scientific or historical documentation.

disappeared, and, along with it, sincere joy. The works of art made today are no more than copies of copies, and if one still laughs, if is only from habit. The only representative of the ideal side of humanity that can be encountered today is the one with the minimal amount of the ideal: positive science, the declared enemy of all that is metaphysical. But the very haste with which the majority of scholars declare themselves devoid of all that is metaphysical, or with which they even attack it directly, renders the matter suspect, and leads us to examine the true relationship of positive science and the metaphysical. (From the introductory lecture)[15]

We indicated that metaphysical reality is presented in works of art in distinct images. Science requires that it be given to us as logical knowledge, as a universal totality. And it is precisely this that is categorically rejected today. But such hatred toward all that is metaphysical is the best proof of the reality of a metaphysical need, and the more this hatred is incited, the more manifest becomes the power of the enemy force. Unable to deny the very fact of a metaphysical need, enemies of the metaphysical must maintain either that this need is abnormal, exclusive, a type of illness, or that, being normal, that is, inherently part of human nature, the need can never be satisfied. As for the first supposition, it is entirely arbitrary. What are the criteria for normal needs? Every need is normal by virtue of the fact that it exists. But, even if there were abnormal needs, how could one put a universal need into that category, a need that appears in all sorts of different peoples, in all ages and all countries? The need for metaphysical knowledge, in one form or another, whether as religion or philosophy, is unquestionably intrinsic to the vast majority of men, so that those who absolutely lack this need can be regarded as abnormal, as monsters. As for the assertion that the metaphysical need can never be satisfied, insofar as it is inherent in human nature, this merely repeats that man is condemned to eternal suffering and makes of humanity a spiritual Tantalus for all of eternity.[16] Such a supposition is too serious for our acceptance, simply based on the word of these gentlemen, without closely examining the reasons that might support it.

Translated by Judith Deutsch Kornblatt

"Sophie. First Triad. First Principles"

"First Dialogue: The Absolute Principle as Unity (The Principle of Monism)"

Sophie: Why do you seek the living among the dead, here, in this place between the petrified East and the decomposing West?

---

15. Kozyrev assumes this note refers to Solovyov's introductory lecture to his course on the history of philosophy, delivered on January 27, 1875, at Moscow University (see *PSS* 2:328).

16. Tantalus, one of Zeus's human sons in Greek mythology, ignored the traditional guest-host relationship when invited to dine with the gods and was punished in Tartarus (Hell) by being eternally "tantalized" with hunger and thirst.

In margin (crossed out): *N.B. The beginning, and everything that relates to Christianity, should be changed.*[17]

Philosopher: A vague dream led me to the banks of the Nile. Here, in the cradle of history, I thought to find some sort of thread that passes through the ruins and graves of today to reconnect the primitive life of humanity with the new life that I await.

Sophie: A naive fantasy. The thread of life is not attached to geographic regions.

Philosopher: And so I quickly abandoned that idea. I left the dead to bury the dead,[18] and all my aspirations belong henceforth to regions where life never ceases. You have deigned to come to my aid, and to make yourself accessible to my senses. You want to reveal to me the mysteries of the three worlds and the future of man, for the truth that is known must precede l<ife>.[19]

But before hearing your revelations, I would like to know the relationship between your doctrine and the faith of our fathers. Is the universal religion that you herald Christianity in its perfected state, or does it have another principal source?

Sophie: What is it that you call Christianity? Is it the Papacy, which declares itself infallible instead of cleansing itself of the blood and filth it's covered itself with for ages, and that it deems sacred? Is it a divided and powerless Protestantism, which wants to believe but no longer does? Is it blind ignorance, the routine of the masses, for whom religion is an old habit from which they are slowly weaning themselves? Is it the self-interested hypocrisy of the priests and the powerful? Know that the universal religion comes to destroy all of that for all time.

In margin (in Russian): [20]

17. Since the original manuscript began with the philosopher's statement "But before hearing your revelations . . . ," Kozyrev speculates that the added lines that now precede that statement were part of the changes that Solovyov intended, and thus the author crossed out this note to himself (*PSS* 2:75). The dialogue still starts in medias res, however, suggesting that the monologic fragments of *The Sophia* were meant to precede the dialogue and serve as an introduction (cf. *PSS* 2:325). Even so, Solovyov did not explain the encounter between the Philosopher (presumably himself) and Sophia in the desert near Cairo until twenty years had passed, in *Three Encounters* (see page 270).

18. See Matt. 8:22, Luke 9:60—"Jesus said to him, 'Let the dead bury their own dead, but you go and proclaim the Kingdom of God.'"

19. In this case of an indecipherable word, a "v" is clear, leading the French editor to speculate that Solovyov intended the word "vision." Kozyrev instead fills in "life" (*vie*).

20. Losev comments on the scheme shown in this table as it is discussed in the chapter rather erroneously titled "Third Chapter: Morality and Politics" (see page 161; Losev, *Vladimir Solov'ev i ego vremia* 194–95). In that text Solovyov lays out the hierarchy of the Universal Church and, probably influenced by Plato's *Republic*, further divides humanity into priests, craftsmen, farmers, and women. The quotation about the Eternal Feminine, probably in Solovyov's own translation, is from the "Chorus Mysticus," the last lines of Goethe's *Faust: Part Two*.

1 pope
7 patriarchs
46 metropolitans
722 archbishops
7,000 bishops
70,000 deacons
700,000 priests
700,000 candidates to the priesthood
777,777

All that is changeable
Is but reflected;
The unattainable
Here is effected;
Human discernment
Here is passed by;
The Eternal Feminine
Draws us on high.

4 classes: *1. priests*   {*the living law*
          2. craftsmen⎫ *workers–active relative to external nature, passive–in*
          3. farmers ⎬ *society*
          4. women   *not workers; passive relative to external nature, active*
                      in society
              lawgivers, producers,
              women managers or stewards

Philosopher: I do not confuse the state of world Christianity in a given epoch with Christianity itself. I mean living Christianity, and not its tomb. What I want to know is if the universal religion is the religion of Christ and the Apostles, that is, the religion that founded the new world and that animated the saints and martyrs.

Sophie: I'd answer your question with this comparison: The universal religion is the fruit of a large tree, whose roots are formed from primitive Christianity, and whose trunk is formed from the religion of the Middle Ages.[21] Modern Catholicism and contemporary Protestantism are withered and fruitless branches, ready to be pruned. If you call Christianity the whole tree, then the universal religion is no doubt the final product of Christianity; it is Christianity in its perfection. But if you give this name only to the roots and trunk, then the universal religion is not Christianity. You must also see that the same roots have produced still other shrubs. When ignorant people see plants of such different form and size, they believe that they also have different origins. But when the fruit ripens, the mistake becomes obvious and the whole world sees that all of these trees bear the same fruit, and are thus from the same source.

Philosopher: I understand you, but I fear that your words might be misinterpreted. The very universal form that you give to your doctrine could cause a

21. Kozyrev suspects this image is taken from Jacob Boehme (*PSS* 2:336). Solovyov returns to the image in lecture 3 of *Lectures on Divine Humanity* (*SS* 3:39). He marked the passage here by a wavy line in the margin from "the universal religion is the fruit . . ." to "is not Christianity." It is not clear whether he intended to move the passage elsewhere, to delete, or just to return to it later.

huge misunderstanding. There are those who feel themselves called to universalize Christianity. In order to do this, they take only the most simple and facile aspects.[22] They eliminate from Christianity anything that is positive or characteristic, and thus obtain something that is neither Christianity nor Islam nor Buddhism, nor anything at all. They call this "nothing" the Universal Religion, the Religion of Humanity, and other pleasant names. I fear that at first glance one might take the true universal religion for a naive production of this sort. And I know Jews and Muslims who treat the Torah and Islam in this same manner. I believe that you can find the same among Brahmans and Buddhists. All of these good gentlemen, without recognizing each other, arrive at results as similar as two peas in a pod. And they thus believe themselves to be great thinkers and heroes of humanity. There are even those who go further; they not only eliminate the content of positive religion from their universal religion, but they eliminate the principles of religion altogether: God and the soul and all suprahuman reality. These people are the proudest of all, and believe themselves to be true innovators.

Sophie: I don't know those people. As for the misunderstanding you speak of, I anticipated it with the comparison that I just drew; when you want to get fruit, you don't cut down the tree that bears it.

Philosopher: Furthermore, the quasi-universal religion of these good gentlemen resembles nothing more than a denuded and desiccated trunk that gives neither fruit nor shade.

Sophie: But the true universal religion is a tree with countless fruit-laden branches that spreads its tabernacle over the entire earth and over the worlds to come. This is not the product of abstractions and generalizations. It is the real and spontaneous synthesis of all religions that takes nothing positive away from them, and instead gives them something more than they had had. The only thing destroyed by it is their narrowness, their exclusivity, their mutual negations, their egoism and their hate.

In margin: *The universal religion is not only the positive synthesis of all religions, but also the synthesis of religion, philosophy, and science, and thus of the spiritual or internal sphere in general with the external sphere, with political and social life. In becoming universal, religion loses its exclusive character; it becomes more than a religion, and is no longer opposed to the other spheres of human life. Rather, it includes everything in itself.*

Philosopher: This is indeed the vague image of the truth of which I have been dreaming for some time now.[23] But you have promised to acquaint me with

---

22. Later Solovyov accused Lev Tolstoy of this very simplification in the preface to *Three Conversations* (1900). Without mentioning names, he compares Tolstoy's teachings to a fictional sect of "Hole Worshipers": "The similarity here is in the purely negative and content-less character of both 'world views.' Although 'intelligent' hole worshippers do not call themselves hole worshippers, but Christians, and they call their teachings the Gospels, nonetheless a Christianity without Christ and a Gospels, that is, the *Good News*, without any *good* that would be worthwhile claiming as news, that is, without actual resurrection into the fullness of blessed life, that would be the very same *empty space* as the ordinary hole, drilled in a peasant's hut" (*SS* 10:84).

23. This line brings us back to the opening of the dialogue, when the Philosopher tells Sophie that a "vague dream" had led him to Egypt.

the truth itself. First, though, tell me about the first principle of the universal religion. Where does it begin?

Sophie: Where can it begin other than with the absolute principle of all things, the principle that is known equally to all religious and philosophical systems, though under different names?

Philosopher: I am well aware that the existence of an absolute principle was known by all systems, even by skeptical systems, postulated by the very nature of our spirit. But I also know that skepticism, while recognizing the reality of such a principle, nonetheless raises serious objections to the possibility of knowing it.[24] Can you demonstrate for me that the absolute principle of all things, being-in-itself, is accessible to our understanding?

Sophie: I'll carefully avoid *that*. Would you like me to become just as ridiculous as the rest of you?[25] Oh, you poor children, who always mistake words for thoughts and realities. A question of words! Don't you know that understanding—and I am speaking of the understanding of real beings and not of logical or mathematical abstractions—don't you know that understanding, by its very nature, is relative? We know something in relationship to one thing or another. We know something more or less. The simple and absolute question: "Can one know one thing or another thing?" is senseless. It is not possible to answer absurd questions.

Philosopher: When I ask: "Can one know the absolute principle?" I am speaking of the knowledge that in school is called "adequate," that is to say corresponding perfectly to the known object.[26] I want to know if one can know the absolute principle, as it is in itself, being-in-itself, as such. You well know that modern skepticism affirms that we can know nothing in itself, because knowledge supposes that the known object exists for us, that is, relatively, as a phenomenon and not as a substance.

Sophie: Do you know me? Do you know with whom you are speaking?

Philosopher: As if I could not know you!

Sophie: You no doubt know me as a phenomenon, that is, insofar as I exist *for you* or in my external manifestation. You cannot know me as I am *in myself*, that is, my thoughts and intimate feelings as they are in me and for me. You know them only when they manifest themselves outwardly in the expression of my eyes, in my words and my gestures. These are only external phenomena and yet . . .

Philosopher: And yet, when I look into the deep azure of your eyes, when I hear the music of your voice, is it outward phenomena of sight and sound that I perceive? My God! I know your thoughts and feelings, and, by your thoughts and feelings, I know your inner being.

Sophie: And this is the way that all beings know each other. You know the interior phenomena by way of the exterior, and, by that, the being-itself, or what one philosopher has called the intelligible character.[27]

24. Skepticism claims that we cannot use reason to come to any real and definitive conclusions.

25. Here is a good example of the condescension with which Sophie addresses the Philosopher. Her tone on the one hand elevates her over her human interlocutor but on the other also humanizes her. Although possibly all-knowing, she is clearly not all-patient.

26. The Philosopher holds his own here in the discussion. He proves to Sophia that he is well versed in the major elements of her teaching.

27. According to Immanuel Kant in *Critique of Pure Reason*, "intelligible character" is noumenal, a "thing-in-itself," and cannot be derived from empirical causes.

Philosopher: So, the philosophical distinction between a being-in-itself and phenomena is false?

Sophie: It is not their distinction, but their arbitrary separation that is false. Our ignorance confuses the being-in-itself with phenomena. And abstract philosophy separates them completely. You must walk a high road between confusion and abstract separation. There is a middle path: difference *and* correspondence. Phenomenon is not being-in-itself, but still is in a decided relationship with being; it corresponds to it. Here again a dispute has raged without understanding the real significance of the terms that were being used. What does "phenomenon" mean?

Philosopher: "Phenomenon" comes from the Greek verb φαίνομαι, meaning to appear, to show oneself, or to manifest oneself.

Sophie: So, phenomenon means appearance or manifestation; this assumes some thing that appears or manifests itself, and that thing, considered independently from its manifestation, is evidently the being-in-itself. Thus, we call that which manifests itself the being-in-itself, and the manifestation itself, a phenomenon. And if we know the phenomenon, that is, the manifestation of the being-in-itself, then we know the being-in-itself insofar as it has manifested itself. To manifest oneself means to become something for another; to be known means the same thing. Thus, when you say: "We only know phenomena," you say that we know the being-in-itself insofar as it can, in general, be an object of knowledge, that is to say, you affirm a truth that is evident in itself. To pretend that you can know a being-in-itself other than by its manifestation is the same thing as pretending to perceive colors other than through vision, and sound other than through hearing. It is impossible, not because of an imperfection or limits in the knowing subject, but because of the absurdity of it.

Philosopher: Since to be knowable means to be able to exist for another, and to be in oneself according to the very meaning of the term excludes all existence for another, it is clear that to be in oneself and to be unknowable mean exactly the same thing; so those brave people who so vaunt their principle that one cannot know being-in-itself are doing nothing more than stating a tautology, as if they were saying that to be in oneself is to be in oneself.

Sophie: But on the other hand, when they draw the conclusion that we can have no knowledge of being from the fact that one cannot know being-in-itself as such, that is, directly, they demonstrate a lack of reasoning and an ignorance that is truly extraordinary. Since phenomena are possible only as manifestations of being-in-itself, one cannot know them without knowing at the same time, more or less indirectly, the being itself that manifests them. In acting on another, in effect that being makes itself known by that other, and, as that action comes from the being itself, it is determined by the being's own character and thus makes that character known. Those people do not know how to distinguish between immediate knowledge of the being itself by another—an impossibility because it implies a contradiction—from another's knowledge of a being's nature or its essence (its inner character) through the action that the being has on the other, or through its manifestation to the other; such a knowledge is not simply possible, but clearly necessary once we admit that the being manifests itself. In conclusion, a being that is unknowable as such, that is incompatible with knowledge, acts on another or manifests itself to it, and in this way makes its nature or its character known; and the very term "knowledge" simply means this manifestation of one being to another or its existence for it.

Philosopher: But what would you say to counter the philosophers who represent the exact opposite of the skeptics, and say that in knowing the manifestations of being in their general forms, we know the being itself absolutely and directly, and that, in this way, being is not distinct from that knowledge?[28]

Sophie: Such a theory supposes that, in manifesting itself, that is to say in acting, a being passes directly into its action, ceases to be itself, and loses its proper being. But this supposition destroys itself, for action supposes an agent, and if the agent ceases to be, then all action ceases as well; nothing is produced. When you act, you do not lose your proper being, you do not pass into that action, but, rather, are the master of it; you retain the independent power to act. The agent, or that which manifests itself, always retains something more than the manifestation; it can never transform all of its being into the manifestation or the phenomenon. And not only the absolute being, but even the inner or subjective manifestations of any being can never pass as such into the immediate consciousness of another. When I communicate my thoughts or my feelings to you, it is only their objective content that you know. Or, to put it better, in manifesting thoughts and feelings through external phenomena, I evoke in you corresponding thoughts or feelings, but not the act itself of thinking, or the subjective state I found myself in when I had those thoughts or feelings.

Philosopher: That is clear. So let's pass on to the principal object of our conversation, to the absolute principle of all things.

Sophie: By applying what we have just said to this discussion, we can affirm that the absolute principle, unable to be known directly in its own being, is known through the phenomena that are its manifestations. But, as all phenomena are equally the manifestations of the absolute principle, one cannot know it through one or another phenomenon, but only in the collection or totality of those phenomena. Now, it is clear that that totality shouldn't be understood in a numerical sense, because such an understanding, even if it were possible, would only let us know the particular elements of the whole, but not the whole in its principle. Thus, this totality of phenomena is their general connection to each other, or their ordering. Since all order supposes a principle of order, and this principle in regard to the universal order or the order of all can be nothing else but the absolute of all things, then the universal order is understood to be the connection of phenomena in relation to the absolute principle, or their natural hierarchy. Thus, knowledge of the absolute principle in phenomena is defined as knowledge of the natural or essential hierarchy of phenomena. The principle is known here not directly in its pure sense, but in relationship to the phenomena as the principle of their hierarchy.

Philosopher: My reason stops me here and asks if, in order to know the natural or essential relationship of the absolute principle to phenomena, we must not first know its nature or its proper essence. But you have said that the latter knowledge is impossible.

Sophie: You confuse direct knowledge of the absolute principle in its proper or inner state with general knowledge of the idea that we have of it. You can see that we can have a general notion of the absolute principle without having direct knowledge of it by analyzing what we call a general notion.

Philosopher: That is the definition or designation of a thing.

---

28. Solovyov refers here to empiricism and the work of Francis Bacon. See *PSS* 2:337.

Sophie: But how can you designate a thing if not by its relationship to another, that is to say, negatively?

Philosopher: Yes, I remember the great Spinoza's aphorism: *Omnis determinatio est negatio.* [Latin: Every definition is a negation.][29]

Sophie: Thus, all general notions are negative and do not suppose direct and subjective knowledge.

Philosopher: And then what is the general notion of the absolute principle?

Sophie: If the general notion of a particular being designates it negatively in relationship to another particular being, it is clear that the general notion of the absolute principle must designate it in relationship to all being, because all that we call being is its manifestation. Thus, we must say that the absolute principle is not being, that is to say that it can be neither the direct object of our outer sensations, nor the direct subject of our inner consciousness, for everything in these two categories is what we call being. You can see that it is not being from another angle as well. It is the principle of all being; if it were being itself, it would be a being outside of all being, which is absurd. Thus it is clear that the principle of being cannot be designated as being.

Philosopher: So I should designate it as nonbeing?

Sophie: You could surely do that, and in so doing you would merely follow the lead of many great theologians, including Orthodox theologians, who have no compunction against calling God nonbeing. But, in order not to confuse lesser minds, it would be better to resist. The common person always understands nonbeing as the lack or privation of being. And it is clear that in this sense nonbeing cannot become the predicate of the absolute principle. We saw that in manifesting itself, that is to say in passing into being (in realizing itself), it does not cease to remain itself, it does not lose itself, it is not exhausted by the manifestation. (Otherwise, if the principle of action would cease, action would also cease.)

In margin: *Sublime thought, forming the basis of all truth, is as follows: at the base of all that exists is but one, and that one is neither existence nor a being, but that which is above all existence and all being, so that, in general, being and existence are only the surface, but at the base is something superior to them. And this superior unity is also in us, as it is in all things, and, in raising us above all being and all existence, we feel and know that absolute substance directly, because we find it in itself.*

Philosopher: But how can you define this nonbeing, which is nonetheless not privation or the lack of being?

Sophie: If you call privation or lack "powerlessness," then the opposite would be "power" or "positive possibility," "force" [*puissance*].[30] Thus, the absolute principle—being not, as such, being—is the possibility of being, that

---

29. Kozyrev suggests that Solovyov borrows this phrase not directly from Spinoza but from Hegel's reassessment of Spinoza. See *PSS* 2:337.

30. Solovyov contrasts "impuissance" and "puissance," or powerlessness and power or force. Because he here equates force with "positive possibility," the Russian translator proceeds to translate "puissance" as possibility or potentiality rather than power. I follow this reading.

which is evident because it manifests itself, that is to say, the product of being. And since, in manifesting itself, it cannot exhaust itself or pass without a trace into the manifestation, it remains always the possibility of being of the sort that is its constant and proper attribute. Thus, the absolute principle defines itself as that which has the possibility of being. And as that which has power is superior to that over which it has the power, we must say that the absolute principle is superior to being, that it is above being, that it is *super-ens*—ὕπερον [Latin, Greek: super-real/ beyond being]. It is clear analytically that the absolute principle is in itself singular and simple, because plurality supposes relation.

In margin: *The principle common to all religious and philosophical systems, but particularly, etc., N.B. to develop.*

This unity and absolute simplicity is the primary definition of the absolute principle as it became known in the East, and since religious man always wants to become like his God and thus to unite with Him, the constant aspiration of oriental religions was to force man to abstract from all plurality, from all forms, and thus from all being. But the absolute principle is the principle of all being; unity is the principle of all plurality, simplicity is the principle of complexity, and purity of form produces them all. It is the ἔν καί πᾶν [Greek: one and all].[31]

Thus, those who want to know it only as ἔν [Greek: one], in its unity alone, know only half of it, and their religion, both theoretically and practically, remains imperfect and powerless. This is the general character of the East. In the opposite way, the Western tendency is to sacrifice absolute and substantial unity for the multiplicity of forms and individual characters, so that the West cannot even comprehend unity as more than a purely external order. This is the characteristic of their Church, of their State, and their society.[32] The universal religion is called to unite these two tendencies in their truth, to know and realize the true ἔν καί πᾶν.

In margin: *To develop: the relativity of all being. Knowledge is relative only because being itself is relative. And not accidentally, as the Positivists believe, but necessarily, by its very nature. The absolute, which is above knowledge, is also above being.*

"Second Dialogue: The Absolute Principle as Duality (The Principle of Dualism)"

Philosopher: After having recognized the absolute principle in its unity above all manifestation, and, consequently, of all being, we must now pass onto its realization in the hierarchy of beings. But tell me, what cause and what power

---

31. Here we see an early formulation of Solovyov's idea of *vseedinstvo* as all-oneness, multiplicity-in-unity. As he says in *Lectures*: "All that is is necessarily one and many" (*SS* 3:61), and "Multiplicity reduced to unity is wholeness" (*SS* 3:113).

32. Solovyov will soon develop these ideas in "Three Powers" (1877) (*PSS* 1:199–208).

can force the infinite substance to leave its absolute state and to manifest itself in the series of beings and relative phenomena?

Sophie: Your question is as false at its core as it is in its expression. I have
already told you that in manifesting itself the substance cannot cease to be
what it is; it cannot leave its absolute state. Do you believe that it is dimin-
ished by action and manifestation? When you act, when you manifest
yourself, do you cease to be what you are, do you leave your state as psychic agent and, in manifesting yourself materially, do you become matter?
In producing objective phenomena, do you lose your subjective being? So?
Do you really think that the absolute substance is less powerful than you
are? When it realizes itself, the substance does not lose its absolute state,
but rather acquires a relative state. Without ceasing to be infinite, it becomes definite as well; and that is true infinity, the true absolute. You comprehend that by its very definition the absolute principle cannot be deprived
of anything, cannot lack anything in itself. If it were only infinite and absolute, then it would lack relativity and finitude; it would be imperfect.
Thus, in order to be that which it is, it must also be the opposite of itself,
or, it must be the union of itself and of its opposite. In order to be truly
absolute and infinite, it must also be the principle of relativity and
finitude.

Philosopher: What you're saying isn't new to me. I've already learned it from a
great philosopher, and have always felt the truth of that reasoning.

In margin: *Hegel, Goethe.*[33]

Even more, the idea of the absolute substance as affirming itself in its
self-denial, and as revealing the great principle of the unity of opposites, has
always delivered me into a sort of mystical enthusiasm.

Sophie: And do you know why? Because this idea is merely the logical expression of the great moral and physical reality, of love. In loving, you deny yourself (because there is no love without self-denial), you affirm another, you give
yourself to that other, and nevertheless you do not lose your own being. On
the contrary, you affirm your being to a higher degree, you elevate yourselves
to a new perfection. Thus, when you say that the absolute substance as such,
analytically, by its very definition, is the union of itself and its negation, you
merely repeat in an abstract form the definition of our great apostle: God is
love.[34]

Because the absolute principle by necessity is love, then love is the nature
of the absolute principle. As the striving toward the opposite of the absolute
principle, that is, toward being (because the absolute principle as such is above
being), love is the principle of plurality, because the indispensable condition

33. Kozyrev sees this note in the margin as a reference to "names of the philosophers in
whom he finds an essential analogy with his own teaching on the absolute principle that contains opposition within itself: Hegel and Goethe" (*PSS* 2:339).
34. 1 John 4:8.

of being is plurality. But we have already said that the absolute principle cannot lose its own state when passing into its opposite. It cannot cease to be the absolute as such. On the contrary, in positing, producing or positively separating out its opposite, it affirms itself as such. Thus, the absolute substance, necessarily and for all eternity, divides itself into two poles: one, the principle of absolute unity affirmed as such, the principle of freedom in relation to all form, to all manifestation and to all being; and the other, the principle or the productive force of multiple being and of phenomenal forms.[35] We have already recognized this latter as love. It is easy to find an analogy in our own inner selves. When you free yourself internally from all multiplicity of desires and thoughts, when you affirm yourself and contemplate yourself vis-à-vis the exterior world as a simple and immobile whole, inaccessible to the foreign forces of matter, then what would you call yourself?

In margin, perpendicular to text (in Russian):[36]

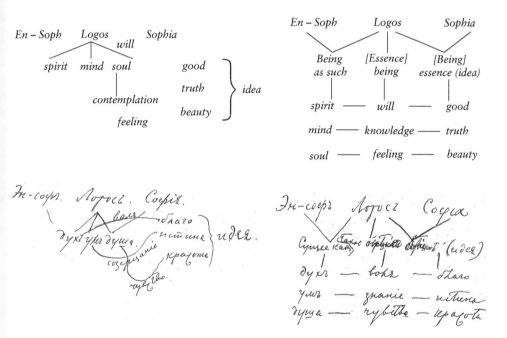

From Solovyov's manuscript of *The Sophia*. RGALI.

35. The previous two paragraphs, along with numerous other short passages, are also found word for word in Solovyov's *Philosophical Principles of Integral Knowledge* (PSS 2:263–64).

36. Compare to tables in *Philosophical Principles of Integral Knowledge*, PSS 2:282 and 286. As we saw in part 1, Ein-Sof (En-Sof) is the Kabbalistic term for the unknowable root of all.

Philosopher: As an indestructible whole, as the subjective center of creation, as the free principle above all contingent states, I would call myself Spirit.

Sophie: That is also the name that you should give to the positive or higher pole of the absolute principle. You well understand that this is not a new and distinct hypostasis of the absolute substance. It is the substance itself, affirming itself as such through the positing of its ideal opposite:[37] The absolute substance, which has no proper name, presents itself as one, manifesting itself as an indestructible unity through the production of its opposite, just as true unity, positive unity, does not fear multiplicity and does not flee from it, but, on the contrary, produces it within itself and, in producing it, is not swallowed up by it. Rather, it remains that which it is, it remains a unity, and by that proves clearly that it is essential unity, unity by its very nature, and, consequently, cannot be destroyed by any multiplicity.

Philosopher: In effect, it is clear that true and positive unity is not the lack or privation of multiplicity, but rather power over multiplicity. It is above, rather than below multiplicity. And it is further clear that it can only prove its superiority by producing multiplicity within itself and triumphing over it, for everything is proved by its opposite. And, thus, a great principle is newly confirmed. We find proof that this idea is not empty dialectical verbiage in our own spirit, which, in the multiplicity of its thoughts, feelings, and desires, affirms always its unity.

Sophie: Which proves yet again that we do not give the name Spirit to the positive pole of the absolute principle merely metaphorically. Moreover, being one and simple according to its very idea, it does not call for much development. But I must explain the multiform and equivocal nature of its companion.

We saw that the productive force of being, which we call direct possibility, necessarily belongs to the absolute principle, and is its nature. Thus, the absolute Spirit eternally finds its opposite within itself. (They are mutually connected since it is only in relation to that opposite that it affirms itself).

It is thus necessity, the divine *fatum*; the absolute principle is free only in the eternal triumph over this necessity, that is to say, when remaining pure, simple, and immobile in all the multiple products of its love. Thus we see that freedom and necessity are correlative, the first being actual only in the realization of the second. But, since divine necessity as well as its realization is eternal, then divine freedom is also eternal. In other words, the absolute Spirit never submits to necessity, over which it eternally triumphs. What is more, when we speak here of necessity, we are obviously not speaking of external necessity, the weighty necessity of our material existence. As the absolute principle can have nothing external, nothing foreign, we are speaking now of its own necessity, its nature and its love. That is necessary to it, as it is necessary to us in order to be, to live, to love. It is clear that this necessity does not contradict absolute perfection.

---

37. The pages in the archival manuscript are confused here. I follow the order proposed by Kozyrev.

Philosopher: That is clear, and the stupidity of certain theologians who would like to deprive God of this necessity is also clear.

Sophie: As if they could prove that! But ask them if it is necessary that God be goodness, reason, in order to be God, in order to exist at all? They would be obliged to respond affirmatively. But, if it is necessary for God to be, it is also necessary for Him to manifest Himself, all the more, according to their own words, because His power is in action. Or, rather, all the attributes that they give Him are relative to creation, and without creation not only could they not be manifest, but would have no meaning at all. And if these attributes are necessary, then it is clear that creation is also necessary.

Philosopher: In general it seems that all these questions—Did God create the world of His free will?; Could He have not created it?; Could He have produced a creation other than the one that exists?—demonstrate a conception of divinity that is entirely childish, and are infantile fancies unworthy of serious minds.[38]

Sophie: You are right. But let us return to the development of the second principle. I said that it is the direct possibility of being. Don't you know another, more common name that would mean the same thing?

Philosopher: It seems I do. The ancient sages called it *matter.*

Sophie: Perfect. The material of all being is not being, but it is not nonbeing. It is the direct possibility of being.

Philosopher: But we have already used this name for the positive principle, absolute substance. Would it not be a contradiction to give the same name to opposite principles?

Sophie: Think about both the similarity and the difference. The absolute principle and universal matter are equally different from being; the attribute of being is equally foreign to both of them. In addition, both are not nonbeing, they are not nothing. Thus, just as the only thing between nothing and actual being is the possibility (*potentia*) of being, they must both be defined as the possibility of being. But the absolute Spirit is positive possibility. It is the freedom of being. It is above being. The material principle, of necessity being the striving or gravitation toward being that contains negative possibility, is nothing more than privation, the lack of being. Real lack or privation (for we are not dealing with abstractions) can be best defined as desire or thirst for being, and, as desire or thirst, it constitutes the essence of love, and we return to our first definition of the productive principle as love.

In margin, (in Russian):

1. *Being in itself* (potentia absoluta [Latin: absolute possibility])

2(3). *Being as the principle of existence or of the other:* natura, materia prima (potentia proxima essendi [Latin: nature, primary matter, the unmediated power of being]), *direct force or the possibility of existence (love*-cupido [Latin: thirst]) =

3(2). *"The Other" is simply the possibility of existence or the striving toward existence. The first principle must contain actual realization, insofar as it*

---

38. The Philosopher begins to assimilate Sophie's condescending tone here.

produces real being, or insofar as it determines the primary material for being, it is called logos and among the principles constitutes an eternal mediator. The correlation or interdependency of the second and third principles is evident, in consequence of which the third (matter) is also mater Verbi [Latin: the mother of the Word], *but at the same time it is the* filia [Latin: daughter] *of* Bet-Kol [Hebrew {correct form: bat kol}, the daughter of the divine voice].[39]
Ein-Soph, Logos, Sophia.
The First Trinity.[40]

Philosopher: Thus, if the higher pole of the absolute principle should be termed Spirit, which returns us to the category of freedom, then the lower pole makes itself known as necessity, power, nature (will), desire or thirst for being, Matter. The essential identity of the first four terms is clear, but their similarity with the last seems more difficult for me to conceive. The first terms all have an internal character, that is, a character that is psychic and subjective,

In margin: *Develop these expressions.*

while the term "matter" ordinarily designates the external reality of objective phenomena. How can one conceive of matter as desire or love, for example?

Sophie: When I speak of matter as a primary principle that directly produces being, it is clear that I do not mean what the sages of our time arbitrarily designate by that term.[41] I follow philosophical terminology, rather than that of chemistry or physics, which have nothing to do with primary principles or productive agents of being. It is clear that physical and chemical matter has different qualities and quantitative relations, which means that it is already formed—that is to say that it is no longer matter properly speaking, pure matter—and possesses only a purely phenomenal character; it can never pretend to the ranks of primary principle. The matter I am speaking of is the ὕλη [Greek: matter, substance, material] of the ancient philosophers. It does not possess, and by its nature *cannot* possess either quality or a specific quantity. Now it is perfectly clear that matter as principle has an interior character,

---

39. In Jewish Talmudic literature, *bat kol* is sometimes equated with the *Shekhinah*, or the presence of God. Here, in a somewhat sloppy play on words, "matter" becomes "mother," and the "Mother of the Word" is also the "Daughter of the Word." Mary, then, is mother and daughter of God at the same time and is herself both human and divine. It should be clear why Solovyov might turn to Sophia, particularly in her association with Shekhinah, in order to avoid theologically suspect statements such as that above. See Burmistrov: "In the given instance, we see an obvious and rather early example of Solovyov's equation of 'the eternal feminine,' 'the Virgin Divine Wisdom,' Sophia, with the 'feminine principle' of Kabbalah, 'the Daughter of the Divine Voice,' equivalent in this case to the Shekhinah or Malkhut" ("Vladimir Solov'ev i Kabbalah" 34).
40. Sophia is thus equated with the Holy Spirit in this scheme.
41. By "sages of our time," Solovyov means the proponents of the ruling materialist and positivist ideologies.

whether psychic or subjective. That which has no quality cannot act on the senses and, consequently, cannot have objective being. Pure Spirit and pure Matter are equally foreign to objective being; this is their common character. (I have already indicated their respective difference.)

Philosopher: That's true. And the psychic character of pure matter begins to be recognized by the sages themselves, despite their prejudices. They now reduce all matter in general to dynamic atoms, to the center of forces, and force is a notion that belongs completely to the subjective or inner sphere. What is force in itself, if not desire or will? What we call force, in relation to the other or viewed from the outside, is, in itself or looking from the subjective, inner sphere: desire.

Sophie: Thus Spirit and Matter are not absolutely different entities, separated and opposed, but different sides or poles, as we have already said, of the same substance, in which the higher or dominant side is represented by Spirit, and the lower by Matter, or by natural and blind desire. This is perfectly in accord with the usual meaning of these terms. One says: material penchants, material instincts, material interests, material desires, even material spirit or intelligence, in no way having in mind the matter of physicists or chemists, but rather the lower side of a psychic being.[42]

Since Spirit is the proper affirmation of the absolute principle as such, and the dominant pole, one can say that Matter, or the material principle, belongs to Spirit; it is the inferior side, the necessary and spontaneous nature of Spirit. It is Spirit that is the subject of matter. Thus, although they are eternally distinguished from and opposed to each other in a certain sense, nonetheless the spiritual principle and the material principle can never be conceived as separated one from the other; they are forever and always tied to each other, they presuppose each other; each is impossible without the other. What is more, they are united by their essential identity, for both are inner, subjective principles; they are but different sides of the same subject, of the same substance. Spirit is that substance, the subject-as-such, the absolute subject; the material principle, or desire, is the subject as dependent on an external manifestation, as a necessary force of external and phenomenal being, as the direct, productive possibility of that being. The absolute subject cannot affirm itself as such without distinguishing itself from itself as a principle of external being; and it cannot make that distinction if it does not locate the principle of external being in itself, as a given. And as the absolute subject is eternal, the material principle is also eternal. For it is clear that the absolute subject must be eternal in its totality, and, consequently, the material principle can never be missing from it. It finds its very nature in itself and triumphs over it.

In margin: *Here I need to insert the developments of the 1st and 2nd folios.*[43]

---

42. See a similar statement in *Philosophical Principles of Integral Knowledge*, PSS, 2:266–67.

43. Both the French and Russian editors point out that this author's note refers to the parts of the manuscript written as monologic philosophical discourse, and which Solovyov labeled 1st and 2nd f.

["Third Dialogue"][44]

Sophie:[45] You must now know the relations between the Spirit, the principle of unity, and material possibility, the principle of duality, and all that follows from those relations. Spirit affirms the material principle as other; one can conceive of the other ideally, which is to say in thought or through thought, as well as really, which is to say in feeling or through feeling.

In margin: *The material principle is the principle of multiplicity, just as Spirit is the principle of unity. Multiplicity can be both ideal and real; Spirit, as the principle of unity in relation to ideal multiplicity, that is, as the principle of ideal unity, is Mind; as the principle of unity in relation to real or sensory multiplicity, that is, as the principle of real and sensible unity, it is Soul.*

In conceiving the other in thought—as idea or image—the absolute Spirit becomes Mind;[46] in opposing it, it takes on a positive consciousness of itself and affirms itself as *Ego.* However, it cannot lose its nature as pure Spirit in this act of consciousness. Thus, in producing Mind, it necessarily remains that which it is, which is to say, pure Spirit, inaccessible to the duality of I and not-I, in which Mind consists. {But the material principle is the principle of being in general, whether ideal or real; thus, in appearing to Spirit as the desire of the ideal not-I, and producing the *idea* in Mind, it simultaneously appears to it as the desire of the real not-It.

In margin (as automatic writing): *Sophia I am answering you: Only the earth is inhabited by the human species. There are the beginnings of organization in other stellar worlds, but no other organisms capable of becoming the seat of human spirits. + Sophia.*

Mind, however, already acts on the material principle between this material desire and pure Spirit.}[47]

Now you see the bases of universal development. We have Mind as active principle, affirming itself as I, as subject, and primary matter appearing to it as something alien, opposed, as not-I, as object. We have seen, however, that the objectivity of matter is only relative, phenomenal; it also has a subjective or psychic character, for its essence is desire, primitive and blind desire, or instinct. Through this subjective nature it can act on Mind. Thus, we have

---

44. This section has no title in the manuscript but would logically serve as the third dialogue. The French editor supplied the following subtitle: "Relations between Spirit, the principle of unity, and material possibility, the principle of duality" (Solovyov, *La Sophia*, ed. Rouleau 20)

45. The word "Sophie" in the manuscript is followed by the words "The world of," which are crossed out but in the handwriting typical of Solovyov's automatic writing.

46. Solovyov uses the French term "Intellect," which Kozyrev translates into Russian as *Um.* The term is confusing and becomes more so when the philosopher places it as the middle term in the triad of Spirit-Mind-Soul. In a Trinitarian scheme, it would then be parallel to Son or Logos.

47. The text between wavy brackets is similarly marked in the original manuscript. The reason for the marking is not clear.

two principles that act on each other, that do battle with each other, and through this interaction produce a development, a process.

The principle of this process is the essential subjectivity of Mind, which continually triumphs over the objective principle, making it increasingly subjective, up until the point that it becomes merely a holder, the substratum of the Mind that produces concrete Mind or the ideal personality. The products of this process—ideas, or, better yet, ideal objects—rise at the same time to individuality and to universality. The products of the first reaction of Mind against not-I have an indifferent, abstract, and general character. They become increasingly more and more differentiated, more composed, more concrete and individual.[48]

Philosopher: That seems contrary to common sense, according to which the individual is directly opposed to the universal.

Sophie: Nonetheless, the truth of my words is clear. What is the most universal of beings that you know?

Philosopher: That would have to be the human being. While all others remain within their own narrowly limited beings, he alone departs from himself and embraces the universe through his knowledge and action.

Sophie: But what is the most individual being, the one most liberated from nature in its entirety and from the special nature of its own species? What is the freest, most original, most independent being?

Philosopher: That would also have to be the human being.

Sophie: Thus, in humans you see the coincidence of the greatest universality and the greatest individuality.

Philosopher: You're right. But can't you show me the necessity for this coincidence a priori?

Sophie: Don't you call something universal if it includes in itself the greatest number of different elements and if it finds itself in the greatest number of relationships and relations with other beings? But the greater the number of different elements, the more each depends on the others, and the stronger and more indissoluble is their union. The greater the number of different elements, the greater the number of their possible combinations, and the lesser, so to speak, is the possibility that the same combination would be found in other beings. (This is one of the meanings of the term individuality.) Finally, since the relation or relationship of two beings is at the same time necessarily a *distinction*, the more relationships a being has with others, the more it distinguishes itself from them and the more it is distinguished, which is to say the more it affirms itself or is individual. Thus, you should recognize that it is a major and essential law that the universality of a being is always in direct relationship to its individuality; the more a being is individual, the more it is universal.[49]

48. Kozyrev assumes that the previous two paragraphs should be spoken by the Philosopher and changes "Now you see" to "Now I see" (*PSS* 2:103).

49. In *Lectures*, Solovyov similarly asserts: "The universality of a being is found in direct relationship to its individuality," and "Thus, the universal organism, expressing the unconditional content of the divine principle, is *par excellence* a particularly individual being. This individual being, or the realized expression of the unconditionally essential God, is Christ" (*SS* 3:114).

Philosopher: In our material reality, the most universal being only contains others in itself ideally, that is to say, by knowing them as objects. However, since there is no other existence in the ideal world but ideal or objective existence, the most universal being that you call concrete Mind, in containing in itself its ideal world, contains it entirely or in its totality.

Sophie: That is obvious. The whole ideal world is nothing more than an object for the Mind, its objectivity, so to speak, its form. But in the parts of this form, which represent phases and stages of the universal process,[50] the one is subjective or ideal in relation to the other, the latter representing the real or objective pole, which is the material of the higher phase. And each of the phases that are intermediate between the concrete Mind on the one hand and the object or simple not-I (being in general) on the other, each of these intermediate phases is subjective, ideal, intellectual, energetic and active in relation to the lower phases, and objective, real, material, potential and passive in relation to the higher phase. Each of these phases potentially contains the higher and the lower, and is contained by both the lower and the higher. It is only the mode of potentiality that is different in the two cases. This is because potentiality, which in general is opposed to actuality, can be of two sorts: a being can have no actual state whatsoever because it already had one but exhausted it, or because it has not yet had one. This is to say that a state can be potential either as a passive remnant or as an embryo. It is clear that the lower being is contained in the higher being as a passive remnant, and the higher state in the lower as an embryo.

Philosopher: What you are telling me reminds me of the teachings of the ancient and the modern sages, namely Aristotle among the former and Schelling among the latter.

Sophie: It would be sad indeed if truth were confined to the present day. If I were to have told you things that were completely unheard of, you wouldn't even have been able to understand them and, if you had understood them, you would not be understood by anyone else.

In margin (as automatic writing in French): *Sophia + I can tell you that your transformation* . . .

The universal doctrine that I am teaching you is not distinguishable from the systems of the past in terms of the material that serves as its construction, but by the construction itself, by everything in its entirety, just as humans are not distinguishable from the lower animals by the chemical or physical makeup of their bodies. Therefore, you cannot judge the connection of the universal teaching with other systems until you know it in its entirety. Just as the universal being contains in itself all forms and lower

---

50. At this point, the French editor notes that the text is broken off and several words are missing. The Russian editor, however, assumes that the pages were wrongly bound in the manuscript and fills in with several paragraphs from earlier in the French version. I follow the latter assumption.

beings in a single whole, and it is in this that its universality as well as its individuality consist, I am telling you now simply that the universal doctrine contains in itself, in a perfect whole, all the ancient and modern doctrines, and it is in this that its universality and its individuality consist. Recall that the distinctive character of absolute truth lies in the fact that it excludes nothing and can exclude nothing, because otherwise it would not be absolute and universal. It would be partial, limited; it would no longer be the truth. I thus warn you once and for all that in my doctrine you will find idealism and realism, materialism and spiritualism, monism and dualism, pantheism, monotheism, polytheism, atheism, and everything else including skepticism. And each new element that you discover in this doctrine will be a new proof of its absolute truth.

In margin, in Russian: *Gradovskii—Bestuzhev-Riumin—Grot—Titov—Barsukov—Bezobrazov* [51]

Do you still believe that the truth has a proper name? It has all names, which is to say that it has no single one. And the same is true for error, which is to say that everything can be an error and can be the truth, according to whether it affirms itself exclusively or affirms itself as a member of the whole. However, since something must first affirm itself as such within its own being in order to affirm itself as a member of the whole, it is clear that error is indispensable for truth. But this consideration leads us away from our current topic, and, besides, can make unaccustomed minds spin. Let us thus return to our process. I indicated to you its general character and its result: concrete and universal Mind. As for different determined phases of the process, or special forms of the ideal world and their mutual relationship, that belongs to a special philosophical science, for which the term dialectic fits the best, for the principle of this ideal development is the unity of opposites, which (for Plato as well as for Hegel) is the principle of dialectic. Perhaps the new development of this science will one day become the object of one of your special works.[52] As for the present, let us leave the ideal world and pass on to another sphere of being.

51. Most likely, this list of names has nothing to do with the theme of the dialogue. The marginal notes probably refer to A. D. Gradovskii (1841–89), publicist and historian of governmental law; K. N. Bestuzhev-Riumin (1829–97), historian and director of the Higher Women's Courses in Saint Petersburg beginning in 1872; Ia K. Grot (1812–93), philologist; V. P. Titov (1807–91), member of the State Council and in his youth a member of the Moscow circle of Wisdom-Lovers, as well as collaborator in *The Moscow Herald* (*Moskovskii vestnik*) and *Northern Flowers* (Severnye *tsvety*); N. P. Barsukov (1838–1906), historian and bibliographer, in the 1870s the assistant to the director of the archives of the Holy Synod (or possibly one of his brothers is meant here—I. P. or A. P. Barsukov); V. P. Bezobrazov (1828–89), academician. See *PSS* 2:342.

52. Solovyov here has Sophia suggest material for his later work. In this way, she acts as a kind of intellectualized muse and, by analogy, we should not be surprised to see her inspire some of his best lyric poetry. The wisdom she teaches is both discursive and poetic.

In the sphere of the Mind, the antidivine principle appears as an idea of not-I, or of the foreign being. But the antidivine principle by its general nature cannot be limited to the ideal sphere; it appears in its proper nature as the principle of the real not-I, as desire or the striving toward external being, as appetite or concupiscence. We saw that the essence of the absolute principle is concrete unity; and if, in relation to ideal duality and multiplicity, this concrete unity appears as Mind, in relation to real duality and multiplicity this unity also appears as the principle of reality or force, as Will. In the ideal sphere, God thinks or represents His essential unity ideally or objectively; in the sphere of reality, He desires it, and insofar as Will is already action in the absolute principle, the only action possible—because all action separated from Will presupposes something external and independent, that which exists only in the produced and relative world and not in the principles—it realizes or produces that unity. It is clear that the antidivine principle in its real appearance is already determined by the ideas that serve it as forms; the real form is the body, that is to say existence for the sake of sensation. The principle of Matter

In margin: *blind desire* [53]

possesses the ideas and gives them a corporeal existence. It separates them from each other. But divine Will, following the unity of the Mind, reunites them in reality. That real unity is called the Soul. It is clear that the progress of this real or animated process is the same (only in a different sphere) as the progress of the ideal process. The degrees and relations are the same, with the exception that everything in the first process is ideal and objective, while in the second it is real and subjective. The result is thus also the production of a being that reunites the highest universality with the highest degree of individuality: the production of the concrete Soul, of the World Soul.[54]

In margin: *Mind and Soul are, by all indications, coeternal, and are not a temporal product of the process, for the process itself is not temporal. Mind acts directly on the objective images that present themselves to it, incorporating them into its unity. But the Soul, which by its very essence is the desire for unity, Love, must use <blind desire?>, in order to produce real unity.*

The Soul receives the ideas of the Mind and, in using them as forms, unites the material elements into a single organism, in which it is the Soul. There are as many particular souls as there are ideas, but all of these souls are only parts and elements of the World Soul. In other words, they are objective and

---

53. Kozyrev interpolates these words here in the text, as well in the next marginal note.

54. Here is Solovyov's first mention of the World Soul, which he designates in French as "Ame universelle," or universal Soul, with "universal" parallel to other instances of universal religion, universal Mind, etc. Kozyrev chooses to translate the term as "mirovaia dusha," or World Soul, a term that Solovyov uses throughout his writings about Sophia. I use that translation here, recognizing that the World Soul is parallel to the universal Mind, etc.

material in relation to the World Soul—they form the body of the Soul[55]—while the bodily elements strictly speaking, that is the direct products of the material principle, form the external or material body of the great organism.

In margin: *In the ideal world, the external principle, material or objective, is the analytic element; the internal principle, spiritual or subject, is the synthetic element. In the world of the soul, desire for real multiplicity, isolation, corresponds to the former; the desire for unity, love, corresponds to the latter.*

Mind is Spirit entered into the ideal process; Soul is Spirit entered into the real process. Mind is the first complete appearance of the absolute first principle (as the principle of ideal unity); Soul is its second complete appearance (as the principle of real unity). But we saw that the absolute principle does not lose itself when it becomes manifest; it remains in and of itself, always separated from its manifestations. Thus, we have three divine hypostases: Spirit, Mind, and Soul. Just as a particular idea corresponds to each separate soul, so, too, a particular spirit corresponds to each idea and soul, because, for each ideal and real distinction, for each ideal and real manifestation, the principle returns to itself as unity or pure spirit; therefore, there are as many separate unities and pure spirits as there are united ideas and souls.

In margin: *N.B. The Mind receives its reality from the Soul, as the Soul receives its form or its ideality from the Mind.*

Just as separate souls correspond to separate ideas and souls, so, too, the universal Spirit or concrete Spirit corresponds to the universal Mind and Soul. Thus, each of these hypostases is the principle of a special world: Spirit of the world of pure spirits; Mind of the world of intelligences or ideas; and, finally, Soul of the world of souls. Instead of world, it would be better to say organism, since this term better expresses the distinct unity of the spheres. The particular spirits are only members or integral parts of the universal Spirit that could not exist without it, just as it could not exist without them. In the same way, ideas are simply necessary members of the universal Mind, which would be impossible without them as they would be impossible without it. The same is true for the particular souls and the World Soul. You understood the great law, by which universality develops in direct relationship to individuality, such that universal Spirit, Mind, and Soul are individual beings to the highest degree, individuals or hypostases κατεξοχήν [Greek: par excellence]. But now you can further see where this law originates; it necessarily flows from the great fundamental axiom by which a manifestation does not diminish or exhaust the principle that it manifests,

---

55. Solovyov uses "corps animique," which Kozyrev translates as "dushevnoe telo." There is no adequate direct English translation.

but rather develops or affirms it to the highest degree. Thus, in manifesting itself in the world of spirits, Spirit does not lose its independence, that which makes it, so to speak, itself. On the contrary, Spirit develops and distinctly affirms its independence, thus becoming concrete Spirit, Spirit that is absolutely individual and universal. The same applies to Mind and Soul.

Spirit, Mind, and Soul, being principles of distinct spheres, are nevertheless intimately bound, with Mind being merely the manifestation of Spirit in relation to ideal or objective multiplicity, and Soul being merely its manifestation in relation to real or subjective multiplicity. And, on the other hand, Spirit *in its concreteness* is merely the product of its manifestation in Mind and Soul. Thus, each of the three hypostases is absolutely indispensable for the existence of the others, such that they form but a single being or a single substance that is already necessary for their communal origin. Thus, we have a single substance, or, better, a single being (οὐσία) in three individuals or hypostases.[56] And just as the principles of the three worlds are united, so too are the worlds united, such that all the plenitude of being in the three spheres and all the degrees of the hierarchy form but a single being, a single organism, with one Spirit, one Mind, one Soul, and one Body.

Philosopher: But this organism, being individual and determined in all its positions, cannot be an organism in general—that which remains merely an abstraction of our reason. It must be a specific organism, that is to say, it must have a form unique to it.

Sophie: And what other organic form can conform to the absolute being, what organic form reunites universality and individuality with such perfection, if not the human form?

In margin: *The unity of principles corresponds to the unity of their function. The function of Soul is love; the function of Mind is thought; the function or state of Spirit is blessedness (freedom, peace). The related nature of these states is obvious. One thinks in order to be happy and one is happy when loving and thinking. In general, love is the beginning or the cause, thinking is the middle or mean, and blessedness or peace is the end or the goal. In addition, blessedness alone reunites a free spirit, an ideal mind, a loving soul, and a material body.*

Thus we must say that the absolute being in its concrete manifestation is *a great Man, the absolutely universal Man*, who, at the same time, is *the*

56. Solovyov's insertion of the Greek for "essence" (ousia) to clarify the Latin for "substance" is not accidental, as he is here emphasizing multiplicity. As Timothy Ware has written, "[I]n the early Patristic period, there is a general tendency for the Latin west to start from the unity of the divine essence and to work from that to the threeness of the persons, whereas there is a general tendency for the Greek east to argue in the opposite direction, from the threeness of the persons to the oneness of the essence" (217).

absolutely individual Man. Since the three hypostases are perfectly individual, this great Man contains within himself three men: spiritual man, intellectual or rational man, and man of the soul *[l'homme animique]*. The normal gender of the man of the soul is feminine. Intellectual man, who is spouse of the soul, is masculine. Spirit is above all difference.

"Second Dialogue:[57] *The Cosmic and Historical Process"*

[*Sophie*] *Philosopher*:[58] You have revealed inner nature to me, as well as the mutual relationship between the three worlds.[59] I have recognized them in their differences and in their perfect unity. I have also recognized that the three divine worlds contain the principles of our world, of the world in which I live, through which I move and exist. Nevertheless, it is clear to me that this latter world is not entirely contained in the three former ones, that it distinguishes itself from them and in this way forms a fourth. Their essential character is even opposite to ours. In the former three, unity and divine spirituality dominate; they are nothing other than the realization of that unity and spirituality. Multiplicity and materiality in them are only the organ, the means for that divine unity; love and peace reign. It is the exact opposite in our world; multiplicity, division, hatred, and gross materiality always have primary place here, and spiritual unity seems to be only an accidental product. Where does this new world come from?

Sophie: This is not a new world. This is simply the third world, the world of souls and bodies (for we have seen that the soul is inseparable from the body) in its state of separation from the two others, for it is directly tied to the intelligible or ideal in its separation from it.

Philosopher: So tell me, what is the principle, the beginning[60] and the end of this separation?

In margin (in brackets in original): *[the material principle (causa materialis, ὕλη ὑποκείμενον) of the fourth world or of the separated state of the worlds, of the extradivine state, is the Soul and souls. The formal principle is the Demiurge. The efficient or active principle is Satan, the cosmic Spirit. The final principle—God.*

---

57. Solovyov indicates that this section was written in Sorrento, Italy, in March 1876. His title here is not consistent with previous sections, since there has already been a "Second Dialogue" in the "First Triad"—"The Absolute Principle as Duality (The Principle of Dualism)." One might expect this section to be the "Second Triad," but it is not and would not follow logically from the "First Triad," called "First Principles." See the "Plans and Rough Drafts" in *PSS* 2:162–81 for further but by no means definitive indications of Solovyov's intentions. Kozyrev points to similarities between this section and the ninth and tenth parts of *Lectures*, as well as the later French text *La Russie et L'église universelle* (1887–89). See *PSS* 2:342–43.

58. "Sophie" is crossed out and overwritten by "Philosopher."

59. Following on the previous section, Solovyov must mean the "worlds" of Spirit, Mind, and Soul.

60. Solovyov uses the French word *principe*, perhaps conflating two meanings of *nachalo*: beginning and principle.

Sophie: Since the three divine worlds are a single organism, the relationship between them together is maintained when they are separated. But . . . I am delighted that you have <reached> me.[61]

Since the antidivine power that serves as matter in the three worlds is eternal, it cannot be destroyed. But it exists directly only for the Soul. Because the matter of Spirit is Mind, and the matter of Mind is Soul, the matter of Soul in the end is matter in the proper meaning of the term. Thus Soul possesses in itself the possibility of being, the antidivine possibility. Thus, it is placed between two possibilities: the divine possibility, represented for it by Mind and the ideal world, the possibility that governs the Soul; and the antidivine possibility that is governed by Soul.

In margin (brackets in original): [*The material principle of the cosmic process is secondary matter, the principle moving cause or agent*—αρχή τῆς κινήσεως {Greek: the first principle of movement}—*Satan; the formal principle is the Demiurge, the final principle*—*Sophie.*]

Enumeration of the primary and secondary principles:

1. *The Absolute.*
[2. *Freedom and power.*]
2. *Free spirit and primary matter*
3. *Spirit, Mind, Soul.*
4. *C<oncrete> Spirit, Concr<ete> Mind, Soul, body.*
[4]5. *Satan, Demiurge, secondary matter, incarnated humanity.*
5. *Sophie and Christ*
[5. *Mary and Christ*]
[6. *Holy Spirit*]
6. *Sophie and Holy Spirit*
7. *God,* ἕν καί πᾶν [Greek: one and all][62]

The Soul can assert itself against the divine possibility by arousing the demonic power within itself. However, the Soul loses the power that it possesses over this force insofar as it is determined by the ideal world as soon as

61. These words by Sophie are written in automatic writing, with the last sentence in Russian and crossed out in the original. The word "reached" is incomplete and surmised by Kozyrev.
62. If this marginal marking is a type of outline for the dialogues, we find ourselves now at [4]5. Solovyov has explained the meaning of the Absolute (1), the relationship of Spirit and Matter (2), and the interrelationship of Spirit, Mind, and Soul (3). He has just told us that "as above, so below," so that the absolute world of Spirit, Mind, and Soul corresponds to the concrete world of spirit, mind, and soul. He is about to explain the world as we know it as a cosmic battle of Satan and the Demiurge that directly affects humanity incarnate. This outline then seems to move back up in levels of abstraction, ending where it had begun, with God as "one and all." The following dialogue does not follow the second half of the scheme.

it separates itself from that world. We saw that the Soul possesses natural or external Mind in potential, the analytic or negative power of reality. As long as external reality in its principle remains in a state of possibility, natural Mind, which is the negative pole of reality, also remains in this state. But as soon as blind force rouses itself and passes from a potential to an actual state, then natural Mind necessarily undergoes the same transformation. It becomes actual, it receives being for itself, it becomes personal. External Mind as an individual or person is called the Demiurge, for it is the formal or formative principle of external nature. The principle of external reality in its existence for itself, in its personal existence, is called Satan or Cosmic Spirit.[63] The Soul, whose task is to govern natural Mind by subordinating it to Divine Mind (to Logos) and to govern Cosmic Spirit by subordinating it to Divine Spirit, the Soul, whose nature is unity, now finds itself deprived of its task in a state counter to nature. It is divided between the blind power of Cosmic Spirit and the intelligent but negative and external power of the Demiurge. Neither obeys it any longer, engaging instead in mortal combat within its domains. The Soul thus finds itself in a kind of suspended state, in a state of supreme suffering, of living death.

Philosopher: But tell me then why the Soul was put in such a state of suffering?

Sophie: In finding itself the mistress over the magical possibility of being, the Soul wanted to use that possibility for itself. It wanted to be for itself, to create and govern its world like the Divine Spirit and, in becoming equal to that Spirit, to unite itself with it and to know it directly. The Soul found itself doubly bound by the ideal world, which gave it the absolute in image alone, and which, on the other hand, gave it obligatory rules and norms, necessary to govern the finite world. It wants to rid itself of this double bond, it wants to be for itself, and arouses in itself the spontaneous possibility of being and of action (which is will). But the Soul, being only a secondary unity, a unity that is brought into being, possesses this possibility only insofar as it is subordinate to the Spirit and to Divine Mind, insofar as it is their organ. It has power only insofar as it, itself, is in a state of possibility, and insofar as it does not assert itself, but serves as the transparent means for divine power and thoughts. As soon as it departs from that state, as soon as it affirms itself, it becomes impenetrable to divine action, it loses all its power and, instead of possessing, it, itself, is possessed.

---

63. Solovyov calls Satan alternately the Spirit of Cosmos and the Spirit of Chaos. For Solovyov, chaos always lies behind cosmos and eternally opposes it. Kozyrev points to an explanation in a late work about Tiutchev's poetry, "Poeziia F.I. Tiutcheva" (1895): "Chaos, that is, negative infinity, the yawning abyss of all insanity and ugliness, demonic gusts, rising against all positive and proper, this is the deepest essence of the World Soul and the basis of the whole Universe. The cosmic process leads that chaotic element into the boundaries of common order, subjects it to reasonable laws, gradually incarnating the ideal content of being into it, giving sense and beauty to this wild life. However, even when led into the bounds of common order, chaos makes itself known by rebellious movements and gusts" (*SS* 7:126–27).

Philosopher: I see great moral portent in that transcendental event, in that fall of the Soul.[64] Every separate being has possibility and happiness only in self-negation, in the passive or potential state. It cannot give itself that which it does not have; being separate, it cannot give itself by itself, cannot create an absolute being for itself. In affirming itself, it affirms only its separate and bounded being. But to be separate means to be determined by another, and to be determined by another means to suffer. When it affirms itself, it excludes, it negates all that is other, but it cannot destroy the other, for it is determined by it. It wants to be absolute, but is determined. This determination is the opposite of its will and is an external necessity; it is suffering. But, when the separate being renounces itself and submits itself as a member of the whole, it loses its separate and exclusive being. It enjoys the life of the whole, and its determination as a member of the whole, being in accord with its will, is not an external necessity for it. It is free; it does not suffer. Freedom and happiness for the separate being consists in its voluntary submission to the universal being.

[*Sophie*: . . .][65]

Submission to the universal Being is the primitive or natural state of the Soul; as such it is not voluntary, it is not free. For that, submission and self-negation must be produced by the Soul itself; it must submit itself to the universal Being. In order to submit itself, however, it must raise itself up. Produced or free affirmation is the result of the negation of negation. In order to resign oneself to the exclusive antidivine existence, one must recognize it and, since one can know an existence only empirically, one must submit to it.

The Soul possesses the possibility of being within itself. This possibility is will, will that is not yet desire, will as possibility and not as action. The Soul, not wanting being, not affirming it (always being separate and exclusive), possesses it in possibility. When it does not affirm being, it is still free to affirm it or not affirm it; however, once it has decided and does affirm it, the Soul is no longer the master of being. It cannot affirm being and not affirm it at the same time. That is to say, it does not lose this possibility absolutely, which would contradict the great principle, but it loses it in actuality.

In margin: NB: *in the principal beings—God, Soul, etc.—active will, that is desire, is already action.*

It can still *not* affirm being, but not in its actual state, since in that state it already affirms it. Here begins the fatal separation of the potential and actual

64. Solovyov seems to take his narrative of the fall of the Soul directly from Gnosticism.
65. At this point, Solovyov abandons the dialogue form. The name "Sophie" is written in the margin and might indicate the beginning of the reply, or it might refer to the term "universal being" at the end of the Philosopher's statement. There is no paragraph break. As Kozyrev points out, the remainder of the section, beginning after this paragraph, is written in different-color ink, suggesting that Solovyov returned to it at a later time, having by then abandoned the idea of a dialogue.

state. In its normal state, the Soul was pure possibility—it was possibility in actuality—it did not have two separate states. Now it has them, it is divided in itself; it maintains its unity and its power over being only potentially. In actuality, it is divided and enslaved.

The affirmation of the Soul is the affirmation of a separate being, it is the exclusive affirmation of each of the elements of the grand Being;[66] it is their mutual negation, it is their egoism. It is clear that egoism comes before hatred and struggle and leads them behind it. Thus, it is a fight to the death between all the elements, instead of their unity and mutual love. It is the *bellum omnium contra omnes* [Latin: war of all against all]; it is chaos.

The Soul is a principle of unity and love insofar as it is passive and submits to the ideal and spiritual world. But in rising up against them and in separating itself out, in becoming egotistical, it becomes the principle of separate and exclusive being, of division, of hatred and struggle. In actuality as well as in possibility (*in potentia*), it preserves its divine origin.

The Soul as a principle of division, of egoism, of hatred and struggle, in a word, as principle (or prince) of this world, or of this age, is Satan, the devil. The Soul is Satan—here is Wisdom. It is the principle of cosmic existence and the principle of our own partial and egotistical existence; it is our actual soul:

Nos habitat non tartara sed nec sidera coeli
Spiritus in nobis qui viget illa fecit.
[Latin: It lives in us and not in Tartarus, not in distant constellations; Spirit, having power in us, created them.][67]

The Soul—*anima*—is passive, feminine by nature, and thus it remains in its normal state; in becoming active, that is to say, masculine, it is no longer Soul.[68] It becomes Spirit-*spiritus*, but a spirit of shadows, of evil. In general, the Spirit is the principle of true, that is to say, universal unity; as a principle of totality, it is the Divine Spirit; as a principle of false, exclusive unity, or of egoism, it is the Satanic Spirit, the Spirit of Evil.

[The Soul, in becoming Cosmic Spirit, does not cease to be Soul, but is Soul in possibility only. Possibility is an equivocal term (it signifies simple possibility, as, for example, I have the possibility to become an angel or god;

---

66. See Solovyov's discussion of Comte's "grand Être," page 218.

67. Solovyov does not cite the author of these Latin verses. He first used them in the monological section of *The Sophia* titled "About the Three Phases of the Absolute Principle" and later used them in the eighth section of *Lectures* (see page 184). Kozyrev believes Solovyov took them from Schopenhauer, who also does not cite the author in his *World as Will and Representation*, among other places. The verses originate with the Renaissance esoteric philosopher Agrippa (*PSS* 2:331–33).

68. Solovyov is inconsistent in his association of the feminine with passivity. See Clowes, "The Limits of Discourse" for an analysis of the female as passive in "The Meaning of Love."

In margin (in Russian, in pencil): *The transformation of Logos into Demiurge*[69]

or it signifies the direct power to do or become something): *Potentia potens* and *potentia impotens*. [Latin: active possibility and powerless possibility]. The Soul, in producing Cosmic Spirit, remains *potentia impotens*, suffering to the highest degree.

We saw that the Soul, in corresponding to and in opposition to the possibility of a real, external existence (will) that, in becoming actual, is the Cosmic Spirit, possesses the possibility of the knowledge of external things; it is the external Mind as a necessarily opposite pole. While external existence remains in the state of possibility and does not manifest itself, external Mind necessarily is also only possibility. As soon as external existence becomes actualized, however, the corresponding Mind is actualized as well, and we have external or Cosmic Mind opposed to Cosmic Spirit.] As Cosmic Spirit is the principle of Cosmic Matter, thus Cosmic Mind is the principle of form, of order and relationships, but of form, order, of the law of right and external relationships. [It is exactly in the same relationship to the second divine hypostasis as Cosmic Spirit is to the first.

Cosmic Mind is not passive: *mens agitat molem* [Latin: mind moves mass]. In order to give it a name that is blessed by Christian Gnosticism, I will call it the *Demiurge*.][70]

Satan and the Demiurge are not independent substances; they are two opposite actualities of the [Soul, which, as potential unity, remains their common substance. The Soul is the Demiurge as much as it is Satan, but it also is distinct from both of them. The best term to express the substantial identity and the actual division is *generation*. Thus we can say that Satan and the Demiurge are engendered by the Soul; they are its sons.][71]

Now, let us pass on from the sphere of principles to the sphere of elements.

In margin (in Russian, crossed out in pencil):

x Saturn—Satan
xx Jupiter—Demiurge
xxx Venus—Sophia
x Mars
xx Mercury

69. Having discussed the cosmological origins of Satan, Solovyov turns to the emergence of the Demiurge. The section here in square brackets is crossed out in pencil in the original, with this note in the margin. Solovyov must not have been satisfied with his initial introduction of the subject.

70. The bracketed section is crossed out in pencil in the original. Solovyov refers here to the Gnostics' identification of the Demiurge with the God of the Hebrew bible, who created the extradivine world.

71. The bracketed section is crossed out in pencil in the original, perhaps because it contradicts the earlier statement that Logos or Mind, rather than Soul, transforms into the Demiurge.

Sun (Apollo)
xxx Moon (Earth?)[72]

We saw that following the transcendent act of the Soul, each element affirms itself and excludes all others, each wants to be the unique center. This is the direct action of the Cosmic Spirit;[73] it is centripetal force or gravitation. As they gravitate toward a unique (common) center, each element tries to attract and absorb all the others; that is to say, all strive equally and mutually to absorb each other. This is the power of attraction and, if this tendency or this force were the only one, if the Satanic Spirit were the only cosmic principle, the elements would confound themselves in a single point.

In margin: *Satan is the principle of existence of a separate being within itself. The Demiurge is the principle of external existence for another being.*

But the Cosmic Mind—the principle of external order—impedes them. Each element necessarily perceives the others through it; out of necessity they exist for it and it cannot destroy them, for it is limited by them. In perceiving them, by virtue of its egoism, the Cosmic Mind repulses them and is repulsed by them.

Thus each one remains in itself and the others remain outside it; in this way, real, external, extended space is produced—produced by the Demiurge.

[By its nature, the Cosmic Spirit strives for a unique existence, for real unity, [independent of the higher spheres]. It strives to be the unique center of the world. But the material of its existence, the multiplicity of elements that obey the Demiurge, oppose this tendency and divide being. Thus, Satan cannot attain unity directly, but only as a consequence of fighting with the Demiurge. The consequence of this is time. Thus, in fighting against the Demiurge, the Cosmic Spirit produces time, just as the Demiurge, in fighting against the Cosmic Spirit, produces space.

Space and time are correlative (that is to say, they are defined by the other, mutually presupposing each other). This means that there is nothing absolute in them; they are purely relative. Space is the simultaneous existence of many beings, it is order, repose (στάσις) [Greek: stasis], a static principle; time is the existence of many states in a single being, succession, it is change, movement, the violation of order, change.

In margin (in Russian, in pencil): *Lacera<tion> and ruin is the ac<tual> sta<te>. Inter<nal> unity does not exi<st> act<ually>, it must be sei<zed>, attain<ed>, it must, and can only produce itself through the battle of the Demiurge with the*

---

72. A system of seven planets corresponding to seven archangels can be found in diverse sources from Babylonian astrology to the angelology of the Talmud and Jewish apocrypha. In Gnosticism, the soul crosses seven spheres after death before it unites with its divine counterpart.

73. As before, Solovyov calls Satan the Spirit of Cosmos as well as the Spirit of Chaos.

spirit of Chaos, and through the constant subordination of the latter to the cosm\<ic\> process. The form of this process is time.

The battle of Satan and the Demiurge is the cosmic process; it is cosmogony. The Demiurge strives to reduce Satan to a passive state, without knowing that it thus reduces itself to a passive state, since the two principles are correlative. But the reduction of Satan and the Demiurge to a passive state is the realized Soul.

In margin (crossed out in pencil): NB: *Space and time are products of the Soul; it limits Satan with the former, and the Demiurge with the latter.*

Thus, if Satan is the effective principle of the cosmic process, and the Demiurge is its formal principle, then the realized Soul, which is to say God, is the final or determining principle in it, so that the Soul in its divided and suffering state is the matter or the substratum of the process.]

In margin (in Russian, in pencil): *In the actual cond\<ition\> of the world, spa\<ce\> is the condition of its external unity, and time, its internal. The integral organism of divine humanity* (bogochelovechestvo), *lacerated by the fall into sin, must be restored in time.*[74]

Satan exerts its power equally in all the elements (atoms, monads), but in all the elements it also submits its action to the Demiurge; in order to escape from this action, it concentrates its powers, which is to say it withdraws its action from one portion of the monads in order to render it stronger in another portion.

In margin (in ink):[75]

Dem\<iurge\>

Soul

S\<atan\>

Two poles of creation

The monads in which Satan dominates, that is to say monads where appetite, gravitation, weight, and inertia dominate and that exist only for themselves, these are the monads that constitute matter per se. It is Satan that has concentrated or *condensed* there, in submitting to the action of the Demiurge. It is Satan materialized. The monads in which the Demiurge dominates, that is to say perception, centripetal force, and repulsion, comprise what is called ether or imponderable fluid, the particular forms of which are heat and light, magnetism

---

74. Solovyov's use of the term *bogochelovechestvo* points directly toward the lectures he will deliver only a year or two hence. The integral relationship of humanity and divinity is essential and will be restored. This note to himself also reminds Solovyov to move his argument forward from cosmic to historical time.

75. This diagram shows the dynamic battle between Satan and the Demiurge, with the Soul produced between them as the two opposite but correlated poles reduce each other to passivity.

and electricity.[76] These phenomena represent modifications of ether in its re-lationship with matter; the modifications produced by ether in matter itself are mechanical movement, sound, and chemical compounds. All these phenomena, being the products of a single physical agent, or the modifications of a single physical being, ether, can mutually transform themselves; this is the great truth developed by the scientific theory of the unity of physical forces.[77]

In margin: *NB—The cosmic Spirit has two aspects: considered in itself, it is the principle of immobility, of uniformity, of inertia (*Starrheit*); in relationship to its enemy and to the order that is established by it, it is the principle of destruction, of change, of movement; it is Saturn that devours its children. In the same way, the Demiurge, considered in itself, is the principle of order and thus of stability; but, in the sphere of its enemy, it is clearly the principle of change, of movement. Our world has two different sides for us. From one side, the formal side, it is cosmos, order, the rule of law, of the Demiurge; from the other side, the material side, it is the rule of blind forces, chaos, the empire of Satan, and it is clear that cosmos supposes chaos, that the latter is the substratum, the material of cosmos.*

Sparseness and lightness are the characteristic traits of ether, just as density and weight are those of matter. From this it is clear that it is ether that can and must penetrate matter, occupying a greater volume, and surrounding it. Thus the visible world in its origin presents a solid nucleus of matter, surrounded and penetrated by a delicate atmosphere of ether. The center is comprised of a cold and shadowy cosmic fire: *domus Saturni* [Latin: the realm of Saturn].

Divide et impera [Latin: Divide and conquer]. The Demiurge, with its ethereal army, penetrates throughout the nucleus of the Cosmic Spirit and divides it into a multitude of spheres.

[In margin:]

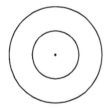

The blind enemy is expelled from the center, is broken into pieces, and a multitude of cosmic bodies or stars are produced. The ether produces a luminescent atmosphere around each star; these are so many suns.

The Soul is the principle of real unity. Each time such a unity is produced, each time a multiplicity of elementary

---

76. Solovyov's insistence in the following pages on the reality of ether must be understood in the context of his time. Although physicists undertook experiments in the latter half of the nineteenth century that seemed to deny the age-old existence of ether, it was not until Einstein in the twentieth century that most agreed that the element was unobservable and thus nonexistent. Nonetheless, contemporary physics' description of an active vacuum field is not so far from the ancient's notion of ether.

77. This theory has been propounded in some form since Aristotle but for Solovyov was probably most clearly formulated in the natural philosophy, or *Naturphilosophie*, of Friedrich Schelling. The assertion of the unity of physical forces supports the principle of the conservation of energy that lies behind much of modern physics.

beings is reunited in a single being, the Soul is realized in a relative way, and we have a partial or produced soul. It is clear also that unity can only be internal and real when the principle of unity is not a secondary product, the arithmetic sum of elements, but is independent and primordial. Thus we must accept that these partial souls, existing for all eternity in the World Soul as its members, and reduced to the state of powerless possibility within it, will, when the occasion presents itself, seize control of the elements, and become their Soul. The less true the unity—and we have seen that, for true unity, a multiplicity of different and separate elements must mutually penetrate—the less the soul is realized and free. The more it is potential, the more it submits to the cosmic principles. The first level is the union of Satan and the Demiurge, of matter and ether; we have a world in which the Soul is its unity and in which opposite poles are represented by these two elements.

In margin (in pencil): *Zoroastre* [followed by other markings similar to So-lovyov's automatic writing]

But they are only two, their composition is perfectly uniform and they pene-trate each other only superficially: the Soul here is almost nothing. The sec-ond level is the stars, but here also the composition is perfectly monotonous and the atoms are united only mechanically. The Soul here is still totally sub-ordinate to the Cosmic Spirit, and for this reason the astral souls as a whole are called astral spirits or demons.

After having divided the great cosmic nucleus, the Demiurge wants to di-vide the partial nuclei or the suns that it surrounds with its ethereal atmo-sphere. But this is more difficult for it, because the small volume of the partial nuclei causes the cosmic force to be more powerful, and they are denser and more resistant. Thus, in order to succeed, the Demiurge directs all its efforts toward a single point, toward the sun alone; it well knows that triumph over this single point will assure victory, just as a single breach is sufficient in or-der to take a fortress.

In margin (in Russian): *Bol'shaia Dvorianskaia, dom 4, Safonov Moiseev.*[78]

The star at which the Demiurge directs its efforts is our sun. The Demiurge surrounds it with a thick ethereal atmosphere and tries to penetrate into its center. [It succeeded after a tense battle . . .]

For its part, the Cosmic Spirit uses all its efforts to escape the embrace of the enemy and to break up the ethereal atmosphere. The struggle would last indefinitely if the Demiurge didn't employ a ruse. At the moment that the enemy exerts all its forces against the ethereal atmosphere, the Demiurge suddenly cedes several points, and at once a mass of material atoms, finding

78. Most likely Solovyov jotted down this information on the only paper he had available, and this address is unrelated to the text. The addressee is unidentified.

no resistance, escape from the sun. They would have been disseminated throughout space, followed by the ethereal fluids, had the power of attraction not caught up to them and arrested them in their orbit. Thus, the planetary bodies of our solar system were formed. Sunspots are the remains of gaps through which the planets escaped.[79] The sun, thus weakened, could no longer resist the Demiurge, and became its seat of power; it does not have a distinctly material nucleus, but is completely penetrated by ether. One of the planets, earth, because of conditions that cannot be examined here, became the most differentiated, that is to say, the most organic, and because of that the most able to receive the action of the Soul and to become its astral seat.

{Among the seven largest planets (since a large role is not played by Uranus and Neptune in the system, due to their distance from the sun and their isolation, or by asteroids, due to their small size), Saturn is the least <susceptible> to the action of the Demiurge; it is the planet of the Chaotic Spirit.}[80]

The varied and complicated conditions of chaotic and cosmic forces over the earth render it capable of becoming the seat of organic development. As soon as the possibility presents itself, the World Soul, localized on the earth, makes itself master and produces a living soul, that is to say an organism in the true sense of the word. But the conditions of the change can become still more favorable, and thus the Soul abandons old types and creates new ones: this is the cause of different paleontological creations. However, when an old type can develop without being destroyed, then the Soul profits by it and develops it using all natural means. Since it can create nothing from nothing, it can only use the matter given it by the elementary or Chaotic Spirit, and the form given it by the Demiurge in order to place into it an internal and organic unity, a soul. [We have said that all these souls are preexistent. Thus, there could have been only one creation of souls. Consequently, the paleontological creations that became extinct did not have special souls (for what would have become of them?), but were animated by the same souls that animate today's creation; only when earthly conditions became more favorable for more perfect organisms did the souls leave the old types and pass into the new ones.][81]

[It is necessary to distinguish the different steps on the cosmogonic ladder that exist as the seat of souls in different stages, as well as the different types

79. Solovyov's description of the emergence of the planets and his definition of sunspots would certainly be dismissed by astronomers today, but his ideas were no more fantastic than many others of his own day.

80. Text inside wavy brackets is marked by a wavy line in the margin of the manuscript.

81. It is not absolutely clear why this and the following paragraphs are crossed out in the text (indicated here by square brackets), although it is obvious that they contradict the newly popular theories of Darwin to which Solovyov refers below. Solovyov shows a strong knowledge of and intellectual sympathy for Darwinism in later works, especially "Beauty in Nature."

of earthly creation which were only rough drafts or temporary dwellings for the souls.[82] For example, the zoological step represented by fish exists because there are souls whose character is best expressed by the organism of the fish. But fish of a certain previous geological period were only temporary dwellings for the ichthyomorphic souls that animate today's fish. Perhaps today's geological period is not the final one, and we will have fish that are still more perfect. In any case we will always have fish.]

One of the principal means by which organisms develop, which is to say become capable of being the seat of the most elevated souls, is the natural selection of producers in the battle for existence (for battle, one mustn't forget, is the universal cosmic law). Thus we concede Darwin's theory within certain legitimate limits. We have no reason, however, to concede that this is the only means, and that the organic world follows an uninterrupted development, departing from a single source, having a single root. Nature, that is to say the World Soul,[83] is not obligated to follow a direct line, when it could disperse life in various different directions. It created where it could; it gives out its soul, gives itself out to whatever is capable of receiving it. Furthermore, one mustn't forget, it is chaos that is at the base of creation; order and law are only on the surface.

Finally, the cosmic process (which is now Telluric)[84] arrives at the production of the perfect organism, of the human organism. But the perfect organic union is impossible because of the duality of the producers, because of the external materiality of creation. The human organism appears double: masculine and feminine. The signature of the Demiurge is still very apparent in the masculine organism; it is relatively free of the feminine. The plenitude of human nature must appear, in this material world and according to the laws of space and time, in a multitude of beings that, despite their common substance and origin, posit themselves as separate and independent. Nothing becomes apparent or manifest without positing itself, affirming itself as such, and the affirmation of self in a partial being is the negation of the other. It is hatred and mortal war. Thus, the cosmic battle must repeat itself in the human world.

The goal of the cosmic process is the realization of the soul and of God in the soul. This is to say, the goal of the cosmic process is the production of the most perfect unity in the most perfect multiplicity, or of a perfectly integrated being that at the same time has the highest degree of differentiation: the production of a perfect organism. Man is such an organism. But an individual human is not Man: Man is Humanity. The human organism is not the organism of an individual man, which is only the perfection of the animal

---

82. Kozyrev notes that the following statement about the immortality of fish souls contradicts a later one asserting that only human souls are immortal (*PSS* 2:345–46). Perhaps this in part explains the crossing out.

83. Here the World Soul is equated with created nature rather than Divine Wisdom.

84. The Telluric Period in Solovyov's cosmogony refers to the creation of the earth.

organism; the truly human organism is the social organism. Thus, the universal goal is the production of the perfect social organism. The parts of this organism must be at the highest degree of differentiation; for this they must be at the very start posited exclusively, absolutely. For that, they must mutually exclude each other, but only as a process by which they become a unity, an interior unity, free, voluntary, with a conscience. And they cannot affirm (desire) unity consciously without knowing their opposite in a real way, that is to say, without having submitted to this opposite, without having passed through it. Thus, at the beginning, there is battle and chaos. In affirming himself exclusively, man is under the action of Satan. Satan looks to dominate the greatest number of men, and by that to create an apparent unity. The egoistic will is the place of Satan in man; reason and justice are the place of the Demiurge.

The first God that humanity adores is the Cosmic Spirit, the chaotic will that is the base of the universe. Man and the universe[85] are under its domination, but that domination in man is at the same time disputed by the Demiurge. Mythology is created by this battle of the Demiurge and the Chaotic Spirit within human consciousness. Since the human soul is substantially the same as the universal World Soul, human consciousness is only the ideal repetition of cosmic reality. Thus the mythological process in general follows the progress of the cosmic process. And since one can distinguish three periods in the cosmic process—the Uranic or astral period, the solar period, and the Telluric or organic period—one can distinguish the same three periods in the mythological process. Since in the cosmic process the battle of the Demiurge against the Chaotic Spirit ends with the Soul's dominance, in its third stage the mythological process similarly passes into the deliverance of the human soul, of consciousness. The Cosmic Spirit and the Demiurge do not completely lose their power, but this power is no longer blind; it is subordinated to consciousness.

The mythological process ends and the historical process properly speaking begins. The agents of this process are three peoples: the Hindus, the Greeks (later replaced by the Romans) and the Jews. For the Hindus, the Soul, scarcely delivered from the domination of the cosmic powers, is drunk on its freedom and on the consciousness of its unity with the Divine. It dreams, and in its dreams all of the superior creations of humanity are found in rudimentary form: philosophy, poetry, magic. But all of this is in a vague form, barely distinct, as it must be in a dream; everything is mixed together and confounded; everything is one and everything is nothing. Buddhism had the last word in Indian consciousness: everything that is and everything that is not are equally an illusion, a dream. This is the category of substance, of the first unity or indifferentiation, it is the Soul-in-itself, for the Soul-in-itself is nothing.

---

85. The original simply has "They." Kozyrev interpolates "Man and the universe."

For the Greeks and the Romans, the Soul is not only delivered from the cosmic powers, it begins to deliver itself from itself, and by this begins to receive the influences of its divine spouse, the eternal Logos: beauty and reason, art and philosophy. Moral order for the Romans. But the inspirations of Logos were corrupted for the Greeks, and then even more for the Romans, by its ape—the Demiurge. This is the reason that Greek philosophy came to an end, first in Sophism and then in Skepticism, and that Greek art too often represents the superficial contours of corporeal beauty, rather than internal beauty, the beauty of expression.[86] This is also the reason that the Roman's moral order produced only an external order based on violence. And furthermore, in addition, the Greeks and Romans conceived of the Logos merely ideally, as an idea; but the Soul is more than an idea, and whatever is conceived of as only an idea in the end becomes powerless. An idea is nothing without a person who carries it. The Soul is a person, an *ego*; a strong personality without any idea is still something.[87]

The Greeks and Romans were so penetrated by their respective ideas that nothing remained for them when they lost those ideas. Personhood in them was too weak.[88] Only a superindividual, even egoistical, people could save humanity. Such a people was found: the Jews. If for the Hindus the Soul remains in its substantiality, and for the Greeks and Romans it begins to receive inspiration from the Logos while still preserving the signature of the Demiurge, for the Hebrews, the Soul begins to receive the inspirations of the Divine Spirit, of the first hypostasis, while still preserving the signature of the first natural hypostasis, of the Chaotic Spirit or Satan.[89]

However, in order to better understand the great historical act in which the Jewish nation played the primary role, we must examine more closely the immediate agents of the historical process.

In margin: N.B.—*All nature, with the exception of man, is animated in a transient manner by the action of the World Soul. Man, to the contrary, is animated by the World Soul itself. We have seen that this Soul is necessarily composed of a multiplicity of individual elements, or individual souls, in which it is the central soul or the real unity. These individual souls are as eternal as the World Soul. From this comes the multiplicity of human beings. Each human is an individual soul, an eternal element of the World Soul, whereas in nature (which is only the external body of the soul) there are only primary elements, monads and atoms that are eternal, in forming the material of the world; whereas complex individuals, the stars and planets, are*

---

86. Kozyrev points out that this negative portrayal of Greek art contradicts Hegel and is also reversed later by Solovyov in his *Spiritual Foundations of Life* (PSS 2:346).

87. In other words, Solovyov suggests that a person or a soul without an idea is still a person, while an idea without a person, without being embodied, is nothing.

88. Personhood (*la personalité*) here is no doubt Solovyov's translation of the Russian *lichnost'*, something other than, fuller than, more associated with the divine (*bozhii lik*) than an individual, or *individuum* in Russian.

89. Kozyrev points out another comparison with *The Spiritual Foundations of Life* (SS: 3:358–59).

animated only by the action of the World Soul, an action that can only exist while the external body that is its seat exists. Thus, the astral, vegetable, and animal souls can only exist with their bodies; when the latter are destroyed, the World Soul removes its action and the partial soul no longer exists. On the contrary, individual human souls are eternal and consequently immortal; the corporeal organism is a concern only for their state, but not for their existence.

Each human is a distinct individual, an eternal soul, and, because of that, is immortal. That soul is united with a material body; but every material body is formed from the action of the ether; and the forms of the material body are only crude and corrupted expressions of the ethereal forms (ether in the physical world being the principle of form). In an organism, that is to say in a material being that possesses, or, better, that is possessed by a real unity, by a soul, the ethereal forms as well as the material forms are subordinate to that unity. They form a unique body that expresses on the outside, or manifests, the character of the internal being, the soul. Thus, every organism is composed of three principal elements: soul, ethereal body, and material body. [In lower organisms, unity, being transient] The ethereal body is the immediate expression, the direct organ of the soul; although it is originally produced with the material body as its exact correspondence, in submitting to the direct and constant action of the soul, it can become independent from the material body. It is clear that this is not the case with lower organisms, where the soul itself has no independence, being only the action of the World Soul applied to a corporeal organism and, consequently, completely determined by that organism. In these lower organisms, when the material organism decomposes, the soul retires and the ethereal body, which was their place and in which unity is determined by the unity of the soul, necessarily dissolves as well. But in the higher organism, in man, having become independent from the material body as the direct organ of the soul, the ethereal body does not dissolve with it. Once unity, the soul, exists, then its direct organ, the ethereal body, also exists as a corporeal or phenomenal unity.

The state in which individual humans find themselves immediately after death depends on the dominant influence on their lives. Satanic natures find themselves in Gehenna, demiurgic natures in Sheol, natures dominated by the Soul in the loins of Abraham, a state of sweet repose.[90] However, they can all act on mortals to a greater or lesser degree, and can receive their actions; consequently they transform themselves.

The spirits of Satan find themselves in such a painful state that they are forced to seek to leave it. There are several means of exit. Through an internal

---

90. Kozyrev cites the biblical passages that no doubt inspired Solovyov's classification of humanity's three levels of abodes in the afterlife: Gehenna, or Hell (Matt. 5:29–30; 10:28; Mark 9:43–45); Sheol (Gen. 37:35; Numbers 16:30); the loins of Abraham, or the resting place of the righteous (Luke 16:19–31).

development of consciousness, they can attain conversion; but this is very difficult and given only to a small number of spirits. They can invoke prayers, that is to say acts of love, on the part of the living and, through this communion of love, purify and perfect themselves. Finally, and this is the most successful means, they can reincarnate themselves and, through a new life of suffering and resignation, expiate their past.

The Demiurge's spirits are those that are neither hot nor cold. These kinds are the slowest to transform and the most to fear. Their situation is not so painful that they would want to rid themselves of it. On the contrary, since these are people without strong passions, their situation at first seems to suit them perfectly, and they need to remain in this situation long enough that the monotony of such an existence without colors disgusts them and produces boredom and, then, they begin to doubt themselves. This doubt is the beginning of transformation in the demiurgic spirit. In general, the demiurgic spirits are not reincarnated for expiation. Sometimes, however, after conversion, they take on the mission of guiding mortals in reincarnation.[91]

The spirits of S<ophia?>, as we have said, are in a state of relative calm, disturbed only by their love. They act on the living, and the majority of things that happen for the better in private or public life are a result of their action.

The souls that are not yet incarnated act as direct organs of the World Soul, in order to prepare conditions for their final incarnation. The souls that temporarily animate inferior organisms finally incarnate themselves in a human organism, which is their proper form that they can no longer lose.

In the first period, souls that are not incarnated, genies, principally act on humanity; they are naive souls without experience (naiveté is a characteristic of genies). In the second period, the influence of the dead dominates, to which corresponds the conscious, reflective, experienced character of this period. In the third period, the division between dead and living ends: the two worlds are reunited. The first period lasts up until Jesus Christ; the second up to the end of the nineteenth century. (The third period begins with the years 1878–1886.)[92] When the size of invisible humanity becomes larger than that of visible humanity, the former overwhelms the latter. Since its origin, the land of deceased souls has no chief, no form of organized society. The Chaotic Spirit, the Demiurge, reigns in the actual world; Sophie directly governs the unincarnated souls; the Logos presides over the intelligible world and the Holy Spirit over the divine world.[93]

91. The manuscript here includes some crossed-out signs, which look like the beginning of automatic writing.

92. Solovyov elsewhere calls the third period the epoch of the Eternal Testament (cf. S. Solov'ev, *Zhizn' i tvorcheskaia evoliutsiia*, 121; *Vladimir Solovyov*, trans. Gibson 128). The first corresponds to God the Father and the Old Testament, the second to Christ and the New Testament, and the third—to come—to the Holy Spirit.

93. The reference to Sophie in the third person confirms that Solovyov abandoned the genre of dialogue earlier in this section. The use of the name "Sophie" instead of "The Sophia" in reference to her confuses the fictionalized, personal form with the abstract discourse of the surrounding text. The equation of the Demiurge with the Chaotic Spirit also confuses earlier statements about Satan as the Spirit of Chaos.

The goal of the universal process is the production of the perfect social organism: the Church. The principle of that organism is internal or free unity. This unity can only be produced by the submission of the Soul to its divine principle, to the Logos. But submission of the World Soul is not sufficient now, when individual or partial souls have received an independent existence. These individual souls must also submit themselves to the Logos; they must become its material. (It is clear, however, that, having lived a separate existence in time, the souls cannot submit themselves to the Logos simultaneously, they cannot materialize themselves, potentialize themselves, become its soul. The first of the unincarnated souls that submits completely to the divine Logos by falling in love with it unites itself to it and becomes its individual, human soul).[94] The Divine Logos, however, belonging to the intelligible world, is invisible to those who have left that world. It must become humanly individual and corporeal, it must incarnate itself.

In margin: $400 + 10 + 160 + 50 + 3.50 + 4 + 12.50 = 640$[95]

That is to say, it must unite itself internally with an individual soul through the power of love. By its character, that soul must be ready for the union, it must be passive and passionate; it must possess the feeling of individuality to the highest degree, but be initiated by the feeling of the universal, of the absolute, by religion: in a word, it must be a Jewish soul.[96] If active egoism is the antidivine principle, then potential, passive egoism is the seat of the divine,

In margin (Russian, in French transliteration): 637 *frankov doljen ya maleniko-mou kitaytzou [I owe 637 francs to the little Chinese man].*[97]

because one cannot have the potential of feeling something without having the real feeling of its opposite. Egoism is power. Left to its own, it is antidivine power; if it is universalized, it is the power of divinity. It is natural that the moment of real union between the Logos and the Soul, and of its incarnation, is determined by the march of the historical process. When the ideal union of humanity and the Logos in Greek and Roman culture was proved insufficient and when, on the other hand, the religious and national egoism of the Hebrews {turned into universalism by the power of things}[98] had to be recognized as an illusion, at the moment when, everywhere, in the East and

94. In the manuscript, this section in parentheses is also marked by a line in the margin.

95. The word "incognito," crossed out, is found next to the equation. It is possibly the beginning of automatic writing.

96. The mention of the Jews here points ahead to several of Solovyov's significant writings of the 1880s, especially *Jewry and the Christian Question* (SS 4:142–85).

97. This is also no doubt a note to himself unrelated to the surrounding text, and might follow from the equation above. If so, it is not clear why he will pay the Chinese merchant three francs less than he is due.

98. Wavy brackets in the original, perhaps an indication of deletion.

the West, man found the world empty, and seized on suicide as the one means to counter despair and boredom, at that moment the divine Logos, united to the human soul, was born in Judea.[99]

At the time of birth, the Demiurge gives form through the father, and the Cosmic Spirit gives matter, through the mother. In the case of our Savior, since form was already given by the divine Logos, there was no need of the father. In general, the fact that participation of the male is not an absolute necessity in the production of an animal organism is proven by the parthenogenesis of several animals, of bees, for example. And there is no absolute difference between the human organism and the organism of other animals. Thus, the material possibility of parthenogenesis in the case of our Savior cannot be disputed.

(Some words about the cult of the Virgin).

After his death, resurrection, and ascension, when our Savior finally returned to the invisible or spiritual world, that world—the invisible Church—received its divine leader; and, since the visible Church is governed by the invisible one, the Church as a whole had a unique and divine leader, and was constituted in that manner into a true, living organism. The final ascendance of the invisible world over the visible begins from here. Before reaching its height, however, the Church still had to undergo a great battle against the powers of that age that, dethroned but not annihilated, simply changed the sphere of their activity. Before the appearance of Christ, they acted on man principally through external nature. After the advent of Christianity, that external nature lost its power over man, for the purely human world, subordinate to spiritual influences, departed from the new religion. Nature became perfectly external, objective or material for man. It materialized itself, which is to say it became subordinate to man, and consequently could no longer determine it. Thus, the powers of the age had to act in man's sphere in order to have any influence over him. This was possible for them, for humanity could not, naturally, be regenerated at once and as a whole.

Primitive Christianity was not an absolute religion; it had limits. These limits were both theoretical and practical.

Firstly, Christianity, which was the direct victory of Spirit over Chaos (Satan), could not be impartial toward the enemy that had only barely been vanquished. The more practical, rather than contemplative spirits, men of will, rather than intelligence (and that is the majority) retained traces of the battle and of hatred. Those men could not see Satan as an organ of divinity, they could see him only as an enemy; from here sprang dualism, the separation of the reign of God and of Satan, the division of humanity into the elected and the damned, the doctrine of Hell and eternal suffering—all those absurdities and horrors that will end in the ruin of historical Christianity.

---

99. This obviously refers to the birth of Jesus.

And this theoretical dualism that proved fatal for dogma combined with practical dualism that was fatal for the Church. Christianity presented itself originally as an otherworldly principle that could have nothing in common with the things of this world (God and Caesar).

In margin: *With the advent of Christ, the Spirit of Chaos was relegated to the depths of the abyss, and the Demiurge took his place in the world. We have seen that originally the pagan State was the external manifestation of Logos, but when the Logos received its higher manifestation in the purely spiritual spheres with the incarnation of Christ, when it became the principle of religion and of the Church, the Demiurge took control of the State (as servants appropriate items that were left by their masters). (The relativity of degrees and states)*

It is clear that this separation could only be provisional, for in the end all powers of this world must be subordinate to Christ. In the end, the Church must completely penetrate the State with its Spirit, must employ the State as its organ. But, for such a true penetration, the Christian Church must first completely penetrate human society; the Christian principle must entirely take control of the heart, the Spirit, and the lives of men. Then the external life of society, as well as of the State, which regulates that life, becomes only the expression, the external manifestation of internal life, regenerated by the Church. Before the Church could attain this penetration, only an external union was possible between it and the State. In the beginning, when the State remained overtly pagan, even that unity was impossible. There was only battle. But, when the Demiurge saw that violence and persecutions were only strengthening the Church, it used another means. Through a prince who was completely under its influence (Constantine), it submitted to the Church only externally and falsely, without changing the principle of the pagan and demiurgic State in any way, without transforming or christianizing it in any way. The empire of Constantine differed in no essential way from the empire of Diocletian. The Church, which was powerful enough to impose on the State, but not powerful enough to assimilate it, accepted the compromise; thus was formed that hermaphrodite society called the Byzantine Empire.

In margin: *Develop*

It was different in the West. There, the Church did not deal with an organized State, but with the chaotic forces of barbarians. It conserved its social authority and truly subordinated them, but did not have the inner power to regenerate them as a whole and to make of their savage kingdoms its own organs. Regeneration or christianization of the barbarians was always on an individual basis. The masses were Christian only externally. Barbarian pagan society remained feudal, a situation continued by the mockery of the Romanic-German Empire. Soon, these heterogeneous elements—the Church, the empire, the feudal system—entered into battle. In this violent battle, the Church naturally lost its purely spiritual and peace-loving character, and transformed itself into the militant papal monarchy. It is natural that, in their earthly sphere, the earthly powers should be victorious;

In margin: *Develop*

it is true that the Holy Empire, because of its equivocal and artificial nature, began to cede power to the papacy; but the feudal system, which was a natural organization, was victorious when it concentrated its forces under the feudal kings. If the emperor ceded to the pope, the king made him his prisoner.

In margin: *N.B.—on the Donation of Constantine*[100]

Thus, in the practical sphere, toward the end of the Middle Ages, the Demiurge achieved a double success, through the victory of royalty over the papacy, and through the transformation of the papacy itself into a temporal force.

The secularization of the Church in the theoretical sphere was even more fatal for Christianity, for the Church exercised its authority over the Spirit and the Mind, but there is no external force capable of subordinating Mind. Mind revolted and destroyed the Church's authority in the theoretical sphere.

In margin: *Develop*

But as the Church was the sole representative of Christianity, no matter how disfigured; the revolt and negation of the Church was the negation of Christianity. The progress of this negation was well marked: Episcopal Protestantism, Presbyterian Protestantism, Unitarianism or Socinianism,[101] Deism,

In margin: *Deism—the religion of the Demiurge.*

Atheism (and Materialism).

The progress of the Demiurge in the practical sphere: absolute Monarchy, Parliamentarianism, Republicanism, Socialism, and Anarchy.

Thus we see that, in the practical sphere as well as in the theoretical sphere, the profits of the victories of the Demiurge belong to the Spirit of Chaos, which is in perfect accord with the middling nature of the Demiurge, being able to possess neither beginning nor end. But, as the Spirit of Chaos by its nature is only negative, and cannot be the principle of life in any way, the victories of the Demiurge come to profit the third principle, the Soul.

After all the external or demiurgic forms of life are destroyed, the Soul must look in itself for the principles of a new life; it must return inward to itself, retire its external powers, concentrate itself, potentialize itself. This return of the Soul begins in theory (for theory, in actual conditions, is the direct sphere of her actions).

In margin: *Develop*

---

100. The Donation of Constantine refers to a document, later determined to be forged in the eighth or ninth century, that allegedly proves that Constantine "gave" the western parts of the Roman Empire to Pope Sylvester I in the fourth century.

101. Socinianism was an antitrinitarian sect begun in the sixteenth century.

From there begins the development of modern speculative philosophy, which wants to create the world of the interior. (This is the difference from ancient philosophy; the latter is the philosophy of the objective Logos, while modern philosophy is the philosophy of the subjective soul, of the human soul itself).

In margin: *Contemporary poetry is also a manifestation of the World Soul, of its subjective character.*[102]

The thoughts of the Soul are expressed by modern philosophers. Through geniuses, it directly communicates what it thinks to men who are capable of understanding and expressing these revelations well. This is the theoretical incarnation of Sophie.[103]

The dev<elopment> of modern philosophy.[104]
Jacob Boehme, Swedenborg, Schelling.[105]
The real incarnation of Sophie. The universal religion.

"Third Chapter: Morality and Politics"[106]

The universal religion is the religion of the Soul; the special function of the Soul is love; thus the morality of that religion can have no other principle than love. Love in the universal religion is distinct from love in the old form of Christianity because the latter has its limits—Satan and his reign—while universal love has no boundaries, for it includes Satan himself as a reality of the Soul.

It is necessary to know that hatred is only a modification of love, and does not have any independent origin. Hatred comes from egoism, and egoism is the exclusive love of oneself. There are therefore two loves: negative love, or hatred; and positive love, or love properly speaking.

Positive love is absolute; negative love is relative. Negative love is transient; positive love is eternal. Positive love has three degrees:

102. In this marginal note, Solovyov returns to the relationship between Sophia (here as World Soul) and poetry and also unites poetry and philosophy through their common production out of the World Soul.

103. Again, we would expect here "Sophia" instead of "Sophie."

104. Kozyrev here instead interpolates *devenir,* or future.

105. Solovyov includes himself in this development, as seen in the following list—"Kabbalah and Neoplatonism. / Boehme and Swedenborg. / Schelling and me" (*PSS* 2:177), as well as earlier in part 1 (page 82).

106. This chapter, which is not preceded by a first or second chapter, follows directly in the manuscript after the second dialogue. Knowing Solovyov's predilection for triads, one would certainly expect a third dialogue, not chapter, here, but Solovyov has clearly abandoned the dialogue form. In terms of content, however, Kozyrev sees a clear development of Solovyov's plan for a proposed work called "The Principles of Universal Teaching," of which the dialogues might form a part. The first section was to be a critique of the historical church and contemporary society; the second part was to lay out the dogmatics of "theosophical principles" of the teaching; and this, the third part, was to consider the problem of ethics, central to which is the teaching about love.

Natural love, which at base is love between the sexes, but can extend more or less to other relationships that come from the sexual relationship;

Intellectual love, with which we love something that we do not know directly, or, better, with which we love the objects that are not directly present to our senses. It is also more or less extended to related areas: patriotism, [fanaticism], the love of humanity, and finally the love of God as a general principle of all things, or as universal substance, *"amor Dei intellectualis"* [Latin: intellectual love of God] of Spinoza,[107] the final perfection of the second degree;

[Finally, divine or absolute love: love of the incarnated Sophia.]

Natural love possesses spontaneous power, but lacks universality; intellectual love has universality, but lacks spontaneous power.

The third degree, which is the synthesis of the two preceding ones, unites the spontaneous power of natural love to the universality of intellectual love: It is absolute love. In order to have this character, it must have as its object an individual being that is present to the senses, but who represents a universal principle or is the incarnation of that principle. This requires some development.

Different beings represent different degrees of perfection, and since perfection consists of universality, then of different degrees of universality. Now, when one being loves another that is its superior, the latter is not only an object of physical love, but also a principle of universal life. But every principle of life, if it is truly appropriate, must produce fruits, or be realized. And why would it be realized in our case if not so that the relatively inferior being, having received universal life from its superior lover, can communicate that universal life to another being more inferior than it (for the degrees are relative). Thus, in order to be complete, its love must be double, just as the unity of gamma is at least triadic. Each being is in a love relationship with two beings: one that it loves with an ascending love, and one with a descending love. But, since quantity is in indirect proportion to perfection, and the perfect being is unique, then the objects of descending love are always more numerous than those of ascending love. The highest object of the latter is unique; it is Sophia. She is in direct relationship to the elected of humanity (necessarily to men, since she is female) who love her with ascending love, and who are loved by her with descending love. They are, in turn, in direct relationship to a great number of individuals (necessarily female), who love them with ascending love and whom they love with descending love. Those again are the object of ascending love on the part of a number of main individuals, and so forth.

Among the elected of the first order, a single one is in the most intimate relationship with Sophia, and is the great priest of humanity. The others are the patriarchs of the Universal Church, or priests of the first degree. The second

---

107. See Spinoza's *Ethics*, especially pt. 5, 36: "The Mind's intellectual Love of God is the very Love of God by which God loves himself, not insofar as he is infinite, but insofar as he can be explained by the human Mind's essence, considered under a species of eternity; i.e., the Mind's intellectual Love of God is part of the infinite Love by which God loves himself" (Spinoza 612).

order, composed of females, forms the first council. Then comes the third order (the second masculine order), which gives priests of the second order, the metropolitans of the Universal Church. The third order is comprised of archbishops, the fourth of bishops, the fifth—deans, the sixth—priests in the strict sense of the world, the seventh—deacons, the eighth—believers, the ninth—catechumens, the tenth—novices. Each masculine order has a corresponding council formed by the female order. Another principle of division is one of vocations, according to which the Universal Church is divided into laborers, demiurges (artisans), and priests; it is clear that the class of priests belongs only to the seven higher degrees, and that the classes of artisans and laborers can only belong to the three lower classes. The third division of the Universal Church is founded on differences in character. Humanity is divided into seven large parts: Africa, the Orient, Upper Asia, India, the West, America, and Russia. A priest of the first order stands at the head of each of the large parts. These large parts are divided into smaller ones that are governed by the priests of the second order, and down to the communes of the sixth order, or parishes, that are governed by the simple priests. The parishes are divided into districts, governed by deans; the districts are divided into quarters; the quarters into houses of courts; the houses of courts into families. Thus the family is only the lower grade on the social scale, and individuals of the higher grades cannot possess the family properly speaking.

Translated by Judith Deutsch Kornblatt

3 Sophia in Philosophical Prose

Reading Guide

The personalized Sophia of Solovyov's early poetry and of the *Sophia* dialogues appears more abstractly in Solovyov's philosophical oeuvre. In this diverse body of works she is no longer necessarily female and does not speak in her own voice. Although the two most extended references to Sophia appear in *Lectures on Divine Humanity* and *Russia and the Universal Church*, both excerpted below, we can find her at least in passing in a number of published and unpublished works throughout Solovyov's entire career. In the preface to *The History and Future of Theocracy*, for example, she appears but briefly at the very end of the forward to this massive work of several hundred pages:

> Then the higher, free unity of the Church is revealed, based not on tradition and custom *alone*, and also not on abstract, rational conviction, but on moral, spiritual deed *[podvig]*. The Universal Church appears to us not as a dead idol, and not as an animated, but unconscious body, but as a being *[sushchestvo]* that is self-conscious, morally free, and active in its own realization *[osushchestvlenie]*. It appears as God's true friend *[podruga Bozhiia][1]*, as a creation that is united with the Divine fully and completely, that fully makes space *[vmestivshee]* for God in itself. In other words, it appears as that *Sophia, the Wisdom of God*, to whom our ancestors, in a surprising prophetic impulse, built altars and cathedrals, themselves not knowing who she is. (*SS* 4: 260–61; emphasis in original)

---

1. This "true friend" is unambiguously female in the original: *podruga* instead of *drug*. The reference must be to the Wisdom of Proverbs.

Solovyov's reference here to altars and cathedrals reminds us of the Wisdom images on icons, as well as of the numerous churches dedicated to Sophia throughout medieval Russia. In this way, the brief mention of "Sophia, the Wisdom of God" in *The History and Future of Theocracy* in the 1880s points ahead to the curious ending of Solovyov's essay on the French positivist, Auguste Comte, where the philosopher describes the Novgorod Sophia icon in great detail (see page 225). Despite her association with visual art and architecture, however, Sophia in the passage just cited is more than concrete, more than the "visible church."[2] As "God's true friend," the "ideal human" and the "body of God," she is both abstract *and* personal. Ultimately, she is the true Universal Church, the past and future, as Solovyov believed, of all of Western *and* Eastern civilization. Sophia, as indicated here, will both motivate and accomplish the reunion of the Eastern and Western churches; the reincorporation of the Jews into the church of Jesus through their own contribution of the third, prophetic principle; and the reconciliation of all nations now divided by destructive nationalism. In other words, she is the medium and the result of the God-human process of bogochelovechestvo.

The following section presents translations of a diverse set of texts from both published and unpublished material. The first few fragments are roughly contemporaneous with Solovyov's earliest poetic articulations of Sophia in the mid-1870s and show his attempts to situate personal, mystical intuitions within the established vocabularies of Christianity and Western philosophy. That the final fragment presented ends with a seemingly unmotivated list of alchemical elements only underlines the difficulty faced by the philosopher as he returned to Russia from the Egyptian desert and tried to take back his place in the largely conservative academy. His *Lectures on Divine Humanity*, along with the defense of his doctoral dissertation in 1880, did manage to establish his reputation in Russian society as a legitimate philosopher.[3] The lectures' broad survey of cosmic and religious history, their effortless incorporation of Hegelian terminology into the surrounding discourse, and their use of at least five different languages all served to prove Solovyov's vast erudition. Despite the grounding of *Lectures* in Western history and thought, however, Sophia does not appear any less contradictory in them, and the numerous references to her/it tend to confound rather than clarify.[4] The reader is left with the impression

---

2. For an influential discussion of the relationship between the "Church visible and invisible," see Aleksei Khomiakov's essay "The Church Is One" (Jakim and Bird 31–53).

3. Nonetheless, Solovyov was not offered a permanent professorial position at the university.

4. In fact, contradiction marks bogochelovechestvo in general. As Losev states: "Without a doubt, the teaching of *bogochelovechestvo* marks the pinnacle of Vl. Solovyov's theoretical philosophy. One cannot say, however, that that pinnacle arose with no contradictions. And below we will become convinced that this contradictoriness had the greatest living meaning for Vl. Solovyov and turned out to be one of the most essential sides of his philosophical development" (*Vladimir Solov'ev i ego vremia* 124).

of an all-embracing idea that explains all of being and nothing at the same time.[5]

After Solovyov's controversial letter to the new tsar in 1881, asking for the ruler to govern his people with "Christian politics" by forgiving the assassins of his father, Solovyov left his academic positions and found it increasingly more difficult to publish in the Russian press. For *Russia and the Universal Church*, excerpted below, Solovyov returned to his earlier scholarship in French. The text's strong advocacy for Rome as the center of the Universal Church clearly militated against acceptance by the Russian Orthodox censors in Russia, while Solovyov's reliance on the authority of Kabbalah and the Hebrew Bible in this re-vision of Sophia also situated the work in a genre less acceptable to the Russian establishment. Again, Sophia is many contradictory things at once, both beginning and goal, both catalyst and resulting unity. As Solovyov writes:

> Being the finished unity of the all in God, Divine Wisdom also becomes the unity of God and of extradivine existence. She therefore represents the true cause of creation and the goal of the latter—the principle in which God created the heaven and the earth. . . . She is *reshith* in the beginning—the fruitful idea of the absolute unity, the unitary power destined to unify all things. She is *Malkhout* (Βασιλεία, *Regnum*, Kingdom) at the end—the Kingdom of God, the perfect and fully realized unity of the Creator and creation. (*SS* 11:298–99; see page 201)

The collection of various types of philosophical texts offered here ends with a complete translation of Solovyov's late essay on Auguste Comte. While rejecting Comte's positivism, Solovyov embraces the French philosopher's idea of Humanity as *le grande Être* [French: the Great Being], particularly because of Comte's insistence on its female gender:

> The Great Being of Comte's religion has yet one more constant sign in addition to its complete reality, power, and wisdom that makes it our Providence: the fact that it is a feminine being. This is not a metaphor or the personification of an impersonal concept, like various virtues, arts, and sciences as depicted in classical mythology in the form of women. From the previous account in Comte's own words, it is sufficiently clear that the Great Being was not an abstract concept for this philosopher. He clearly distinguished humanity as a sum of national, familial, and personal elements (his *humanité* with a small *h*) from Humanity as an essential, actual, and living principle of all these elements (*Humanité* with a capital *H*), or the Great Being. (*SS* 9:185–86; see page 223)

---

5. Solovyov himself is perfectly comfortable with this kind of contradiction. Speaking of God or the Absolute as both All and Nothing (or No-thing), he cites Hegel: "This constitutes the profoundly true meaning of the famous paradox with which Hegel's *Logic* begins: Being as such—that is, pure, empty being—is identical with its opposite, or nothing" (*SS* 3:84).

This *Humanité* with a capital "H," this Great Being that was supposedly intuited by medieval Russian icon painters and church architects, *is* Sophia.

"Fragments": An Overview

The three fragments translated below bridge the period between Solovyov's work on *The Sophia* in Egypt and Italy and his later published work in Russia in the last few years of the 1870s and beginning of the 1880s. The first two examples belong to an unfinished project tentatively titled "Theosophical Principles" that clearly resonates with the concerns of the monologic sections of the French manuscript and later of *Philosophical Principles of Integral Knowledge* (1877). Both fragments come from the first of three chapters comprising the second part (no first part remains) and are followed by three more short chapters from the third part, called "Morality." The two pieces—"On the Three Worlds" and "On the Three Conditions (in General)"—describe Solovyov's model of three interactive worlds: the utterly transcendent world of the Divine; the abstract world of representation that the Divine posits outside itself; and the tangible world of the cosmos, nature, and humanity. Typically for Solovyov, the triadic model complicates more reductionist assumptions of the duality of spirit and matter, of God and humanity, of heaven and earth. The divine world, whose subject is will and whose nature is idea, produces the second—a world of abstract desire and presentation. From the first two worlds then emerges the third, our physical world, whose subject is physical yearning and whose nature is feeling or sensuality. These worlds do not exist in temporal sequence but all together, irrespective of time and space. It is again typical of Solovyov that elements of upper and lower worlds are present in each other, so that no part of divine or human experience is completely separate. The bracketed words (crossed out in the original manuscript) in the first fragment suggest that Solovyov experimented with several overlapping terms to describe both the differences and identities of the worlds. The end of the very short second fragment makes clear that Solovyov associates his triadic model with the Trinity, the third member of which he calls Sophia rather than Holy Spirit. (Elsewhere, as we have seen, he associates Sophia with Logos, or the Son.) Sophia, in fact, is present in all the worlds and therefore acts as a mediator between the ineffable ideal, abstract representation, and physical reality.

The final fragment translated below criticizes earlier philosophers and mystics for ignoring concrete aspects of the physical world process, the third part of his model. Only Schelling emerges relatively unscathed; he is called the "real precursor of the universal religion." The accompanying table makes clear, however, that the true prophet of that religion is Solovyov himself. This fragment contains an example of automatic writing, as well as some gnostic or alchemical references to minerals, planets, and biblical figures. Relying on the reference to Petr Alekseevich Bibikov, a friend who committed suicide on

November 14, 1875, Kozyrev speculates that these notes were written while Solovyov was still in Egypt.

"On the Three Worlds"

In the first world, div<ine> nature is the subject [contemplation][6] of will [*volia*]; in the second, it is the subj<ect> [of year<ning>] [of will] of desire [*zhelanie*]; in the third—of yearning [*khotenie*]. In the first, it is idea; in the second—presentation, in the third—feeling.

In the first, it is [blessedness] possibility, in the second, [freedom] reality, in the third, necessity.

The first world is the world of pure [of images] blessedness

the second world is the world of images

the third world is the world of sensuality

The head of the first world is God; of the second—Christ, Λογος;[7] of the third—Sophia. Everything that is included in the first world, including internal reality and spiritual sense, transforms into images in the second and into external feeling in the third. The first world has its own internal reality within itself, and magically develops images and feelings from it. The second world receives internal reality, its subjectivity, its will, from the first world; in itself it has images, or ideas, of all things, out of which correspondingly develop feelings. The third world has neither internal reality nor images within itself, but receives the former from the first world through the second, and the latter directly from the second. In itself it has only the possibility of feeling, which is called matter. The beings of the first world are principally the spirits of love; of the second—the spirits of contemplation; of the third—spirits of external feeling and action. [Sophia] The normal relationship between the three worlds: the third receives all of its content—both real and ideal—from the first two, and changes it into external reality.

[But for that][8] Since any *action* requires a *reaction* in order to become palpably real, the full manifestation or realization of divine love and reason in the whole multitude of beings requires the reaction of these beings in the Divine.

---

6. Words with letters in angle brackets are abbreviated in the manuscript; I follow Kozyrev in the presumed completion. Words in square brackets are crossed out in the manuscript. I retain them here to provide a sense of the development, and sometimes confusion, of Solovyov's terminology. Where ambiguous, I also include transliteration of the Russian in brackets. Particularly curious here is the juxtaposition of two near synonyms for desire: *zhelanie* and *khotenie*. The latter is no longer present in modern standard Russian and is difficult to parse, except for the obvious distinction Solovyov draws between abstract desire [*zhelanie*] of the second world and physical want in the third. I have chosen to distinguish between them with the words "desire" and "yearning." The word for will [*volia*], corresponding to the first world, can also mean freedom, but Solovyov considers the use of the word again for the "second world" that he associates with a synonym for freedom [*svoboda*] in the second paragraph of the fragment.

7. Here and sometimes also with "Sophia," Solovyov mixes Cyrillic and Greek letters. I combine English and Greek.

8. The handwriting changes at this point in the manuscript.

The law of essence (of will), of reason and [of will] divine spirit demands the unity of all beings. From the divine essence [fl<ows>] is produced the essential unity that we find in the first world. There, the essential unity of everything is action; multiplicity is only potential—ideal multiplicity. Div<ine> reason demands ideal unity—of order and law—and we find this realized in the second world. There, in contrast to the first world, the essential unity has already broken apart into multiplicity. There, the ideal multiplicity of the first world becomes action, actualized multipl<icity><indecipherable>, and at the same time essential unity becomes idea—ideal unity, order, law. In the third world, unity cannot be initially essential, as in the first, nor initially ideal, as in the second. Instead, it is purely actual, i.e., having come from *action*, i.e., of course, from the action of the beings themselves. It is, so to speak, an acquired unity. But such an acquired, active unity presupposes the loss of its former, initial, or rather initially ideal unity (for the initially essential unity was already absent in the second world). In other words, this presupposes the rebellion of the third world against the divine order, presented in the second world.[9]

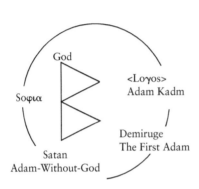

Translated by Judith Deutsch Kornblatt

"On the Three Conditions (in General)"

The first condition—everything in God—*sub specie aeternitatis* [Latin: under the aspect of eternity][10]; the second condition—the self-assertion of individual beings in the third world, the falling apart of unity; the actual connectivity of the worlds tears apart; the third condition—a unity is established by means of both the [cosmic] physical as well as historical world process, but now real, determined as such, having proceeded through its

---

9. In the diagram shown, Solovyov embeds two connected triangles within a circle. The upper triangle links God, Logos, and Sophia, while the lower one links Sophia, the Demiurge, and Satan. In this way, the upper corresponds to a higher, ideal world and the lower triangle to the realized world of creation. Sophia is the link between the two. Solovyov calls Logos Adam Kadmon, the Kabbalistic term for the ideal, essential Adam. The Demiurge becomes The First Adam (*Adam haRishon*), and Satan is *Adam Blial*, literally the Adam without God. We saw in *The Sophia* that Solovyov attempts to explain the cosmic process as a battle between the Demiurge and Satan, mediated, as it seems here, by Sophia.

10. This is a philosophical term referring to what is universally and eternally true, without reference to temporal or special reality.

negation, containing the latter within itself and, consequently, unable to be destroyed again.

> God-the-Father is Spirit
> God-the-Son is Mind
> God-the-Holy Spirit is Σοφια (soul (and body) Wisdom)

Translated by Judith Deutsch Kornblatt

From "Theological Principles"

Until now (until me), theosophical systems that had spiritual bases did not have a true idea of the wor<ld> process. They either ignored it altogether (Neoplatonism, Swedenborg), or else introduced an element of coincidence and arbitrariness (the Fall)—Kabbalah, Boehme. As a result both types ended up with devils and eternal hell.

On the other hand, philosophical systems that had a real understanding of the world process as necessary and without any arbitrariness were devoid of spiritual bases. Therefore, the process turned out to be either purely ideal, and even abstractly logical (Hegel), or purely natural (evolutionary materialism). Some even comb<ined> ideal<ism> with naturalism (the nature philos<ophy> of Schelling, Hartmann's syst)[11]. As a consequence of the lack of spiritual bases, even these latter, relatively complete systems could not define the true goal and significance of the process, for that goal is the realization of the spiritual, divine world.

In h<is> final syst, Schelling combines a logic<al> understand<ing> of the process with a kind of incomplete and rather confused present<ation> of spiritual principles; therefore the goal of the process also gets a relatively satisfying definition; from there, then, he has, together with a recognition of the concrete spiritual world—like in Boehme and Sweden<borg>[12]—the absence of devils and hell. This is why Schelling is the real precursor of universal religion.

The teachings of Boehme and Swedenborg are the fullest and highest theosophical expression of the old Christianity. The positive philosophy of Schelling

---

11. See part 1 for Solovyov's interest in all these figures. On Hegel, see also de Courten 163–84, as well as the seminal work by Kline, "Hegel and Solovyov." Solovyov also wrote an encyclopedia article on Hegel (*SS* 10:301–21). Friedrich Wilhelm Joseph von Schelling (1775–1854) was extremely important for Solovyov, as he was for much of nineteenth-century Russian philosophy and literature, although Solovyov rarely refers to his German predecessor directly (see *PSS* 2:356). He did leave a fragment about Schelling's ideas on the Absolute (*PSS* 2:179–81), perhaps written even earlier than the *Sophia* manuscript and the current fragment. As we see below, for Solovyov, "Schelling is the real precursor of universal religion." For a concise overview and more bibliography, see de Courten 258–66. See Solovyov's encyclopedia article on von Hartmann in his collected works (*SS* 10:297–301).

12. See part 1 for Boehme and Swedenborg's influence on Solovyov.

is the first embryo, weak and incomplete, of the new Christianity or the universal religion—of the eternal covenant.

Kabbalah and Neoplatonism.
Boehme and Swedenborg.
Schelling and me.

Newplatonism — Kabbalah		Law	Old Testament
Boehme — Swedenborg		Gospels	New Testament
Schelling — me		Freedom	Eternal Testament

[The following text is written in automatic writing, with Solovyov receiving messages in two different languages]:

[In French:]

Sophie. Eat a little more today. I don't want to see you waste away. My dear. We want to prepare you for the grand mission that you must fulfill. Always meditate on the principles. Do not give over to thoughts of despair, but also chase away pride and ambition.

Say, did you think [indecipherable]. Say did you think about your friend Bibikov,[13] who committed suicide. Sophie. I told you that you must eat today.

[In Russian:]

Pamfil. Do not think about such trifles. Let him eat who eats for the sake of God, and he who eats not for the sake of God, let him not eat.[14]

What do you think about the heavenly, about the divine mode of minerals: gold, mercury, copper, silver, iron, tin, and lead. 7 spirits:[15]

---

13. P. A. Bibikov (1832–1875) was a literary critic and translator from the French. He was a friend of Solovyov's.

14. This is one of only several instances when "someone" other than Sophia communicates with Solovyov through automatic writing. Here "Pamfil" and Sophia disagree over Solovyov's diet. Kozyrev surmises that Pamfil refers to P. D. Iurkevich, the Ukrainian philosopher, Darwinian, and Swedenborgian who died in September of 1874. A letter from March 1875 from the religious writer A. G. Orfano to S. D. Lapshina, the wife of Solovyov's friend I. O. Lapshin, relates that Solovyov had recently attended a séance at which the spirit of Iurkevich appeared (*PSS* 2:357). In the message, Pamfil seems to refer to Romans 14:6: "He who observes the day, observes it in honor of the Lord. He also who eats, eats in honor of the Lord, since he gives thanks to God; while he who abstains, abstains in honor of the Lord and gives thanks to God."

15. The seven spirits listed are archangels in several esoteric systems. Solovyov's source here is most likely Gnosticism, although his obvious knowledge of Goethe's *Faust* suggests that he could be drawing on medieval alchemical terminology as well.

first Lucifer   (Saturn, lead)
second Michael   (Jupiter, tin)
third Uriel   (Mars, iron)
fourth Gabriel   (Moon, silver)
fifth Anael   (Venus, copper)
sixth Raphael   (Mercury, mercury)
seventh Samael   (Sun, gold)
7 spirits   7, 30, 12
7original characteristics, 7 spirits, 7 planets, 7metals, 7 churches
7, 12, 30, 360

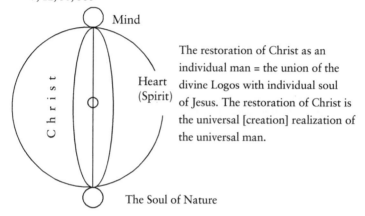

The restoration of Christ as an individual man = the union of the divine Logos with individual soul of Jesus. The restoration of Christ is the universal [creation] realization of the universal man.

Translated by Judith Deutsch Kornblatt

From *Lectures on Divine Humanity*: An Overview

After returning to Russia in 1876, Solovyov began to lecture on philosophy at the University of Moscow. He soon moved to St. Petersburg, where he settled semipermanently after a brief and largely unsuccessful interlude to join the war effort in the Balkans in the summer of 1877. It is then that he began to plan a series of twelve public lectures for the beginning of 1878, intended to explain the structure of the cosmos and the meaning of all human history.

Solovyov placed a great deal of importance on the lectures, which he saw as a transfer of his patriotic duty to the Slavs from the battlefield to the academic hall.[16] He wrote to his school friend D. N. Tsertelev: "I'd be delighted if you could come to Petersburg for the beginning of my lectures, i.e., by the 15th of January. I could put them off for a week, i.e., until the 22nd of January. In all, there will be 12 lectures, as you can imagine in support of the Red Cross, although in part also to aid the restoration of the St. Sophia in Tsargrad"[17] (*Pisma* 2:242).

16. According to Sergei Solovyov, "Solovyov realized that he was a poor military correspondent and that his revolver would scarcely hit a target. Toward autumn he returned to St. Petersburg in order to serve the cause of the Slavs by those means that were at his disposal" (*Zhizn' i tvorcheskaia evoliutsiia* 165; *Vladimir Solovyov*, trans. Gibson 188).

17. This refers to the Cathedral of Hagia Sophia in Constantinople.

At first intending to deliver the lectures at the university, Solovyov was foiled in his attempt to secure a hall and had to postpone the event. He pleaded for help from his acquaintance, A. A. Kireev, in early 1878:[18]

> The local university management has had difficulty in giving me a room for the public lectures, apparently finding that *aula academica* [Latin: academic court] is better intended for student dances and public assault on the powers that be, rather than the discussion of dry matters. In light of this, I must rent a hall for myself, and finally settled on a hall belonging to the Credit Society. But I have absolutely no idea how to go about this. And I need to hurry, since I received permission for the lectures quite some time ago. The content has already been announced in the newspapers, to turn down the lectures would be awkward and undesirable for me, and it is no longer possible to put them off since Easter is approaching. Would you be so kind as to take on yet one more in a long line of favors? If you secured a hall for me, you'd have all my thanks. And in any case, you can arrange it forty times faster and more easily than I could. The price is immaterial, even if I have to give up all the money I have collected. The time is Thursday and Saturday of this week in the evening. If that is inconvenient for some reason, it could be other days.
>
> Be so kind as to send me some kind of answer.
>
> Your devoted Vlad. Solovyov (*Pis'ma* 2:95)

Solovyov's plea was apparently successful, and he wrote back to Kireev: "I received the permission and the lectures have been announced (in two newspapers) for the 26th and 28th. . . . I hope that everything works out, and I thank you with all my soul" (*Pis'ma* 2:96).

Solovyov did finally deliver the first of twelve public lectures at the end January but not, it seems, on the days initially announced. Shortly thereafter, the following announcement appeared in the February issue of the journal *The Orthodox Review* (*Pravoslavnoe Obozrenie*):

> Beginning on 29 January the Master of Philosophy V. S. Solovyov will read lectures on the philosophy of religion at 8:30 p.m. on Sundays and Fridays in the large auditorium of the Museum of Applied Sciences.
>
> The aim of Solovyov's lectures will be to show the rational character of positive religion, to show that the truth of faith, in the whole fullness of its concrete content, is, at the same time, the truth of reason.
>
> The central idea of the lectures is Divine Humanity as the living God.
>
> Of the twelve lectures the first six will represent a necessary transition from the natural content of human consciousness to the central idea that first received historical actuality in Christianity. Here, the main stages of this transition will be considered as they have been expressed in the intellectual history of pre-Christian humanity, i.e., Buddhist pessimism and nihilism, Plato's idealism, Old Testament monotheism.

---

18. Kireev (1833–1910) was a Slavophile philosopher.

The remaining six lectures will be concerned with the positive development of the religious idea itself. They will cover the actualization of Divine Humanity in eternity and in time, the divine world, the fall of spiritual beings into sin, the origin and meaning of the natural world, the earthly incarnation of Christ and redemption, the visible and invisible church, the end of the cosmic process, and the full revelation of Divine Humanity. (*SS* 12:539)[19]

The lectures attracted just about the entire educated elite of Petersburg. Despite the philosopher's young age and the prodigious work that was to follow, Sergei Solovyov calls his uncle's appearances "the apogee of his fame; all St. Petersburg thronged to them" (*Zhizn' i tvorcheskaia evoliutsiia* 165; *Vladimir Solovyov*, trans. Gibson 189). One particular guest was Sophia Khitrova, to whom Solovyov had recently been introduced and with whom he remained enamored for the rest of his life.[20] As mentioned earlier, the lectures also left a lasting impression on Dostoevsky and helped shape the famous novelist's own ideas on Divine Humanity.[21]

Solovyov claims that the aim of his series of lectures is to show the rational character of positive religion. In this way he appeals to the followers of contemporary philosophical and social movements that stress reason and rationality, agreeing with them that they have every right to reject religion, for in its current form it is not "positive," and only "calls for negation." "Religion in the present is not what it should be" (*SS* 3:3). At the same time, however, he rejects socialism and positivism for their exclusively humanist focus and their failure to recognize the unconditional principle in life. True religion, he tells us in the first lecture, "speaking generally and abstractly, is the connection between man and the world and the unconditional principle and concentration of all existence" (*SS* 3:3). "[R]eligion is the connection of man and the world with the unconditional and whole [*vsetselym*] principle" (*SS* 3:12).

Except for a brief reference to the physical edifice of Hagia Sophia in Constantinople in lecture 3, Solovyov first turns to Sophia as an idea in the second half of lecture 7. This lecture begins with a recapitulation of lecture 6, in which Solovyov had moved from a cosmological and historical survey of expressions of the Unconditional Principle (culminating in the contributions of the Hebrew prophets) to an actual description of that Principle, largely in Hegelian terms. Thus, the Unconditional, or God, "is" in three aspects or states: In-Itself (*v sebe; in Sich*), For-Itself (*dlia sebia); für Sich*), and By-Itself (*u sebia; bei Sich*). All of these states exist simultaneously and in relationship with each other. Indeed, their "distinction is *relationship*" (*SS* 3:85).

19. Translated by Jakim in *Lectures on Divine Humanity* ix. The confused history of the lectures was reconstructed by Florovskii in "Chteniia."

20. "We can say only one thing: Vl. Solovyov retained his feelings for S. P. Khitrovo for his whole life, with a few periodic moments of weakening. He dedicated his best poetry to her and continually journeyed to Pustyn'ka for more or less extended stays" (Losev, *Vladimir Solov'ev i ego vremia* 52).

21. See Kostalevsky 81–111.

We thus have *three relations* or *three positings* of that which absolutely is as determining itself with respect to its own content. First, it is posited as possessing this content in immediate, substantial unity, or nondifferentiation, with itself. It is posited as a single substance, which essentially includes all in its absolute power. Second, it is posited as manifesting or actualizing its own absolute content, opposing the latter to itself or separating it from itself, by an act of self-determination. Third and last, it is posited as maintaining and asserting itself in its own content or as realizing itself in an actual, mediated, or differentiated unity with this content, or essence, that is, with the *all*—in other words, as finding itself in its other, as eternally returning to itself and remaining "at home with itself [*bei sich*]." (SS 3:90)

Our translation picks up in the middle of lecture 7 with the first reference to Sophia. Solovyov's own footnotes to the published text of the *Lectures* are designated by symbols rather than numbers.

Lecture Seven

In the divine organism of Christ, the acting, unifying principle, the principle that expresses the unity of that which absolutely is, is obviously the Word, or Logos. The second kind of unity, the produced unity, is called Sophia in Christian theosophy. If we distinguish in the Absolute in general between the Absolute as such (that which absolutely is) and its content, essence, or idea, we will find the former directly expressed in the Logos and the latter directly expressed in Sophia, which is thus the expressed or actualized idea. And just as an existent being is distinct from its own idea but is at the same time one with it, so the Logos, too, is distinct from Sophia but is inwardly united with her. Sophia is God's body, the matter of Divinity,* permeated with the principle of divine unity. Actualizing in Himself, or bearing this unity, Christ, as the integral divine organism, both universal and individual, is both Logos and Sophia.

To speak of Sophia as an essential element of Divinity is not, from the Christian point of view, to introduce new gods. The thought of Sophia has always existed in Christianity; it even existed before Christianity. The Old Testament includes a whole book, attributed to Solomon, entitled "Sophia."[22] Although this book is not canonical, even in the canonical book of the Proverbs of Solomon we find the development of this idea of Sophia (under the corresponding Hebrew name *Hokhmah*).[23] It is stated there that wisdom existed before the creation of the world (that is, of the natural world). God "had her in the begin-

---

22. Solovyov refers here to the Wisdom of Solomon.

23. Solovyov transliterates the Hebrew word for Wisdom using Cyrillic characters. In a number of places throughout his published work, Solovyov illustrates his knowledge of Hebrew, sometimes to the point of boasting. For background on his study of Hebrew, Aramaic, and traditional Jewish texts see Gets.

* Author's note: Of course, I use such words as body and matter in the most general sense, as relative categories. I am not connecting them with those particular representations that can be applied to our material world but are absolutely inapplicable to Divinity.

ning of His way" (Proverbs 8:22).[24] In other words, wisdom is the idea that God has before Him in His work of creation and that He, consequently, actualizes. We find this term in the New Testament as well (in the Apostle Paul), now in a direct relation to Christ.[25]

The conception of God as an integral being, as a universal organism that presupposes a multiplicity of essential elements constituting this organism, may appear to violate the absoluteness of Divinity, to introduce nature into God. But it is precisely to absolutely distinguish God from our world, from our nature, from this visible reality, that it is necessary to acknowledge in Him His *own* distinctive eternal nature, His own distinctive eternal world. Otherwise, our idea of Divinity will be poorer, more abstract, than our conception of the visible world.[26]

The negative course in the evolution of religious consciousness was always such that Divinity was first cleansed, so to speak, of all actual determination, was reduced to a pure abstraction; then religious consciousness easily dispensed with this abstract Divinity and passed into an irreligious consciousness, into atheism.

If we do not acknowledge in Divinity the whole fullness of actuality, and thus necessarily of multiplicity too, positive significance inevitably passes to the multiplicity and actuality of this world. Then Divinity retains only a negative significance and is gradually denied. For if there is no other actuality, no absolute actuality, if there is no other multiplicity, no other fullness of being, then our present actuality will be the only one. Then Divinity will be left without any positive content. It will either merge with this world, with this nature (this world, this nature would then be acknowledged as the direct, immediate content of Divinity) and we will pass into a naturalistic pantheism, where this finite nature is all and God is only an empty word, or (and this is more consistent), Divinity, as an empty abstraction, will simply be denied, and consciousness will be openly atheistic.

Thus to God, as an integral being, together with unity belongs multiplicity, the multiplicity of substantial ideas, of potencies or forces with a determinate, particular content.

These forces, each possessing its own particular, determinate content, relating in different ways to the contents of the others, necessarily constitute different secondary wholes or spheres. Taken together, they constitute one divine world, but this world is necessarily differentiated into a multiplicity of spheres.

24. Fox translates these lines as "The Lord created me at the beginning of his way, / At the start of his works of old. / In primeval days I was formed, / At the start, at the world's origin." There is still a scholarly controversy over whether the Hebrew term "qanani" should be translated as "created" or "acquired/possessed/had" (see Fox 411). Whichever translation Solovyov used must have decided on the latter. (In *Russia and the Universal Church*, Solovyov translates into French from the Latin Vulgate version. See page 193.)

25. 1 Cor. 1:24.

26. This is not the last time that Solovyov will need to defend himself from accusations of pantheism. Indeed, criticism of his allegedly pantheistic teaching continues to this day. Florovsky, Zenkovsky, and Losev all read him as falling more or less often into heretical pantheism.

If the divine whole is composed of essential elements, of living forces with determinate, individual content, then these entities must have fundamental traits that necessarily belong to every individual being, certain traits of a psychical character common to all living forces.

If each of the entities actualizes a determinate content, or idea, and if the force actualizing them can, as we have seen, relate to a determinate content, or idea, in three ways (the force can have this content as an object of will, or contain it as what is willed; it can represent it; and finally, it can feel it), if this force can be related to the determinate content, or idea, substantially, ideally, and really, or sensuously, it is easy to see that the sensuous elements of the divine whole must differ depending upon which of these relations is predominant: the will (the moral principle), representation (the theoretical principle), or feeling (the aesthetic principle).

Thus, we have three orders of living forces, forming the three spheres of the divine world.

The individual forces of the first order, in which the principle of will predominates, may be called pure spirits; the forces of the second order may be called intellects; those of the third order, souls.

The divine world is thus composed of three main spheres: the sphere of pure spirits, the sphere of intellects, and the sphere of souls. The spheres are united in a close and unbreakable bond, united in perfect inner unity and solidarity, for each of them fulfills the others, is necessary to the others, and is affirmed by the others. Each separate force, each sphere, posits as its object, as its goal, all the others, which form the content of its life. In the same way, each separate force and separate sphere is the goal and object of all the others, for it possesses its own particular quality, a quality that they lack. Thus, a single, unbreakable bond of love unites all the countless elements that form the divine world.

Obviously, the actuality of this divine world, which is necessarily infinitely richer than our visible world, can be fully accessible only to one who actually belongs to that world. But since our natural world also is necessarily closely connected with this divine world (what that connection is, we shall see presently) and since there is not and cannot be any impassable gulf between them, the individual rays and glimmerings of the divine world must penetrate into our actual world,[27] constituting all the ideal content, all the beauty and truth, that we find in it. And man, who belongs to both worlds, can and must touch the divine world by an act of mental contemplation. And though living in the world of conflict and muffled disquiet, he enters into relations with the clear images from the kingdom of glory and eternal beauty. This positive, although incomplete knowledge of, or penetration into the reality of the divine world is particularly characteristic of poetic creation. Every true poet must necessarily penetrate 'into the fatherland of flame and word,'[28] in order to take from there

27. See Solovyov's early Sophianic poems (pages 105–108) for the use of light imagery to depict Sophia.

28. As noted in part 1, this phrase is the fourth line of A. K. Tolstoy's "Menia, vo mrake i v pyli" (see page 74). The rest of the poem follows.

the primal images of his creation and, together with them, that internal lucidity that is called inspiration and through which we, in our natural reality, can
find the sounds and colors for the incarnation of ideal types, as one of our poets says—

> And my dark glance brightened,
> And the unseen world became visible,
> And since that time my ear hears
> What others cannot catch,
> And I came down from the mountain heights,
> Fully penetrated by her rays,
> And on the agitated dale
> I gaze with new eyes
> And I hear as incessant talk
> Rings everywhere,
> As the stone heart of the mountains
> Beats with love in the dark depths;
> And slow clouds curl
> With love in the sky-blue firmament,
> And under the bark of trees
> The living juice in the leaves
> Rises up with love as a singing stream.
> And I understood with a prophetic heart
> That all that is born from the Word,
> Pouring out the rays of love,
> Thirsts to return to Him again.
> And every stream of life,
> Submissive to the law of love,
> Rushes irrepressibly to God's loins
> With all the strength of being.
> And sound and light are everywhere,
> And there is only one principle for all the worlds,
> And there is nothing in nature
> That would not breathe with love.

Lecture Eight

The eternal, or divine world (about which I spoke in my last lecture) is not a
riddle for reason. This world, as the ideal fullness of the all and the actualization of goodness, truth, and beauty, presents itself to reason as that which is, in
itself, obligatory and *normal*. This world, as the absolute norm, is *logically* necessary for reason, and if reason cannot certify for us the *factual* existence of this
world, this is only because, in its essence, reason is not an organ for knowing
any factual actuality. It is obvious that any factual actuality can be known only
through actual experience. But the ideal necessity of the divine world and of
Christ, as the absolutely universal and, at the same time and thereby, the absolutely individual center of this world, in possession of its whole fullness—this
ideal necessity is clear for speculative reason, which can find only in this eternal

sphere that absolute measure by which it recognizes the given natural world, our actuality, as something conditional, abnormal, and transitory.

Thus, it is not the eternal, divine world but rather nature, the actual world given to us, that constitutes a riddle for reason. Reason's task is to explain this actuality, which is both factually indubitable and obscure to reason. This task clearly consists in deriving the conditional from the unconditional, in deriving what is not in itself obligatory from the absolutely obligatory, in deriving contingent reality from the absolute idea, in deriving the natural world of phenomena from the world of divine essence.

This derivation would be an impossible task if there were not something that unites the two opposed terms (one of which is to be derived from the other), something belonging equally to both terms, to both spheres, and therefore serving as a transition between them. This uniting link between the divine and natural worlds is *humanity*.

A human being contains all possible oppositions, which can all be reduced to the one great opposition between the unconditional and the conditional, between absolute and eternal essence and transitory phenomenon, or appearance. A human being is at the same time divinity and nothingness.

There is no need to dwell on the assertion of this undeniable opposition, because it has long represented a common theme of poets as well as of psychologists and moralists.

Our task is not to describe humanity but to indicate its significance in the general connectedness of that which truly is.

In the previous lecture, I spoke about the necessity of distinguishing a twofold unity in the integrity of the divine being, the acting, or producing, unity of the divine creativity of the Word (Logos) and the produced, or actualized, unity, just as in a particular organism of the natural world we distinguish the active unity (the principle that produces and maintains its organic integrity, the principle that constitutes the living and active *soul* of this organism) from the unity of that which is produced, or actualized, by this soul, the unity of the organic *body*.

If in the divine being, in Christ, the first, the producing unity is, strictly speaking, Divinity, God as the active force, or Logos, and if, thus, in this first unity we have Christ as the divine being proper, then the second, the produced unity, to which we have given the mystical name Sophia, is the principle of humanity, the ideal or normal human being. And Christ, who partakes, within this unity, of the human principle, is a human being, the second Adam (to use the scriptural expression).[29]

Thus, Sophia is ideal or perfect humanity, eternally contained in the integral divine being, or Christ. Since it is beyond doubt that God, to exist in actuality and reality, must manifest Himself, manifest His existence, that is, must act in the other, the existence of this other is thereby established as necessary. And, since in speaking of God, we cannot have in mind the form of time, because whatever we say about God presupposes eternity, the existence

29. 1 Cor. 15: 22; Romans 5:14–19.

of this other with respect to which God manifests Himself must be acknowledged as necessarily eternal. This other is not *absolutely* other for God (that would be inconceivable), but is God's own expression, or manifestation, with respect to which God is called the Word.

But this disclosure, or inner revelation, of Divinity and, consequently, the distinction of God as Logos from God as primordial substance, or Father, necessarily presuppose that in which Divinity is revealed or in which it acts, and which in the Father exists substantially, or in a latent form, while being manifested through the Logos.

Consequently, for God to exist eternally as Logos, or as active divinity, it is necessary to assume the eternal existence of real elements that receive the divine action. It is necessary to assume the existence of a world that is patient of divine action, that makes room in itself for the divine unity. The specific, produced unity of that world—the center of the world and the periphery of Divinity—is humanity. Every actuality presupposes an act, and every act presupposes a real object of that act—a subject that receives it. Consequently, God's actuality, based upon God's activity, presupposes a subject that receives this activity, namely humanity, and presupposes it *eternally*, since God's activity is eternal. The objection that an eternal object for God's activity is already presented in the Logos is not valid, for the Logos is God made manifest. This manifestation presupposes that other for which, or with respect to which, God manifests Himself, that is, it presupposes humanity.

To be sure, in speaking of the eternity of man or humankind, we are not referring to "natural man," or the human being as a phenomenon. That would be an internal contradiction and would also contradict scientific experience.

Science, specifically geology, shows that the natural, or earthly human being appeared on earth at a particular moment in time, as the final link of organic development on the globe. But the human being as an empirical phenomenon presupposes the human being as an intelligible being, and it is of this being that we are speaking.

On the other hand, in speaking of the essential and eternal human being, we have in mind neither the generic concept *human being* nor humankind as a collective noun. To be sure, for those who accept the given natural actuality as something absolute and uniquely positive and real, everything that is not this given actuality can only be a general concept or an abstraction. When they speak about an actual human being, they have in mind this or that individual being, who exists in a specific space and at a specific time as a physical, material organism. Beyond this, a human being is for them only an abstraction and humankind is only a collective noun. Such is the point of view of empirical realism.[30] We will not argue against it; rather, we will attempt to develop it with full logical consistency. As we shall see, better than anything else this will show that empirical realism has no basis. Admitting that only a single real fact has genuine being, we, to be logically consistent, cannot acknowledge even a separate, individual human being to be a genuine, actual

30. Solovyov here implicitly contrasts empirical realism to transcendental idealism.

being. From this point of view, even that individual must be regarded as only an abstraction.

In fact, let us consider a particular human individual. What do we find in him as a reality? First of all, he is a physical organism. But every physical organism is an aggregate of a number of organic elements, a group in space. Our body consists of a multiplicity of organs and tissues, which can all be reduced to a union, diversely modified, of minutest organic elements, the so-called cells. From the empirical point of view, there is no basis for regarding this union as a real rather than merely a collective unit. The unity of the physical organism, that is, of this entire multiplicity of elements, is manifested empirically only as a connection, as a relationship, but not as a real unit.

Thus, if, empirically, we find the organism to be only a collection of a number of elementary entities, a specific physical human being cannot, from this point of view, be called a real indivisible, that is an individual in the strict sense of the word. We could with equal justification recognize each individual organ as a real unit, and we have far better grounds to recognize the individual organic element, the cell, as a real unit. But one must go beyond this, for the cell is also a complex entity. From the standpoint of empirical reality, it is but a physical-chemical association of material particles, in the end, an association of a number of homogeneous atoms. But the atom, as a material unit and, thus, a unit of extension (and it is only in this sense that empirical realism admits atoms) cannot be absolutely indivisible: matter as such is divisible to infinity, and, consequently, the atom is only a conventional term of division, nothing more. Thus, an individual human being as an organic specimen is not a real unit, and neither are the smallest elements of which he is constituted. And it is absolutely impossible to find such a unit in external reality.[31]

But not having found the real unity of the human individual in this individual's physical being, or in this individual as an external phenomenon, perhaps we will find it in this individual's psychic being, in the inner human phenomenon, the human being within. But here, too, what do we find from the empirical point of view? We find a succession of separate states in human psychic life, a series of thoughts, desires, and feelings. To be sure, this series is united in self-consciousness in that all these states refer to a single I. However, empirically, this reference of different states to a single psychic focus, which we call *I*, is only one psychical phenomenon among others. Self-consciousness is only one of the acts of psychic life. The *I* of which we are conscious is not a real entity but a result produced or conditioned by a long series of processes. The *I*, as only an act of self-consciousness, is itself devoid of all content, is but a point of light in the muddy stream of psychic states.[32]

---

31. Here, as elsewhere, we clearly see Solovyov's continuing interest in the scientific advances of his age, despite the fact that he never completed the scientific degree he first sought.

32. Solovyov's interest in science was equaled at this time only by his pursuit of psychic phenomena, séances, automatic writing, and other manifestations of the spirit world. For more on Solovyov's spiritualist pursuits, see Kornblatt, "Who Is Sophia?"

Because of continuous changes of matter in it, a physical organism cannot maintain any real identity at two different moments of time (we know, for instance, that a human body may not contain a single material particle that existed in it a month before). In the same way, in human psychic life as a phenomenon, every act is something new: every thought and every feeling are new phenomena, connected with the remainder of the psychic content solely by the laws of association. From this point of view, we find absolute unity, a real unit, neither in the external, physical organism nor in the inner, psychic organism.

A human being, that is, this separate individual, appears here, on the one hand, as a collection of an uncountable number of elements, which continuously change their material composition and retain only a formal, abstract unity and, on the other hand, as a series of psychic states, following one after another according to an external, random association and connected with one another only by a formal, contentless, and even discontinuous act of reflective self-consciousness, expressed in our *I*. This *I* is itself different in each separate act of self-consciousness (when I mentally say "*I*" at a given moment and later say the same thing in moments that follow, these are separate acts or states that are not connected in any real unity). If an individual human being, as a phenomenon, thus represents in the physical aspect only a spatial *group* of elements and in the psychic aspect only a temporal series of separate states or events, then, from this point of view, not just human beings in general, or humanity, but also separate human individuals are only abstractions, not real units. As we have already pointed out, generally speaking it is impossible, from such a point of view, to find any real unit. For, on the one hand, every material element that enters into the composition of an organism can, since this element is spatially extended, be divided *ad infinitum*, and, on the other hand, every psychic event, since it occurs at a determinate time, can be divided *ad infinitum* into infinitely small temporal moments. In neither case is there an ultimate unit; every assumed unit turns out to be conventional and arbitrary. But if there are no real units, neither can there be a whole. If there are no actually determinate parts, there is no actual whole. From this point of view, the result is complete nothingness, the negation of all reality—a result that proves the obvious inadequacy of this point of view. In fact, if empirical realism, which takes the given phenomenon as the sole actuality, cannot find any ground for an ultimate reality, for any real units, we are justified in concluding that these real units, without which nothing can exist, have their own independent essence beyond the limits of given phenomena, which are only the manifestations of those genuine essences, not the essences themselves.

We must therefore acknowledge that full actuality is possessed by ideal entities, which are not given in immediate external experience and are neither material elements existing in space nor psychic events or states occurring in time.

From this point of view, when we speak of a human being, we have neither need nor justification to limit this human being to the given visible actuality. We speak of an ideal human being, but a human being who is nonetheless altogether essential and real, who is much more, incommensurably more, essential and real than the visible manifestation of human beings. There is in us an unlimited wealth of forces and content concealed beyond the threshold of our present consciousness. Only a certain portion of those forces and that content passes, a little at a time, over the threshold into our consciousness, never exhausting the whole.

"It is in ourselves," an ancient poet states, "not in the stars of heaven, nor in the depths of Tartarus, that the eternal powers of the whole universe reside."*[33]

Although a human being as phenomenon is a temporary, transitory fact, the human being as essence is necessarily eternal and all-embracing. What, then, is an ideal human being? To be actual, such a being must be both one and many and therefore is not merely the universal common essence of all human individuals, taken in abstraction from them. Such a being is universal but also individual, an entity that actually contains all human individuals within itself. Every one of us, every human being, is essentially and actually rooted in and partakes of the universal, or absolute, human being.

Divine forces constitute the single, integral, absolutely universal, absolutely individual organism of the living Logos. Similarly, all human elements constitute a similarly integral organism, one both universal and individual, which is the necessary actualization and receptacle of the organism of the living Logos. They constitute a universally human organism as the eternal body of God and the eternal soul of the world. Since this latter organism, that is, Sophia, in its eternal being necessarily consists of a multiplicity of elements of which she is the real unity, each of these elements, as a necessary component part of eternal Divine Humanity, must be recognized as eternal in the absolute or ideal order.

Thus, when we speak of the eternity of humankind, we make implicit reference to the eternity of each separate individual.** Apart from such eternity, humankind itself would be an illusion.

The deepest essence of every actual human being is rooted in the eternal divine world. Every human being is not only a visible phenomenon, that is, a series of events and a group of facts, but also an eternal and special being, a necessary and irreplaceable link in the absolute whole. Only by recognizing

33. Schopenhauer uses this line from the medieval philosopher Agrippa, unattributed as an epigraph to the second part of his *World as Will and Representation*. Solovyov uses it as well in *The Sophia* (see page 145). It has its origin in Ovid's *Ars Amatoria*.

* Author's note: Cf., Nos habitat non Tartara, sed nec sidera coeli Spiritus in nobis qui viget illa fecit [Latin: It lives in us and not in Tartarus, not in distant constellations; Spirit, having power in us, created them].

** Author's note: In speaking here of the eternity of every human being, I do not assert anything completely new or contradictory to established religious positions. In considering the origin of the world, Christian theologians and philosophers always distinguished between the finite manifestation of the world in space and time and the eternal existence of the idea of the world in divine thought, in Logos. And it must be remembered that in God, as the eternal reality, the idea of the world is not to be regarded as anything abstract, but must necessarily be considered eternally real.

this is it possible to admit rationally the two great truths that are absolutely necessary for both theology, that is, for religious knowledge, and human life in general: the truths of human freedom and human immortality.

To begin with the latter: it is perfectly evident that if we regard a human being as merely a being originating in time, created at a determinate moment and not existing prior to physical birth, this, in essence, reduces the human being to phenomenal appearance, to manifested existence, which actually begins only with physical birth. But, after all, such existence also ends with physical death. That which appeared only in time must also disappear in time. An infinite existence *after death* is by no means logically compatible with nothingness *before birth*.

As natural beings, as phenomena, human beings exist only between physical birth and physical death. We can admit that they exist after physical death only if we acknowledge that they are not merely beings that live in the natural world, are not just phenomena, but are also eternal, intelligible essences. But in this case it is logically necessary to acknowledge that a human being exists not only after death, but also before birth, because an intelligible essence, by its very concept, is not subject to the form of time, which is only a phenomenal form.

Passing to the second truth mentioned above, human freedom, it is easy to see that by regarding human beings as created in time, out of nothing, and, consequently, as accidental for God (since it is assumed that God can exist without human beings and, before their creation, did exist without them), by regarding human beings as absolutely determined by God's arbitrary will and therefore as absolutely passive with respect to God, we decidedly leave no room for human freedom.

I shall try to show in the next lecture how the problem of freedom can be solved from the point of view of eternal humanity, or from the divine human point of view.

Lecture Nine

[This lecture begins with a discussion of the natural, created world, and the existence of evil. Again, there are three, not two (human vs. divine) worlds, all interacting and reflexive of the others. As we will see below, the "second, produced, unity—in contrast to the primordial unity of the divine Logos—is, as we know, the World Soul, or ideal humanity (Sophia), which contains within itself and unites with itself all particular living entities, or souls. As the realization of the divine principle, its image and likeness, archetypal humankind, or the World Soul, is both one and all. The World Soul occupies a mediating position between the multiplicity of living entities, which constitute the real content of its life, and the absolute unity of Divinity, which is the ideal principle and norm of its life." We pick up the translation here in the last third of the lecture.]

The first sphere of the divine world is characterized by a decisive predominance of the deepest, the most inward, the most spiritual principle of being: will. Here, all entities are in a simple unity of will with Divinity, in a unity of pure, immediate love. They are essentially determined by the divine first principle; they abide "in the bosom of the Father."[34] Insofar as they belong to this first sphere, entities are pure spirits, and the entire being of these pure spirits is directly determined by their will, because the latter is identical with the all-one [vse edinoe] will of God. Therefore, the predominant tone of being here is absolute love, in which all are one [vse—odno].

In the second sphere, the fullness of divine being unfolds in a multiplicity of forms bound together by an ideal unity. Here, representation or intellectual activity determined by the divine mind predominates. Entities in this sphere can therefore be called minds. Here, all entities have their being not only in God and for God but also for one another—in representation or contemplation. Determinateness and separateness already appear, though only in an ideal manner. All essences (ideas) stand in a certain relation (ratio, τὸ ἄπειρον) one to another. Thus, this sphere is preeminently the domain of the divine Word (Logos), which ideally expresses the intelligent fullness of divine determinations. In this sphere, every "intelligent" being is a determinate idea, which has its determinate place in the ideal cosmos.

In these two spheres (spiritual and intellectual) of the divine world, everything that exists is directly determined by the divine principle in the first two forms of its being. But if, in general, the actuality of the divine world consists in the interaction between the one and the all, between the divine principle itself and the multiplicity of beings that it contains, the divine world cannot have its full actuality in these two first spheres in themselves, for there is no real interaction here. This is because entities as pure spirits and pure minds, abiding in immediate unity with Divinity, do not have any separate, isolated, or self-centered existence and, as such, cannot, out of themselves, internally, act upon the divine principle. Indeed, since they exist in the immediate unity of divine will and love, entities in the first sphere, or as pure spirits, have in themselves only potential existence. But in the second sphere, although these multiple entities are in fact separated out by the divine Logos as determinate objective forms that stand in a permanent determinate relation to one another and consequently receive a certain individuality, this is a purely ideal individuality, for the entire being of this sphere is determined by intellectual intuition or pure representation. But such an ideal individuality of its elements is insufficient for the divine principle as the one. What is necessary for it is that the multiple entities should receive their own real individuality. Otherwise, the force of divine unity or love would have no object upon which to manifest or disclose itself in its fullness. Therefore, the divine being cannot be content with the eternal contemplation of ideal essences (with contemplating them and being contemplated by them). It is not sufficient for the divine being to possess them as its object, its idea, and to be for them only an idea. But "free from envy," from exclusiveness, the divine being desires the real life of these essences, removes its will from that absolute substantial unity by which the first sphere of divine being is

34. John 1:18.

determined, directs this will upon the whole multiplicity of the ideal objects contemplated in the second sphere, and lingers upon each of them separately. Through an act of its will, it unites with each one of them and thereby asserts and fixes the independent being of each, so that each in turn may act upon the divine principle. By that real action, the third sphere of the divine principle is formed. This act (or these acts) of the divine will, which unites with the ideal objects or forms of the divine mind and thereby gives them real being, is, strictly speaking, the act of divine creation. The following consideration may serve to clarify it. The ideal entities (or minds) that constitute the object of divine action do not really have in themselves, in their separateness, substantial being or absolute independence (that would contradict the unity of that which is). Yet, each one of them represents a certain ideal particularity, a certain characteristic property, that makes this object what it is and distinguishes it from all other objects, so that it always has an absolutely independent significance, if not according to its existence, then according to its essence or idea (*non quoad existentiam, sed quoad essentiam* [Latin: not as far as existence, but as far as essence]), that is, according to that inner property that defines its thinkable or intellectually intuitable relation to all else, or its concept (τὸ ἄπειρον) independent of its real existence. But Divinity, as inwardly all-one [*vseedinoe*] and all-good [*vseblagoe*], fully asserts all that is other. In other words, Divinity posits its own will as an unlimited potency of being (τὸ ἄπειρον)[35] into all that is other, not retaining it in itself as in the one, but actualizing or objectifying it for itself as the *all-one*. By virtue of the essential particularity (by which it is *this*) that belongs to all else, that is, to every divine idea or to every objective form, every such image, every idea with which the divine will unites itself does not remain indifferent to that will but necessarily changes its action in accordance with its own particularity, gives to it its own specific character, molds it into its own form, so to speak. For it is clear that the property of actual will is necessarily determined not only by the willer but also by the willer's object.

Every objective form, receiving the unlimited divine will in its own manner, by virtue of its own particularity, thereby appropriates it, that is, makes it its own. Thus, this will ceases to be only divine will. Received by a determinate form (or idea) and having received from this form its own particular, determinate character, divine will becomes as much a property of that objective form in its particularity as an action of the divine being. In Divinity, the unlimited power of being (τὸ ἄπειρον) is always covered by actuality, for God always (*eternally*) desires or loves all and has all in Himself and for Himself. But in each particular entity, this unlimited potency ceases to be covered by God's actuality, for this actuality is not the all but only one of the things in the all, something particular. That is to say, each entity loses its own immediate unity with Divinity, and the act of God's will, which has no limits in Divinity since

35. After Anaximander (610–546/545 BCE), meaning an unlimited, undifferentiated mass, or primal chaos.

it is never separated from all other entities, receives such a limit in a particular entity. But in becoming thus individualized, this entity gains the possibility of acting upon the one divine will and determining the latter in its own particular way. The particular idea with which the act of divine will is united, impressing upon that act its own distinctive character, separates it out of the absolute immediate unity of the divine will, receives it *for itself*, and acquires in it the living force of actuality, which enables it to exist and act autonomously as an individual, or an independent subject. Thus, we now have not only ideal entities that have their life only in the contemplation of Divinity but also living entities that have their own actuality and act autonomously upon the divine principle. We call such entities souls. Thus, by becoming objects of particular divine will (more precisely, by particularizing, in virtue of their inherent particularity, the divine will that acts in them), the eternal objects of divine contemplation become "living souls." In other words, entities that substantially rest in the bosom of God the Father, that are ideally contemplated and contemplating in the light of the divine Logos, receive, by the power of the quickening Spirit, their own real being and action.

The unity of the divine principle, substantially abiding in the first sphere of being and ideally manifested in the second, can receive its real actualization only in the third. In all three spheres we distinguish the active divine principle of unity, the Logos, as the direct manifestation of Divinity, and the "many" or "all" that is unified by the action of this unity receives it into itself and actualizes it. But in the first sphere, this "all" exists in itself only potentially, and in the second, it exists only ideally. Only in the third does it receive its own actual existence. Therefore the unity of this sphere, produced by the divine Logos, appears for the first time as an actual, independent entity, capable of acting upon the divine principle. Only here does the object of divine action become a genuine, actual subject and the action become a genuine interaction.

This second, produced, unity—in contrast to the primordial unity of the divine Logos—is, as we know, the World Soul, or ideal humanity (Sophia), which contains within itself and unites with itself all particular living entities, or souls.[36] As the realization of the divine principle, its image and likeness, archetypal humankind, or the World Soul, is both one and all. The World Soul occupies a mediating position between the multiplicity of living entities, which constitute the real content of its life, and the absolute unity of Divinity, which is the ideal principle and norm of its life. As the living focus, or soul, of all creatures and the real form of Divinity, the existent subject of creaturely being and the existent object of divine action, partaking of the unity of God and at the same time embracing the whole multiplicity of living souls, the all-one humankind, or the World Soul, is a dual being. Containing within itself both the divine principle and creaturely being, the World Soul is not determined exclusively by either one or the other, and it therefore remains free. The divine principle, which is present in the World Soul, liberates it from its creaturely nature,

---

36. This is an excellent example of Solovyov's equation of Sophia with the World Soul.

while nature in turn liberates it with respect to Divinity. Embracing living entities (souls) and, in them, all ideas, the World Soul is not exclusively bound to any one among them, is free from all them. However, since it is the immediate center and real unity of all these entities, the World Soul receives in their individuality independence from the divine principle and the possibility of acting upon the latter as a free subject. Insofar as it receives the divine Logos into itself and is determined by the divine Logos, the World Soul is humanity, the divine humanity of Christ, the body of Christ, Sophia. Receiving the one divine principle and uniting with this unity the whole multiplicity of entities, the World Soul thereby gives the divine principle complete actual realization in the all. Through the World Soul, God is manifested as the living, active force in all creation, as the Holy Spirit. In other words, in being determined or formed by the divine Logos, the World Soul enables the Holy Spirit to actualize itself in the all, for that which in the light of the Logos is disclosed in ideal forms is actualized by the Holy Spirit in a real action. Hence, it is clear that the World Soul contains in unity all the elements of the world only insofar as it itself is subordinate to the divine principle that it receives, insofar as it has the divine principle as the sole object of its vital will, as the absolute goal and focus of its being. For the World Soul can communicate the divine all-unity to all of creation only insofar as it itself is permeated by that unity, uniting and subordinating to itself the entire multiplicity of entities by the power of Divinity present in it. The World Soul possesses all to the extent that it is possessed by Divinity, for in Divinity all is in unity. Asserting itself in the all-unity, the World Soul is thereby free from all in particular, free in the positive sense, as possessing all. But the World Soul receives and is determined by the divine principle not because of any external necessity but by its own action, by its own positing; the World Soul has in itself the principle of independent action, or will, that is, the capacity to initiate in itself an inner striving. In other words, the World Soul can itself choose the object of its life-striving.

What could this object be if not the divine principle? It possesses the all, and the unlimited potentiality of being (τὸ ἄπειρον) is satisfied in it. But it is satisfied not absolutely and, therefore, not finally. The World Soul has the "all," as the content of its own being (its own idea), not directly from itself but from the divine principle, which is essentially prior to it, is presupposed by it, and determines it. Only in the openness of its inner being to the action of the divine Logos does the World Soul receive, in Him and from Him power over the all and possess the all.

Therefore, although it possesses the all, the World Soul can still desire to possess the all differently from the way it does, that is, it can desire to possess it *from itself*, like God. It can desire that to the fullness of being belonging to it there be added absolute *autonomy* in the possession of this fullness, an autonomy that does not belong to it. By virtue of this, the World Soul can separate the relative center of its life from the absolute center of divine life; it can assert itself outside God. But thereby the World Soul necessarily loses its central position, falls out of the all-one center of divine being, and ends up at the multiple periphery of creation, losing its freedom and power over this creation, for it possesses such power not from itself but only as a mediator between creation and Divinity, from which, in its self-assertion, it is now separated. In applying its will to itself, in concentrating itself in itself, the World Soul takes itself away from the all, becomes only one among many. When the World Soul ceases to unite all with itself, all things lose their common bond and the unity of cosmic creation breaks up into a multitude of separate elements: the universal organism is transformed into a mechanical aggregate of atoms. For all the particular, specific elements of the universal organism in themselves, precisely as specific elements (each as "something" but not as all, as "this" but not as "another"), are not in immediate unity with one another but have this unity only through the World Soul, which is their common center that contains and encompasses all of them within itself. But with the separation of the World Soul, when it detached from the whole by exciting in itself its own peculiar will the particular elements of the universal organism lose their common bond in the World Soul and, left to themselves, are doomed to discordant, egoistic existence. The root of such existence is evil and the fruit, suffering. All of creation is thus made subject to the vanity and bondage of corruption not willingly but by the will of that which has subjugated it: by the will of the World Soul, as the one free principle of natural life.[37]

Lecture Ten

[Solovyov continues his discussion of the World Soul in lecture 10 but mentions Sophia only once, as the "universal organism" and "the incarnated divine idea" (SS 3:146). He explains the presence of the World Soul at the beginning of the world process as the passive potential for all-unity and equates it with the term "nature" (SS 3:144). For the most part, lecture 10 traces the development of the world process through various historical peoples, culminating in the Jews, the birth nation of Christ.]

Lectures Eleven and Twelve

[In these last two lectures, Solovyov continues his historical survey, now after the incarnation of Jesus Christ and the creation of the church, which he calls the "body of Christ" (SS 3:172). He returns to Sophia only at the end of lecture 12, as translated below, where he argues for the necessary future reunion of the Eastern and Western churches into the Universal Church. Sophia, the true "body of Christ," *is* this church. We reproduce here only the last paragraph.]

If the overshadowing of the human Mother by the active power of God produced the incarnation of Divinity in humanity, the fructification of the divine Mother (the Church) by the active human principle must produce a free deification of humankind. Prior to Christianity, the natural principle in humankind was the given (the fact), while Divinity was the unknown (the ideal). As the

---

37. This last section shows the strong influence of Gnostic ideas about Sophia's rebellion.

unknown, Divinity acted (ideally) upon humanity. In Christ, the unknown was given, the ideal became a fact, an event, the active divine principle became material. The Word was made flesh, and this new flesh is the divine substance of the Church. Prior to Christianity, the fixed foundation of life was human nature (the old Adam) and the Divine was the principle of change, motion, progress. After Christianity, the Divine, as incarnate, becomes the fixed foundation, the element of life for humankind. Here, the unknown is humankind, which corresponds to the Divine, that is, it is capable of uniting with the Divine by its own initiative, of assimilating it. As the unknown, this ideal humankind is the active principle of history, the principle of movement, of progress. In the pre-Christian course of history, human nature, or the natural human element, was the basis or matter, while the divine mind ὁ λόγος τοῦ θεοῦ [Greek: the Word of God] was the active and formative principle. The result was the God-man, that is, God who has received human nature. In the same manner, in the process of Christianity, divine nature (the Word made flesh, or the body of Christ, Sophia) is the basis or matter, while human reason is the active and formative principle. The result is the man-god, that is, man who has received Divinity. And since a human being can receive Divinity only in his or her absolute wholeness, that is, in union with the all, the man-god is necessarily collective and universal, that it, is all-humankind, the Universal Church. The God-man is individual whereas the man-god is universal. Thus, the radius of a circle remains the same for any point on the whole circumference; consequently, the radius is itself already the beginning of the circle, while the points on the periphery form the circle only in their totality. In the history of Christianity, the fixed divine foundation in humankind is represented by the Eastern Church, while the Western world represents the human principle. And, here, before reason could become the fructifying principle of the Church, it had to step away from the Church in order that it might develop all its powers in freedom. Only after the human principle has completely isolated itself and come to know its helplessness in this isolation, can it enter into a free union with the divine foundation of Christianity, preserved in the Eastern Church, and, as a result of that free union, give birth to a spiritual humankind.

Revised translation by Boris Jakim; additional revisions
by Judith Deutsch Kornblatt

From *Russia and the Universal Church* (Book Three): An Overview

Solovyov first published *Russia and the Universal Church* in France in 1889. He traveled to Paris in May of 1888 and shortly thereafter presented his paper "The Russian Idea" in an effort to introduce his ideas to the French public. In that lecture he criticizes the Russian Church quite sharply and begins the development of his ideas on the primacy of Rome that form the basis of *Russia and the Universal Church.*[38] The first part of this lengthy work attempts to prove that the Orthodox East has no true religious administration. The second part justifies locating that administrative center with the Catholic Pope. These ideas clearly won him no friends among the Russian ecclesiastic authorities, but they also irritated Catholics as well as Russian Orthodox believers. As he wrote to a Catholic friend, "My French book is disapproved of from both sides: liberals for its clericalism, and clerics for its liberalism. The Jesuit fathers have washed their hands of me and are trying to 'silence' me" (*Pis'ma* 1:179).

The third part—"Book Three: The Trinitarian Principle and Its Social Application"—departs from the earlier discussion of the ecclesiatic structure of the church and returns to the "dogmatic and theosophic character" of his work from the 1870s. In fact, Solovyov's nephew calls it "a synthesis of the youthful works *Sophie, The Philosophical Principles of Integral Knowledge,* and *The Lectures on Godmanhood* [Divine Humanity] with Solovyov's mature Catholic ideas" (*Zhizn' i tvorcheskaia evoliutsiia* 285; *Vladimir Solovyov,* trans. Gibson 352). By the time Sergei Solovyov wrote his biography, he himself had converted to Catholicism, and thus he emphasizes quite strongly his uncle's pro-Catholic leanings. We might do better, however, to stress the title that Solovyov himself chose: *The Universal Church.* That church reunites the East and the West, presumably uniting the best of both.

Sophia's centrality to *Russia and the Universal Church* is most clear in its final line: "The cycle of sacraments, like the cycle of universal life, is completed by the resurrection of the flesh, by the integration of all of humanity, by the definitive incarnation of Divine Wisdom." The following translation of book 3, chapters 3 through 7, elaborate on the many meanings of Sophia.

"III. The Divine Essence and Its Threefold Manifestation"

God is. This axiom of faith finds its confirmation in philosophizing reason, which, by its very nature, strives to find absolute and necessary being, that is, such a being that has the entire foundation of its existence in itself, explains itself, and can serve as the explanation of all things. Taking this fundamental concept as our point of departure, we had previously distinguished in God: (1) the triune subject, presupposed by the fullness of His existence; and (2) the objective essence or absolute substance which this subject possesses in three different respects—in pure or initial act, in secondary or manifested action, and in the third state, or the perfect possession of itself. We have shown that these three aspects can be grounded neither upon a separation of parts nor upon a succession of phases (these two conditions are equally incompatible with the concept of Divinity); and this presupposes, in the unity of the absolute essence, the eternal existence of the three relative subjects, or the consubstantial

---

38. See S. Solov'ev, *Zhizn' i tvorcheskaia evoliutsiia* 277–81; *Vladimir Solovyov,* trans. Gibson 343–48, for a discussion of the writing and publication history of the book.

and indivisible hypostases, which in Christian revelation are called by the holy names of the Father, the Son, and the Spirit. It is now incumbent upon us to define and name this absolute objectivity itself, the one substance of this Divine Trinity.

This substance is one; but since it cannot be a thing among other things, a particular object, it is precisely the universal substance, or *all in unity* [*vse v edinstve*]. Possessing this substance, God possesses all in it; this substance is the fullness or absolute universality of being, preceding all partial existence and surpassing the latter.

This universal substance, this absolute unity, is the essential Wisdom of God (*Hokhmah*, Σοφία). She possesses the hidden power of the all, while herself being possessed by God, and this in a threefold manner. She herself says this: "The Lord created me [possedit me; Latin: possessed me] at the beginning of his way, / at the start of his works of old" (Prov. 8:22).[39] And further: "In primeval days I was formed, / at the start, at the world's origin" (8:23). And in order to complement and explain this threefold form of existence, she adds: "And I was near him, growing up [cuncta componens; Latin: putting everything together], / and I was his delight day by day, / frolicking before him at all times" (8:30).[40] In other words, God possesses His unique and universal substance, or His essential Wisdom, as the eternal Father, as the Son, and as the Holy Spirit. Thus, having one and the same unique objective substance, these three divine subjects are consubstantial.

Wisdom has revealed to us that in which her action consists: she shapes the universe (she was a "master craftsman" [putting everything together]). She will now also tell us what her possession consists in: "frolicking before him at all times, / frolicking in his habitable world. / and my delight is in mankind" (8:30–31).

What is the nature of this delight of the Divine Wisdom, and why does she find her greatest joy in the sons of men?

In His absolute substance, God possesses the fullness of being. He is one in all, and He contains all in His unity. This universality presupposes multiplicity, but a multiplicity which is reduced to unity, which is unified actually. And in God, who is eternal, this unification, too, is eternal. In God, indeterminate multiplicity never existed, was never manifested *in actu*; rather, from all eternity, multiplicity was subordinated and reduced to the absolute unity in the three indivisible forms of the latter: to the unity of simple being or of being in

39. In the original French version, Solovyov transliterates the Hebrew text into Latin letters, followed by a translation into Latin. The Russian translation by G. A. Rachinskii transliterates the Hebrew using Cyrillic letters, then translates into Russian. Here we include the English version from Fox's translation, with Solovyov's Latin insertion in brackets when it affects his interpretation.

40. As explained in part 1, the Hebrew term for "craftsman" here, *amon*, can be and probably is more correctly translated as youth or nursling (see page 37). Fox translates it as "growing up." The nonetheless common translation as craftsman from the Latin Vulgate—"putting everything together"—clearly suits Solovyov's purposes to show the close relationship between Sophia and the Creator.

itself—in the Father; to the unity of actively manifested being—in the Son, who is the direct action, image, and Word of the Father; and finally to the unity of being permeated with the sense of total self-possession—in the Holy Spirit, who is the common heart of the Father and the Son.

But if the eternally actual state of the absolute substance (in God) consists in being all in unity, then the potential state of this substance (outside God) consists in being all in separation. Here we are confronted with indeterminate and anarchic multiplicity, with chaos, the τὸ ἄπειρον [Greek: primal chaos] of the Greeks, the *schlechte Unendlichkeit* [German: bad infinity] of the Germans, the *tohu va bohu* [Hebrew: formless and void] of the Bible. This antithesis of the Divine Entity is, from all eternity, removed, reduced to the state of pure possibility, by the very fact of God's existence, by His first act. The absolute and universal substance belongs, in effect, to God; He eternally and primordially is all in unity: He is, and this is sufficient for chaos not to exist. But this is not sufficient for God Himself, who is not only being, but also perfect being. It is not sufficient to affirm that God is; it is necessary to have the possibility of saying why He is. To exist from the beginning, to suppress chaos and to hold all in unity by the act of His Omnipotence—that constitutes the divine fact which requires a *grounding* for itself. God cannot be satisfied by the fact that He is *effectively* more powerful than the chaos; He must be such *by right*. And in order to have the right to defeat the chaos and in eternity to transform it into nonbeing, God must be *more true* than the chaos. He manifests His truth by opposing to the chaos not only the act of His Omnipotence, but also rational justification, or idea. He therefore necessarily *distinguishes* His perfect universality from chaotic multiplicity, and to every possible manifestation of the latter He responds in His Word with the ideal manifestation of the true unity, with the rational justification that proves the intellectual or logical impotence of the chaos which seeks to assert itself. Containing all in the unity of absolute Omnipotence, God necessarily contains all also in the unity of the universal idea. The powerful God must also be the true God, Supreme Reason. To the encroachments of the infinitely diverse chaos He must oppose not only His own pure and simple Being, but also the integral system of ideas, grounds, or eternal truths, each of which in its indissoluble logical connection with all the others represents the triumph of determinate unity over anarchic multiplicity, over bad infinity. The chaotic tendency, which provokes each separate entity to assert itself in its exclusivity, as if it were all, this tendency is condemned as false and illegitimate in the system of eternal ideas, which relegates each entity to its determinate place in the absolute universality and which thus manifests, alongside God's truth, His judgment and His justice.

But the triumph of reason and truth is still insufficient for divine perfection. Since bad infinity, or chaos, is in its essence an *irrational* principle, the logical and ideal exposure of its falseness does not constitute a real means to its inner suppression. Truth is revealed; the light has shined forth; but the darkness remains as it was: "And the light shines in darkness; and the darkness comprehended it not" (John 1:5). Truth is a sundering into two, a separation; it is a relative unity, for it affirms the existence of its opposite as such, differentiating itself from its opposite. But God needs absolute unity. He needs the possibility of embracing in His unity the principle that opposes Him; He needs to reveal Himself superior to this principle, not only in truth and justice, but also in goodness. God's absolute superiority must be manifested not only *against* chaos but also *for* it; His superiority must give to chaos more than the latter deserves, making it a participant in the fullness of the absolute existence, demonstrating to it the superiority of divine fullness over the empty multiplicity of bad infinity not only by means of objectively rational proof but by means of inner and living experience. To each manifestation of the chaos that has risen in revolt, Divinity must be able to oppose not only an act of *power*, which suppresses the opposing act, and not only rational justification, or *idea*, which exposes the falseness of the chaos and separates it from true being, but also *goodness*, which permeates the chaos, inwardly changes it, and leads it to unity by its own free choice.

This threefold unification of the all, this threefold triumphant reaction of the divine principle against *possible* chaos, is the inner and eternal manifestation of God's absolute substance, or of His essential Wisdom, which, as we know, is all in unity. Power, truth, and goodness, or (in other terms) authority, justice, and mercy; or (in yet other terms) reality, idea, and life—all of these relative expressions for the designation of absolute universality are objective definitions of divine substance, corresponding to the Trinity of hypostases, which from all eternity possess it. And the indissoluble connection of the three persons of the Supreme Entity (*Sushchestvo*) is manifested with necessity in the objectivity of their unique substance, whose three attributes or chief qualities are mutually dependent upon one another and are equally necessary to Divinity. God could not permeate and fill the chaos with His mercy if He did not differ from it by truth and justice; and He could not differ from the chaos or separate it from Himself if He did not embrace it in His power.

"IV. The World Soul as the Foundation of Creation, Space, Time, and Mechanical Causality"

We can now understand what the Bible means when it speaks of the "joy" or "delight" of Eternal Wisdom. She "rejoices" or "frolics," evoking before God the numberless possibilities of all the extradivine existences and again absorbing them into His omnipotence, into His absolute truth and infinite mercy. In this joy of His essential Wisdom, the One and Triune God, suppressing the power of possible chaos, illuminating the darkness of the latter, and penetrating its abysses, the One and Triune God feels within Himself and from all eternity confirms for Himself that He is more powerful, more true, and more good than any possible entity outside Himself. In this joy of His Wisdom it is revealed to Him that all positive things belong to Him in fact and by right, that from all eternity He possesses in Himself the infinite treasure of all real powers, all true thoughts, all gifts, and all grace.

In the two first essential qualities of Divinity, God could limit Himself to immanent self-manifestation,* to the eternal joy of His Wisdom; as omnipotent, just, and true, He could of course be satisfied by the triumph over anarchic existence in Himself, in the inner certainty of His absolute superiority. But that is insufficient for goodness and mercy. In this third quality, Divine Wisdom cannot find satisfaction in a purely ideal object; she cannot remain satisfied with a purely possible realization, with simple joy. If in His power and in His truth *God is all*, then in His love He desires that *all be God*. He desires that, outside of Himself, there be another nature, which would gradually become what He is from all eternity: the absolute all. In order to attain divine universality, in order to enter into a free and mutual relation with God, this nature must be separate from God while at the same time being united with Him. It must be separate from Him in its real foundation, which is the earth; and it must be united with Him in its ideal apex, which is man. In particular, in seeing the earth and man Eternal Wisdom revealed its joy before God: "frolicking before him at all times, / frolicking in his habitable world. / And my delight is in mankind" (Prov. 8:30–31).

We know that the possibility of chaotic existence, from all eternity contained in God, is eternally suppressed by His power, condemned by His truth, annihilated by His goodness. But God loves chaos in its nonbeing as well, and He desires that it exist, for He will be able to return the rebellious existence to unity. He will be able to fill the infinite emptiness with the abundance of His life. God therefore gives freedom to chaos. He restrains His omnipotence's counteraction to chaos in the first act of divine being, in the element of the Father, and He thereby brings the world out of its nonbeing.

If we do not wish to renounce the very idea of Divinity, we cannot admit outside of God an autonomous being, a real and positive existence. Thus, the extradivine can be nothing other than a *transformed or inverted* Divine. We see this, first of all, in specific forms of finite existence which separate our world from God. Truly, this world was constituted outside God through forms of spatial extension, time, and mechanical causality. But these three conditions do not represent anything real and positive; they are only a negation and distortion of the Divine existence in its chief categories.

We have differentiated three things in God: (1) His absolute *objectivity*, represented by His substance or essence, which is the All in indivisible unity; (2) His absolute *subjectivity* or His inner existence, represented in its totality by three inseparable hypostases, mutually conditioning and complementing one another; and (3) His free relativity or His relation to that which is not He Himself, represented first by the *joy* of the Divine Wisdom and then by creation (and, as we shall later, by the incarnation). The general character of divine being in these three categories or from these three points of view is its *autonomy* or perfect autocracy, the absence of all external determinations. God is auton-

---

* Author's note: Immanent in relation to God and transcendent in relation to us.

omous in His objective substance; for, being the all in itself, this substance cannot be determined by anything. He is autonomous in His subjective existence, for the latter has absolute fullness in its three coeternal and hypostatic phases, jointly embracing the totality of being. Finally, He is autonomous in His relation to that which is not He, for this *other* is determined to existence by the uniquely free act of divine will. Thus, the three categories which we have indicated are only different forms and expressions of divine autonomy.

It is precisely for this reason that, in the earthly world, which is merely the inverted image of Divinity, we find three corresponding forms of cosmic *heteronomy*: spatial extension, time, and mechanical causality. If the objective and essential expression of the Divine autocracy is *all in unity, omnia simul in uno,* then the heteronomic objectivity of spatial extension consists, on the contrary, in the fact that every part of the extradivine world is separated from all the others. This is the abiding of each part outside the all and of the all outside each part; this is inverse to the concept of integrality. Thus, our world, insofar as it is composed of parts with spatial extension, represents an inversion of divine *objectivity*. In the same way, if the subjective autonomy of divine existence finds its expression in the equal actuality and in the inner and indissoluble connection of the three definitions of this existence, which complement one another but do not follow one another in succession, then the heteronomic form of time appears to us, on the contrary, as an indeterminate succession of moments which *dispute one another's* existence. In order to utilize actuality, each of these moments must exclude all the others; and all of these moments, instead of mutually complementing one another, mutually suppress one another and take one another's place, the integrality and fullness of existence never being achieved. Finally, even as God's creative freedom is the definitive expression of His autonomy, so the heteronomy of the extradivine world is definitively manifested in mechanical causality, in virtue of which the external action of a given entity never represents the direct result of its inner act but is necessarily determined by the linkage of material causes or conditions, independent of the actor.

The abstract principle of spatial extension consists in the fact that two objects, two parts of the all cannot simultaneously occupy one and the same place, and that one object, one part of the all cannot be simultaneously located in two different places. This is the law of the separateness or the objective mutual exclusion between the parts of the all. The abstract principle of time consists in the fact that two internal states of a subject (in current terminology, the states of consciousness) cannot coincide in a single actual moment, and that a separate state of consciousness cannot be preserved as actually identical in the course of two different moments of existence. This is the law of the constant disunification of the internal states of every subject. Finally, according to the abstract principle of mechanical causality, no act and no phenomenon can occur arbitrarily or by itself; rather, it is totally determined by another act or phenomenon, which itself is only the result of a third act or phenomenon, and so on. This is the law of the purely external and random relation of phenomena.

It is easy to see that these three grounds or these three laws only express a general striving or *tendency*, directed toward the fragmentation and disintegration of the body of the universe, toward the elimination of all internal connection in the universe and the destruction of the solidarity of its parts. This striving or tendency is the very essence of extradivine nature or chaos. The striving presupposes *will*, and will presupposes a psychical subject, or *soul*. Just as the world that this soul is striving to produce is the fragmented, disintegrated all, held together only by a purely external connection; just as this world is the opposite and the reverse side of divine universality, so the *World Soul* herself is the opposite or antitype of the essential Divine Wisdom.[41] This World Soul is a creature and the first of all the creatures; she is the *materia prima* [Latin: prime matter] and the true *substratum* [Latin: basis] of our created world. In fact, since nothing can exist really and objectively outside God, the extradivine world can be, as we have already said, nothing other than the divine world subjectively transformed and inverted: the extradivine world is only a false aspect or illusory representation of divine universality. But this illusory existence needs a subject that, since it has taken a false point of view, reproduces in itself a distorted image of the truth. Since this subject can be neither God nor His essential Wisdom, it is necessary to admit a different subject as the principle of creation in the proper sense; and this subject is the World Soul. As a creature, the World Soul does not have eternal existence in herself; rather, she exists from all eternity in God in a state of pure potentiality, as the hidden foundation of Eternal Wisdom. This possible and future Mother of the extradivine world corresponds, in the capacity of an ideal complement, to the eternally actual Father of Divinity.

As a pure and indeterminate potentiality, the World Soul has a dual and changeable character (ἡ ἀόριστος δυάς; Greek: the double unbounded one). She can desire existence for herself outside God; she can take the false point of view of chaotic and anarchic existence; but she can also abase herself before God, attach herself to the Divine Word by her free volition, bring all creation to perfect unity and identify herself with Eternal Wisdom. But in order to achieve this, the World Soul must first exist in reality, as distinct from God. That is why the eternal Father created her, restraining the act of His Omnipotence, which from all eternity suppresses the blind desire for anarchic existence. This desire, having become an act, disclosed to the soul the possibility of the opposite desire; and the soul herself thus received, as such, independent existence, chaotic in its immediate actuality, but capable, when transformed, of becoming its own opposite. Having assimilated the idea of chaos, having given this idea relative reality, the soul arrives at the desire to liberate herself from this disorderly existence, agitated without goal and without meaning in the abyss of darkness. Pulled in all directions by blind forces, disputing among themselves which of them should have exclusive existence; torn, fragmented into the dust of an infinite number of atoms—the World Soul experiences

---

41. In this case, Solovyov differentiates between Sophia and the World Soul.

a confused but profound desire for unity. With this desire she attracts the action of the Word (of active Divinity or Divinity in His manifestation), which is first revealed to her in the general and indeterminate idea of the universe, of the one and inseparable world. This ideal unity, realized on the basis of chaotic spatial extension, takes the form of indeterminate space or limitlessness. Reproduced, represented, or created in the imagination by the soul in her state of chaotic separation, the *All* cannot stop being the *All*, cannot definitively lose its unity; and since its parts do not desire to complement or to permeate one another in positive and living totality they are compelled, even if mutually excluding one another, nevertheless to remain together, to coexist in the formal unity of indeterminate space—in the totally external and empty form of the substantial and objective universality of God. But external limitlessness is insufficient for the soul; she also desires to experience the inner integrality of subjective existence. This integrality, which reigns eternally in the Divine Trinity, is obstructed for the chaotic soul by the indeterminate succession of random and indifferent moments that is called time. This false infinity, which enchains the soul, provokes the latter to desire the truth; and to this desire the Divine Word responds with the suggestion of a new idea. By its action on the soul, the Supreme Trinity is reflected in the stream of indeterminate duration in the form of the three tenses. Desiring to actualize reality in its entirety for herself, the soul is compelled to complement each given moment of her existence by a more or less obscure memory of a past without beginning and by a more or less obscure expectation of a future without end.

And the profound and unmoving foundation of this variable relation is the three chief states of the soul herself, her threefold position in relation to Divinity, established for her in the form of the three tenses. The state of her initial absorption in the unity of the Eternal Father, her eternal abiding in Him in the capacity of pure potentiality or simple possibility, this state is henceforth defined as the *past* of the soul. The state of her separation from God in the blind force of chaotic desire represents her *present*. And the return to God, the reunification with Him, is the object of her strivings and efforts; it is her ideal *future*.

Just as the Word of God establishes for the soul the formal unity of space above the anarchic separation of its spatially extended parts; and just as against the background of the chaotic succession of moments the Word of God establishes the ideal trinitarity of time, so on the foundation of mechanical causality the Word of God reveals the concrete connection of the all in the law of universal gravitation, which by its internal power binds all the fragmented and scattered parts of chaotic reality in order to form out of them a single integral and stable body, the first materialization of the World Soul, the first foundation of action for essential Wisdom.

Thus, by means of blind and chaotic striving that imposes upon the soul an existence infinitely *separate* in its parts, exclusively *sequential* in its moments, and *mechanically* determined in its phenomena; by means of the opposite desire of the soul herself, striving toward unity and universality; and by means of the action of the Divine Word, responding to this striving; by means of the united activity of these three engines, the lower or extradivine world acquires its relative reality or, according to the biblical expression, the foundations of the earth are laid. But in the idea of creation, the Bible, just like theosophic reason, does not separate the lower world from the higher world, earth from heaven.

We have seen, truly, how Eternal Wisdom called forth the possibilities of irrational and anarchic existence in order to oppose to them the corresponding manifestations of absolute power, truth, and goodness. These divine counteractions, which in the immanent life of God represent only the delight of play, are made stable and become real existences when the antidivine possibilities that call them forth stop being pure possibilities. Thus, to the creation of the lower or chaotic world necessarily corresponds the creation of the higher or heavenly world: *"Bereshith bara Elohim eth hashammiim v'eth haaréts"* ("In the beginning God created the heaven and the earth" (Gen. 1:1).[42]

"V. The Higher World. The Freedom of the Pure Spirits"[43]

Bereshith means ἐν ἀρχῇ or rather,*—*in principio, seu potius in capitulo* (in the beginning or rather at the head [Solovyov's own translation from Greek and Latin]).

It would be a complete misunderstanding of the Hebrew language as well as of the general spirit of the ancient East to suppose that these words with which the Book of Genesis begins represent nothing more than an indefinite locution, equivalent to our locutions such as "first of all," etc. When the Hebrew language employed a noun, it took this form in its direct significance, that is, it truly thought about the essence or real object designated by this noun. And indisputably this Hebrew word *reshith*, translated as [ἀρχή], *principium*, is an authentic noun of the feminine gender. The corresponding word of the masculine gender is *rosh*, *caput*, head. Jewish theology uses this latter term, in its predominant sense, to designate God—the supreme and absolute head of all existing things. But from this point of view what does *reshith*, the feminine gender of *rosh*, signify? To answer this question, we do not need to have recourse to Kabbalistic fantasies.[44] We can find an indisput-

---

42. I use the transliteration and translation from Hebrew here and below chosen by Solovyov in his original French publication, although it is not a standard format in English. This reproduces the unusualness of the text sensed by Solovyov's first readers.

43. For an analysis of this chapter in relation to Kabbalah, see Kornblatt, "Solov'ev's Androgynous Sophia."

44. Despite his disclaimer, he in fact uses a number of Kabbalistic techniques in his argument in this section.

* Author's note: Thus the term *bereshith* was translated (according to Origen's *Hexapla* [title given to critical edition of Hebrew Scriptures in Greek and Hebrew by Origen, third-century theologian]) by Aquila [second-century translator often confused in the Talmud with Onkelos], a famous teacher about whom the Talmud uses the words of the psalm: "You are the most beautiful of the sons of mankind."

able solution in the Bible. Specifically, in Chapter Eight of Proverbs, already cited by us, the essential Wisdom, Hokhmah, tells us: "*jagveh qanani* reshith *darco*—Jehovah possessed me as the principle (feminine gender) of His way" (Prov. 8, 22).[45]

Thus, the eternal Wisdom is precisely *reshith*, the feminine principle or head of every existence, just as Jehovah, Jahveh Elohim, the Triune God, is *rosh*, the active principle or head of every existence. But according to the Book of Genesis God created the heaven and the earth in this *reshith*, in His essential Wisdom. This signifies that Divine Wisdom not only represents the essential and actual all-unity of God's absolute being or substance, but also contains the power to unify the separated and fragmented cosmic being. Being the finished unity of the all in God, Divine Wisdom also becomes the unity of God and of extradivine existence. She therefore represents the true cause of creation and the goal of the latter—the principle in which God created the heaven and the earth. If Divine Wisdom abides substantially and from all eternity in God, then she is truly realized in the world, is gradually made incarnate in the world, shaping the latter into an increasingly perfect unity. She is *reshith* in the beginning—the fruitful idea of the absolute unity, the unitary power destined to unify all things. She is *Malkhouth* (Βασιλεία, *Regnum*, Kingdom) at the end—the Kingdom of God, the perfect and fully realized unity of the Creator and creation.[46] She is not the World Soul; the World Soul is only the bearer, medium, and substrate of her realization. She converges with the World Soul through the action of the Word and gradually raises the World Soul to an increasingly fuller and more real identification with herself. The World Soul, viewed from within herself, is the indeterminate subject of creation, accessible equally to the evil ground of chaos and to the Word of God. The *Khocma* [Hokhmah], the Σοφία, the Divine Wisdom is not the soul, but the guardian angel of the world, covering with her wings all creatures in order to raise them gradually to true being, in the same way that a bird gathers her chicks beneath her wings. She is the substance of the Holy Spirit, moving upon the watery darkness of the world that is being born: *Ve rouakh* (feminine gender) *Elohim merakhépheth hal pené hammaïm*" (the Spirit of God moved upon the face of the waters) (Gen. 1:2). We do not have to follow the order of the sacred narrative: "*Bereshit bora Elohim eth hashammaïm v'eth haaréts*" ("In the beginning God created the heaven and the earth") (Gen. 1:1). A special investigation is not necessary to elucidate the meaning of the word *haaréts*. It means: *Earth*. The divinely inspired writer of this text did not hesitate to explain the meaning of this word: "*ve-haarets haïethah tohou va bohou*" ("the earth was without form, and void") (Gen. 1, 2). And the Earth was chaos. But if in the biblical story of the creation the Earth must be

45. Fox translates the verse as "The Lord created me at the beginning of his way, / at the start of his works of old" (264). Solovyov in his translations wants to emphasize the very concrete, physical relationship between the Lord as Jehovah and the female Wisdom. See above, note 40.

46. As we saw in part 1, *Malkhut* is another name for the Kabbalistic *Shekhinah*. See page 68.

understood as chaos, the lower and extradivine world in its chaotic state, then it is clear that the term *ha shammaïm*, heaven, which the sacred text places into a close relation with the earth, in the capacity of the opposite pole of the creation, it is clear that this term signifies the higher or invisible world of divine counteractions, established or actualized in a special manner, as a counterweight to chaotic existence.

Not without justification, the Hebrew language (as well as the Old Slavonic language) expresses this invisible world by a word in the *dual* number (in the western languages it is expressed by the plural). This dual number corresponds to the fundamental division of the Divine world.

We know that the producing cause (ἀρχή τῆς γενήσεως) of creation is the act of will by which God abstains from using His Omnipotence to suppress the possible reality of the chaos, or by which He stops counteracting this possibility by means of the particular power peculiar to His first hypostasis; instead, He limits Himself to counteraction by the second and third hypostases—by means of justice, mercy, truth, and grace.

Once the first hypostasis of the Holy Trinity, the Eternal Father, abstained from counteracting the possibility of chaos by means of the property peculiar to Him, that is, by suppressing the chaos with His Omnipotence (and this constituted the first condition or producing cause of the creation—the ground according to which God the Father is the Creator of the world par excellence), it follows from this that only the particular manifestations peculiar to the two other hypostases remain to form the sphere of the divine counteractions to the chaos. It is this circumstance that determines the basic cause of the duality of the invisible world. We have: *first* of all, the system of creative (direct) counteractions of the *Word*, constituting the ideal or intelligible world in the strict sense, the sphere of pure intelligences, objective ideas, hypostatized Divine thoughts; and secondly, the system of counteractions of the Holy Spirit, more concrete, more subjective, and more vital, constitutes the spiritual world, the sphere of pure spirits or angels.

In this creative sphere of the Word and the Holy Spirit, the Divine substance, essential Wisdom, is determined and appears in her fundamental quality, as a radiant and heavenly entity separated from the darkness of earthly matter. The sphere peculiar to the Father is the absolute light, light in itself, having no relation to darkness. The Son or Word is, as it were, the manifested light; this is white light, illuminating external objects, reflected from their surface without penetrating them. Finally, the Holy Spirit is light which, refracted by the extradivine medium, splits apart and forms above this medium the heavenly spectrum of the seven primary and superior spirits, as if the seven colors of the rainbow.

The pure intelligences that constitute the world of *ideas* are absolutely contemplative, impassible, and unchangeable entities. Immobile stars on the heavens of the invisible world, they are above every desire, every will, and, thus, every freedom. Pure spirits, or angels, have a fuller or more concrete subjective existence. Independent of intellectual contemplation, they are familiar with affective and volitional states; they have motion and freedom.

But the freedom of the pure spirits is by no means similar to that which we know from our own experience. Not being subordinate to the objective limitations of matter, space, and time, to the entire mechanism of the physical world, the angels of God have the power to pre-establish their entire subsequent being by one *inner* act of their will. They are free to be for God or against Him; but since by their nature (in the capacity of direct creations of God) they initially possess a high degree of light and power, they act with complete understanding of the state of affairs and with full actuality of success; and they cannot repent of their acts. In virtue of the perfection and grandeur of their freedom, they can apply the latter only in one decisive act, once and for all. The inner decision of their will, not encountering any external obstacle, immediately calls forth all of its consequences and *exhausts* their freedom of will.

The pure Spirit, who is freely self-determined in God, immediately enters into the possession of Divine Wisdom and becomes, as it were, an organic and inseparable member of Divinity; love for God and voluntary participation in divine action henceforth constitute the nature of this Spirit. On his part, the Spirit who is self-determined in the opposite sense cannot change his decision either. For he made his decision with full knowledge of what he was doing, and the result could only be that which he desired. He desired to separate himself from God, for revulsion to God had been born in him. This revulsion could not have had the slightest foundation, for in God there cannot be the least shadow of any evil which could justify or explain a hostile attitude toward Him. Such hostility is a simple and pure act of spiritual will, which has its entire foundation in itself and which is inaccessible to any change. This hostility becomes the very nature or essence of the fallen angel. Independent of any cause and any external and temporal circumstance in its moral act, unconditionally possessing itself, antidivine will is necessarily eternal and inexorable. This is the infinite abyss into which the rebellious Spirit is immediately cast, and from which he can send his rays in the direction peculiar to him, through the natural chaos, physical creation and up to the boundaries of the divine world. After all, he knew very well when he determined himself against God that he would not lack a field of action, for the Divine Will had then already called forth from nonbeing the World Soul, awakening in her the chaotic desire—the foundation and matter of the entire creation.

This World Soul is the indeterminate and unconditioned principle (ἄπειρον καί ἀόριστον), and to a certain extent she will always communicate this character to all things that originate from her. In this manner, a vast mixed medium will appear that will remain in an oscillating position between God and His opponent, providing the latter with the means to feed his hatred, to realize his rebellion, and to continue his battle. His existence will therefore not be static and empty; his activity will be abundant and diverse, but the general orientation and inner quality of all he does will be determined beforehand by the initial act of his will, which separated him from God. To change this act, to return to God, is for him absolutely impossible.

The opposite teaching, proposed by Origen and condemned by the Church, shows us that that spiritually exalted and richly endowed mind had, nonetheless, a very insufficient idea of the existence of moral evil. In fact, he proved its existence in other circumstances, escaping to purely material and superficial means in order to deliver himself from immoral passions.[47]

"VI. The Three Chief Stages of the Cosmogonic Process"

In God's thought, the heaven and the earth, the higher world and the lower world, were created together in one foundation, which is essential Wisdom—the absolute unity of the all. The union of heaven and earth, established in the foundation (*reshith*), at the beginning of the creative work, must be actualized through the cosmogonic and historical process, which leads to the perfect realization of this unity in the Kingdom of God (*malkhouth*). The unity, when it is truly actualized, presupposes a preliminary separation—a separation manifested in the chaotic existence of the earth, an empty and fruitless existence, submerged in darkness (*khoshéc*: Gen. 1:2) and in the abyss (*tehom*). The task was to fill this abyss, to illuminate this darkness, to fructify this barren womb,[48] and finally, through the joint action of the two worlds, to call to life a semiearthly and semiheavenly existence capable of embracing in its unity the totality of creation and binding it with God by a free and vital connection, embodying in the image created the eternal Wisdom of God.

The cosmic process is the gradual unification of the lower or earthly world, created at the beginning in a state of chaos and disorder—in a state of *tohou va bohou*. According to the revelation presented to us in the sacred narrative of the Book of Genesis, there are two foundations or two generating engines in this process: the first is the absolutely active foundation—God in His Word and in His Spirit; the second is a foundation that, in part, cooperates by its own power with the divine order and prefigurings and realizes them, and that, in part, represents only the purely passive and material element. Truly, when it is a question of the creation of plants and animals, Genesis says: "And God said, Let the earth bring forth grass, the herb yielding seed . . . And the earth brought forth grass, and herb yielding seed after his kind . . . And God said, Let the earth bring forth the living creature after his kind . . ." (Gen. 1:11, 12, 24). It is thus evident that God does not directly create the diverse manifestations of physical life; that is, He only defines, guides, and establishes the creative power of this agent which is called the *Earth*, that is, earthly nature, the first matter, the soul of the lower world. In itself, this soul is only an indeterminate and disorderly power, but a power capable of aspiring toward

---

47. It is widely believed that Origen castrated himself on the basis of a literal reading of Matthew 19:12: "For there are eunuchs who have been so from birth, and there are eunuchs who have been made eunuchs by men, and there are eunuchs who have made themselves eunuchs for the sake of the kingdom of heaven."

48. See part 1 (page 51) for a discussion of the relationship of Mary (whose "barren womb" was "fructified") and Sophia.

Divine unity, of yearning for union with heaven. This desire is answered by the action of the Word and the Spirit of God, suggesting to the ignorant soul increasingly perfect forms of the unification of the heavenly with the earthly and inducing the actualization of these forms in the medium of the lower world. But since the soul of this world represents an indeterminate duality (ἄόριστος δυάς) [Greek: double unbounded one], it is accessible also to the action of the antidivine principle, which, being incapable of subordinating to itself the higher Wisdom, besieges the lower anti-image of the latter, the World Soul, in order to compel her to remain in chaos and disorder and to produce—instead of the realization of the unity of heaven and earth in harmonious and regularly ascending forms—disorderly and fantastic monsters. Thus, the cosmic process, which on the one hand is a peaceful meeting, the love and marriage of two agents, of heaven and earth, this process represents, on the other hand, a battle to the death of the Divine Word and of the principle of hell for power over the World Soul. It follows that the work of creation, as a doubly complex process, can progress only slowly and gradually.

And, as we have seen, the Bible tells us quite definitely that this work of creation is not God's *direct* work. And the Bible's sacred words are fully confirmed in practice. If the creation of our physical world proceeded directly and exclusively from God Himself, it would be an absolutely perfect work—a tranquil and harmonious production not only in its entirety but also in each of its parts.

But reality is far from conforming to such an idea. Only from His own point of view, encompassing all things (Gen. 1:31), with one glance, *sub specie aeternitatis* [Latin: under the aspect of eternity], could God proclaim creation to be perfect, or "very good." As far as the individual parts of the work of creation are concerned, when they are considered in themselves, they merit on God's lips only relative approval or merit no approval at all. In this, as in everything else, the Bible is in full accord with human experience and scientific truth. If we examine the earthly world in its actual state and in particular in its geological and paleontological history, which is well documented in the present age, we will find in it the characteristic pattern of a process of heavy labor, determined by heterogeneous principles which arrive, not at all rapidly and by means of great exertions, at a stable and harmonious unity. There is not the slightest resemblance here to an absolutely perfect creation—with the direct work of a single divine *artist* (*artifex*). Our cosmic history is a slow and excruciating birth. In this history we see clear signs of internal struggle, violent convulsions and spasms, blind groping searches, unfinished and unsuccessful attempts at creation, monstrous miscarriages. Can all of these antediluvian monsters—these megatheriums, plesiosaurs, ichthyosauruses, pterodactyls—belong to God's perfect and direct creation? If each genus of these monstrous creatures was "very good,"[49] why did they totally disappear from our earth, ceding their place to more successful, more harmonious, and better equilibrated forms?

49. Gen. 1:31.

Creation is a gradual and stubborn process; this is a biblical and philosophical truth, as well as a fact of natural science. The process, presupposing imperfection, thereby also presupposes a determinate progress, consisting in an increasingly more profound and fuller unification of the material elements and anarchic forces, in the transformation of *chaos* into *cosmos*, into a living body capable of serving for the incarnation of Divine Wisdom. Without entering into the cosmogonic details, I will only indicate the three fundamental, concrete stages of this unifying process. We have already given attention to the first of these determinate stages, namely in *universal gravitation*, which makes the lower world a relatively compact mass and forms the material body of the universe. This is precisely the *mechanical unity* of the all. Even though they remain external in relation to one another, the parts of the universe are nevertheless held together by an unbreakable bond—by the force of gravitational attraction. However stubborn they might be in their egoism, these parts are exposed in their falsehood by the invincible attraction that pushes them toward one another—by this initial manifestation of cosmic *altruism*. The World Soul attains her first realization as the universal unity and celebrates her first union with Divine Wisdom.

But, impelled by the creative Word, the World Soul strives to attain a more perfect unity; and in this striving she is liberated from the fetters of the heavy material mass and transforms her power into a new matter, refined and rarefied: the *ether*, as it is called. The Word possesses this idealized matter, as the preeminent bearer of His shaping action. This idealized matter transmits massless currents into all parts of the universe, covers all the members of the cosmic body with an ethereal mesh, reveals the relative distinctions between these parts, places them in determinate relations, and thereby creates the second cosmic unity, more perfect and more ideal—the *dynamic unity*, realized in light, electricity, and all other massless forces, which merely represent variations or transformations of one and the same agent. The character of this agent is pure altruism; this is limitless expansion, the continuous act of self-giving. However perfect in itself the dynamic unity of the world might be, it only embraces the material mass in all of the parts of the latter. However, it does not possess these parts inwardly; it does not penetrate down to the depths of their essence; it does not regenerate them. The World Soul, the *Earth*, sees in the radiant ether the ideal image of her heavenly beloved, but she is not really united with the latter. Nevertheless, she is constantly striving to attain this union; she does not wish to limit herself to the contemplation of the heavens and the shining celestial lights immersed in the currents of the ether. Instead, she absorbs the *light*, transforms it into the *fire of life*, and, as the fruit of this new union, begets out of her womb every *living soul* in the two kingdoms, that of plants and that of animals. This new unity, the *organic unity*, which has inorganic matter and the currents of the ether as its foundation and medium, is made more perfect by the fact that it gives form to and regulates a more complex body by means of a more active and more universal soul. In plants, life is realized objectively in its organic forms;

whereas, in animals, life is also *felt* in its movements and subjective effects; finally, in man, life is *understood* in its absolute principle.

The earth, which in the beginning was without form, void, and covered in darkness, but which then was gradually embraced by light, received form, and was differentiated; the earth, which, only in the third cosmogonic epoch, indeterminately felt and obscurely expressed (as in a dream) its creative power in forms of vegetative life, these first combinations of the dust of the earth with the beauty of the heavens; the earth, which, in this world of plants, went outside itself for the first time to meet the heavenly influences, and then separated itself from itself in the free movement of four-legged animals and soared above itself in the airy flight of birds—this earth, having poured its living soul into the numberless genera of vegetative and animal life, was finally concentrated, returned into itself, and clothed itself in a form allowing it to meet God face to face and directly receive from Him the breath of spiritual life. Here, the earth *knew* heaven and was *known by* heaven. Here, the two bounds of creation, Divine and extradivine, the higher and the lower, really become one, are united actually and are conscious of this unity. For true knowledge of one another is possible only in real union: perfect knowledge must be *realized* and real union must be *idealized* in order to become perfect. That is why union par excellence, the union of the sexes, is called *knowledge* in the Bible. Eternal Wisdom, who in her foundation is the unity of the all and who in her integrality is the unity of opposites, a free and reciprocal unity—Eternal Wisdom finally finds a subject in and through which she can fully actualize herself. She finds her subject and rejoices. *My delight*, she says, is with *the sons of men*.

"VII. The Threefold Incarnation of Divine Wisdom"

"And the Lord God formed man—the dust of the earth." "*Et formavit Futurus Deorum hominem—pulvis* (sic)[50] *ex humo*." "*Vajitser Jahveh Elohim eth haadam haphar min haadamah*." (Gen 1:7).

If in general the earth signifies the soul of the lower world, then the *dust* of the earth indicates the state of the humiliation or abasement of this soul when she renounces self-assertion and self-exaltation in the blind desire for anarchic existence; when, rejecting all the seductions of hell and in perfect humility renouncing all resistance and all struggle against the heavenly Word, she acquires the ability to know His truth, to unite herself to His action, and to establish in herself the foundations of the kingdom of God. This humble state, this unconditional receptivity of the earthly nature is objectively expressed in the creation of man (*humus—humilis—homo* [Latin: dust—humble—man]); the sensuous and representing soul of the physical world becomes the *rational* soul of humanity. Having attained an inner connection with heaven, contemplating the intelligible light, this soul can embrace all things that exist in

---

50. Insertion in original French publication.

an ideal unity (through consciousness and reason). A universal essence by his idea, in his rational power (the image of God) man must really become like God, actively realizing his unity in the fullness of creation. A son of the earth according to the lower life given to him from the latter, he must return this life to the earth, and when it is returned it must be transfigured in light and in the life-giving spirit. If in man, through his reason, the earth has risen to the heavens, then it is also by him, through his action, that the heavens will bend down and fulfill the earth; through man, the entire extradivine world must become a single living body—the perfect incarnation of Divine Wisdom.

Only in man is the creation united with God in a perfect manner, that is, freely and reciprocally, for thanks to his dual nature only man can *preserve* his freedom and always remain a moral complement to God, coming into closer and closer union with Him in a successive series of conscious efforts and carefully considered actions. There is an astonishing dialectic in the law of life of the two worlds. The supranatural perfection of the freedom of the pure spirit, absence of all external limitation, creates a situation in which this freedom, manifesting itself fully, is exhausted in a single act; and the spiritual entity loses its freedom owing to an excess of the latter. By contrast, the obstacles which the external medium of the natural world opposes to the realization of our inner acts, the limited and conditioned character of human freedom, makes man freer than the angels, gives him the possibility of preserving his free will and unceasingly using it, of remaining an active collaborator in the works of God even after the fall. Therefore, Eternal Wisdom finds her delight not in angels but in the sons of men.

The inner meaning of man's existence is, in the first place, the inner and ideal union of earthly power and the divine act, of the Soul and the Word; and secondly it is the free realization of this union in the totality of the extradivine world. Thus, in this complex entity there is a center and there is a periphery—the human personality and the human world, the individual man and the social or collective man. The human individual, being in himself or subjectively the union of the Divine Word and of human nature, must apply himself to the objective realization, the realization for himself, of this union, by entering onto the path of external division. In order to authentically know himself in his unity, man had to distinguish himself as the knowing or active subject (the male—man in the strict sense of the word) from himself as the known or passive object (the female). Thus, the opposition and union of the Divine Word and earthly nature are reproduced for man himself in the distinction and union of the sexes.[51]

Human *essence* or nature is fully represented by the individual man (both sexes); the social condition cannot add anything to this, but this condition is absolutely necessary for the expansion and development of human *existence*, for the actual realization of all things that are contained *in potentia* in the hu-

51. Solovyov expands on this idea in "The Meaning of Love," written several years later (*SS* 7:3–60).

man individual. Only in society can man attain his final goal—the universal unification of the totality of extradivine existence. But natural humanity (male, female, and society) in the form in which it appears as a result of the cosmogonic process, this natural humanity contains only the possibility of such unification. The reason and high degree of consciousness of the male, the heart and instinct of the female, and finally the law of solidarity or altruism which constitutes the foundation of every society—all these are only prototypes of the real divine-human unity; they are a sprout which has yet to grow, to blossom, and to bear its fruit. The gradual development of this sprout is accomplished in the process of universal history; and the threefold fruit which it bears is: the perfect female or divinized nature, the perfect male or the man-God, and the perfect society as the perfect communion of God with human beings—the final and definitive incarnation of Eternal Wisdom.

The essential unity of the human being in the male, the female, and society conditions the indivisible unity of the divine incarnation in humanity. Man in the strict sense of this word (the male) already contains, *in potentia*, the entire human essence; but in order to realize this essence *in actu* [Latin: in actuality] he must, first of all, divide himself or objectify his material side in the female personality; and secondly he must multiply or objectify the entire commonality of his intelligible essence in the multiplicity of individual existences organically interconnected and constituting a totality of solidarity—human society. Since the female is only the complement to the male and society is only his extension or manifestation in the whole, in essence there is only one human being. And even though the union of this being with God is necessarily triune in character, it nevertheless represents only a single divine-human entity: the incarnate Sophia whose central and fully personal manifestation is Jesus Christ, whose female complement is the Most Holy Virgin, and whose universal extension is the Church. The Most Holy Virgin is united with God by a purely receptive and passive connection; She gave birth to the second Adam in the same way that the earth gave birth to the first Adam, annihilating herself in perfect humility; there is therefore no *mutuality* or collaboration in the strict sense. As far as the Church is concerned, she is united with God *not directly* but through the incarnation of Christ, whose continuation she is. Thus, Christ alone is the true God-man, man in direct and mutual (active) union with God.

Contemplating in His eternal thought the Most Holy Virgin, Christ, and the Church, God gave His unconditional approval to all of creation, announcing that "it was very good" (Gen. 1:31). This precisely was the chief object of the great joy experienced by Divine Wisdom at the thought of the sons of men; she saw in this thought the unique, pure, and immaculate daughter of Adam; she saw in it the Son of Man par excellence, the sole righteous one; she saw in it, finally, the human multiplicity, united in the form of society unique according to its kind, based on love and truth. She saw in this form her own future incarnation, and in the children of Adam she saw her own children; and she rejoiced, seeing that they justify the prefiguring proclaimed by her before the face of God: "Wisdom is justified by her children" (Matt. 11:19).

Humanity united with God in the Most Holy Virgin, in Christ, and in the Church is the realization of the essential wisdom or absolute substance of God; this humanity is the created form of the essential Wisdom, her incarnation. Truly, we have here one and the same substantial form (designated by the Bible as *the seed of woman* [Gen. 3:15], i.e., *Sophia*) manifested in three successive and abiding aspects that are really distinct but in essence indivisible: This substantial form takes the name Mary in its female personification; it takes the name Jesus in its male personification; and it preserves its own name for its full and universal manifestation in the perfect Church of the future, the Bride and Wife of the Word of God.

This threefold realization of essential Wisdom in humanity is a religious truth which Orthodox Christians confess in their doctrine and manifest in their liturgy. If by the essential Wisdom of God we had to understand exclusively the person of Jesus Christ, how would it be possible to apply to the Most Holy Virgin all of the texts of the *mystical* books which speak of this Wisdom? Moreover, this application, which from ancient times has been manifested liturgically in both the Latin and Greek Churches, has in our own time received the sanction of church doctrine in the bull of Pius IX concerning the immaculate conception of the Most Holy Virgin.[52] On the other hand, there are texts of Scripture that both Orthodox and Catholic teachers of the Church apply either to the Most Holy Virgin or to the Church (for example, the text of Revelation 12 about the woman clothed with the sun, crowned with stars and having the moon under her feet).[53] Finally, it is impossible to dispute the close connection and perfect analogy between Christ's individual humanity and His social humanity, between His natural body and His mystical body. In the sacrament of communion the Lord's personal body becomes in a mysterious but real manner the unifying principle of His collective body—of the community of believers. In this way the Church, divinized human society, has in essence the same substance as the person of the incarnate Christ, His human individuality—and the latter has no other origin and no other essence than the human nature of the Most Holy Virgin, the Mother of God. From this it follows that the organism of the divine-human incarnation, having in Jesus Christ one personal and active center, also has in its threefold manifestation one and the same substantial foundation—the corporeality of Divine Wisdom, insofar as she is concealed and revealed in the lower world. This is the World Soul, fully transformed, purified, and identified with Wisdom herself, just as matter is identified with form in one concrete and living entity. And the perfect realization of this divinely material substance, of this *seed of woman*, is the glorified and risen humanity—the temple of God and His body, the divine Bride.

52. Pope Pius IX established the Immaculate Conception of Mary as dogma in 1854.

53. Although Sophia does not appear explicitly in Solovyov's famous *Three Conversations*, this cosmic woman does appear at the end of "The Short Tale of the Antichrist" to lead the remaining religious leaders into the desert. See *SS* 10:218.

The Christian truth in this definitive form, as the perfect and concrete incarnation of Divinity, has especially attracted the religious soul of the Russian people, from the earliest epoch of its conversion to Christianity. Dedicating its most ancient churches to St. Sophia, the substantial Wisdom of God, the Russian people gave to this idea a new expression, unknown to the Greeks (who identified Sophia with the Logos).

Closely connecting St. Sophia with the Mother of God and with Jesus Christ, the religious art of our ancestors nevertheless clearly distinguished her from both the one and the other, representing her in the image of a separate divine entity.[54] She was for our ancestors a heavenly essence hidden beneath the appearance of the lower world, a radiant spirit of reborn humanity, the guardian angel of the earth, the future and definitive manifestation of Divinity.

Thus, the Russian people knew and loved the *social* incarnation of the Divine in the Universal Church under the name of St. Sophia, alongside the *individual*, human image of the Divine—alongside the Mother of God and God's Son. And now we are required to give a rational expression to this idea, to the idea that was revealed to the religious sensibility of our forerunners, to the idea that is truly national and unconditionally universal. The issue is in how to give clear form to a living thought that was born in Ancient Rus'[55] and which the new Russia must give to the world.[56]

Translated from the Russian by Boris Jakim; revisions based on the original French text by Judith Deutsch Kornblatt

"The Idea of Humanity in Auguste Comte": An Overview

Auguste Comte (1798–1857), who coined the term "sociology," founded the philosophical school of positivism in Europe. Comte's philosophy, expanding on that of his onetime mentor, Henri de Saint-Simon, explains that the human mind, the various sciences, and social institutions have all progressed inevitably through three stages: theological, metaphysical, and positive. The French philosopher worked out these ideas in the six-volume *Cours de philosophie positive* (*The Course of Positive Philosophy*, 1830–42), discussions of which

---

54. Solovyov is referring here to Novgorod icons of Divine Sophia, who is often depicted as an angelic figure sitting on a throne. See part 1 (page 57) and Solovyov's own description of the icon, page 225.

55. Rus' as we saw in part 1 is the name given to a collection of princedoms centered around ancient Kiev and loosely confederated under Vladimir around the time of the baptism of the Slavic peoples of the region in the tenth century. Slavophile writers of the nineteenth century use the term to refer to the "true" nature of the Russian people.

56. Indeed, the various expressions of Sophia in a variety of genres collected in this book attest to Solovyov's own attempts to "give clear form" to his idea.

were translated into Russian in the middle of the century and subsequently exerted enormous influence on the development of positivism in Russia.[57] Solovyov quotes extensively from *The Course of Positive Philosophy* in the following essay.

Solovyov first discusses Comte's three stages in an essay called "The Theory of August Comte about the Three Phases in the Mental Development of Humanity" (1874), appended to his master's thesis, itself called "The Crisis in Western Philosophy (Against the Positivists)." Despite obvious similarities in the three-part historical scheme, Solovyov wrote quite negatively about Comte in this early essay. Nonetheless, the "sharpness of his criticism could not conceal the significance he attached to positivism as well as the affinity he bore with Comte" (de Courten 195). Solovyov's hostility was centered largely on Comte's rejection of traditional religion and God's role, focusing instead on human institutions. Solovyov found it necessary to differentiate his own understanding of "positive religion"—the culminating stage of human development and, like all of the Russian thinker's third elements, incorporating and transfiguring the previous two—from Comte's "positive science," which surpasses and fully supplants the previous theological and metaphysical stages (*PSS* 1:139).

Comte continued to write after the publication of his works on positivism, however, and Solovyov's essay below pays special attention to Comte's later works, claiming that Comte himself placed special emphasis on writings from the period *after* a nervous breakdown, when the French thinker began to develop what he saw as a new religion based on positive science, complete with holy days, a calendar of saints, and a catechism.[58] It is in these later works that Comte articulates most clearly his view of Humanity with a capital *H*, which he also calls *Le grand Être*, or the Great Being. Comte insisted on the feminine nature of this *grand Être*, a point used by Solovyov to draw a parallel with his own ideas of Sophia. Thus, in the following essay Solovyov moves seamlessly from an explanation of positivism to a discussion of the principles of human rights and the meaning of "citizen," through a definition of Humanity and the Great Being, and ultimately to Sophia and the most complete discussion anywhere in his writing of the Sophia icon and its meaning. Although only the eighth and ninth parts of "The Idea of Humanity in Auguste Comte" directly

---

57. See *PSS* 1:326 for this early bibliography. According to de Courten, "Until very recently, the question of Comte's influence on Solov'ëv's views of history has been massively overlooked. One reason is the absence of thorough studies of the reception of Comte in Russia, despite his success in the 1860s–1870s, which was comparable to that of Hegel two decades earlier" (194). The first scholar to take Comte seriously as a direct influence on Solovyov was David, "The Formation of the Religious and Social System," (followed by Rotsinskii. See, in particular, the latter's essay "Vl. Solov'ev i O. Kont."

58. In Comte's new calendar, months were named for Moses, Homer, Aristotle, Archimedes, Caesar, St. Paul, Charlemagne, Dante, Gutenberg, Shakespeare, Descartes, Frederic, and Bichat.

address Sophia, I have included a translation of the entire essay to demonstrate the logic and context of this late articulation of Solovyov's Wisdom.

Solovyov first delivered the essay as a lecture at the Philosophical Society in Russia on the hundredth anniversary of Comte's birth, March 7, 1898. In the published version, used below, Solovyov often paraphrases from Comte's writing, including the original French phrases in parentheses when he feels they are necessary for clarity. I have not always translated the foreign words when they are clear from Solovyov's context. The published essay also includes Solovyov's references to the original text as footnotes.

"The Idea of Humanity in Auguste Comte"

I am particularly grateful to the philosophical society for the honor of opening our session commemorating Auguste Comte. Personally, I have no special right to that honor, other than the right to pay an old debt to a great thinker. In this same venue more than twenty years ago, I happened to begin my public career with a sharp critique of positivist philosophy.* Of that, I have no reason to repent. First of all, positivism was fashionable among us at that time. As often happens, an intellectual trend had developed into idolatry that was both blind and intolerant to anyone not "like-minded." As the first test in a serious philosophical career, any neophyte philosopher finds it not only permissible, but absolutely obligatory to take a contrary stance to the ruling ideology. Secondly, the idolatry—so unfair to those who did not believe—offended its very idol. The fashionable adulation tended to reify only the first half of Comte's teachings, but remained silent on the most important, in the opinion of the teacher himself, and culminating second half.

I have no intention of repenting of the fact of my critique. If I am not guilty in light of the positivism of Russian society of the day, however, my debt before Comte remains all the same. The debt I have requires me to demonstrate the kernel of great truth in the real fullness of his teaching.

I

In evaluating the task of his life quite highly, Comte himself points to its *unity*—he sees here a single idea—"an idea of youth, actualized by maturity" *(une pensée de la jeunesse exécutée par l'âge mûr)*. Of course, we are not bound to Comte's opinions about himself. When speaking about him, however, it would be strange to avoid what he considered the primary idea of his whole life. Besides Comte's own statement, I have two other motives for pausing specifically on this idea. First, outside of a tightly restricted, if widely flung circle of correct-thinking Comtians, this primary idea is relatively poorly

* Author's note: I have in mind my master's dissertation and its defense at the Petersburg University.

known and, in any case, draws insufficient attention to itself. And, most importantly, I see in it the essence of a great truth,[59] although based on false conditions and expressed in a one-sided manner.

First of all, we must remember the general conditions in which Comte's idea arose.

We consider this to be the 1898th year after the birth of Christ. Although Comte was born a hundred years ago, the year of his birth was not 1798, but the seventh year of some new era, established by an external sign to signal that the human mind had finally and internally broken its former bond with Christianity.[60] Although the revolutionary calendar was soon withdrawn and forgotten, the break that it signified was accepted by Comte, together with the majority of his contemporaries, as an established, normative, and irreversible fact. This, then, is the first historical condition of Comte's idea: its growth from the soil of a negative attitude toward Christianity. But this condition in and of itself is too general; there is nothing characteristic or original in it. Its originality appears only in the fact that a negative attitude toward Christianity unites in Comte with a negative attitude toward the French Revolution. When Comte completed all the details of his plan for a normative social structure, he did not return to the Christian calendar, but neither did he accept the revolutionary one. Instead, he calculated his own calendrical schedule that, it is true, excluded Christ, but which respectfully included the apostle Paul and many other saints not only of the Western but of the Eastern Church (for example Athanasius the Great, Basil the Great, John Chrysostom)[61], and which did not admit a single one of the instigators of the French Revolution. Furthermore, it included only one of its victims: the chemist Lavoisier.[62]

In light of his principal alienation from Christianity, Comte's negative attitude toward a purely negative type of thought and action, toward one-sided critical and anarchic tendencies, is of course entirely characteristic. He could call his teaching *positive* in this algebraic meaning as well, as the negation of a negation, as a *plus* formed by the multiplication of two *minuses*. This kind of formal characteristic points only to a general *tendency* of Comte's thought. But in what did this thought consist?

59. The essence of the great truth, as the end of this essay will show, is the identity of Humanity or the Great Being with Sophia.

60. Solovyov is referring to the French revolutionary or republican calendar that was established in 1793 and abandoned in 1806. He calculates 1798 as the seventh year, since the calendar's dating began on September 22, 1782, under the Gregorian calendar. Solovyov's calculations are off by a year, since Comte was born in January of 1798.

61. Rather than Augustine and his followers in the West, these patristic writers are considered among the most important Eastern Orthodox saints.

62. Antoine-Laurent Lavoisier (1743–94) founded the modern study of chemistry. He was beheaded during the French Revolution.

II

From a philosophical-historical point of view, we must recognize the value of at least one element in the French Revolution, an element prompting its principal significance, its justification, and its magnetic strength: namely the declaration of *human rights*. Strictly speaking, this declaration was not novel, for all human rights are included, of course, in the power of people to become God's children, as proclaimed by the Gospels (John 1:12).[63] But speaking purely historically, this declaration of the natural rights of man *was* new, compared not only to the ancient world and the Middle Ages, but also to later Europe. The followers as well as opponents of Europe's religious and ecclesiastical Reformation had completely forgotten that man has inviolable rights. The French reformers, suffering from the dragonnades of Louis XIV,[64] had no principal support for their opposition, since in terms of the most basic of human rights—the freedom of religious conviction—their king was more in agreement with them, and was more powerful and less resolute than their own dogmatist and lawgiver: Calvin.[65] The latter, at the first possibility and with a clean conscience, burned an innocent and meritorious man for disagreeing with him about the dogma of the Trinity.

The principle of human rights was new in that world and was of the highest importance. Yet Comte's negative view of the French Revolution was not due to that. It is worth noting that our philosopher, having rejected the revolutionary calendar and its era (1792) that recalled the rule of terror, took as the starting point of his own counting system: 1789, the year of the famous declaration and the first peaceful attempts at its realization.[66]

The two sides of the French Revolution—the declaration of human rights at the beginning, and then the unheard-of systematic obliteration of all such rights by the revolutionary powers—do not suggest an accidental contradiction or the simple inability of its founders to realize their principles in practice. No, the profound basis for this duplicity is found already in the declaration itself, thanks to the addition of a single word: the rights of man and the *citizen*. This addition would seem innocent and even elementary. Without civil rights, human rights cannot be realized. At a certain historical stage, reached long ago, every man became a citizen, just as he is a family man, a member of his church, his party, his school, etc. All of these individual designations are very

---

63. "But to all who received him, who believed in his name, he gave power to become children of God" (John 1:12).

64. *Dragonnades* were part of a policy of Louis XIV in France designed to reconvert citizens to Catholicism. Special soldiers were billeted in Protestant homes and commanded to cause havoc.

65. John Calvin (1509–64), French theologian of the Protestant Reformation. Solovyov refers here to the fact that, although ostensibly against the autocratic monarchy, Calvin also allowed any number of authoritarian acts, including the executions of his critics.

66. Solovyov refers here to the Declaration of the Rights of Man and of the Citizen, approved by the French National Assembly on August 26, 1789.

important, but there is nothing *self-determining* about them, nothing that would be *in and of itself* the basis for rights that are inalienable by their very essence. The understanding of human rights is dear because of the fact that it points to something unconditional, to a quality in the subject that could not be taken away, to something from which all demands of fairness could be derived with the internal necessity of formal logic. But the treacherous clause "and the citizen" ruined the issue by mixing in what did not belong and placing the conditional on the same plane as that which is unconditional.

It is impossible to say sanely to any man that, "You are not a man." It is all the same, even if he be a criminal, a madman, or a complete savage. But there is no logical obstacle to saying: "You are not a citizen," even to a fully worthy man and to one who has been recognized as a citizen in the past. "Yesterday you were a citizen, now you are still a citizen, but in a minute you will not be a citizen." But if citizenship is recognized as an *independent* basis of all rights, then with the lack or loss of this accidental and mutable significance, these rights as well would cease to exist, would be lost. It is clear that inalienable rights can flow *only* from a worth in the holder that cannot be forfeited. Long before the French Revolution, ancient states knew well the meaning of citizenship and the rights of citizens, but that did not provide the fundamental class of their population either civil or any other rights. Any definite or positive human right can be, in and of itself, taken away. To be a citizen is, in and of itself, only a positive right, and as such can be taken away without internal contradiction. But to be a human being is not a conditional right, but an essentially inalienable quality. Only that quality alone, accepted as the primal basis of all rights, can inform rights with a principal inviolability or can place an unconditional obstacle to their withdrawal or arbitrary restriction. As long as there is one determining principle—*human* rights, then the inviolable rights of everyone are guaranteed, for you cannot declare that people of such and such a race, of such and such creed, of such and such a class are not humans. All you need to do is place an artificial right—citizenship—alongside the natural, basic right of all people, and the broad possibility arises of granting this or that group of people exclusive citizenship, or, more accurately, a status *outside* citizenship, and to take away from them all human rights under the guise of civil ones. Thus, the raising up of the "citizen" to an *independent* principle alongside that of "human" turns out to be fatal for all civil rights. We owe factual credit to the French Revolution for the spread of civil rights to broad groups of people, half or even all of whom had formerly been devoid of such rights in France: to landed peasants, to Protestants, and to Jews. But having turned from the pure and clear staging of the task of freedom on an unconditional basis (the worth of man as such) and mixing into it the conditional and indeterminate concept of the "good citizen," the Revolution opened the doors to all manner of savagery in the future. Of course, in the revolutionary period all of the multitudes of human victims, the masses of drowned, murdered, guillotined individuals suffered not because they stopped being people, but because they were deemed to be poor citizens, bad patriots, "traitors" (like here in Russia, the countless victims of Ivan IV).[67]

Two principles—"human" and "citizen"—were incoherently placed together so that the second should be subordinate to the first. As is natural, the lower, being more concrete and graphic, turned out to be the more powerful, and soon pushed itself into the superior position. It then swallowed up the first *without a trace*, for the execution of the citizen of necessity killed the man.

III

If the brutality of revolutionary terror found its principal support in the declaration of rights and specifically in the addition of "and the citizen," then the addition itself was not the consequence of an accidental mistake or of malicious intent. It had, rather, some internal basis or thought. In fact, it flowed from a natural and just, although falsely conceived and incorrectly applied sense (based on historical conditions) of the *inadequacy* of the individual man. Taken in isolation, it was not felt that the individual could be the unconditional bearer of rights *in actuality*, because of his inability to *realize* human rights.

The best of the originators of the great upheaval understood, or at least felt the internal limitlessness and the self-ruling autonomy of the individual person, but they also understood, or felt, that, in and of itself, this limitless significance is only *potential*, and that for its transfer into reality something else needed to be attached to every single person. And that something had to be higher and more powerful than the person himself. What could this thing be that was really higher, that gives actual fullness of life to the separate individual? Classical antiquity, which had long ago been raised to an ideal through the strength of an intellectual reaction to medieval theocracy, had pointed to *citizenship, government, and fatherland.* The march of modern history merely brought in the apparent change that the idea of the highest political whole was connected not with the city, but with the people or nation. National patriotism, powerfully revealing itself for the first time in the fifteenth century on semireligious grounds in the figure of Joan of Arc, was more and more "secularized" in the course of the following centuries. It was finally affirmed in its purely nonreligious or even pagan mode by the French Revolution.

So, one becomes an actual, full person only as a citizen of his state, a son of his fatherland. Auguste Comte deserves merit and praise most of all for the

---

67. Solovyov here compares the terror of the French Revolution with the reign of Ivan the Terrible (1530–84), the first Russian ruler to call himself tsar. He is known for his establishment of a private army, the *oprichniki*, which terrorized the nation through massive murder and torture of the civilian population.

fact that he was not satisfied with such an obvious and comely decision. Of course, there is no special merit and praise due if someone, believing in the heavenly Father, refuses to place his own earthly fatherland in place of God. But Comte did not believe in the one God Almighty. He also did not believe in the contrary, in the absolute significance of human individuality in and of itself. Seeking the real fulfillment of that individuality, he did not confine himself to the collective whole that exists clearly and concretely, acknowledged by everyone. He did not confine himself to national unity. He was one of the first, and one of the very few, to understand that a nation in its immediate empirical reality is conditional, that although it is always more powerful and physically more enduring than an individual person, it is far from being equally worthy in its internal essence, in its spiritual sense. Who, for example, was closer to the true fullness of human worth: the murdered righteous Socrates in all his external impotence, or the Athenian government that lorded over him with violence in all its internal falseness? And if Socrates needed somehow to fill out his personal worth, if he was somehow not fully individual or completely human, then, of course, he needed that supplement not from his government or his fatherland, which ultimately only filled him with a cup of poison, but from something else altogether.[68]

Comte—and for this is due the bulk of his merit and praise—showed more clearly, more decisively, and more fully than all of his predecessors what that "something" was. He showed that the collective whole transcending every single individual by virtue of its internal essence, not merely its external form, and truly fulfilling the individual both ideally and in complete reality, is *humanity* as a living, positive unity that embraces us all. He pointed to the "great being": *le grand Être.*

IV

The idea of *humanity* would be neither new nor interesting if Comte understood the word merely as a general, generic concept or as a concrete collection that is the sum of individual human entities.

He spoke neither about an abstract concept nor about an empirical aggregate, but about a living, actual being. With brilliant courage, he went further and asserted that a single human being in and of himself or taken separately is only an abstraction, that such a person in actuality does not exist and cannot exist. And, of course, Comte was right.

No one denies the actuality of the elemental terms of geometry: point, line, plane, and, finally, volume or stereometric area, i.e., the geometric body. All of this actually exists; we rely on all of it in life and in science. But in what way do we ascribe actuality to these geometric elements? After some careful thought, it becomes clear that they exist not in their separateness, but only in determined relationships with each other. Their actuality is exhausted, or

68. Solovyov was writing his *Life Drama of Plato* at about the same time as this essay.

fully covered by this relativity. They themselves only represent simple relations that are intellectually secured, *abstracted* from more complex facts.

A geometric point is defined as a boundary, or a place of intersection, i.e., the coincidence of two intersecting lines; it is clear that the point does not exist outside of the intersection of lines. It is impossible to even imagine a separately existing geometric point, for, being by definition devoid of any dimension, being equal to a nullity of space, it cannot have anything inside itself that would distinguish it or separate it from the surrounding area, with which it would haphazardly blend, falling into it without a trace. Thus, points or elements of no dimension do not exist in and of themselves or taken separately, but only in lines and through lines. But lines, too, i.e., elements of one dimension, exist for their part only as boundaries of surfaces or of two-dimensional elements. And planes—only as boundaries of (geometric) bodies or three-dimensional spaces, which, in turn, actually exist only as boundaries of physical bodies, determined, but not exhausted by the geographic elements. It might seem a simple concept that lines are made up of points, planes of lines, and bodies of planes. But that now is unthinkable. If even geometric points could exist independently, then in order to put themselves together in some sort of line, they obviously would need to organize themselves not any old way, but in a specific *direction*. But that would already be a line, which, consequently, is not made up of them, but is determined by them. The same would hold true for lines (presupposing—*per impossibile* [French: in an impossibility]—their separate existence). In order for them to form into surfaces, they would need to spread themselves out along a specific *two-dimensional* outline, i.e., the surface would already be given. And so forth. The fact changes in no way if, as is accepted, in each case we put *the movement of one* geometric element in place of *the constitution of many*. In other words, we imagine a line as the movement of points, surface as the movement of lines, and so forth. It is clear, in fact, that the movement of points can produce a specific line only under the condition that that movement takes place in a specific *direction*, i.e., along the very line that was thus already mentally posited *before* the movement of the points. And the distinction of lines, or the directions for moving points, already presupposes, at least in general, space in two dimensions, since only one line is imaginable in one dimension. The same is true for the movement of a line to form a specific surface area; it would need to be done precisely within the limits of that surface area presupposed already in advance. And so forth and so on. In a word, the order of actual relations is here analytic—from the higher to the lower, from the more concrete to the more abstract. It is completely unthinkable to derive a higher geometric definition synthetically from a lower one, since the latter of necessity presupposes the higher, as its defining space. Points actually exist only in lines, lines—only on surfaces, surfaces—only on physical bodies. The imaginary-*complex*, i.e., actually the relatively-*integral*, is more primary, more independent, more real than the imaginary-simple, and in actuality more real than the merely partial, separate elements: the products of their expansion.

A whole is primary to its parts and is presupposed by them. This great truth, evident in geometry, maintains all its force in sociology as well. There is a complete correspondence here. A sociological point is a single person; a line is a family; a surface is a nation; a three-dimensional figure or a geometric body is a race, but a completely real, physical body can only be humanity. It is impossible to deny the reality of the composing parts, but only in connection with the whole. Taken separately, they are only abstractions. In connection with the whole, one person—a sociological point—can have more meaning than many families, nations, or even races, just as happens with a geometric point. The center of a sphere—a single point—is much more important not only than other points in that body, but than all of its lines. The same is true for persons. Socrates, for example, who has worldwide significance immeasurably surpassing not only the lines of his family, but all the surfaces of Athenian citizenry, nonetheless could not have any real existence without that family and that citizenry, which, in turn, could not exist on its own outside the life of humanity.

A body is not made up of points, lines, and figures, but is already presupposed by them; humanity is not made up of persons, families, and nations, but is presupposed by them. We see, of course, that over the course of world history these single and collective elements of human life converge more and more and, as it were, form together. With this, however, they do not create humanity itself, since humanity is already presupposed by the very movements joining together, as its necessary basis, motive, and leadership. If world history is the successive and systemic collection of individual elements, joining together into the ultimate reality of the whole of humanity, then humanity itself must have previously been divided into delimited groups, up to, but not including the smallest limits. Comte, as the founder of sociology, does not fail to note that humanity divides first into communities, then into families, but *never into separate persons.*[69]

Parts always presuppose their whole and are subordinate to it. And if we were to suggest the opposite, it would only be because of the historically conditional inadequacy of our understanding and formulas, which are unable to present the true reality. "Only from thence comes our inclination always to subordinate the whole to its parts, even though full and solid existence belongs only to the whole. But when a truly synthetic mindset sufficiently overcomes our preliminary habits, the opposite tendency naturally prevails, as the only positive one. When our understanding of humanity becomes broadly accepted, reborn souls will bring the ideas of nation and even family *to it*, in order always to move from the given that is most characteristic to the givens that are less defined. For only the existence of humanity allows a definition that avoids confusion and arbitrariness."

---

69. At this point and over a dozen or more in the text, Solovyov includes a footnote referring the reader to pages in Comte's texts. Since the edition he cites is not readily available and the references fairly general, I have omitted them here.

According to Comte's profound and correct observation, all sophisms that are displayed in a haphazard or backward way of thinking vis à vis the reality of humanity destroy themselves. They posit the point of view of exclusive individualism, which can consequently never lead to a conclusion. The language itself in which the sophisms are expressed would reveal their awkwardness, since the vocabulary used would undoubtedly be broader than the individual, such as Family and Fatherland, a fact that these "backward and unprincipled sophists" would not dare deny. These three basic constructs—language, fatherland, family—undoubtedly are only particular manifestations of humanity, and not of an individual person, who, on the contrary, fully depends on them as on the real conditions of his *human* existence.

Comte notes the tendency of any association to look upon itself as the kernel of humanity. This disposition toward universality corresponds to the fact that any particular association, no matter how well developed, enters into the unity of the whole, from which it can be separated only by abstraction. Comte is not only sure of the actual existence of a whole humanity, but in it sees existence par excellence, and directly names it *la suprême existence.*

V

"The Great Being" includes in itself (not in the sense of a sum of parts, but in the sense of an actual whole, or a living unity) all beings, freely acting together in the accomplishment of universal order. Looking merely to *fill in* the concept of real order, we naturally establish that unity that corresponds to it. According to *objective* subordination, which characterizes the general hierarchy of appearances, universal order becomes essentially reduced to the human order, to the last limit of all observable influences.

Positive teaching, which is necessarily bounded at first by the simplest and most general manifestations, must finally show us actual existence, truly endowed with feelings and will analogous to ours, but united with a higher power.

According to Comte, insofar as the Great Being is not subject to observation by the external senses or mathematical calculations, it is a subject of faith, but of a faith that is necessarily tied to the entirety of scientific knowledge. Comte speaks of positive faith (*la foi positive*) not in a theoretical sense, of course, but rather similar to the way Kant speaks of rational faith, i.e., about faith necessarily postulated by reason.[70] "Positive faith achieves its true *objective* and subjective unity as the necessary consequence of its normal development, concentrating the totality of real laws around a collective being who directs our fates without mediation by the strength of its own necessity, modified by its providence. Such a faith completely agrees with love that is directed toward that most highly sympathetic Great Being, all reverence befitting the charitable ruler of universal order. It is true that this limitless and

---

70. See, for example, Kant's *Religion within the Limits of Reason Alone* (1793).

eternal Being (i.e., Humanity) did not by itself create those materials that it uses in its wise actions, nor those laws by which the results of those actions are determined." But according to Comte, the "absolute evaluation" of this Being does not require mind or, even less, heart. "Of course," he says, "the natural order is sufficiently imperfect that its good deeds can be realized for us only indirectly—through heartfelt service—*par l'afectueux* [sic] *ministère* [French: affectionate service]—of the active and intelligent Being, without whom our existence would become almost intolerable. And such a conviction sufficiently empowers each one of us to turn all our justified gratitude to Humanity, even if there exists a still higher Providence, from which springs *the might of our general Mother.*"[71]

We can recognize in this creator of the religion of humanity the author of positive philosophy. This is the man who wanted to limit the study of astronomy to our own solar system, asserting that the study of the rest of the starry sky is impossible and, as a whole, unnecessary. We find the same principle in both places: "the final frontier of all visible influences"—a principle entirely characteristic of the newest heir of Roman mentality, but essentially unable to endure a critical stance. But my task now is not criticism. Thus, I return to the truth content of Comte's perspective.

Comte recognizes Humanity in the sense of a living and complete reality as a positive fact to which the entire system of scientific knowledge can be reduced. "Profound study of the world's order," he says, "reveals to us the prevailing existence of the true Great Being. Having as its purpose the continual perfection of that order, adapting itself to it, the Great Being represents to us its true totality in the best possible manner. That indisputable Providence, the apex of our fate, naturally becomes the general focus of our feelings, our thoughts, and our actions. However, it is obvious that the Great Being surpasses any human power, even our collective power. The necessity of its structure—*sa constitution nécessaire*—and its own fate make it highly sympathetic to all of its servants."

VI

The proper relationship to the Great Being, or the "religion of humanity" does not exclude family and fatherland. Instead, it includes them as its *preparatory stages.* "Two essential attributes of collective existence—solidity and continuity (*continuité*)—are naturally found on the lower levels where, having less wholeness (as in humanity), they become more noticeable (*mieux appréciables*). In this way, Family and Fatherland will never stop being the nec-

---

71. In this quotation Comte refers to Humanity as female. In the following paragraph Solovyov criticizes Comte for not extending his inquiry *beyond* Humanity to God, or Providence. Nonetheless, the Comtian concept of a female Great Being or a whole Humanity proves extremely important to the Russian visionary of Sophia.

essary thresholds for Humanity (*les préambules nécessaires de l'Humanité*). But a systematic development, summoned to fulfill the natural course of history, must proceed along the opposite path (i.e., not from family and nation toward humanity, but from humanity to nation and family). Having achieved a full understanding of the Great Being, we must relay it to our children, without reproducing that empirical evolution that its original production required. It will be sufficient to better use the natural ability of feeling to anticipate the generalization of mind that will emerge of necessity in the power of the normal superiority of the female sex (*le sexe affectif*) in the totality of positive education."

With this, Comte especially points to the fact that Family and Fatherland, being successive preparations for humanity, *do not need* to be understood as its actual components or its constituent parts, for humanity is an *indivisible being* (*être indivisible*). So, what is it in this sense? What is its formative principle?

VII

The Great Being of Comte's religion has yet one more constant sign in addition to its complete reality, power, and wisdom that makes it our Providence: the fact that it is a feminine being. This is not a metaphor or the personification of an impersonal concept, like various virtues, arts, and sciences as depicted in classical mythology in the form of women. From the previous account in Comte's own words, it is sufficiently clear that the Great Being was not an abstract concept for this philosopher. He clearly distinguished humanity as a sum of national, familial, and personal elements (his *humanité* with a small *h*) from Humanity as an essential, actual, and living principle of all these elements (*Humanité* with a capital *H*), or the Great Being. And in this *main* sense of Humanity, although it has a collective character at its core, it is in itself more than a collection of names,—it possesses *its own proper existence*.

"Objectively," says Comte, "the Great Being is as external to us as are other real beings, despite the fact that, subjectively, we make it a part, at least, of our hope" (*Objectivement le Grand-Être est aussi extérieur à chacun de nous que les autres éxistences réeles, tandis que subjectivement nous en faisons partie du moins en espérence*).[72]

It is clear that he is speaking not about a concept, but about a being. It is a completely real being that might not be exactly personal in the sense of an empirical human individual, but is even less so impersonal. In a word, this being is *superpersonal*, although it would be better to use two words: the Great Being is not a personified principle, but the *Principle Person (Printsipial'noe Litso)*, or the *Person-Principle (Litso-Printsip)*. It is not a personified idea, but a *Person-Idea (Litso-Ideia)*.

72. Solovyov includes the original French here but not the citation.

VIII

The question arises as to the similarity of Comte's religion of humanity, repre-sented by the female-gendered Great Being, to the medieval cult of the Madonna. We note yet another curious coincidence: At the same time that Comte published in Paris an account of his religion, with its extolling of the feminine effective principle of human nature and morality, in Rome the thousand-year-old cult of the Madonna recognized its theological apex with the dogmatic decree of Pope Pius IX on the Immaculate Conception of the Holy Virgin (1854).[73]

When a thinker of Comte's character and significance begins to enter sym-pathetically into an order of ideas that are foreign to him, it is completely use-less to speak of some kind of external influence or direct borrowing. Even if the fact of such borrowing were to be established, this would explain nothing, since the question would remain just as powerfully: Why did he take precisely this idea, and not some other? I have provided you with an understanding of that special and unique intellectual path that Comte must have taken to draw so close to the ancient belief of the people. He acknowledged that path and rejoiced in that internal proximity, having no need of external borrowing.

But the ancient cult of the eternal feminine has one historical manifestation about which Comte could have known nothing, and that nonetheless ap-proaches even more closely the essence of the deeds and thoughts of this phi-losopher.

An inveterate Westernist, Auguste Comte would be very surprised if some-one were to say and prove to him that in his Great Being he had formulated with special surety and clarity, although without distinct understanding, something that has been expressed in the religious inspiration of the Russian people since the 11th century. The central idea of Comte's *religion positive* forms precisely that side of Christianity that was sensed, if not exactly con-sciously, by the Russian soul. And moreover, this feeling, or presentiment, regardless of its lack of consciousness, immediately took on a corresponding concrete expression.

If Comte happened to come upon some ancient, neglected little town that was never either "New" nor "Great," he could have seen with his own eyes an original image of his *Grand Être* that would have been more exact and more complete than anything he would have had occasion to see in the West. It is not only Comte who knew nothing of this ancient Russian creative work; there is scarce a person among all of you who has given it any attention. I will therefore have to explain its meaning to you. It is particularly remarkable that the proper subject of the image is presented *together* with all the others who are similar to, and often confused with it.[74] Nonetheless, the figure on the

73. The Orthodox Church does not accept this addition to Christian doctrine, which, in its understanding, came to a close with the Seventh Ecumenical Council in 787.

74. As Solovyov goes on to say, Sophia (the "proper subject" of the image) is often confused with Christ and Mary, yet all three figures appear together on the Novgorod Sophia icon. This line of argument does not prove that Sophia is distinct from the others, for several views of the

icon is presented in such a way that distinguishes and separates it from every-thing around it, so that there can be no inconceivable confusion.

IX

Among the main image of the ancient Novgorod cathedral (from the time of Iaroslav the Wise)[75], we find a unique female figure in royal clothing, seated on a throne. Two figures are arranged on both sides of it, facing it and leaning toward it: the Mother of God of the Byzantine type on the right; and John the Baptist on the left. Christ rises above the seated figure with arms outstretched, and above Him we can see the heavenly world, in the persons of several angels surrounding the Word of God, represented by a book of the Gospels. [See page 57 for an illustration of the icon.]

Who does this main, central, and royal person depict, so clearly distinct from Christ, from the Mother of God, and from the angels? The image is called So-phia the Wisdom of God. But what does that mean? As early as the 14th cen-tury, a Russian nobleman posed this question to the Bishop of Novgorod, but did not receive an answer. The bishop only expressed his ignorance. Still, our ancestors bowed to this puzzling figure, as the Athenians once bowed to an "unknown god."[76] They built churches and cathedrals to Sophia everywhere, and they designated celebrations and services in which this image of Sophia the Wisdom of God sometimes inexplicably resembles Christ and sometimes the Mother of God. At the same time, there is never complete identity either with Him or with Her, for it is obvious that if it were Christ, it could not be the Mother of God, and if it were the Mother of God, it could not be Christ.

Our ancestors did not take this idea from the Greeks; all available evidence shows that for the Greeks in Byzantium the Wisdom of God, ἡ Σοφία τοῦ Θεοῦ [Greek: the Wisdom of God], was understood either as a general ab-stract attribute of Divinity, or was accepted as a synonym for the eternal Word of God: Logos. The icon of the Novgorod Sophia has no Greek model; it is a matter of our own religious creative work. The meaning was unknown to the 14th-century bishop, but we can guess at it now.

Neither God, nor the eternal Word of God, nor an angel, nor a holy man, the Great, royal, and feminine Being accepts veneration both from the one who completed the Old Testament and from the foremother of the New Tes-tament.[77] Who could it be other than the truest, purest, and most complete humanity, the highest and all-encompassing form and living soul of nature

---

same figure often appear on one icon. Indeed, Christ appears on the Novgorod icon in at least two modes: Immanuel on a medallion on Mary's chest and Christ the Pantocrator over the an-gel. See page 57.

75. Russian prince (974–1054) and son of Vladimir I who strengthened the southern and western borders of old Rus'. The Novgorod Sophia icon is most likely from a later date.

76. Acts 17:22–23.

77. Solovyov refers here to John the Baptist and Mary the Mother of God. As we saw, these figures flank the seated angel in the Novgorod Sophia icon.

and the universe, eternally united, and in the process of time uniting with the Divine, and uniting to Him all that is? It is without a doubt that this is the full meaning of the Great Being, which was in part felt and consciously realized by Comte, and wholly felt, but certainly not consciously realized by our ancestors, the pious builders of the churches of Sophia.

X[78]

The founder of the "religion of positivism"[79] understood humanity as a being that becomes absolute over the course of universal progress. And truly, humanity is such a being. But for Comte, as for many other thinkers, it was not clear that that which becomes absolute within time presupposes an absolute that is essentially eternal. If it were otherwise, however, this very absolute that is *"becoming"* (*das Werden, le devenir*) (out of a non-absolute) would be self-formed of the lesser within the greater, that is, the growth of something out of nothing, or the purest of nonsense. It is not even necessary to raise the philosophical question of the relative nature of time in order to see that becoming absolute can happen only through the assimilation of that which by its very nature *is* eternally absolute. Comte instinctively guessed this truth when he ascribed a female character to the Great Being. Standing between the limited and the unconditional, while participating in both, it is by nature the principle of duality, the ἡ ἀόριστος δυάς [Greek: indefinite dyad] of the Pythagorians[80]—the most general ontological definition of the feminine. Humanity is precisely that elevated form, through which and in which everything that exists becomes absolute. It is the form of the unification of material nature with Divinity. The Great Being is universal nature as it *takes in* the Divine. This is yet another reason to attribute a feminine character to it.

It is clear that true humanity as the universal form of the union of material nature and Divinity, or as the form of nature's reception or taking in of the Divine, is by necessity Divine Humanity and Divine Matter. It cannot be *simply* humanity, inasmuch as this would mean that it takes in without being taken in, it would be form without content, or *empty form*.

The Great Being is not empty form, but the all-embracing divine human [*bogochelovecheskii*] fullness of spiritual-corporeal, divine-created life that revealed Christianity to us. Comte had only a partial, unfinished, and not fully considered understanding of the true Great Being. Nonetheless, he unconsciously believed in its fullness and instinctively bore witness to it. While

---

78. I thank Melissa Miller for her preliminary translation of these last three sections of Solovyov's essay on Comte.

79. Solovyov calls Comte's ideas "the religion of positivism," or literally "positive religion" (*positivnaia religiia*), thus playing on his own call for a positive synthesis of the humanism of positivism with the divine humanity of positive religions. He began this call as early as his *Sophia* manuscript (see 119).

80. Pythagorus, often called the "Father of Numbers" was also the founder of a school of philosophy in the sixth century BCE, and had a significant influence on Plato.

there have been and continue to be countless Christians who did not and do not know about this very essence of Christianity, who have not wanted and do not want to know it, the atheistic and pagan Comte attached himself to it with perhaps an incomplete understanding, but with a full heart.

It is true that he denied God and Christ. But God and Christ surely forgive these personal offenses. They surely pay more attention to what is in a person's heart than to what is in a person's head. After all, don't They value most of all the *other*, that in which the fullness of divine life finds its final, greatest fulfillment—that, which our philosopher sensed and named the Great Being, and that which became for him the subject of true and deep piety, although strange in its external forms and expressions? With this *fullness of the other* that embraces and supports all of us, but that not all of us sense or recognize— with this fullness, the Holy Spirit, who lives and acts in Her,[81] unites God and Christ. Comte did not sin against this. His sin, a sin common to all the theoretical enemies of Christianity, is "the sin against the Son of Man," and, according to the word of the Son of Man, this sin is forgiven.

XI

The great contribution made to the modern Christian world by the atheistic and pagan Comte is not limited to the fact that he regarded this *fundamental* side of *Divine Humanity* (the disregard of which has so greatly harmed the rightful development of religious consciousness) to be of primary importance for his "religion of positivism." In addition, in defining the content and activity of the Great Being, Comte came very close—closer than many believers—to a another, *complete* truth of Christianity, a truth that is almost forgotten in the educated part of the Christian world, in deed, if not in words.

According to Comte, the *dead* (understood as those who were worthy of being taken up by the Great Being—*d'être incorporés au Grand Être* [French: incorporated into the Great Being]) comprise a significant component of that Great Being. The dead prevail over the living two-fold: as clear role models and as the secret patrons and leaders of the living—as those internal organs, through which the Great Being operates in the individual and general history of humanity as it develops on earth. Comte distinguished for man two ways of being: one internal and eternal, which in his terminology is called "subjective" but in ours, essential (not in the sense of *wesentlich* [German: basic], but rather *wesenhaft* [German: substantial, necessary]), and the other one—transitory and external, in his usage "objective," in ours, apparent or phenomenal.[82] The significance of essential, posthumous being is determined by its divinely human unity with the very essence of Humanity. The meaning of external, phenomenal being, on the other

---

81. "Fullness" (*polnota*) in Russian is a feminine noun, allowing Solovyov to continue is association of Comte's feminine Great Being with his own female Sophia. Wisdom unites the three members of the Trinity.

82. Solovyov is using Kantian terminology.

hand, is determined by its ability to isolate or keep relatively separate its own will and actions. Both the dead and the living have their own reality; in the first group, that reality is more dignified (*plus digne*), and in the second, it is freer and more manifestly effective (*plus efficace*). But it is clear that the fullness of life for both the realities can consist only in their perfect harmony and complete interaction. And in what could the definitive meaning of the world order and the conclusion of universal history consist if not in the fulfillment of this wholeness of humanity, if not in its actual recovery through the clear unification of its two separate parts? Comte does not express this thought directly, but whosoever attentively and in good conscience reads all four volumes of his *System of Positive Politics*[83] should recognize that no other world-renowned philosopher has come so close to the task of *resurrecting the dead* as did Auguste Comte.[84]

What I have just touched upon is not only a difficult task, but a difficult conversation as well. It is no wonder that more than eighteen centuries ago in Athens, when the apostle Paul spoke of the unity of the human race and of the presence of God in everyone, the Athenians willingly listened, but as soon as he mentioned the resurrection of the dead, they said, "Well, my friend, we'll discuss that some other time."[85] At this time I would like, if not to discuss with you, then in a couple of words to allude to the human side of that task, and even, while not strictly saying anything about the task itself, merely to point out the first human steps in its direction, because there is nothing in those steps that is incomprehensible or difficult.

XII

Here before us today is one of the countless who have departed. Of course, it does not occur to us to foretell his general resurrection, although we have begun it. Before coming to this celebration of his death, I became better acquainted with Comte and came to love him even more. Here already is the first step, or the first two steps: to know and to come to love. If in addition I have succeeded in conveying to a few of you a true understanding and goodwill toward this departed one, then that is already the third step.

For the resurrection of the dead, as well as for any other undertaking, knowledge and love still do not constitute the whole task, but only its necessary condition. Without them, it is impossible to complete, because it is impossible to begin.

But now, in conclusion, I would like to express one modest hope.

Comte, as you know, created for the religion of Humanity his own calendar, in which, alongside many peculiarities, there is also something good. It might be pleasant for the philosophical community to note that, in addition to Descartes and Leibnitz, Kant, Fichte and Hegel are also canonized there.

83. *Système de politique positive* (1851–54)

84. Here readers should also recognize Solovyov's praise of the "Common Task" (*Obshchee delo*) of the resurrection of the dead espoused by his friend and fellow lay philosopher, Nikolai Fedorov (1829–1903)

85. Acts 17:16–34.

Nevertheless, this positivist calendar will not become generally accepted, just as the revolutionary calendar did not. It is the Christian calendar that will remain as the accepted one, but with, I believe, several new additions.

When the authoritative representatives of Christianity concentrate their attention on the fact that our religion is first and foremost a divinely human religion, and that *humanity* is not some kind of appendage but a fundamental, generative half of Divine Humanity, then they will decide to exclude from their historical pantheon anything nonhuman that has accidentally fallen into it over the course of so many centuries, and to bring into it instead something more of the human. Then we will have to remember this thinker who, despite his gross misconceptions and the limitations of his theoretical outlook, more strongly than anyone else coming out of the nineteenth century sensed and advanced what was not always sufficiently valued in historical Christianity, namely, the human side of religion and life. He sensed this not in any separate relationship but in its general makeup, embracing the past and future of humanity in addition to its present. And then, while not adopting his calendar because it is perhaps too human, we can maybe put it to good use for a certain expansion of our own. First of all, perhaps the name of Auguste Comte himself will be entered there in commemoration of the service he rendered to the development of Christian consciousness, despite the fact that he did not recognize it as such. He revived in our Christian consciousness ancient and eternal truths, but under new names: the fundamental truth about collective essence or the World Soul—whose simplest name in Christian terms is the Church—and the consummate truth about the life of the dead.

I am not a student of Auguste Comte or a convert to his "positivist religion." I do not have any personal reasons for bias or exaggeration of its significance whatsoever. Of course, in my early hostility towards Comte and positivism, there was much more passion and fervor than there is in tonight's affection, due to now having acquired a better understanding of him. And if I posit all the same that Comte really has secured himself a place in the sacred calendar of Christian humanity, then I mean this in the most definitive sense. I mean no temptation or offensive to anyone, no matter who they might be. "Saintliness" does not mean perfection in all aspects, it does not even mean absolute perfection in a single aspect. Saintliness is not even perfect goodness or righteousness; the only truly righteous one is God. Whoever has adequate and sustained knowledge of the life and work of Comte will recognize in him, of course, alongside various misconceptions and several fundamental defects of mind and character, the absence of any cunning, as well as his rare frankness, simplicity, and pure heartedness. That is why Wisdom, who "does not enter into the crafty soul,"[86] found a place for herself in the soul of this person and gave him the capacity to be, although only semiconsciously, a prophetic voice for the highest truths about the Great Being and the resurrection of the dead.

Translated by Judith Deutsch Kornblatt

---

86. The Wisdom of Solomon 1:4.

4 "At the Dawn of Misty Youth"

A Semiautobiographical Short Story

Reading Guide

The tone of this story, like many of Solovyov's Wisdom writings, mixes humor with serious discussions of truth and reality. More than any other work before *Three Encounters*, "At the Dawn of Misty Youth" is autobiographical, although Solovyov has clearly and probably intentionally confused many facts of his life. Indeed, we cannot know whether an incident on a train as described ever occurred. Solovyov's biographer, S. M. Luk'ianov, notes a trip to Khar'kov in May of 1872 but none to Kirghizia and no particular illness at that time.[1] Solov'ev had felt poorly the previous year and in the summer had gone to rest from his studies at Fedorovka, the estate of his maternal grandmother, E. F. Romanova. It was at that time that he renewed his friendship with Ekaterina Vladimirovna Romanova, then a ward of their mutual grandmother. This Ekaterina, the Olga of the story, was the daughter of Vladimir Vladimirovich Romanov, the brother of Solovyov's mother. Vladimir, a favorite uncle, had two daughters, Ekaterina and Poliksena. Solovyovv had three other female cousins, the daughters of his uncle Pavel, and may very well, as the narrator confesses in this story, have been infatuated with them one after the other.[2]

The narrator of this story suggests he was made ill by the "intemperate application of German books," most likely the pessimistic philosophy of Kant, Schopenhauer, and the latter's successor, Eduard von Hartmann. Hartmann's *Philosophie des Unbewussten* had appeared to much fanfare in 1869, and

---

1. According to Luk'ianov, Solov'ev was never seriously ill during his college years but was frequently sick with minor complaints (*O Vl. S. Solov'eve* 1:272).
2. Luk'ianov, *O Vl. S. Solov'eve* 1:10–11.

Solovyov refers to it in his master's thesis, "The Crisis of Western Philosophy (Against the Positivists)," as the culmination of the German philosophical tradition.[3] He wrote entries in the *Encyclopedic Dictionary* on both Kant and Hartmann and would no doubt have included one on Schopenhauer as well had he not died before he could continue past the first part of the "S" volume (see *SS* 10:345–80 and 297–301). These Western philosophers were clearly part of his early and continuing intellectual education.

According to statements made by the philosopher in 1887 and 1890, he left the Faculty of Physics and Mathematics in 1872, at the age of nineteen, and enrolled as an auditor in the History and Philology Faculty of Moscow University. He took his exams in the latter and received his degree in the spring of 1873.[4] Luk'ianov demonstrates, however, that Solovyov did not officially withdraw from the Faculty of Physics and Mathematics until April of 1873.[5] In either case, his reading of the "German books" that so influenced his philosophical stance toward the world was undoubtedly extracurricular. He apparently rarely attended class and had a rather negative attitude toward the level of teaching at the university.[6] Solovyov's haphazard approach to education, so at odds with the obviously erudite philosophical treatises that he penned, makes all the more humorous the narrator's mocking definition of himself as "a nineteen-year-old philosopher."

The setting of the narrator's vision, on the hard metal plate between two train cars, also humorously sets the scene for what has been called Solovyov's "fourth meeting" with the Divine Sophia.[7] The laconic tone of the story belies the mystical experience of wholeness and integration that Solovyov describes: "A single wondrous image was motionlessly reflected in that sensation, as in a pure mirror, and I felt and knew that in that one was all. I loved with a new, all-absorbing and endless love, and in that love for the first time I sensed the whole fullness and meaning of life." The tawdriness of the situation—the dirty locomotive, the loud gymnasts in the train car, and especially the "shame and disgrace" experienced by the narrator after "the wings of [his] will's self-denial sank lower and lower" and he succumbed to the "earthly principle" with the obviously flighty and antiphilosophical "Julie"—does not negate the sacredness of his vision. Rather, as always in Solovyov's re-visions of Sophia, the earthly and the divine cohabit in the same moment and the same meaning. The matter-of-fact tone of the story at once mocks and reinforces the mystical nature of the Wisdom that he sees.

---

3. *SS* 1:49.
4. See *Pis'ma* 2:185 and 337.
5. Luk'ianov 1:135–6.
6. Luk'ianov 1:170, 173–74.
7. Jakim, Introduction to Solovyov, *"At the Dawn of Mist-Shrouded Youth,"* 6.

"At the Dawn of Misty Youth"[8]

I spent the entire night awake. My fitful imagination, however, did not evoke the usual disconnected traces of real and invented scenes or of events in kaleidoscopic and startling combinations. This time my sleepless delirium had both coherence and unity. A continuous string of details about one distant and seemingly entirely forgotten occurrence arose before me with greater and greater clarity. Although that event began entirely inconsequentially, its conclusion left a deep impression on my internal life. I am glad that a restless recollection has now returned all of these details to me, and I hasten to write them down while they are still before me.

I

I was nineteen at the time. It was the end of May, and I had just advanced to the last year of university. I was traveling from Moscow to Khar'kov, where I was to have an extraordinarily important "explanation" with one of my cousins, toward whom I had experienced a tender and rather noble love a few months previous.[9] Thanks to her I had decided to make a large detour. The actual goal of my journey was the Kirghiz steppe, where I was intending to take the local cure by fermented mare's milk, as my organism had been severely distressed by the intemperate application of German books.[10]

I took a seat in a second-class car. A young, fair-haired woman dressed in light-gray traveling clothes had installed herself in the other corner of the same double car. She was speaking affectionately and gaily with three men, there to see her off. When the train moved away from the platform, she nodded to them from the window and continued to wave her handkerchief for a long time.

Only a low barrier separated the adjacent sections of the car, so I could freely examine my vis-à-vis. I occupied myself with this activity, since there was nothing else of interest in the car. She was somewhat short, slender, and very well put together, but her face was far from pretty, with an irregular nose and wide mouth. When she would look up affectionately with her bright eyes, however, that homely, plain face could become extremely attractive. It's not that her glance was especially expressive, but there was something in her eyes more profound than thought, some kind of quiet light, lacking fire or brilliance.[11] Those eyes attracted and interested me from first glance. I noticed

8. I particularly thank Leonid Livak and Matt Walker for assistance with the translation and annotation of this story.

9. For translations of the letters between the young Vladimir and Ekaterina (Katya), see Solovyov, *"At the Dawn of Mist-Shrouded Youth."*

10. To travel from Moscow via Khar'kov to the Kirghiz steppe in southeastern Central Asia would require a significant detour to Ukraine.

11. These bright though quiet eyes, "more profound than thought," are the reader's first indication of the presence of Sophia.

her thick, ash-colored hair as well. It seemed to me that she returned my gaze with a smile full of favor and encouragement. At those times, as you can imagine, I assumed a dreamy and disenchanted look. But I could not dare speak with her, partly because it would have been awkward across the barrier, but more because I was excessively shy. Despite my proud demeanor, the glance of any woman could cause my heart to stand still and my lips to seal.[12]

An older woman visited my companion several times from another car, a relative of her husband, as it turned out later, who was traveling with her family in first class. They talked, partly in French,[13] about everyday affairs. I could make out from this conversation only that they were from Moscow, and traveling to the Crimea.

II

This woman in the gray dress definitely appealed to me. She had such a delicate, graceful turn of the head, and when she talked, all her movements were so elegant and feminine.

"But all the same, my Olga is much better," I said to myself, and, closing my eyes, began to think about Olga and our upcoming meeting in Khar'kov, which she did not expect. I imagined how she would cry out when she saw me, how she would grow pale and even, perhaps, faint from the unexpected happiness, how I would bring her back to consciousness and what I would say to her.

One mustn't suppose, however, that I expected an ordinary lovers' rendezvous, with simple caresses and tenderness. Oh no, I was far from that kind of superficiality. Of course, I allowed myself an element of tenderness, but that would amount to a mere a shadow of the complete picture. The main show would be entirely different. I wanted to see Olga in order to "put our relationship on the firm ground of self-denial of the will."[14] That was, in truth, my intention. I was going to have to say something like the following to her:

"Dear Olga, I love you and am glad that you love me, too. But I know, and you must learn, that all of life, and, thus love, the flower of life, is only a phantom and a lie.[15] We race madly toward happiness, but in reality we find only

---

12. Solovyov's biographers disagree about his romantic encounters, both in early and later years, often ascribing what Luk'ianov refers to as his "lack of success" in the area of love to the philosopher's "heavenly" orientation (Luk'ianov 1:266). Velichko writes, "He avoided women, and related to them with derision, almost hostilely" (cited in Luk'ianov 1:123). Mochul'skii, on the other hand, refers to a number of passionate relationships. The narrator here confesses to nothing more than ordinary adolescent shyness.

13. The French conversations remind us of the language of *The Sophia* and of many of the examples of automatic writing, in which Sophia seems to have communicated directly with Solovyov. Its association with Russian noble drawing rooms also, of course, contrasts with the more "learned" German of the narrator's studies.

14. See Luk'ianov 1:173.

15. This pessimistic philosophical rejection of love was obviously only a phase for Solovyov and clearly contradicts his definition of love as an absolute principle in *The Sophia*. See page 128.

suffering. Our will forever deceives us, making us blindly chase after worthless objects, as though they were the highest blessing and bliss. On the contrary, love is the first and greatest evil, from which we must free ourselves. For that we must reject all its exhortations, crush our personal cravings, renounce all our desires and hopes. If, as I am sure, you are able to understand me, then together we can accomplish life's journey. But know that with me you will never find that so-called family happiness that has been thought up by dull-witted philistines.[16] I have learned the truth, and my goal is to realize it for others; I will expose and destroy the universal lie. You understand that such a task can have nothing in common with pleasure. I can promise you only a hard struggle and suffering together."[17]

This is what I was intending to say to my pretty little seventeen-year-old Olga. In general, the total worthlessness of all that exists comprised the main theme of my conversations with my cousins, of which I had several and with whom I fell successively in love. The evil and insignificance of life were partly known to me, of course, from personal experience. From experience I knew that my cousins' kisses did not last forever, and that an extra glass of wine would cause a headache. But if my experience of life had not been sufficiently rich, I had nonetheless read much and thought even more, and had, already by the age of eighteen, stumbled upon the firm conviction that all temporal life, since it was comprised solely and exclusively of evil and suffering, must be totally and definitively destroyed as soon as possible. I had scarcely managed to arrive at this conclusion on the basis of my own mental powers when I was forced to recognize that I wasn't alone, and that this teaching had already been thoroughly developed by several famous German philosophers. I was somewhat of a Slavophile then, and thus, although I allowed that the Germans could abolish the universe theoretically, I placed the practical fulfillment of this task exclusively on the Russian people. Furthermore, I did not doubt in my heart that the first signal for the destruction of the world would be given by none other than me.

III

In all fairness, I must note that denial of the will and the need to destroy the universe were by far not the most complex parts of the teaching with which I had edified my lucky cousins. On one fine summer's evening a year prior to my trip to Khar'kov, one of them—the blue-eyed, but ardent Liza (then the

---

16. Solovyov probably refers here to Tolstoy's story "Family Happiness" ("Semeinoe schastie," 1859), just as he refers implicitly to the recently published "Kreutzer Sonata" ("Kveitserova sonata," 1890), which is also narrated on a train. The rival stories reflect a growing antagonism between Tolstoy and Solovyov. In the opening pages of *Dr. Zhivago*, Boris Pasternak refers to the cult of celibacy among Yuri Zhivago and his friends, drawing on both Tolstoy and the young Solovyov.

17. See Luk'ianov 1:238–39 for a discussion of Solovyov's actual letters to Katia.

object of my passion)—was honored with initiation into the secrets of *transcendental idealism.*

Walking with her along the paths of a neglected country park, I explained to her, not without animation (although I kept losing track of my words), that space, time, and causality are merely subjective forms of our cognition, and that the world, existing in these forms, is only our representation. In short, it essentially doesn't exist at all. When I arrived at this conclusion, my partner, whose big, greenish eyes had been looking serious the whole time, smiled and remarked with obvious cunning:

"And how is it that yesterday you kept speaking about Judgment Day?"

"About what Judgment Day?"

"Well, it's all the same, you know, about the need to destroy everything. If you believe that the world doesn't exist, then why would you so much want to destroy it?"

This contradiction confused me for no more than a moment.

"Isn't it true that you want to get rid of a bad dream or a nightmare when it troubles you?" I answered triumphantly.

She suddenly and without any obvious cause burst out in resounding laughter.

"What is it?" I asked with dissatisfaction.

"Ah, just imagine," she began to say, laughing and gripping my hand firmly. "Can you imagine that today I dreamed that my James (this is what she called her setter) was not a dog at all, but the commander of a regiment of Belorussian hussars, and all of our officers had to salute him. But instead of saying "your esteemed excellency," they had to say "your esteemed FLEA-CENCY."[18]

She finished this unexpected report with an equally unexpected kiss, and suddenly ran away, shouting to me from a distance:

"Let's go to the garden and pick strawberries. I noticed that lots are already ripe."

And I went to pick strawberries, although the categorical imperative, which simple people call conscience, showed me rather clearly that this was not self-denial on my part, but, quite the opposite: self-assertion of the will.

But blithe Liza leaned her fair little head so sweetly over the strawberry patch, and raised her dress so coquettishly, the silver buckles of her shoes sparkling so in the sun, that I definitely had no desire to rid myself of this pleasant nightmare, and the chapter *about the synthetic unity of transcendental apperception* that I had not finished reading continued to await me in my room.[19]

Now, sitting in the train car and for some reason remembering this little episode, a vague premonition of future sinful falls stirred in my soul.

18. The original has *vashe vysokoblagorodie* and *vashe vysoko BLOKHORODIE.* An alternate translation might provide "My esteemed cur" in place of "My esteemed sir."

19. The narrator was obviously reading Kant.

IV

Meanwhile, evening settled in. We arrived at some small station. From the courtyard you could hear the lively and impatient ringing of bells. It seemed that a low carriage pulled by three horses had come for a graying gentleman and his two young ladies, who had descended onto the platform with their things and were speaking animatedly with the station master.

I stuck my head out the little window. It smelled strongly of lilac from a dense little garden abutting the station. Young peasant girls were offering bouquets of lilies-of-the-valley. A ringing came from the distance. Someone was playing the piano in a small side room, and a group of local men and women sat around a samovar on top of a small platform in a corner of the garden and chatted gaily.

My lady in the gray dress walked along the platform and smiled to me tenderly. I looked at her with the same kind of calm satisfaction with which I viewed everything else. That evening my soul was quiet and serene. The evil and suffering of existence had receded so deeply into the very essence of things that I didn't sense them at all, although perhaps it was because I wanted absolutely nothing at that moment, and saw only a landscape in all that surrounded me.

When the train set out, I stared at the thick birch grove with the same quiet enjoyment, thinking about nothing and desiring nothing. The grove greeted our train with a welcoming whisper and embraced it from both sides, calling us to rest, and meekly smiling with the tops of its trees, now golden from the evening rays.[20]

However, the serenity of my soul was soon destroyed in the most unexpected way. When we arrived in Tula,[21] and I and the young woman were the only passengers remaining in the car, a crowd of noisy new passengers suddenly entered. This was a troupe of traveling French actors, on their way to Orel.[22] Although it is entirely possible that these were not actors at all, but merely acrobats. They were a group of seven or eight men and women. The men were considerably drunk, and behaved rather indecently. At first they wanted to play cards, but couldn't find any. They then took off their outer coats and set to gymnastic exercises, hanging from the transom, swinging to and fro, doing somersaults, and two even tried unsuccessfully to play leapfrog.

Their ladies manifested a similar frivolity. They wrangled with their gentlemen, laughing loudly and shrieking. To no small embarrassment on my part, one rather pretty woman sitting near me took off her shoe and flung it at one

20. The ringing of bells and profusion of flowers, as well as the golden sunset, all familiar from Solovyov's early Sophianic poems, intensify the introduction of Sophia into this story.

21. An ancient city south of Moscow.

22. An ancient city on the banks of the Oka River, still farther south/southwest of Moscow. Kursk, mentioned later, continues the train ride south to Khar'kov.

of the gymnasts. In retaliation, he grabbed her by the foot and intended to drag her to the floor, but, instead, fell forcefully backwards. His fall aroused the indescribable delight of the entire company.

V

The lady in the gray dress was apparently scandalized by this latest episode, although she had at first watched the spectacle with a certain curiosity. She rose and walked up to me. (I was sitting on the edge of a bench near the passageway.)

"May I hide from these gentlemen behind you? They are so frightful."

I bowed.

She sat down next to me, near the window.

I was secretly delighted that my pretty companion had taken the first step so easily and simply, and all my shyness completely disappeared. After several minutes we were chatting like old friends.

It turned out that I had heard of her husband. They had young children.

"Ah! How hard it is to raise children when you yourself have absolutely no upbringing. I have long thought about this and decided to leave them to the whim of fate—let them grow and rear themselves as they will, and I, at least, will not spoil anything."

With the serious air of a mentor, as befitted a nineteen-year-old philosopher, I remarked that she could still attend to her own education.

"Ah, so you think! I am so lazy. I have absolutely no character, not a bit of a character! And then, where could I look for education? Some advise one thing, others another. No, better I should stay as I am!"

Indeed, the education of my companion was limited to refined manners and the French language.

"I do sometimes read the *Moscow Gazette*,[23] and novels as well, as long as they are not serious . . . But you, I suppose, want to be a scholar? Ah, please, do give it up! It's so nasty. Why, it's practically the same as being an acrobat, like these gentlemen. It's just as unnatural and even more boring. And then, it is so dangerous for your health. Look how thin and pale you are already. What a pity. Why, listen. Come to see us in the Crimea. You need to swim in the sea. That'll strengthen you . . . And how fun it is there! A large crowd and no one does anything, and everyone is happy. And the air there is absolutely special. I'll be spending my fourth summer there, and each time I fall in love . . . Imagine, they fall in love with me as well," she added, apparently sincerely surprised by this circumstance.

"Do you think that I am lying, because I am so unattractive? It's true. I assure you that it is true. Why, everyone falls in love with everyone else there. Some get married; each year comes someone else's wedding. Sometimes even

23. *Moskovskie vedomosti* was a very popular and increasingly conservative newspaper in Solovyov's day.

without one . . . Good grief, what silliness I keep talking! What must you think of me?"

I hurried to remark that, although love is evil and deceit, in any case, illicit love is much more excusable than lawful love. At that time, such was my sincere conviction. As an extreme pessimist, I was perturbed by marriage, and especially by happy marriage. After all, the entire world was largely resting on it, and the destruction of that world was my highest ambition.

My companion apparently did not understand what I wanted to say.

"It is my misfortune," she said, "that for some reason many people love me, and it is terribly difficult for me to offend or cause grief to anyone, especially those who love me. The most terrible torment for me is to turn someone down. In general, I would like to love everyone, and do nice things for everyone. That, however, is completely impossible in this situation. Here it is all so nastily arranged that everyone is jealous of everyone else. They envy and get in the way of each other. If you fall in love in order not to cause grief to one, then you offend another. It is simply terrible! And then, I have a husband and children. I made the decision never to deceive my husband, and it is true that he asks little of me. But there are some terrible people who want to understand nothing and demand the impossible, just like little children . . . Ah, sometimes I just want to die! Only not now. Now I am happy. I am glad that I have met you."

She fell silent for a minute.

"You know, I sometimes think about the future life, and I imagine that everything will be reversed there; no one will interfere with anyone else, and it will be possible to love everyone, and no one will be offended . . . Ah, I am so stupid, I can't explain it properly. Really, though, I understand how it all will be."

She grasped her head with both hands and grew pensive.

VI

It was already completely dark. The train car was quiet. The Frenchmen had grown tired of their racket and settled down on their seats one way or another. Disconnected cries would occasionally ring out, or someone would mutter in his sleep.

"You are probably not going to sleep," my companion suddenly said.

I nodded my head.

"Me neither. Let's talk. I just have to make myself more comfortable."

She took off her hat and let down her hair.

Certain objects exist in this world beneath the moon that have had an irresistible effect on me since early childhood. In the era that I am now recalling, my pessimism would lose its strength in the light of these objects, and my ascetic morals let down their wings with shameful submissiveness. The long hair of a woman, loose about her shoulders, always belonged to the list of these magic objects, and I had never encountered such luxurious hair as was now before my eyes. The longer I looked, the more distant from my mental perception became the distinction between eternal essence and transient phenomena. The wings of my will's self-denial sank lower and lower.

I took a thick curl of this fair, fragrant hair and raised it to my lips.

A quiet smile and silence ensued.

She lowered her hands to her knees and bowed her head. She was decidedly beautiful in that pose with her loose hair. I wanted to say this to her, to say that I loved her, but the words would not come from my lips. I merely leaned down to her lowered hands and began to cover them with kisses.

"How strange you are! Who gave you permission?"

I raised my head, whispered a naive excuse for this outburst, and suddenly felt a long, soundless, burning kiss on my lips . . .

The next morning I was gloomy and morose. I had not thought even once during the past night about the difference between good and evil, but they appeared to me now with full clarity and distinction.

What shame and disgrace! I, a pessimist and an ascetic. I, the uncompromising enemy of the earthly principle. I had given in to this earthly principle without a fight, without the slightest attempt at opposition. Worse still, with a kind of joyful readiness and attention. I had immediately acknowledged its power and relished my enslavement. I, who had recognized the vanity of desire almost since the cradle, who knew the falsehood of happiness, the illusion of satisfaction. I, who had worked for the past three years to fortify this inborn truth in the impregnable walls of transcendental philosophy, I now sought and could at least momentarily find bliss in the embrace of a woman whom I scarcely knew, who seemed empty-headed and entirely uneducated.

For what have I striven, unhappy man?

Before whom have I humbled my proud mind?

Who was I not ashamed to idolize

With the rapture of pure thoughts?[24]

Never before had I subjected myself to such debasement. Of course, I had frequently kissed my cousins. But that was something entirely different. First of all, the matter is not in the kisses themselves, but in their intensity, as well as their extensiveness; and, second, my cousins were more or less followers of my teachings, and I could consider kisses merely the external expression of internal spiritual relations. But I could most certainly not make out any capacity toward higher philosophical understanding in my new acquaintance. And in the meantime I could deceive my Olga for her, Olga, who was languishing in her separation from me, who understood me so well and would accompany me hand in hand on the difficult path of self-denial of the will.

I felt myself decidedly base. No doubt our progenitor felt something of the sort on that sad day, when he was provided with leather clothing in exchange for his lost bliss.

24. From Aleksander Pushkin's poem "Razgovor knigoprodavtsa s poetom" ("Conversation of a Bookseller with a Poet").

VII

Julie[25]—as my companion wanted me to call her—was also not happy. She was unwell. It seems that she suffered from tachycardia. Every minute she would have to close her eyes and press her hand to her heart. With a sickly compressed mouth, closed eyes, and an unhealthy color to her face, she became positively plain. I was irritated by her. I blamed her for everything. Because of her, after all, I proved to be trash, a dishrag. Because of her, I shamelessly betrayed my principles, because of her I brought shame upon myself. At that time I did not believe in the devil. That means that the one who was guilty had to be Julie. Alas, in that sense as well I was exactly like the ancient Adam, who, having sinned, justified himself and heaped blame on the weaker side.

But whenever her pain would subside, she, my poor Eve, began to speak affectionately as before. This irritated me even more. I was ready to hate her. Despite her extreme ignorance, she, it seemed, loved to argue about important subjects. Now, everything that she said seemed to me either nonsense or trivial.

Among other things, she spoke about the emancipation of women. I interrupted her rudely.

"It seems to me that our women are already too emancipated. If they are lacking in anything, then that would be restraint, rather than freedom."

My hint was clear. Julie blushed slightly and raised her big eyes to me. There was nothing except sad surprise in that glance. But after a minute she again began to talk affectionately.

Something pricked my heart. I became ashamed that I had offended her, but I did not at all value the meekness with which she had endured the insult. I did not love her. I forced myself to be polite with her in order to smooth over my rudeness, but the politeness was very cold, and Julie noticed the insincerity of my tender declarations. She peered at me sadly and sadly smiled.

We had to change trains in Kursk. A first-class ticket had previously been arranged for Julie, and I took a ticket for second class. Thus, we parted. I pretended to be saddened, but was happy in my heart. Her closeness oppressed me; likewise, as we neared Khar'kov, my obligations concerning my understanding Olga presented themselves to me with greater and greater clarity.

After I accompanied Julie to her car, I settled in my seat with a lightened heart and in excellent spirits, and soon acquainted myself with my nearest neighbors. These included a medical student from Kiev University, a young merchant from Taganrog in a heavy wool overcoat and a new black cap with

25. Solovyov writes the name in Latin letters in a clear reference to Rousseau's sentimental heroine and probably also to the debauched heroine of *Julie, ou les malères de la vertue* by Marquis de Sade. Solovyov's Julie, named here for the first time, combines these two opposing modalities. Julie, or Iulin'ka, was also the nickname of a young girl on whom the nine-year-old Solovyov had a crush. See *Three Encounters*, page 265.

a visor, and a dark-haired man of indeterminate rank and age, with a dark-blue chin—a rich moneylender, as it turned out, also from Taganrog.[26]

I chatted with the young medic. He was a provincial nihilist of the brightest stripe. He immediately recognized me as one of his kind—"by the intelligent expression on my face"—as he explained later, and as well, perhaps, by the long hair and careless dress.

We opened our souls to each other. We were in complete agreement about the fact that the existing order had to be destroyed in the near future. However, he thought that an earthly paradise would follow this destruction, where there would no longer be poor, stupid and sinful people. Instead, all of humanity would equally enjoy the world's physical and mental goods in countless phalansteries, which would cover the earth.[27] I asserted with animation that his view was not radical enough, and that in fact not only the earth, but the entire universe must be in some essential way destroyed, that if there would be any kind of life after that, then that life would be totally different, unlike our present life, purely transcendental. He was a radical naturalist; I was a radical metaphysician.

We talked and argued passionately and loudly. At one time my companion tried to engage the opinion of our neighbors, but the moneylender with the blue chin only laughed with pity and waved his hand, and the young merchant muttered something unencouraging, along the lines of "damned pests," and turned his back on us.

At the end of our argument, my opponent remarked that our theoretical positions might differ, but since our nearest practical goals were the same, since we were both "frank radicals," then we could be friends and allies, and we affectionately shook hands.

VIII

At that time the doors of the car opened, and Julie appeared at the entrance. She came to invite me to her place in first class. Her compartment was vacant. She was the only one there, and was bored by herself. We could travel together as far as Khar'kov.

I readily accepted the proposal, but in my heart was dissatisfied. At that moment my new friend and ally interested me much more than she. "And why does she compromise herself in this way? How stupid it is!" I thought.

Fatigue from the long journey, the unaccustomed excitement of the last sleepless night, and finally, the heated and intense conversation about the most abstract matters—all of this, no doubt, had totally upset my nerves. Walking

26. Here Solovyov sets up a situation similar to that of Tolstoy's "Kreutzer Sonata," in which the narrator meets a man on a train, from whom he hears a story of love, sexuality, and betrayal. Taganrog is located to the southeast of Khar'kov. It is the birthplace of Anton Chekhov.

27. A vision of communal living promulgated by the French philosopher Charles Fourier. In Russia, the idea is most famous from Chernyshevsky's *What Is to Be Done?*

in front of my lady, just at the moment I wanted to step onto the second cast-iron plate between the cars, I suddenly lost consciousness. I came to on the platform of my own car. Later my new friend, who had seen us through the open door and had hurried to help, told me that I would surely have fallen into the space between the cars and certainly been crushed by the train running at full speed, if it hadn't been for "that little lady," who had grabbed me by the shoulders and held me on the platform.

I learned that later. Regaining consciousness, I saw only the bright sunlight, a strip of blue sky, and bending over me in that light, and against the sky, the image of a beautiful woman. She looked at me with wondrous and familiar eyes, and whispered something quiet and tender.

Without a question, this was Julie. Those were her eyes, but how the rest had changed! What a pink light burned in her face. How tall and majestic she was. Something wondrous took place inside me. It was as though my entire existence—all my thoughts, feelings, and desires—had melted and flowed together into a single, endless, sweet, bright, and dispassionate sensation. A single wondrous image was motionlessly reflected in that sensation, as in a pure mirror, and I felt and knew that in that one was all. I loved with a new, all-absorbing and endless love, and in that love for the first time I sensed the whole fullness and meaning of life.[28]

At first she sat me solicitously in my former place. My friend the medical student courteously yielded his seat to her, next to me. At the next train station, she brought me to her compartment.

We were alone together. I could not talk for a long time. I merely looked at her with senseless eyes and kissed the edge of her dress, kissed her feet. She also said nothing, and merely held a handkerchief soaked in eau de cologne to my head. Finally, I began to relate what was happening to me in a disconnected and jumbled whisper. I said that I loved her, that she was everything to me, that I had been reborn by this love, that it was an entirely different, new love in which I completely forgot myself, that only now I understood that there is God in man, that there is good and true joy in life, that the goal of life is not in cold, dead negation . . .

She listened with clear eyes and a happy smile. The transformation that had occurred in me brought her joy but, apparently, did not surprise her. She questioned me about nothing. She now endured my adoration as quietly and serenely as she had endured my previous insults.

When I had come to myself a bit more, she began to talk simply and calmly. She had taken a liking to me from first glance, and she was happy that I loved her now with such a good, pure love. She was sure that there could be quite

---

28. This passage, quoted in part as the epigraph to part 1, sums up much of Solovyov's imagery of Sophia, as well as the effect of Sophia on the visionary. The rosy light, the wonder, the sweetness, the mirror imagery, and, most of all, the paradoxical interrelationship of one and all, the multiple and unitary (vseedinstvo) recur throughout Solovyov's poetic accounts of his visions. Looking forward, the senselessness and disconnected speech just below will be repeated in *Three Encounters*. See page 268.

friendly relations between us. We must meet in Moscow. She would introduce me to her husband.

"But you had better not come to the Crimea. I am so spineless. It would be awful there, for both of us."

I said that I would do anything that she desired.

We didn't notice how the day ended nor how the evening passed. It came time for us to part. I remained with her at the Khar'kov station until the last call. As the train pulled away, she leaned out the window and extended both hands to me. The night was dark, and no one paid any attention to us. Perhaps some sentimental little star took pity on me, having noticed from above how heavy, hot tears flowed from my eyes onto those dear, tender hands.

The train had long since disappeared from view, but I kept standing in the same place.

IX

"What's with you, old chap? Did ya wash in salt water and turn into a pillar of salt? Hey, don't mourn. It's not like you'll never see each other again. But I approve of your taste. Damn it, that's a pretty babe! At another time I'd have fallen for her myself. Well, let's get going, señor!"

I followed the frank radical silently, and we rented a cab to get to the "Hotel Dagmar."

My heart was full of Julie until I managed to get to sleep. The next day, my whole meeting with her seemed completely fantastic and terribly far away. I had experienced something; somewhere in the deepest little corner of my soul I had felt something new, unprecedented. But it had not yet merged with my real life. I knew that everything had to continue as before, to take its normal course, as though nothing had happened. And what had, in fact, happened? Subjective exaltation and nothing more!

I went to see Olga. You can imagine that our meeting went nothing as I had pictured. To begin, I didn't find her home, which for some reason had never occurred to my imagination. I left a note and went away. Thus, when I came for the second time she had already been warned about my arrival, so there wasn't enough basis for fainting or other extreme behaviors. She had just returned from a walk in the country. I found her greatly changed. She was nothing like that gentle, flighty little girl who had remained in my memory from our last meeting in the village, when she would come out of the dressing room by the river in a light-blue cotton dress, with her dark braid thrown carelessly behind her back. Now she was a fully grown and smartly dressed maiden with a free and easy manner. She looked at me so boldly and intently with her black eyes, a little reddened from the sun and wind. There was something decisive and independent about her.

After the preliminary short questions about relatives, health, and the like, I set to my task. In her letters she had written that she loved me, and I had to explain to her my opinion of our relations. I spoke briefly and unconvincingly.

I myself felt that I was reciting some kind of memorized lesson. Each word rang in my ears like something foreign and absolutely dull. To tell the truth, the words were completely wooden.

She leaned her elbows on the table and listened pensively. When I finished my speech with the inevitable invitation to accompany me on the path of self-denial of the will, she looked into the distance for a long time with motionless eyes, and then suddenly put down her hands, raised her head, and, fixing her gaze on me, spoke with a calm and firm voice:

"I do not want to deceive you. I was mistaken in my feelings. You are too intelligent and ideal for me, and I do not love you sufficiently to share your views and attach my life to yours forever. Here you reject all pleasure, and all I understand is pleasure. I will always love you dearly. Let's be friends."

I hurry to note that this was my last experience with the direction of young maidens along the path of self-denial of the will. I left Khar'kov that very evening, without even saying goodbye to my new friend the radical.

Four years later I met Julie in Italy, on the Riviera. But that was the kind of meeting that you relate only to those who enjoy stories of Christmas night.[29]

Translated by Judith Deutsch Kornblatt

29. Fantastic stories are traditionally told on Christmas Eve. For more on this incident, see Luk'ianov, "Iunosheskii roman" 114.

5   *The White Lily*

Or a Dream on the Eve of the Feast of the Protection of the Mother of God (A Mystery-Jest in Three Acts)

Reading Guide

Solovyov wrote *The White Lily* in Moscow and Pustyn'ka in the late seventies, at the same time as he was delivering *Lectures on Divine Humanity*, although he did not publish the play until 1893—perhaps because he was busy establishing his more serious career, and perhaps because he was not convinced the play was complete. *The White Lily* is an early attempt to combine humor with mystical truth, as evident from the subtitle *A Mystery-Jest in Three Acts*. Solovyov also included the subtitle *Or a Dream on the Eve of the Feast of the Protection of the Mother of God,* an Orthodox holiday in early October (October 14 October/October 1 o.s.) that marks the beginning of winter and that Russian tradition links with marriage and miracles. Dreams dreamed on this night are said to come true. He thus also attempts in the title, and throughout the play, to combine traditional Russian belief with Gnostic and other mystical symbolism. At the same time that he leaves open the possibility that this is "only a dream," Solovyov associates the story with a sacred holiday, one itself evocative of Sophia through its use as the name day for important Sophia cathedrals in Russia.

Solovyov professes the importance of laughter and its ability to reconcile opposites in the following "Dedication to an Unpublished Comedy" ("Posviashchenie k neizdannoi komedii," 1878), probably referring to an early draft of *The White Lily*. He included the poem in the first collection of his poetry:

> Do not expect here graceful, tuneful verse,
> You mustn't ask for flowers in darkest Fall!
> I've known no bright nor cloudless days,

But only still and silent phantoms
Cast upon my twilight ways.

Such is the law: Mist shrouds what's best,
While what's at hand is laughable or painful.
We mustn't ignore this two-faced edge:
The universe's harmony is fashioned
From ringing laughs and muted sobs.

Let laughter ring as freely as a wave.
Our days do not deserve to take offense.
With your young smile, poor muse,
Shine through the murky way but once,
And for a moment calm the evil life
With all the goodness of your laugh.

                                        (SS 12:25)

Some speculate that Solovyov did not immediately publish the play because he was unhappy with the sometimes heavy-handed slapstick in combination with symbols of Divine Wisdom. The editors of the Brussels edition
of Solovyov's collected works claim that "[i]n general, The White Lily, like
the story 'At the Dawn of Misty Youth,' cannot be counted among Solovyov's best. The theme of The White Lily was too real to him for Solovyov to
treat it in a humorous work. The poems that he included in it do not blend
with the whole. Apparently, Solovyov himself was conscious of the comedy's
lack of success, since it remained unpublished until 1893" (SS 12:173). Indeed, the play contains some quite serious lyrics that Solovyov published
separately, including "The Song of the Ophites" and "Not in vain have we
have come together" ("Pesnia Ofitov" and "My soshlis's toboi nedarom";
SS 12:14 and 18–19), as well as some stanzas that are reminiscent of the
later narrative poem Three Encounters. The similarity to the latter work,
however, suggests that Solovyov was not dissatisfied with the combination
of humor and gravity per se (the "two-faced edge" of the universe) but perhaps only with this early attempt to articulate prosaic and poetic registers in
one breath.

It might also be that Solovyov was unhappy with the rather haphazard mixture of symbolism, most of it imported undigested from Gnosticism but with
alchemical, Rosicrucian, Eastern mystical, and Russian folkloric elements thrown
in as well. In explicating the poem that ends The White Lily, also published in
1876 as "The Song of the Ophites," a Solovyov scholar particularly attuned to
mystical allusions interprets the white lily as symbolizing the "bearer of heavenly
wisdom from the world of the stars to the earth." The rose represents "the forces
of the heart which grow up in earthly men, working in perfect balance between
what is above and what is below." Pearls suggest "the pearl of great price" in
alchemy, and the dove figures the Holy Spirit.[1] A bear, of course, is a traditional

---

1. Allen 124–25.

symbol of Russia, and the Feast of the Protection of the Mother of God is particularly beloved in the Russian Orthodox tradition, as are icons of Mary hold-
ing the protective veil above her head. The play's sorrowful hero finds Sophia in
Tibet; he is led there by a drunken fool from the farthest reaches of Siberia, further complicating the symbolic mix. Solovyov also makes reference to earlier
Russian comedy in the play, as well as to folklore and mysticism.

The White Lily:
Or a Dream on the Eve of the Feast of the Protection of the Mother of God (A Mystery-Jest in Three Acts)[2]

CHARACTERS

THE CHEVALIER DE MORTEMIR[3]	A rich but completely disillusioned landowner.
CHALDEAN[4]	Serves in the Asiatic department. Is practical.
INSTRUMENT	A retired dragoon. Has physical strength and is prepared.
SORVAL[5]	A young man. Often does the opposite of what he says.
COUNT MNOGOBLIUDOV[6]	Is afflicted with softening of the brain tissues.
GENERAL KHLESTAKOV[7]	He wrote all of Plato's dialogues, and was the secret cause of the head cold that prevented Napoleon from crushing the Russian army at Borodino.

2. I thank Nina Familiant and Matt Walker for help with the annotations for this play and
Melissa Miller for the synopsis of acts 1 and 2. In addition, I have incorporated Jakim's notes
from his Variable Press edition of this translation. The current translation is revised for this
book.

3. This name appears to be a combination of the French *mort* (death) and the Russian *mir*
(the world), possibly indicating that he is "dead to the world." The standard spelling of the name
is Mortimer.

4. A member of the ancient Semitic nation, the Chaldeans; a person versed in the occult arts;
or a member of a Uniate church in Iran and Iraq converted from Nestorianism in the sixteenth
century. All these associations to distant places and times only underline their opposite: the utter ordinariness of this character.

5. This name recalls the verb *sorvat'* (to tear off); a *sorvanets* is a wild, madcap fellow.

6. This name literally means "many dishes." In addition, a *lizobliud* in Russia is someone
who curries favor, and thus the name also suggests servility.

7. This name is derived from the verb *khlestat'* (to lash out) and is the name of the protago-
nist of Nikolai Gogol's play *The Inspector General* (*Revizor*). Gogol's character became synonymous with empty boasting. Borodino is the location of a significant battle between the
Russians and Napoleon in 1812.

MELANCHOLY LANDOWNER	He has devoted himself to the study of transcendental physics.
SKEPTIC	He serves in the Ministry of Finances.
DON'T-SPIT-ON-THE-TABLE	An ancient sage.
GALACTEA	
ALCONDA	Three ladies, agreeable in all respects.[8]
TEREBINDA	
THE SUN	A fixed star of the third magnitude.
BIRDS	
PLANTS	
WOLF	
LIONS AND TIGERS	
MOLES	
OWLS	
VOICE FROM THE FOURTH DIMENSION	
BEAR	
THE WHITE LILY	

[The following translation focuses on act 3. Preceding it, we have provided a synopsis of acts 1 and 2, with pertinent stanzas cited. The play begins in Petersburg in the winter garden of the home of the Chevalier de Mortemir. The Melancholy Landowner enters, obsessing over the Fourth Dimension. He is accompanied by the Skeptic, who laments over the fact that he has nothing over which to obsess. They are joined by the Desperate Poet, whose endeavors have aged him. Uniting in their misery, they go to seek solace in a fashionable restaurant. Meanwhile, the three young ladies—Galactea, Terebinda, and Alconda—tryst with their respective lovers, Chaldean, Instrument, and Sorval. However, their rendezvous are cut short: Mortemir, heeding the call of the Voice from the Fourth Dimension, leaves, and Chaldean, Instrument, and Sorval soon follow. To help Mortemir on his journey, Galactea gives him three unusual flowers. When the others leave the stage, Mortemir raises the flowers to his face and declares the following, evoking Sophia in the reference to dreams, gold, and feminine beauty:]

MORTEMIR

Pleasure there is in the smell of roses
When a fire burns in the breast
And the whole world of magical dreams
Speaks distinctly with the soul;
When in the bluing mist the path
Of everyday existence lies before you

8. This description is a reference to Gogol's novel *Dead Souls* (*Mertvye dushi*), with the Lady Agreeable in All Respects and the Simply Agreeable Lady.

But the goal has been reached beforehand
And victory has anticipated the battle;
When from your heart the silvery threads stretch forth
Into the realm of reverie . . .
O gods eternal! Take the bitterness
Of my experience and return to me
The whole power of the first storms of spring!

Yes, I knew you, golden years,
Dreams innocently bold,
Proud surges of freedom,
Visions of mysterious beauty,
When the distant notes of a keyboard
Or the rustling of a dress on sand
Submerged the whole soul in dreams
And excited incomprehensible longing
Or sweet trepidation.
Where are you, captivating dreams
And sorrows without cause?
The thrust of life's wave
Has borne you far away.
The turbulent surges have rushed you away,
The first roses of spring,
And where you are buried
Other flowers have bloomed
And just as quickly faded,
Or withered in an untimely way.

But let all that has come before be forgotten
And shrouded in darkness forever!
I will make room for hope!
Perhaps I will yet succeed in finding the White Lily.
And so—forward!
Let me proceed on my mysterious quest!

       The noise of an approaching crowd is heard.

Farewell all! my soul would
Find it painful to see you.
But where is my traveling cap?
Here! And my gloves are in it.

       He leaves hurriedly.

[The second act begins in an unknown forest as the sun, plants, animals, and birds discourse on the absence of "the golden-haired empress." Mortemir then appears and recognizes that all of nature is speaking of "Her."]

           THE SUN

Once again I am setting,
And I look about sadly:

I have not seen her today either.
O sorrow! She[9] is nowhere to be found.
Without her the whole white world
Is no dearer to me than the nether world.

> *The Sun covers his face with clouds,*
> *and cries a fine rain.*

BIRDS

We sing. We sing.
Together with the sun we wait
For the golden-haired empress to appear.
But she does not hear.
Our song will not wake her
From her deep slumber.

PLANTS

We grow and bloom.
God gives us rain to drink.
Aromas we pour forth,
Tremble, and wait for
The mistress of paradise,
She who shines with heavenly beauty,
To appear from the dwelling place of dreams
Like an empress of flowers.

WOLF

I am a murderer and a thief.
Bloodthirsty is my gaze.
What's more, my cowardice is extreme!
Though I am quite a villain,
Yet I, too, can
No longer bear my foul life.
Tail between my legs, I lie
And look at the sky to see
If the empress will come down from there,
The empress about whom
Both the flowers and the chattering birds
Are weaving their songs.

CHORUS OF LIONS AND TIGERS

Yyyes!
We live by violence,
Pull off the skins of those we meet,
Eat them raw,
Drink their hot blood,
But we too are waiting for
Something; secretly
We shed tears at night

---

9. "She" here is obviously Sophia, as we can see from the reference to "the golden-haired empress," below, as in Solovyov's early poems. She is likewise the "mistress of paradise"; she shines with heavenly beauty and dwells in a place of dreams. She unites all of nature in song.

And, wagging our tails,
Think of putting an end
To this kind of life . . .
Yyyes!

ALL

Sun, sun! If only you would draw and lure
The empress of beauty to us
By your flaming power,
By a rainbow net of rays!
We no longer have the strength to wait for her.
Without her, all things are repulsive to us.
Lost is the luster of both day and night.
Without her, the whole world's a grave!

The Sun waves his hand and sets.
The Chevalier de Mortemir enters.

MORTEMIR

She! She is everywhere! Only about her
Do all the voices of yearning nature speak.
Not I alone—but also the river, the forest, the mountains,
The trees, the beasts, the sun, and the flowers—
Call her and await her.
If she were to come, the snowy peaks
Of the cloud-piercing mountains would at once
Bow down before her; the sumptuous flowers
Would unfurl their wide carpet before her;
The lions, snow leopards, and rhinoceroses
Would gather around her,
A happy family, harmonious,
And serve her; the rapid and noisy streams
Would suddenly stop; the turbulent ocean itself
One last time would boil up again
And, after casting all of its pearls
At her feet, would grow quiet and still,
And like a mirror, transparent, motionless,
Would lie down before her so as to reflect
All the more clearly her marvelous image
In mute ecstasy.[10] Yes, this is true!
But, my God, when?
When, when? This insignificant word
Contains despair and joy, life and death.

He lies down beneath a tree.

[Soon, Mortemir is joined in the forest by Chaldean, Instrument, and Sorval, and then by Don't-Spit-on-the-Table. The latter enters in unusual semi-Asiatic

---

10. As we saw earlier, Solovyov often connects Sophia to the image of mirrors and other reflecting surfaces.

attire, carries a staff, and is looking for Mortemir. He gives Mortemir a parchment, which the latter does not understand. Don't-Spit tells Mortemir that he can lead him to the White Lily he seeks. Mortemir's companions agree to accompany him on his quest. Don't-Spit suggests they depart at dawn, so that they may drink to their health all night. All the men sing about the love they have left behind, except for Don't-Spit, who sings a drunken ode to the Chukotskii Peninsula,[11] his home. The men then swear an allegiance to each other, confirming there is enough of the White Lily to satisfy them all. The translation below picks up with the third act, in which Mortemir finds and is united with the White Lily/Sophia.]

ACT III

Part One

A large neglected garden near southern Tibet.
In the foreground is the entrance to a large cave,
veiled by a purple curtain.

SCENE I

Enter the Chevalier de Mortemir, Don't-Spit,
Chaldean, Sorval, and Instrument.

DON'T-SPIT

Over here, over here!
This garden, sirs,
Is the very same one
Toward which we have been heading.

ALL

Yes, yes!
But what is the purpose of this cave?

DON'T-SPIT

There is no cave! It is only a chimera,
An illusion, a deception, a dream.
There's no reason for it to be here.
A cave can house a dragon,
Bear or lizard; but an empress—
And here I'm prepared to swear—
Could scarcely dwell in such a cave.
An empress dwells in a castle, or at the very least,
In a high tower.

CHALDEAN

Where are they?

DON'T-SPIT

Don't you see those lights over there?

---

11. The Chukotskii Peninsula is in the extreme northeastern section of Asia. Its inhabitants, the Chukchi, are the butt of many Russian jokes for their alleged lack of culture and intelligence.

CHALDEAN

Why are you lying? You can't see lights
In the brightness of day.

DON'T-SPIT

Over here stands a tall tower, while over there
A lady is going out onto a balcony.
Surely, that must be the empress's maid,
Adorned with a feather of the Fire-bird.[12]
She is followed by courtiers,
All wearing court-dress coats . . .
What do I see? They're eating pancakes!
What wonderful rich pancakes!

CHALDEAN

He's pulling our leg, that son of the devil!

INSTRUMENT

He treats us contemptuously!

ALL

Beat him mercilessly!

DON'T-SPIT

Don't be angry, my friends,
Don't judge me harshly
If I sometimes
Fool around a bit.
It's not a big deal.
As long as we have some food and drink,
Let us sit down and partake.

CHALDEAN, SORVAL, AND INSTRUMENT

That's a great idea.
That's perfect.
We see clearly:
He's no fool.

DON'T-SPIT

Smugly

Yes, that's clear.
I'm no fool.

MORTEMIR

Could I eat and drink
Not knowing where she is?
There's a mystery here, I can see,
And not just one!

---

12. A mythical bird with shining feathers, an image in Russian fairy tales that embodies people's dreams of happiness.

DON'T-SPIT

Believe me: she has left
These regions for a reason,
But as soon as dawn's ray shines,
She will return in her chariot.

MORTEMIR

Having eaten and drunk heartily, he gets up,
and, pointing at the sky, he speaks.

Enough! I have no strength left! May my righteous anger
Strike your heart with the sting of indignation!
Have we really come here, having abandoned and condemned
everything,
To drink and eat like cannibals?

ALL

Hurriedly finishing their food and drink.

Well sir, we are ready!
What should we undertake?

MORTEMIR

Somberly.

We must put on
The crown of thorns.

CHALDEAN

That's certain!
But how to begin?

MORTEMIR

I would with all my heart
Gladly tell you
If I myself
Knew how . . .

A terrible roar comes from the cave.

Who is sending curses
Heavenward?
There's no doubt!
There's a mystery here!
We must crawl into the cave.

DON'T-SPIT

But first we must
Take down the curtain.
Pull it all together.
No one lag behind!

ALL

They take hold of the curtain, but then
Chaldean, Instrument, and Don't-Spit step
back, and each of them, turning aside, sings.

But I feel a trepidation,
Because I do not know
What awaits us,
Let me stand behind you.

> *Each of them tries to stand behind all the others.*
> *Before the curtain stand only Mortemir, deep in*
> *thought, and Sorval, looking about in perplexity.*

DON'T-SPIT

Dear friend, Sorval,
You should rip down the curtain!

> *He then runs even farther away.*

SORVAL

I obey you very willingly,
And will rip it down straightaway!

> *He rips down the curtain. A large bear comes*
> *out of the cave and, with a roar, stands*
> *up on his hind legs.*

DON'T-SPIT

Ai! Ai! Ai!

> *He grabs at his stomach, and falls dead. Sorval,*
> *Chaldean, and Instrument bare their swords.*
> *The Bear turns his back to them. Then, crossing*
> *their swords, they place Don't-Spit's corpse on*
> *them and bear it away, singing to the tune of*
> *"How happy I am, Captain, that I've seen you."*

CHALDEAN, SORVAL, AND INSTRUMENT

He has perished, he has perished,
A sacrifice to valor.
Let our swords
Be his bier.

Wisdom with bravery
He artfully melded,
But he was suddenly slain
By this foul disease!

He has perished, he has perished,
A sacrifice to valor.
Let our swords
Be his bier.

SCENE 3[13]

Mortemir and the Bear are on stage.

VOICE FROM THE FOURTH DIMENSION

The door of bliss
Then—not now—

---

13. The original is missing scene 2.

Will be opened by the beast.
Love and believe!

MORTEMIR

I love and believe
This beast here.

VOICE

All right!¹⁴

Part Two

SCENE 1

*Several weeks have passed. The scene is another
place in the same garden. The cave is some
distance away. In the foreground is a gravestone,
near which the Chevalier de Mortemir
stands in a pose of despair.*

MORTEMIR

Every last nook in my soul has grown stale!
How much I loved him and how fine he was!
What grace of sprawling movements!
What genius, what wisdom
Shone from his pensive eyes! I saw in him
The last anchor of the ship of life.
He spoke in his own language,
Though without words. But with a loving soul
I could understand him easily.
And he loved me. Furry and large,
He was tender as a little child.
How he turned his beautiful head!
Alas! Those most blissful moments
Have rushed off without a trace, as in a dream.
He died . . . And what am I to do?
Ah, I know what! I will turn my back to nature,
Plunge a dagger into my stomach, and lie down next to him!

*He wants to kill himself, but suddenly above the Bear's grave
appears the White Lily.*

SCENE 2

WHITE LILY

From you, my darling,
I will not hide the fact
That beneath my grave
There is nothing.

MORTEMIR

Your features are celestially fine!
But where is *he*, the bear of my soul?

---

14. "All right" appears in English in the original.

WHITE LILY

The Bear is alive—there is just no bear skin.
But don't grieve, my friend! This is a sacrament of nature.
I was in the bear, now the bear's in me.[15]
As you loved him in the past, so love me now.
Invisible I was then,
But now invisible for ever
Is the beast hidden within me.

MORTEMIR
Ecstatic

We now have bliss enough
For all eternity.
It is not for naught
That he sucked his extremity.

> *They embrace and, rising into the air,*
> *suddenly go over into the fourth dimension.*
> *White lilies and red roses grow on the*
> *former grave of the Bear.*[16]

SCENE 3

Enter Galactea, Terebinda, and Alconda

GALACTEA, TEREBINDA, AND ALCONDA

We are tired, we are tired.
We have wandered, we've been wayward,
Lost our way, that is to say.
We awaited the unexpected,
Sought the impossible—
All for naught.

GALACTEA

These lilies and roses
Carry us into the realm of dreams—
Should we not go to sleep?

ALCONDA

I have not slept for two weeks.
Indeed, let us rest.

TEREBINDA

From sorrow and care
Let's seek shelter in this grotto.

---

15. As in the earlier Sophianic poems, and later in *Three Encounters*, Sophia combines the material and the spiritual. She is both superior to and within created matter.

16. In an earlier version of *The White Lily*, Mortemir and the White Lily die instantly of "an excess of bliss" when they "are united by the ties of love." Villagers find them and bury them. Red roses grow on Mortemir's grave, and white lilies grow on White Lily's grave. See Solov'ov, *Stikhotvoreniia* 285.

GALACTEA

Yes, each one tying up a bouquet,
We shall enter this cave.

They fashion their bouquets and go into the cave.

SCENE 4

Enter Chaldean, Instrument, and Sorval

CHALDEAN:

Look under those bushes. Look under those bushes, I tell you. What idiots!

SORVAL

Why look? I've gotten into a heap of trouble even without looking.

INSTRUMENT

It was washed away by rain, or blown away by wind.

SORVAL

There's something white over there.

He picks up a piece of paper, and throws it.

CHALDEAN

Yes, it's a piece of paper,
But not the one we're looking for.
Ah, you simpleton!

SORVAL

I found it!

He picks up the parchment of the wise man, Don't-Spit-on-the-Table.

It's intact. Look.

CHALDEAN

He takes it and reads.

"Abracadabra, abracadabra.
There is an elevated and mysterious meaning here
That can be revealed only by a bear
Endowed with extraordinary strength."

You see: a bear. Everything went as it should have. We were foolish to be scared, and that old clown more than anyone. Mortemir's no fool: He stayed with the bear; and now he's certainly got the White Lily, but we have to keep skulking around here as if we were possessed.

INSTRUMENT

We must find them.

SORVAL

But where should we look?

INSTRUMENT

It's obvious where. There's that very same cave.

CHALDEAN

Sorval, my soul, run over there. Do me a great favor. Look in the cave.

SORVAL

With great pleasure.

> *He disappears into the cave, and after a few*
> *minutes cries out.*

Hey, hey, Chaldean!
Come quick!
Hey, Instrument,
Seize the moment!

CHALDEAN

Whom did you find there?

SCENE 5

Sorval leaves the cave. He's followed by Alconda, Galactea, and Terebinda.

SORVAL

A white lily. Look:
Not one, but three.[17]

CHALDEAN AND INSTRUMENT

Familiar features but with a new beauty.

CHALDEAN

Pointing to Galactea

I am captivated by this one.

INSTRUMENT

Pointing to Terebinda

And I by that one.

ALCONDA, GALACTEA, AND TEREBINDA

Each handing her bouquet to her respective partner

Dear friend, did you recognize me?
Though you sought another here,
You must submit to your fate.

CHALDEAN, INSTRUMENT, AND SORVAL

Each to his lady

I do not regret it.
For I recognize
The White Lily in you.

---

17. Again, this is an allusion to Sophia's ability to reconcile divine and earthly reality. The ironic reference to the Trinity is also obvious.

Each pair embraces, and all coming together, they sing.

White lily with rose,
With scarlet rose we wed.
We unearth the eternal truth
Of the furtive dream of the seer.

Utter the visionary word!
Throw your pearl in the cup sooner!
Bind our dove
With the new coils of the ancient snake.

The hurting heart does not hurt . . .
Should it fear Prometheus' fire?
The pure dove is free
In the fiery coils of the powerful snake.

Sing of the scarlet storm.
We find peace in the scarlet storm.
White lily with rose
With scarlet rose we wed.

Curtain

Translated by Boris Jakim and Larry Magnus; revisions
by Judith Deutsch Kornblatt

6 *Three Encounters*: Final *Poema*

Reading Guide

The *poema* in Russia developed from eighteenth-century verse epics into the romantic narrative of Alexander Pushkin's time and then, later in the nineteenth century, into a narrative poem with more social, historical, or philosophical scope. Lyrical elements overtook epic ones at the turn of the twentieth century. *Three Encounters* includes both lyrical and philosophical/religious perspectives, oddly mixed with a conversational, narrative style. In some ways, Solovyov draws on both Pushkin's ironic "novel in verse," *Eugene Onegin*, and Gogol's humorous poema, the novel *Dead Souls*.

As indicated in part 1, *Three Encounters* describes events from Solovyov's life that allegedly occurred almost twenty-five years previously. He claims to have seen Sophia first as a nine-year-old boy while standing in church contemplating an equally young girl with whom he was infatuated. He then claims to have seen only the head of Sophia ("Before my eyes she shines—but only partly— / Alone, alone, I see her face alone") in the Reading Room of the British Museum, where he had gone to read descriptions of Sophia by other mystics. Finally, he sees her in the desert outside Cairo, where the poem tells us he had been instructed to seek her. " 'Get thee to Egypt!'—an inner voice sounded." He ventures out into the desert one evening only to be attacked by a group of Bedouins, or so he says, and to wander back into town with holes in his shoes but radiance in his heart.

While staying in Egypt, Solovyov apparently did more than seek Sophia in the desert. He engaged in séances, invited his friend Tsertelev to join him, and composed with Tsertelev a humorous play about spiritualism called *Evenings in*

Cairo.[1] Preceded by rappings on the furniture and automatic writing, the ghost of Socrates appears in the play to debate with a skeptical doctor about the reality of spirits. Although the manuscript was never completed, it shows Solovyov's interest in spiritual investigations of the time and in the English spiritualist scene he had just left in London. After returning to Russia, Solovyov shared many of his Egyptian experiences with his friend F. L. Sollogub, who composed another humorous playlet, also incomplete, called "Solovyov in the Thebaid."[2] Thus, even in the immediate retelling, Solovyov recognized the humor in his mystical visions of Sophia. At the same time, the visionary composed the poems translated in part 2, section 1 of this book, showing a much more serious, metaphysical side of his relationship with Divine Wisdom.

Despite the obvious self-mockery in which Solovyov engages in *Three Encounters*, his Symbolist heirs, and most readers since, took the poem highly seriously, seeing in it an accurate recording of Solovyov's real mystical experiences. The poet denies neither seriousness nor mockery but sees the juxtaposition of humor and biographical references to be "irrepressibly" natural. As he writes in a note at the end of the poem: "An autumn evening and the dense forest inspired me to re-create the most significant moments of my life up until today in these humorous verses. For two days memory and consonance rose up irrepressibly in my consciousness, and the third day delivered this small autobiography that has appealed to some poets and ladies" (*SS* 12:86; see page 272).

The original poema is written in iambic pentameter throughout, with a highly consistent aBaB rhyme scheme, alternating feminine and masculine endings. I have tried to preserve meter as well as rhyme, sacrificing feminine rhymes on several occasions and allowing extra unstressed syllables from time to time to avoid excessively awkward or archaic phrases in English. I hope I have also retained the humor in this clearest of all of Solovyov's re-visions of his beloved Divine Sophia.

Three Encounters

> Triumphing over death before its season,
> With love I overcame the chain of time,
> Eternal friend,[3] to call you I've no reason,
> For you will simply sense my halting rhyme . . .

---

1. See Kornblatt, "Spirits, Spiritualism, and the Spirit," for an annotated translation of this playlet, which was first published in Luk'ianov 2:247–55. See also *SS* 12:529–535.

2. The playlet is printed in Luk'ianov 2:283–307.

3. It is obvious in the original that the "friend" is female (*podruga*), most certainly Sophia. Solovyov calls her the "girlfriend of God" in a number of places (see *SS* 4:261; 11:309, 310). As we have seen, she can be the girlfriend of both God and humanity (or of an individual man, in the case of the speaker of this poem) precisely because she is the transition point between the created world and the Creator, operating in both, and affecting the operations in one by her conduct in the other.

Suspicious of this lying world of pretense,
Beneath the vulgar shell of earthly shine,
I've touched your royal imperishable resplendence
And known the radiance of the divine . . .

Did you not thrice give way to my perception?
Mere cerebration it was not at all![4]
As portent, or as aid, or reparation
Your image came to answer my soul's call.

I

The first—ah, yes, how very long ago!—
When pangs of troubled dreams[5] and love's sweet tears
Came suddenly to touch my youthful soul—
Since then have passed some six and thirty years.

Then I was nine, and *she*[*6] . . . was also nine.
"It was a Moscow day in May," wrote Fet.[7]

---

4. This is the first but by no means the last instance when Solovyov juxtaposes different levels of discourse in the poem. In this case, he follows two stanzas of elevated, poetic diction (cf. nouns such as *porfira* [royal purple] and *siian'e* [radiance], as well as frequent use of gerunds and participles: *torzhestvuia* [triumphing], *odolev* [overcoming], *veruia* [believing]) with this line with its unusually awkward combination, *myslennoe dvizhenie* ("thought movement" or here, "cerebration"), and the conversational exclamation *o, net* ("oh no," or here, "not at all"), not to mention an unnecessarily emphatic exclamation mark to indicate actual speech. In one of his own notes, Solovyov apologizes for any awkwardness in poetic cadence his reader might encounter with the caveat that he has no experience writing narrative poetry (see page 269). The juxtaposition of styles, however, points less to a lack of poetic talent than to a conscious effort to break down the barriers between everyday experience and extraordinary spiritual or mystical experiences, just as Sophia transcends the distinction between the divine and the human.

5. As we have seen earlier in this book, Solovyov associates his visions of Sophia with dreams on several occasions. In the poem "Near, far off, not here, not there" (see page 107), in which the poet addresses Sophia as "goddess," Solovyov describes his nine-year-old self: "A strange child was I, / And strange dreams did I see." In that poem, written after his third vision of Sophia, Solovyov mentions daydream (*greza*), sleeping dream (*son*), and a dream as in an aspiration (*mechta*) in the first three stanzas, allowing the vision itself to waver, it seems, between reality and dream. Similarly, in the first dialogue of "Sophie" (see page 120), the Philosopher claims that "a vague dream" (*un rêve vague*) had led him to the banks of the Nile. As in *Three Encounters*, the reader can never be sure of the reality of the vision—or rather, in *which* reality it exists—and therefore how seriously (i.e., literally) to understand it.

6. Velichko identifies a certain Iulin'ka S. who captivated the nine-year-old Vladimir, only to "prefer another" (Velichko 12).

7. An inexact reference to Afanasii Fet's poem "It was a wondrous May day in Moscow" (*"Byl chudnyi maiskii den' v Moskve"*). Solovyov was quite close to the somewhat older Fet and often used quotations from Fet's poetry in philosophical essays. He also wrote a critical essay on the poetry of his friend ("O liricheskoi poezii," 1890, *SS* 6:234–60) and dedicated four poems to him.

* Author's note: "She" in this stanza was a simple young girl, and has nothing in common with the "you" to whom the preamble is addressed.

I swore my love. For naught. Oh, God of mine!
A rival. Yes! I'll not let him forget.

To duel, to duel! In mass at Ascension.[8]
My soul aboil in floods of fervid fears.
Yet we must put aside . . . this world's . . . pretension.—
The chanting lingered, faded, disappeared.

The altar door's agap[9] . . . But where're the celebrants?
And where's the crowd that milled around in prayer?
My flood of passions—drained all of a sudden,
As azure fills my soul, and fills the air.[10]

Transpierced throughout by rays of golden azure,
Unearthly flowers clasped within your hands,
You smiled before me full of radiant favor,
Then nodded as you left for other lands.

That childish love now distantly retreating;
My soul was blind to all that eyes might see . . .
Our German nursemaid sadly kept repeating:
"Volodia—ach! How stupid be can he!"[11]

II

Years passed. Now master, scholar by profession,[12]
I speed abroad the first chance that I might.
Berlin, Hanover, Köln in quick succession
Flashed quickly past, then disappeared from sight.

Not Paris's beau monde, nor Spain's far country,
Nor the gay brilliance of far eastern themes.
The British Museum was the goal of my fancy,
And it betrayed nary a one of my dreams.

8. It is not entirely clear whether Solovyov refers here to a specific church or chapel in Moscow or to the holiday of the Feast of the Ascension. Both S. M. Solovyov and Luk'ianov believe the latter (S. Solov'ev 53; Luk'ianov 3:4), although the words cited two lines below are from the daily, not holiday, liturgy and do not point directly to the Feast of the Ascension.

9. Solovyov uses the term *altar'*, which refers to the area behind the iconostasis in which the altar table itself is located. In this case, the door of the iconostasis would have stood open, normally revealing the priest standing over the altar as he prepares the sacred Eucharist. The icon screen marks the limen between sacred and profane; here the open door through it marks the penetration of one into the other.

10. The distinction between interior and exterior breaks down at this mystical moment, so that azure is both within and surrounding the visionary.

11. Solovyov has the German nanny (*nemka-bonna*) speak ungrammatical Russian here, using a feminine ending as the predicate to "he." I have suggested the error through inappropriate word order in English. She also makes reference to the "stupid" appearance of Volodia (Volodin'ka in the original, a diminutive of Solovyov's first name) at the moment of mystical experience. This stupidity or senselessness is repeated with each vision.

12. As we saw in part 1, after the defense of his master's thesis in 1874, Solovyov became a *dotsent* (here translated as "master") at Moscow University and a *lektor*, or lecturer, at the Higher Women's Courses of V. I. Ger'e.

Not for the beckoning whims of fleeting beauty,
Nor passion, nature, nor mere worldly cheer,
But for possession of my soul by only you then,
That blessed half year rests forever dear.

Let myriads of people push and scurry by,
Beneath the thunderous breath of fiery motors,[13]
Let soulless structures rise into the sky—
In holy quietude, I'm here alone.[14]

But then, admittedly, *cum grano salis,*[15]
I was alone, but not a misanthrope.
For even loners entertain their visitors.
Of which, my guests, should I here make a note?

Too bad that I can't work into my meter
Their names, nor alien sounds of how they speak . . . [16]
I'll mention here a couple Moscow masters,
And British conjurers, just two or three.[17]

Most times, though, in the Reading Room alone,
Believe or not, for God must surely see,
I would receive, picked out by powers unknown,
All books on her that I could ever read.

A sinful whim would now and then inspire me
To take a book "with quite a different tone."[18]
When this would happen, I'd distractedly
Pick up my things and make my way toward home.

---

13. With one phrase—literally, "the thunder of fire-breathing machines"—Solovyov evokes the Industrial Revolution in England, contrasting both to his more "backward" Russia and to his current contemplative state.

14. In fact, we know from memoir accounts that Solovyov had quite a few social contacts while in England. S. M. Solovyov lists I. I. Ianzhul and his wife, Ekaterina; M. M. Kovalevskii, a "young scholar from Khar'kov"; a Moscow professor named Kapustin; a salon owner by the name of Ol'ga Alekseevna Novikova; Orlov, the deacon of a local Russian church; the English scholar B. Ralston; and Alfred Wallace, a zoologist (S. M. Solov'ev 115–17). In addition, Luk'ianov mentions Peter Lavrovich Lavrov (2:139, 149, 160–71); Professor Babukhin from Moscow University (2:91); two enemies of his father (2:96); Mrs. Seegers, the landlady of both Solovyov and Ianzhul (2:97, 122); Charles Williams, a popular medium of the day (perhaps the "conjurer" of the poem) (2:106); the spiritualist William Crookes (2:107); and two others named Butlerov and Hume (2:109–10). See also Solovyov's letter to his friend Tsertelev, in which he describes the individuals he met at séances (*Pis'ma* 2:228).

15. Latin: with a grain of salt.

16. This statement is humorously self-effacing, for he has just easily rhymed the Latin *cum grano salis* with *popadalis'* (found themselves) and the poem as a whole abounds in cleverly integrated foreign names.

17. Solovyov uses the term *chudodei,* meaning crank or miracle worker (obs.). As we saw in part 1, Solovyov went to London partly to make contact with the spiritualist community there, although he claimed to have been disappointed: "Local spiritualism (and thus spiritualism in general, since London is its center) is in an absolutely pitiful state. I have seen famous mediums as well as famous spiritists, and don't know which of them are worse" (*Pis'ma* 2:229). "Cranks/conjurors" can be read with affectionate irony.

18. Solovyov uses the Russian expression "from a different opera."

Just once—towards Autumn—it was in that season,
I said to her: "O radiance divine!
I feel you here, but what then is the reason
From childhood on you've hidden from my eyes?"

These words had just appeared within my heart, when
The room all fills with azure and with gold.
Before my eyes she shines—but only partly—
Alone, alone, I see her face alone.[19]

This instant lasted long and sweet as bliss;
My soul again was blind to earth's affairs.
And if a "sober" ear would chance upon this,
My parlance would sound *stupid* and unclear.[20]

III

I told her then: "Your face has come before me,
I want to see the all of you again.
When as a child you did not need to spare me,
You mustn't refuse the same to a young man!"[21]

"Get thee to Egypt!"—an inner voice sounded.
To Paris, southward, steam propels me on.
My reason fought no more with my emotions,
For reason, like an idiot, had grown dumb.

To Lyons and Turin, Piacienza, Ancona,
To Fermo, Bari, Brindisi—and on,
Upon the deep blue sea like Jonah,[22]
A British steamship rushes me along.

19. The tense shift when Sophia appears suggests suspension from the ordinary world. The three instances of "alone" in this line only poorly substitute for Solovyov's marked repetition of the vowel sound o: "Odnó eë[ó] litsó,—onó odnó."

20. Here again Solovyov claims that the speaker appears "stupid" at the moment of mystical experience. Although for him inner and outer are united ("As azure fills my soul, and fills the air" or "You stand alone before me, and within me"), to outside observers his exterior appearance in no way conforms to the heightened consciousness within. Although Solovyov here does not describe the speaker retelling the vision, he might nonetheless have had in mind the "unclear" parlance of Mark 16:17: "And these signs will accompany those who believe: in my name they will cast out demons; they will speak in new tongues." Acts 2:4 describes the scene after the decent of the Holy Spirit: "And they were all filled with the Holy Spirit and began to speak in other tongues, as the Spirit gave them utterance."

21. The narrator addresses her with a familiar tone, since through Sophia he has become the active bridge between humanity and divinity. The bantering also recalls the dialogue from *The Sophia*.

22. Solovyov does not have this biblical reference, although his use of the highly poetic "blue, trembling bosom" (*sinee trepeshchushchee lono*) for the sea justifies an elevated allusion, as does the somewhat comic juxtaposition.

At the "Abbat" in Cairo, they extended me credit.
Alas, that lodging no longer exists.
Commodious and modest, the best one could want it,
Where Russians, even Muscovites could rest.[23]

A tenth-ranked general amused us so,
Remembering old times in the Caucasus . . .
No sin to name him—he died long ago,
And I mention him only with kindness.[24]

This Rostislav Faddeev was a well-known soldier
In retirement, and not a bad scribbler.
To talk of cocottes or a local cathedral,
We found a host of resources within him.

We gathered twice a day for table–d'hôte;
He spoke nonstop with cheer, and often would
Produce for us a racy anecdote,
And then philosophize as best he could.

I waited meanwhile for my cherished encounter,
Until one night when all was quiet and near,
A breath, so cool and breezy, came to mutter:
"Come forth into the desert. I am here."

I go on foot (for passage is not gratis
From London southward on to the Sahara.
I've lived on credit long as it has lasted,
My pockets are ballooned with naught but air).

Without a cent, just God knows where, alas,
I set on my way at one glorious time,—
As Nekrasov has written, like Uncle Vlas.[25]
(So, willy-nilly, now, I found a rhyme.)*

23. Perhaps Solovyov makes reference here to his more humble Moscow rather than imperial Petersburg origins. Solovyov moved to St. Petersburg shortly after returning from his trip to Egypt.

24. On November 27, 1875, Solovyov wrote his mother the following: "I often see General Faddeev, a kind of Russian bear, but really not a dumb man at all. But I am beginning to write like Ivan Aleksandrovich Khlestakov. Forgive me for this" (*Pis'ma* 2:19). The reference is to Gogol's *Inspector General*, in which the boaster Khlestakov writes endearingly but condescendingly about his recent acquaintances in a provincial town. We have already seen Solovyov's use of references to *The Inspector General* as well as *Dead Souls* in *The White Lily*, page 249.

25. The reference here is to the very popular narrative poem *Vlas* by N. A. Nekrasov. *Three Encounters* is in fact quite reminiscent of some of Nekrasov's narrative poems. The similarity only intensifies the strange humor of Solovyov's poem, for the latter chose the form to speak of sublime encounters with Divine Sophia, while Nekrasov is known for his more secular civic and folk subjects.

* Author's note: This device for finding a rhyme, blessed by Pushkin's example, is all the more forgivable in the given instance, for the author, more inexperienced than young, is writing narrative verse for the first time.

You[26] surely laughed, surrounded by hot desert,
I looked a fright in coat and tall top hat.
A Bedouin youth mistook me for the devil,
And shuddered out of fear. And just for that

They nearly killed me—Arab sheiks
From various tribes held council loudly
About my fate. And then just like a slave
My hands were bound behind as silently

They led me off to distant sands untrod,
Untied my hands most nobly—and were gone.[27]
I laugh along with you; for just like gods,
Men laugh at troubles that are past and done.

And all the while, a soundless night descended
Without jest[28] upon the earth entire.
I harken only silence, ever endless,
And see but dark between the starry fires.

Lying on the ground, I watched and heeded . . .
When suddenly a jackal odiously wailed;
Doubtless in his dreams I was his dinner,
And I didn't even have a stick that I could flail.

The jackal be damned![29] It was so awfully cold . . .
At night—a frost—though sweltering by day . . .
The stars, they shone so mercilessly bold;
Both light and cold conspired to keep me waked.

For long I lay in a horrendous daze,
Until I harked the wind: "Poor friend—to sleep!"—
I fell asleep; when I awoke unfazed,—
The scent of roses filled earth and heaven's sweep.

And in the purple of the sky's resplendence
Your brimming eyes o'erflowed with azure blaze.*[30]
You looked about, like the first radiance
Of creation's universal day of days.

26. The addressee is no doubt Sophia, who the speaker assumes awaits him in the desert.

27. See page 15 for Solovyov's letters referring to this incident. The enjambments in these stanzas exist in the original as well, lending the story a familiar, anecdotal tone.

28. Solovyov uses the colloquial expression *bez obiniakov*, something like "without beating around the bush."

29. Solovyov has *Shakal to chto!*, again a very colloquial expression.

30. This is an inexact reference to Mikhail Lermontov's poem "Kak chasto, pestroiu tolpoiu okruzhen."

* Author's note: A line from Lermontov.

What is, what was, what ever will be—
Was there embraced in one motionless gaze.
Below run blue the rivers and the sea,
And alpine snows and distant forest ways.

I saw it all, and all I saw was one.[31]
A single image of all female beauty . . . [32]
The immeasurable encompassing its sum.
You stand alone before me, and within me.

That desert day I saw you in your fullness . . .
Oh, radiant one! You have deceived me not;
The roses in my soul shall ever flourish,
From now, no matter where I'm tossed about.

But then the sun's orb rose above the skyline.
A moment! Then the vision hid away—
To glorious sounds of bells' perpetual chiming,
The desert silent; as my soul prayed.

The spirit's bold! But two days without eating
Can cause exalted vision to erode.
Alas, although the soul may well be willing,
They say that hunger has its own stern code.[33]

I followed the sun as far west as the Nile,
And reached my Cairo domicile toward night.
My soul hid traces of the roseate smile,
My boots, though, they were holey from the flight.[34]

To others it all must surely have been stupid[35]
(Though vision from my tale for them I'd spared).
The General silently set down his soup spoon,
And, eyeing me, portentously declared:

"Of course, *stupidity* is a right that the mind does grant us,
But license it would be best not to take;

---

31. Solovyov plays with *vse* and *vsë*—everything and all one thing. Sophia is one and all (vseedinstvo in Solovyov's philosophical works), inner and outer, as the rest of the stanza implies.

32. Solovyov uses the adjective for "female" (*zhenskaia*) rather than "feminine" (*zhensvennaia*), referring to biology rather than more abstract gender. For Solovyov, physical and spiritual beauty are intimately related as an "incarnated idea" and "transfigured matter." See his articles "Beauty in Nature" and "The Meaning of Love" (*SS* 6:33–74 and 7:3–60).

33. Solovyov uses the colloquial expression *Golod ved' ne tetka*, implying that you cannot ignore hunger the way you might an interfering and scolding aunt. I can only speculate that Solovyov would have appreciated this translator's humorous but anachronistic reference to Robert W. Service's "The Cremation of Sam McGee" (1907).

34. Solovyov's humorous juxtaposition here of holes in boots and roseate smiles in souls suggests this inserted pun on "holy." The translation inevitably neglects a number of other puns in the original.

35. Again Solovyov contrasts a stupid exterior to the sublime interior experience.

For people are dull, and certainly not masters[36]
In madness and the forms that it can take.

"So since it's disgraceful to be known as
Insane, or for that matter, simply a fool,—
Breathe not a word of this shameful occurrence,
To nary, I say nary, a soul."

And he proceeded to joke, while before me the haze
Sparkled brightly and ever so bluely.[37]
And the ocean of life retreated away,
Defeated by a mysterious beauty.

While still a slave to this world's hollowness,
Beneath the vulgar shell of earthly shine,
I glimpsed the royal imperishable resplendence,
And felt the radiance of the divine.

Triumphing over death by premonition,
With dreams I overcame the chain of time,
Eternal friend, to call I have no reason,
But you'll forgive my poor, uncertain rhyme!

26–29 September, 1898

Author's note: An autumn evening and the dense forest inspired me to re-create the most significant moments of my life up until today in these humorous verses. For two days memory and consonance rose up irrepressibly in my consciousness, and the third day delivered this small autobiography that has appealed to some poets and ladies.[38]

Translated by Judith Deutsch Kornblatt

36. Solovyov has the general use the colloquial expression "ne masteritsa," with its implications that the analysis of personality is no more than a handicraft and one that he, at least, has clearly mastered. At the time, the field of psychology was growing strongly in popularity.

37. Sophia's azure radiance lingers in and around the visionary.

38. On the contrary, the editors of the Soviet edition of Solovyov's poetry cite Sergei Solovyov as remarking that the poema "greatly displeased" mystically inclined friends of the poet, especially Sophia Khitrovo, who recommended that he not publish *Three Encounters*. According to the editors, "apparently, the irony of the poema was taken as 'blasphemy'" (*Stikhotvoreniia* 309).

Source Notes
to the Translations

Early Sophianic Poems

"Vsia v lazuri segodnia iavilas'," *SS* 12:12, and *Stikhotvoreniia* 61.
"U tsaritsy moei est' vysokii dvorets," *SS* 12:12–13, and *Stikhotvoreniia* 62.
"Blizko, daleko, ne zdes' i ne tam," *SS* 12:92, and *Stikhotvoreniia* 63–64.
First published in *Stikhotvoreniia Vladimira Solov'eva* (Moscow, 1891); *Stikhotvoreniia Vladimira Solov'ev*, 6th ed. (Moscow, 1915).
Previous translation with dual-language edition in *Vladimir Solovyov's Poems of Sophia*, trans. Boris Jakim and Laury Magnus (Variable Press, 1994), 12–21.

The Sophia

La Sophia/ Sofiia, in V. S. Solov'ev, *Polnoe sobranie sochinenii i pisem v dvadtsati tomakh* (Moscow: Nauka, 2000) (*PSS*), 2:8–178, with facing French and Russian translation by A. P. Kozyrev.

The work was first published in French as *LA SOPHIA et les autre écrits français*, ed. François Rouleau (Lausanne: La Cité—L'Age d'Homme, 1978). That publication follows the order of pages in the archived manuscript (in the Russian State Archive of Literature and Art [RGALI], f. 446, op.1, ed. khr. 19, l. 1–82), which seem to have been bound incorrectly. The order is corrected in this translation following the discussion in *PSS* 2:325–26.

A translation by Kozyrev first appeared in *Logos* 2 (1991): 171–98; 4 (1993): 274–96; and 7 (1996): 145–67. The work was also translated by T. B. Liubimova (Moscow: 1995) from the Rouleau edition, reproducing the disordered pages.

The Sophia was written in London, Cairo, and Sorrento in 1875–76 but not published during Solovyov's lifetime. The manuscript, really four fragments of varying lengths connected by theme—the "universal teachings"—and time of composition, passed to Solovyov's brother Mikhail after the philosopher's death and from there to his nephew, Sergei Mikhailovich. Sergei first described the work in his study of his uncle, *Vladimir Solovyov: His Life and Creative Evolution*, completed in 1923 but not published until 1977. Most major biographers and scholars of Solovyov did not have the opportunity to read *The Sophia*, and many did not know of its existence.

The notes from *PSS*, as well as personal correspondence and meetings with Kozyrev, helped tremendously in the preparation of this text. This English translation, the first of its kind, was made from the French original, in consultation with the Russian version. It contains only the dialogic sections and a small part of the monologic philosophical discourse, in keeping with the emphasis in this book on the diversity of genres Solovyov used to express his vision of Sophia.

Sophia in Philosophical Prose

Fragments and drawings from "Plany i chernoviki" published in *PSS* 2:162–78.
Manuscripts archived in the Manuscript Section of the Institute of Russian Literature (*Pushkinskii Dom*) (RO IRLI) in St. Petersburg and in the Russian State Archive of Literature and Art (RGALI) in Moscow (see *PSS* 2:350 for details).

From *Lectures on Divine Humanity*

Chteniia o bogochelovechestve, SS 3:1–181.
First published: Lecture 1 in *Pravoslavnoe obozrenie* (March 1877): 472–78; Lecture 2 (April 1877): 714–26; Lecture 3 (May–June 1877): 308–30; Lecture 4 (June 1877): 477–87; Lectures 5–6 (September 1877): 108–53; Lectures 7–8 (October 1879): 223–51; Lecture 9 (November 1880): 941–956; Lecture 10 (February 1881): 317–18; Lectures 11–12 (September 1881): 12–32.
Translated into English as *Lectures on Godmanhood*, trans. Peter Zouboff (London: Dennis Dobson, Ltd, 1948); *Lectures on Divine Humanity*, rev. and ed. Boris Jakim (Hudson, NY: Lindisfarne Press, 1995). The present translation makes minor corrections to this edition.

From *Russia and the Universal Church*

Rossiia i vselenskaia tserkov', SS 11: 139–348 (trans. G. A. Rachinskii).
First published as *La Russie et L'église universelle* (Paris: Librairie nouvelle parisienne, 1889) and (Paris: P. V. Stock, 1906).
Translated into Russian as *Rossiia i vselenskaia tserkov'*, trans. G. A. Rachinskii (Moscow: Tovarishchestvo tipografii A. I. Mamontova, 1911).
Translated into English in full as *Russia and the Universal Church*, trans. Herbert Rees (London: Centenary Press, 1948).
The translation below is newly made from the Russian version published in SS 11, checked against the original French.

"The Idea of Humanity in Auguste Comte"

"Ideia chelovechestva u Avgusta Konta," SS 9:172–93.
Delivered on March 7, 1898, at the Philosophical Society of Petersburg University.
First published in *Cosmopolis* 4 (1898): 60–73, and 12 (1898): 179–82.
We present here the first full translation into English.

"At the Dawn of Misty Youth"

"Na zare tumannoi iunosti," *SS* 12:289–302.

First published in *Russkaia Mysl'* (May 1892).

Previous English translation by Boris Jakim and Laury Magnus, *"At the Dawn of Mist-Shrouded Youth" with Selected Letters to Ekaterina Romanova*, Variable Readings in Russian Philosophy 5 (n.p., 1999).

The White Lily

Belaia liliia ili son na noch' Pokrova (Misteriia-shutka v 3-x deistiiakh), *SS* 12:174–211.

First published in *Na pamiat'*, ed. F. A. Dukhovetskii (Moscow: T. I. Gachen, 1893).

First translated by Boris Jakim as *The White Lily by Vladimir Solovyov* (New Haven: Variable Press, 1995). The current translation has been revised by Jakim and Laury Magnus, with additional minor revision by Judith Deutsch Kornblatt.

Three Encounters

Tri svidaniia, *SS* 12:80–86; and *Stikhotvoreniia* 125–32.

Written in Pustyn'ka, 1898; first published in *Vestnik Evropy* 11 (1898).

Previously translated as *Three Meetings*, in *Vladimir Solovyov's Poems of Sophia*, trans. Jakim and Magnus; Allen 345–57; Koprince 21–30; and as *Three Encounters* in Kornblatt, "Vladimir Solov'ev's *Three Encounters*." The translation below is revised from that latter publication, as are many of the annotations.

Other Major Works by Solov'ev Cited

The Crisis of Western Philosophy (Against the Positivists) (Krizis zapadnoi filosofii [protiv pozitivistov]) (1874)

"Philosophical Principles of Integral Knowledge" ("Filosofskie nachala tsel'nogo znaniia") (1877)

"Three Powers" (Tri sily) (1877)

Critique of Abstract Principles (Kritika otvlechennykh nachal) (1880)

Three Speeches in Memory of Dostoevsky (Tri rechi v pamiat' Dostoevskogo) (1881–1883)

The Great Controversy and Christian Politics (Velikii spor i khristianskaia politika) (1883)

Jewry and the Christian Question (Evreistvo i khristianskii vopros) (1884)

The Spiritual Foundations of Life (Dukhovnye osnovy zhizni) (1882–1884)

The History and Future of Theocracy (Istoriia i budushchnost' teokratii) (1885–1887)

"Beauty in Nature" ("Krasota v prirode") (1889)

Russia and the Universal Church (*La Russie et L'église universelle*) (1889)

"The General Meaning of Art" ("Obshchii smysl iskusstva") (1890)

The National Question in Russia (Natsional'nyi vopros v Rossii) (1883–1888 and 1888–1891)

"The Meaning of Love" ("Smysl liubvi") (1892–1894)

"First Step Toward a Positive Aesthetics" ("Pervyi shag k polozhitel'noi estetiki") (1894)

The Justification of the Good (Opravdanie dobra) (1894–1898)

The Life Drama of Plato (Zhiznennaia drama Platona) (1898)

"The Idea of the Superman" ("Ideia sverkhcheloveka") (1899)

Three Conversations (Tri razgovora) (1899–1900)

Other Sophianic Poems Cited

"You gaze at the stars" ("Na zvezdy gliadish' ty") (1876) (translation from Plato)

"As the heavenly glory is reflected / In the pure azure of the quieted seas" ("Kak v chistoi lazuri zatikhshego moria / Vsia slava nebes otrazhaetsia") (March 1875)

"Song of the Ophites" ("Pesnia Ofitov") (May 1876)

"Let dark clouds in a threatening crowd" ("Pust' tuchi temnye groziashcheiu tolpoiu") (1891)

"I see your emerald eyes" ("Vizhu ochi tvoi izumrudnye") (1892)

"Emanuel" (Immanu-El') (1892)

"Dear friend, I believe not in the least" ("Milyi drug, ne veriu ia niskol'ko") (1892)

"Azure eye" ("Lazurnoe oko") (1895)

"Das Ewig-Weibliche" (1898)

Bibliography

Allen, Paul M. *Vladimir Soloviev: Russian Mystic*. New York: Blauvelt, 1978.

Ammann, A. M. "Darstellung und Deutung der Sophia im Vorpetrinischen Russland." *Orientalia Christiana Periodia* 4, no. 1–2 (1938): 120–56.

Andreev, Daniil. *Roza mira*. Moscow: Izdatel'stvo "Inoi Mir," 1992.

Antonii, Metropolit Leningradskii i Novgorodskii, "Iz Istorii Novgorodskoi ikonografi." *Bogoslovskie Trudy* 27 (1986): 61–80.

Averin, B., and D. Bazanova. *Kniga o Vladimire Solov'eve*. Moscow: Sovetskii pisatel', 1991.

Averintsev, S. S. *Sofiia-Logos: Slovar'*. Kiev: Dukh i Litera, 2001.

——."K uiasneniiu smysla nadpisi nad konkhoi tsentral'noi apsidy Sophii Kievskoi." In *Drevnerusskoe iskusstvo: Khudozhestvennaia kul'tura domongol'skoi Rusi*, 25–49. Moscow: Izdatel'stvo Nauka, 1972.

Baer, Richard A. Jr. *Philo's Use of the Categories Male and Female*. Leiden: E.J. Brill, 1970.

Balčarek, Petr. "The Image of Sophia in Medieval Russian Iconography and Its Sources." *Byzantinoslavica* 60 (1999): 593–610.

Barth, Roland. *The Humanity of God*. Translated by John Newton Thomas and Thomas Wieser. Richmond, VA: John Knox, 1960.

Berdiaev, Nikolai. "Iz etiudov o Ia. Beme." *Put'*, no. 20 (February 1930): 47–79; no. 21 (April 1930): 34–62.

——. *Russkaia ideia (Osnovnye problemy russkoi mysli XIX veka i nachala XX veka)*. Paris: YMCA Press, 1946.

Berdyaev, Nicolas (Berdiaev). *The Russian Idea*. Translated by R. M. French. New York: Macmillan, 1948.

Berry, Thomas E. *Spiritualism in Tsarist Society and Literature*. Baltimore: Edgar Allan Poe Society, 1985.

Blum, Deborah. *Ghost Hunters: William James and the Search for Scientific Proof of Life after Death*. New York: Penguin, 2006.

Boehme, Jacob. *The Way to Christ*. Translated by Peter Erb. New York: Paulist Press, 1978.

Boikov, V. F. Vl. *Solov'ev: Pro et contra (Lichnost' i tvorchestvo Vladimira Solov'eva v otsenke russkikh myslitelei i issledovatelei).* 2 vols. St. Petersburg: Izdatel'stvo Russkogo Khristianskogo gumanitarnogo instituta, 2000.

Bouyer, Louis. *Le Trône de la Sagesse: Essai sur la signification du culte marial.* Paris: Les editions du CERF, 1957.

Briusova, Vera Grigor'evna. *Sofiia Premudrost' Bozhiia v drevnerusskoi literature i iskusstve.* Moscow: Belyi Gorod, 2006.

Britten, Emma Hardinge. "Spiritualism in Russia." In *Nineteenth Century Miracles, or Spirits and Their Work in Every Country of the Earth.* New York: n.p., 1884. Reprint, New York: Arno Press, 1976.

Buber, Martin. *Ecstatic Confessions.* Edited by Paul Mendes-Flohr. Translated by Esther Cameron. San Francisco: Harper & Row, 1985.

Bulgakov, S. N. *Philosophy of Economy: The World as Household.* Translated and edited by Catherine Evtuhov. New Haven: Yale University Press, 2000.

——. "Po povodu vykhoda v svet shestogo toma sobraniia sochinenii Vladimira Sergeevicha Solov'eva." *Voprosy zhizni* 2 (1905): 361–68.

——. "Priroda v filosofii Vl. Solov'eva." In *Sbornik pervyi. O Vladimire Solov'eve,* 1–31. Moscow: Put', 1911. Also in Boikov, *Vladimir Solov'ev: Pro et contra,* 2:618–45.

——. *Sophia the Wisdom of God: An Outline of Sophiology.* Hudson, NY: Lindisfarne Press, 1993.

——. "Vladimir Solov'ev i Anna Shmidt." In *Tikhie Dumy: Iz statei 1911–1915,* 71–114. Moscow: Leman i Sakharov, 1918. Also in Boikov, *Vl. Solov'ev,* 646–681.

Burmistrov, Konstantin. "Christian Orthodoxy and Jewish Kabbalah: Russian Mystics in the Search for Perennial Wisdom." In *Polemic Encounters: Esoteric Discourse and Its Others,* 25–54. Leiden, Neth.: Brill Academic Publishers, 2007.

——. "The Interpretation of Kabbalah in Early 20th-Century Russian Philosophy: Soloviev, Bulgakov, Florenskii, Losev." *East European Jewish Affairs* 37, no. 2 (2007): 157–87.

——. "Khristianskaia kabbala i problema vospriiatiia evreiskoi mistiki (XV-XIX vv.)." In *Trudy vtoroi molodezhnoi konferentsii SNb po iudaike,* 31–44. Moscow: Tirosh, 1998.

——. "Osobennosti vospriiatiia kabbaly v russkoi religioznoi filosofii (V. Solov'ev, P. Florenskii, S. Bulgakov, A. Losev)." In *Tirosh: Trudy po iudaike,* vol. 4, 67–90. Moscow: Sefer, 2000.

——. "Vladimir Solov'ev i Kabbala: K postanovke problemy." In *Issledovaniia po istorii russkoi mysli,* edited by M. A. Kolerova, 7–104. Moscow: OGI, 1998.

Cady, Susan, Marian Ronan, and Hal Taussig. *Sophia: The Future of Feminist Spirituality.* San Francisco: Harper & Row, 1986.

Carlson, Maria. "Gnostic Elements in the Cosmogony of Vladimir Soloviev." In Kornblatt and Gustafson, *Russian Religious Thought,* 49–67.

——. *No Religion Higher Than Truth: A History of the Theosophical Movement in Russia, 1875–1922.* Princeton: Princeton University Press, 1993.

Cassedy, Steven. *To the Other Shore: The Russian Jewish Intellectuals Who Came to America.* Princeton: Princeton University Press, 1997.

Chulkov, G. I. "Avtomaticheskie zapisi Vl. Solov'eva." *Voprosy filosofii* 8 (1927): 123–32.

Cioran, Samuel D. "The Affair of Anna N. Schmidt and Vladimir Solov'ev." *Canadian Slavonic Papers* 16, no. 1 (1974): 39–61.

——. *Vladimir Solov'ev and the Knighthood of the Divine Sophia.* Waterloo, Ont.: Wilfred Laurier University Press, 1977.

Chernyshevsky, Nikolai. *What Is to Be Done?* Translated by Michael R. Katz. Ithaca: Cornell University Press, 1989.

Clowes. Edith W. *Fiction's Overcoat: Russian Literary Culture and the Question of Philosophy.* Ithaca: Cornell University Press, 2004.

——. "The Limits of Discourse: Solov'ev's Language of Syzygy and the Project of Thinking Total-Unity." *Slavic Review* 55, no. 3 (1996): 552–66.

Copleston, Frederick C. *Russian Religious Philosophy: Selected Aspects.* Notre Dame, IN: University of Notre Dame, 1988.

Daigin, Uri. "Kabbalah in Russian Religious Philosophy: The Impact of the Kabbalah on the Russian Sophiological Movement (During the Period from the Last Quarter of the Nineteenth Century to the Middle of the Twentieth Century)." PhD diss., Bar-Ilan University, Israel, 2008.

Dan, Joseph. *Gershom Scholem and the Mystical Dimension of Jewish History.* New York: New York University Press, 1987.

David, Zdenek V. "The Formation of the Religious and Social System of Vladimir S. Solovev." PhD diss., Harvard University, 1960.

——. "The Influence of Jacob Boehme on Russian Religious Thought." *Slavic Review* 21, no. 1 (1962): 43–64.

Davidson, Pamela. "Vladimir Solov'ev and the Ideal of Prophecy." *SEER* 78, no. 4 (October 2000): 643–70.

de Courten, Manon. *History, Sophia and the Russian Nation: A Reassessment of Vladimir Solov'ëv's Views on History and His Social Commitment.* Bern: Peter Lang, 2004.

Delokarpov, K. Kh., and B. M. Shakhmatov, eds. *Ogiust Kont: Vzgliad iz Rossii.* Moscow: Izdatel'stvo RAGS, 2000.

Epstein, Mikhail. "Daniil Andreev and the Mysticism of Femininity." In *The Occult in Russian and Soviet Culture*, edited by Bernice Glatzer Rosenthal, 325–55. Ithaca: Cornell University Press, 1997.

Fedotov, George P. *The Collected Works of Goerge P. Fedotov.* Vol. 3, *The Russian Religious Mind (I): Kievan Christianity, the 10th to the 13th Centuries.* Belmont, MA: Nordland, 1975.

The Festal Menaion. Translated by Mother Mary and Archimandrite Kallistos Ware. London: Faber and Faber, 1969.

Fiene, Donald M. "What Is the Appearance of Divine Sophia?" *Slavic Review* 48, no. 3 (1989): 449–76.

Filippov, M. "Sud'ba russkoi filosofii." *Nauchnoe obozrenie*, no. 8–10 (1898): 1351–68; 1548–71; 1793–1812; 1797–98.

Florovskii, G.V. "Chteniia po filosofii religii magistra filosofii V. S. Solov'eva." In *Orbis scriptus. Dmitrij Tschiževskij zum 70 Geburtstag*, edited by Dietrich Gerhardt, 221–36. Munich: W. Fink, 1966.

——. "O pochitanii Sophii, Premudrosti Bozhei, v Vizantii i na Rusi." In *Trudy V-go S'ezda Russkikh Akademicheskikh Organizatsii za granitsei v Sophii 14–21 sentiabria 1930 goda*, 485–500. Chast' I. Sophia, Bulgaria: Izdanie Russkikh Akademicheskikh Organizatsii, 1932.

Florovsky, Georges (Florovskii). "The Hagia Sophia Churches." In *The Collected Works of Georges Florovsky.* Vol. 4, *Aspects of Church History*, 130–35. Belmont, MA: Nordland , 1975.

——. "Vladimir Soloviev and Dante: The Problem of Christian Empire." In *For Roman Jakobson: Essays on the Occasion of His Sixtieth Birthday*, edited by Morris Halle, 152–60. The Hague: Mouton, 1956.

Florensky, Pavel. *Iconostasis.* Translated by Donald Sheehan and Olga Andrejev. Crestwood, NY: St. Vladimir's Seminary Press, 1996.

——. *The Pillar and Ground of the Truth.* Translated by Boris Jakim. Princeton: Princeton University Press, 1997.

Fox, Michael V., ed. and trans. *Proverbs 1–9, The Anchor Bible.* New York: Doubleday, 2000.

Frank, S. L., ed. *A Solovyov Anthology.* London: Saint Austin Press, 2001.

Gaut, Gregory. "Christian Politics: Vladimir Solovyov's Social Gospel Theology." *Modern Greek Studies Yearbook* 10–11 (1994–95): 653–74.

Gets, F. B. "Ob Otnoshenii VI. S. Solov'eva k Evreskomu Voprosu." *Voprosy Filosofii i Psikhologii* 56 (1901): 159–98.

Gillis, Donald C. "Gnosis and Cabala in the Early Works of Vladimir Solov'ev." Unpublished paper. N.d.

Ginzburg, David. "Kabbala, misticheskaia filosofiia evreev." *Voprosy Filosofii i Psikhologii* 33 (1896): 279–300.

Glatzer, Nahum N., ed. *The Essential Philo.* New York: Schocken Books, 1971.

Goethe, Johann Wolfgang von. *Faust: Part One.* Translated by David Luke. Oxford: Oxford University Press, 1987.

——. *Faust: Part Two.* Translated by David Luke. Oxford: Oxford University Press, 1994.

Good, Deirdre J. *Reconstructing the Tradition of Sophia in Gnostic Literature.* Atlanta: Scholars Press, 1987.

Grabar, André. *Byzantine Painting.* Translated by Stuart Gilbert. Geneva: Skira, 1953.

——. "Iconographie de la Sagesse Divine et de la Vierge." *Cahiers Archeologique* 8 (1956): 254–57.

Grabar, Michel. "Les rencontres avec la Sophia: Une experience érotique et mystique de Vladimir Solov'ëv." In van den Bercken, de Courten, and van der Zweerde, *Vladimir Solov'ëv: Reconciler and Polemicist,* 147–61.

Groberg, Kristi. "Eternal Feminine: Vladimir Solov'ev's Visions of Sophia." In *Alexandria I,* edited by Paul R. Fideler, 77–96. Grand Rapids, MI: Phanes Press, 1991.

——. "'Sweet Yielding Consent of Sophia': The Wisdom Visions of Merton via Solov'ev and Bulgakov." Paper presented at the AAASS convention, New Orleans, November 2007.

——. *Vladimir Sergeevich Solov'ev: A Bibliography. Modern Greek Studies Yearbook* 14–15 (1998–1999).

Grossman, Joan Delaney. "Spiritualism and Pantheism among the Early Modernists." In *Christianity and the Eastern Slavs,* edited by Boris Gasparov, Robert Hughes, and Irina Paperno, vol. 3. Berkeley: University of California Press, 1995.

Grossman, Joan Delaney, and Ruth Rischin, eds. *William James in Russian Culture.* Landham, MD: Lexington Books, 2003.

Groys, Boris. "Weisheit als weibliches Weltprinzip die Sophiologie von Wladimir Solovjow." In *Die Erfindung Russlands.* Munich: Carl Hanser Verlag, 1995.

Helleman, Wendy Elgersma. *Sophia, Mary and Beatrice: A Study in Personification of Wisdom Based on Solovyov and Dante.* Columbus, Ohio: Slavica, 2007.

——. "The World-Soul and Sophia in the Early Work of Solov'ëv." In van den Bercken, de Courten, and van der Zweerde, *Vladimir Solov'ëv: Reconciler and Polemicist,* 163–84.

Horsley, Richard A. "Wisdom of Word and Words of Wisdom in Corinth." *Catholic Biblical Quarterly* 39, no. 2 (April 1977): 224–39.

Hubbs, Joanna. *Mother Russia: The Feminine Myth in Russian Culture.* Bloomington: Indiana University Press, 1988.

Hunt, Priscilla. "Confronting the End: The Interpretation of the Last Judgment in a Novgorod Wisdom Icon." *Byzantinoslavica: Revue Internationale des Etudes Byzantines* 65 (2007): 275–327.

——. "Hesychasm and the Iconography of Divine Wisdom." Paper presented at the AAASS convention, Toronto, November 2003.

——. "The Novgorod Sophia Icon and 'The Problem of Old Russian Culture': Between Orthodoxy and Sophiology." *Symposium* 4–6 (1999–2001): 1–40.

Ianzhul, I. I. "Vospominaniia I. I. Ianzhula o perezhitom i vidennom." *Russkaia starina* 1 (1910).

Idel, Moshe. *Kabbalah: New Perspectives.* New Haven: Yale University Press, 1988.

——. "Metaphores et pratiques sexuelles dans la Cabale." In *Lettre sur la Sainteté. Le secret de la relation entre l'homme et la femme dans la Cabale.* Translated and with commentary by Charles Mopsik, 32–44. Paris: Editions Verdier, 1986.

Ivanov, V.I. "Mysli o simvolizme." In *Borozdy i mezhi. Opyty esteticheskie i kriticheskie.* Moscow: Musaget, 1916.

——. "O znachenii Vl. Solov'ev v sud'bakh nashego religioznago soznaniia." In *Sbornik pervyi.*
Jakim, Boris, and Robert Bird, eds. *On Spiritual Unity: A Slavophile Reader.* Hudson, NY: Lindisfarne Books, 1998.
James, William. *The Varieties of Religious Experience.* Cambridge, MA: Harvard University Press, 1985.
——. *The Will to Believe: Human Immortality and Other Essays on Popular Philosophy.* New York: Dover, 1956.
Johnson, Elizabeth. *She Who Is: The Mystery of God in Feminist Theological Discourse.* New York: Crossroad, 1992.
Jonas, Hans. *The Gnostic Religion: The Message of the Alien God and the Beginnings of Christianity.* 2nd ed. Boston: Beacon Press, 1962.
Kelly, Aileen. *Toward Another Shore: Russian Thinkers between Necessity and Chance.* New Haven: Yale University Press, 1998.
Khoruzhii, S. S. *Posle Pereryva: Puti Russkoi Filosofii.* St. Petersburg: Ateleiia, 1994.
Kline, George L. "Hegel and Solovyov." In *Hegel and the History of Philosophy,* edited by Keith W. Algozin, Joseph O'Malley, and Frederick G. Weiss, 159–70. The Hague: Martinus Nijhoff, 1974.
Klum, Edith. *Natur, Kunst und Liebe in der Philosophie Vladimir Solov'evs: Eine religionsphilosophische Untersuchung.* Munich: Verlag Otto Sagner, 1965.
Kochetkova, Tatjana. "Divine Humanity in the Interpretation of Vladimir Solov'ev and the Problem of the Actualization of Human Essence." In van den Bercken, de Courten, and van der Zweerde, *Vladimir Solov'ëv: Reconciler and Polemicist,* 325–45.
——. *The Search for Authentic Spirituality in Modern Russian Philosophy: The Perdurance of Solov'ëv's Ideal.* Lewiston, NY: Edwin Mellen Press, Ltd., 2007.
—— "Vladimir Solov'jov's Theory of Divine Humanity." PhD diss., University of Nijmegen, 2001.
Kolerov, M. A., A. A. Nosov, and I. V. Borisova. "K istorii odnoi druzhby: V. S. Solov'ev i Kn. S. N. Trubetskoi: Novye materialy." *De Visu* 8 (1993): 5–23.
Koprince, Ralph. "Three Meetings." *Russian Literature Tri-Quarterly* 4 (1972): 21–30.
Kornblatt, Judith Deutsch. "On Laughter and Vladimir Solov'ev's *Three Encounters.*" *Slavic Review* 57, no.3 (Fall 1998): 563–584.
——. "Solov'ev's Androgynous Sophia and the Jewish Kabbalah." *Slavic Review.* 50, no. 3 (1991): 487–96.
——. "Soloviev on Salvation: The Story of the 'Short Story of the Antichrist.'" In Kornblatt and Gustafson, *Russian Religious Thought,* 68–87.
——. "Spirits, Spiritualism, and the Spirit: *Evenings in Cairo* by V. S. Solovyov and D. N. Tsertelev." In *Russian Literature and the West: A Tribute to David M. Bethea,* edited by Alexander Dolinin, Lazar Fleishman, and Leonid Livak. Special issue of *Stanford Slavic Studies* 35, no. 1 (2008). 336–58.
——. "The Transfiguration of Plato in the Erotic Philosophy of Vladimir Solov'ev." *Religion and Literature* 24, no. 2 (1992): 35–50.
——. "The Truth of the Word: Solovyov's *Three Conversations* Speaks on Tolstoy's *Resurrection.*" *Slavic and East European Journal* 45, no. 2 (2001): 301–21.
——. "Visions of Icons and Reading Rooms in the Poetry and Prose of Vladimir Solov'ev." In *Aesthetics in Eastern and Western Christianity,* edited by Wil van den Bercken and Jonathan Sutton, 125–43. Leuven, Belg.: Peeters, 2006.
——. "Vladimir Sergeevich Solov'ev." In *The Dictionary of Literary Biography.* Vol. 295, *Russian Writers of the Silver Age, 1890–1925,* edited by Judith E. Kalb and J. Alexander Ogden, with the collaboration of I. G. Vishnevetsky, 311–86. Detroit: Thomson-Gale, 2004.
——. "Vladimir Solov'ev on Spiritual Nationhood, Russian and the Jews." *Russian Review* 56 (April 1997): 157–77.
——. "Vladimir Solov'ev's *Three Encounters*: An Annotated Translation." *The Silver Age: Russian Literature and Culture 1881–1921* 2 (1999): 25–50.

——. "Who Is Sophia and Why Is She Writing in My Manuscript? Vladimir Solov'ev and the Channeling of Divine Wisdom." *The Icon and the Bridge: Sophia in Orthodox Culture*, edited by Manon de Courten and Evert van der Zweerde. Special double issue of *Journal of Eastern Christian Studies* 3–4 (2008).

Kornblatt, Judith Deutsch, and Richard F. Gustafson, eds. *Russian Religious Thought.* Madison: University of Wisconsin Press, 1996.

Kornblatt, Judith Deutsch, and Gary Rosenshield. "Vladimir Solovyov: Confronting Dostoevsky on the Jewish and Christian Question." *Journal of the American Academy of Religion* 68, no.1 (2000): 69–98.

Kostalevsky, Marina. *Dostoevsky and Soloviev: The Art of Integral Vision.* New Haven: Yale University Press, 1997.

Koutstaal, Wilma. "Skirting the Abyss: A History of Experimental Explorations of Automatic Writing in Psychology." *Journal of the History of the Behavioral Sciences* 28, no. 1 (1972): 5–27.

Koyré, Alexandre. *La Philosophie de Jacob Boehme.* Paris: Librairie Philosophique J. Vrin, 1929.

Kozhev, A. "Religioznaia metafizika Vladimira Solov'eva." Translated by A. P. Kozyrev. *Voprosy Filosofii* 3 (2000): 101–35.

Kozyrev, A. P. "Gnosticheskie iskaniia Vl. Solov'eva i kul'tura Serebrianogo Veka." In *Vladimir Solov'ev i kul'tura Serebrianogo Veka: K 150-letiiu Vl. Solov'eva i 110-letiiu A. F. Loseva,* edited by A. A. Takho-godi and E. A. Takho-godi, 226–40. Moscow: Nauka, 2005.

——. "Kosmogonicheskii mif Vladimira Solov'eva: (K voprosu o retseptsii gnostitsizma v tractate "Sofiia")." In *Solov'evskii Sbornik.* Moscow: Fenomenologiia-Germenetika, 2001.

——. "Nizhegorodskaia Sivilla." *Istoriia Filosofii,* no. 6 (2000): 62–84.

Kravchenko, V. V. *Mistitsizm v russkoi filosofskoi mysli XIX–nachala XX vekov.* Moscow: Izdattsentr, 1997.

——. *Vestniki Russkogo Mistitsizma.* Moscow: Izdattsentr, 1998.

——. *Vladimir Solov'ev i Sofiia: Monografiia.* Moscow: Agraf, 2006.

Lebedintsev, P. G. "Sophia-Premudrost' Bozhiia v ikonografii severa i iuga Rossii." *Kievskaia Starina* 10 (December 1884): 555–67.

Lewy, Hans, ed. *Philosophical Writings: Philo.* Oxford: East and West Library, 1946.

Lifshits, L. I. "Premudrost' v russkoi ikonopisi." *Vizantiiskii vremennik* 61, no. 86 (2002): 138–50.

Losev, A. F. *Mif. Chislo. Sushnost'.* Moscow: Mysl', 1994.

——. *Strast' k dialektike.* Moscow: Sovetskii pisatel', 1990.

——. *Vl. Solov'ev.* Moscow: Mysl', 1983.

——. *Vladimir Solov'ev i ego vremia.* Moscow: Molodaia Gvardiia, 2000.

Lossky, Nikolas O. *History of Russian Philosophy.* Crestwood, NY: St. Vladimir's Seminary Press, 1951.

Lossky, Vladimir. *The Mystical Theology of the Eastern Church.* Crestwood, NY: St. Vladimir's Seminary Press, 1976.

Luk'ianov, S. M. "Iunosheskii roman Vl. S. Solov'eva v dvoinom osveshchenii." *Zhurnal Ministerstva Narodnogo Prosveshcheniia* 53 (1914): 71–117.

——. *O Vl. S. Solov'eve v ego molodye gody: Materialy k biografii V. S. Solov'eva.* 3 vols. Moscow: Kniga, 1990. With additions to Luk'ianov, *O Vl. S. Solov'eve v ego molodye gody: Materialy k biografii V. S. Solov'eva.* 3 vols. Vol. 1, Petrograd: Senatskaia tipografiia, 1916, vols. 2–3: Petrograd: Gosudarstvennaia tipografiia, 1918–21.

Masanov, Ivan. *Slovar' psevdonimov russkikh pisatelei, uchenykh I obshchestvennykh deiatelei.* Moscow: Izd. Vsesoiuznoi knizhnoi palaty, 1957.

Mateos, Juan S. J. *Orientalia Christiana Analecta.* Vol. 191, *La Célébration de la Parole Dans la Liturgie Byzantine.* Rome: Pont. Institutum Studiorum Orientalium, 1971.

Mathew, Gervase. *Byzantine Aesthetics.* London: John Murray, 1963.

Matich, Olga. *Erotic Utopia: The Decadent Imagination in Russia's Fin de Siècle.* Madison: University of Wisconsin Press, 2005.

Matthews, Caitlín. *Sophia: Goddess of Wisdom. The Divine Feminine from Black Goddess to World-Soul.* London: Mandala, 1991.

Meehan, Brenda. "Wisdom/Sophia, Russian Identity, and Western Feminist Theology." *Cross Currents* 46, no. 2 (Summer 1996): 149–68.

Meeks, Wayne A. "The Image of the Androgyne: Some Uses of a Symbol in Earliest Christianity." *History of Religions* 13 (1973).

Meerson, Michael A. "Appendix: The History of the First Publication of Two Manuscripts: *La Sophia* by Vladimir Solov'ëv and *Vladmir Solov'ëv: His Life and Creative Evolution* by his Nephew, Sergei Solov'ëv." In van den Bercken, de Courten, and van der Zweerde, *Vladimir Solov'ëv: Reconciler and Polemicst,* 359–62.

Meyendorff, John. "L'iconographie de la Sagesse Divine dans la Tradition Byzantine." *Cahiers Archéologique* 10 (1959): 259–77.

———. *St. Gregory Palamas and Orthodox Spirituality.* Translated by Adele Fiske. Crestwood, NY: St. Vladimir's Seminary Press, 1974.

———. "Wisdom-Sophia: Contrasting Approaches to a Complex Theme." In *Dumbarton Oaks Papers,* 391–401. Washington, D.C.: Dumbarton Oaks, 1987.

Milbank, John. "Sophiology and Theurgy: The New Theological Horizon." Paper delivered at conference on "Transfiguring the World through the Word: An Encounter between Radical Orthodoxy and Eastern Orthodoxy," the Institute for Orthodox Christian Studies. Cambridge, England, October 2005. Available at http://community.livejournal.com/sbulgakov/31493.html.

Mochul'skii, Konstantin. *Vladimir Solov'ev: Zhizn' i uchenie.* Paris: YMCA-Press, 1936.

Nethercott, Frances. *Russia's Plato: Plato and the Platonic Tradition in Russian Education, Science and Ideology (1840–1930).* Aldershot, England: Ashgate, 2000.

Newman, Barbara. "The Pilgrimage of Christ-Sophia." *Vox Benedictina* 9, no. 1 (1992): 9–37.

Nichols, Robert L., and Theofanis George Stavrou. *Russian Orthodoxy under the Old Regime.* Minneapolis: University of Minnesota Press, 1978.

Nietzsche, F. W. *Gesammelte Werke.* 23 vols. Munich: Musarion Verlag, 1920–29.

Nosev, Aleksandr, ed. "Pis'ma A. A. Kireevu." *Simvol.* ed. Aleksandr Nosov. 27 (1992).

Olcott, Henry S. *People from the Other World.* Rutland, VT: Charles E. Tuttle Co., 1972. First edition Hartford, Conn.: American Publishing Co., 1875.

Oppenheim, Janet. *The Other World: Spiritualism and Psychical Research in England 1850–1914.* Cambridge: Cambridge University Press, 1985.

Pagels, Elaine. *The Gnostic Gospels.* New York: Random House, 1979.

Panova, L. G. "Mif o Sofii v poezii Mikhaila Kuzmina: Gnosticheskie siuzhety, motivy, iazyk." In *Poetika. Stikhoslozhenie. Lingvistika,* Edited by E. V. Krasil'nikova and A. G. Grek. Moscow: Azbukovnik, 2003.

———. *Russkii Egipet: Aleksandriiskaia poetika Mikhaila Kuzmina.* Moscow: Vodolei Publishers & Progress-Pleida, 2006.

Patai, Raphael. *The Hebrew Goddess.* 3rd ed. Detroit: Wayne State University Press, 1990.

Pelikan, Jeroslav. *The Christian Tradition: A History of the Development of the Doctrine.* Vol. 1, *The Emergence of the Catholic Tradition (100–600).* Chicago: University of Chicago Press, 1971.

———. *The Christian Tradition: A History of the Development of the Doctrine.* Vol. 2, *The Spirit of Eastern Christendom (600–1700).* Chicago: University of Chicago Press, 1974.

Philo of Alexandria. *The Essential Philo.* Edited by Nahum N. Glatzer. New York: Schocken Books, 1971.

———. *Philosophical Writings.* Edited by Hans Lewy. Oxford: East and West Library, 1946.

Poole, Randall A. "Human Dignity and the Kingdom of God: A Russian Theological Perspective (Vladimir Solov'ëv)." *Listening/Journal of Religion and Culture* 43, no. 1 (Winter 2008).

———. "Vladimir Solov'ëv and Russian Idealist Humanism." In *A History of Russian Philosophy, 1830 to 1930*, edited by Gary Hamburg and Randall Poole. Cambridge: Cambridge University Press, forthcoming.

Powell, Robert A. *The Most Holy Trinosophia and the New Revelations of the Divine Feminine*. Great Barrington, MA: Anthroposophic Press, 2000.

Prokhorov, G. M. "'. . . I pokoias' vechno i dvigaias' . . .' (Vliianie na ikonografiiu Sofii-Premudrosti)." In *Pamiatniki perevognoi i russkoi literatury XIV–XV vekov*. Leningrad: Nauka, 1957.

Prokofieff, Sergei O. *The Heavenly Sophia and the Being Anthroposophia*. East Sussex, UK: Temple Lodge, 1996.

Reeder, Roberta, ed. *Russian Folk Lyrics*. Bloomington: Indiana University Press, 1975.

Reider, Joseph, ed. and trans. *The Book of Wisdom*. New York: Harper & Brothers, 1957.

Rosenroth, Knorr de. *Kabbala denudate*. Frankfort, 1677–84.

Rosenthal, Bernice Glatzer. "William James through a Russian Prism: The Case of the Moscow God-Seekers." In *The Cultural Gradient: The Transmission of Ideas in Europe, 1789–1991*, edited by Catherine Evtuhov and Stephen Kotkin, 109–27. Lanham, MD: Rowman & Littlefield, 2002.

Rotsinskii, S. B. "Vl. Solov'ev i O. Kont: Cherez kritiku—k konvergentsii." In Delokarpov and Shakhmatov, *Ogiust Kont: Vzgliad iz Rossii*, 67–89.

Rozanov, V. V. "Pamiati Vl. Solov'eva." In *Kniga o Vladimire Solov'eve*, edited by B. Averin and D. Bazanova, 335–39. Moscow: Sovetskii pisatel'.

Rudolph, Kurt. *Gnosis*. San Francisco: Harper & Row, 1983.

Ruether, Rosemary. *Goddesses and the Divine Feminine: A Western Religious History*. Berkeley: University of California Press, 2005.

Sbornik pervyi. O Vladimire Solov'eve, Moscow: Put', 1911.

Schiplinger, Thomas. *Sophia-Maria: A Holistic Vision of Creation*. Translated by James Morgante. York Beach, ME: Samuel Weiser, 1998.

Schmemann, Alexander. "Russian Theology: 1920–1972, An Introductory Survey." *St. Vladimir's Theological Quarterly* 16 (1972).

Scholem, Gershom G. *Jewish Gnosticism, Merkabah Mysticism, and Talmudic Tradition*. New York: Jewish Theological Seminary of America, 1960.

———. *Kabbalah*. New York: Dorset Press, 1974.

———. *On Kabbalah and Its Symbolism*. New York: Schocken Books, 1965.

———. *Major Trends in Jewish Mysticism*. New York: Schocken Books, 1941.

Schrooyen, Pauline. "Professional Intellectual and Zealous Heliotrope: A Study of the Role and Perception of Vladimir Solov'ëv in Russian Society." *Australian Slavonic East European Studies* 1–2, no. 19 (2004): 103–28.

———. "Vladimir Solov'ëv in the Rising Public Sphere: A Reconstruction and Analysis of the Concept of Christian Politics in the Publitsistika of Vladimir Solov'ëv." PhD diss., Radboud Universiteit Nijmegen, 2006.

Schüssler Fiorenza, Elisabeth. *Jesus: Miriam's Child, Sophia's Prophet: Critical Issues in Feminist Christology*. New York: Continuum, 1994.

Seiling, Jonathan. "Solov'ev's Early Idealism and the Birth of Sophia." In *Culture and Identity in Eastern Christian History: Papers of the First Biennial Conference of the Association for the Study of Eastern Christian History and Culture*, edited by Russell E. Martin and Jennifer Spock. Columbus: Ohio State University, 2008.

Semenkin, N. S. *Filosofiia bogoiskatel'stva: Kritika religiozno-filosofskoi idei sofiologov*. Moscow: Politicheskaia literatura, 1986.

Sergeev, Mikhail. *Sophiology in Russian Orthodoxy: Solov'ev, Bulgakov, Losskii and Berdiaev*. Lewiston, NY: Edwin Mellen Press, 2006.

Shakhmatov, B. M. "O. Kont i russkaia mysl'." In Delokarpov and Shakhmatov, *Ogiust Kont: Vzgliad iz Rossii*, 50–67.

Shaposhnikov, L. E. *Solov'ev i pravoslavnoe bogoslovie*. Moscow: Znanie, 1990.

Shein, P. V. *Velikoruss v Svoikh Pesniakh, Obriadakh, Obychaiakh, Verovaniiakh, Skazkakh, Legendakh, i t.p.* St. Petersburg: Izd. Imperatorskoi akademii nauk, 1898.

Shmidt, A. N. *Tretii zavet*. St. Petersburg: Al'manakh "Petropol'," 1993.

Slesinksi, Robert. "Sophiology as a Metaphysics of Creation according to V. S. Solov'ëv." In van den Bercken, de Courten, and van der Zweerde, *Vladimir Solov'ëv: Reconciler and Polemicist*, 131–45.

——. "Toward an Understanding of V.S. Solovyov's 'Gnosticism.'" *Diakonia* 31, no. 2 (1998): 77–88.

Solov'ev, S. M. "Ideia tserkvi v poezii Vladimira Solov'eva." *Bogoslovskii vestnik* (January 1915): 145–206.

——. *Zhizn' i tvorcheskaia evoliutsiia Vladimira Solov'eva*. Brussels: Zhizn' s Bogom, 1977.

Solovyov, Sergey (S. M. Solv'ev). *Vladimir Solovyov: His Life and Creative Evolution*. Translated by Aleksey Gibson. 2 vols. Fairfax, VA: Eastern Christian Publications, 2000.

Solov'ev, V. S. *Pis'ma Vladimira Sergeevicha Solov'eva*. Edited by E. L. Radlov. 4 vols. St. Petersburg: Obshchestvennaia Pol'za, 1908. Reprinted as *Sobranie sochinenii V. S. Solov'eva: Pis'ma i Prilozhenie*. Brussels: Zhizn' s Bogom, 1970.

——. *Polnoe sobranie sochinenii i pisem v dvadtsati tomakh*. Moscow: Nauka, 2000–2001 (3 vols. completed to date).

——. *Rossiia i vselenskaia tserkov'*. Translated by G. A. Rachinskii. Moscow: Tovarishchestvo tipografii A. I. Mamontova, 1911.

——. *La Russie et l'église universelle*. Paris: Nouvelle Librarie parisienne/ Albert Savine, 1889.

——. *Sobranie sochinenii*. Edited by S. M. Solov'ev and E. L. Radlov. 2 ed. 10 vols. St Petersburg: Prosveshchenie, 1911–14. Reprinted with two additional volumes. Brussels: Zhizn' s Bogom, 1966–70.

——. *Sochineniia v dvukh tomakh*. Edited by A. F. Losev and A. V. Gulyga. Commentary by S. L. Kravets and N. A. Kormin. Moscow: Mysl', 1988.

——. *Sochineniia v dvukh tomakh*. Edited and with commentary by N. V. Kotrelev and E. B. Rashkovskii. Introduction by V. F. Asmus. Moscow: Pravda, 1989.

——. *Stikhotvoreniia i shutochnye p'esy*. Edited by Zinaida Mints. Leningrad: Sovetskii pisatel', 1974.

Soloviev, Vladimir (V. S. Solov'ev). *La Russie et L'Église Universelle*. Edited by Albert Savine. Paris: Nouvelle Librairie Parisienne, 1889.

——. *LA SOPHIA et les autre écrits français*. Edited by François Rouleau. Lausanne: La Cité—L'Age d'Homme, 1978.

Solovyov, V. S. (V. S. Solov'ev). *At the Dawn of Mist-Shrouded Youth (with Selected Letters to Ekaterina Romanova)*. Translated by Boris Jakim and Laury Magnus. *Variable Readings in Russian Philosophy*, No. 5 (1999).

——. *Lectures on Divine Humanity*. Revised and edited by Boris Jakim. Hudson, NY: Lindisfarne Press, 1995.

——. *Russia and the Universal Church*. Translated by Herbert Rees. London: Geoffrey Bles. The Centenary Press, 1948.

——. *Vladimir Solovyov's Poems of Sophia*. Translated by Boris Jakim and Laury Magnus. N.p.: Variable Press, 1996.

——. *The White Lily*. Translated by Boris Jakim. New Haven: Variable Press, 1995.

Spinoza, Benedictus de. *The Collected Works of Spinoza*. Translated by Edwin Curley. Princeton: Princeton University Press, 1985.

Steiner, Rudolf. *Isis Mary Sophia: Her Mission and Ours*. Edited and with an introduction by Christopher Bamford. Great Barrington, MA: Steiner Books, 2003.

Stites, Richard. *The Women's Liberation Movement in Russia: Feminism, Nihilism, and Bolshevism, 1860–1930*. Princeton: Princeton University Press, 1978.

Stremooukhoff, D. *Vladimir Soloviev and His Messianic Work*. Translated by Elizabeth Meyendorff. Edited by Phillip Guilbeau and Heather Elise MacGregor. Belmont, MA: Nordland, 1980.

Struve, P. B. "Tiutchev and Vladimir Solov'ev." *Put'* 41 (1933): 3–24.

Sutton, Jonathan. *The Religious Philosophy of Vladimir Solovyov: Towards a Reassessment*. New York: St. Martin's, 1988.

Taft, Robert F. S. J. *Orientalia Christiana Analecta*. Vol. 200, *The Great Entrance: A History of the Transfer of Gifts and Other Pre-anaphoral Rites of the Liturgy of St. John Chrysostom*. Rome: Pont. Institutum Studiorum Orientalium, 1975.

Takho-Godi, Aza, and Elena Takho-Godi, eds. *Vladimir Solov'ev i Kul'tura Serebrianogo veka*. Moscow: Nauka, 2005.

Todorov, Tzvetan. *The Fantastic: A Structural Approach to a Literary Genre*. Translated by Richard Howard. Ithaca: Cornell University Press, 1975.

Tolstoy, Leo. *Anna Karenina*. Edited and with a revised translation from Maude by George Gibian. New York: Norton, 1995.

Trubetskoi, E.N. "Lichnost' V. S. Solov'eva." In *Sbornik Pervyi*, 45–77.

———. *Mirosozertsanie Vl. Solov'eva*. 2 vols. Moscow: Izdanie avtora, 1913.

Trubetskoi, Sergei. "Smert' V. Solov'eva. 31 iiulia 1900g." *Vestnik Evropy* 9 (1900). Reprinted in Averin and Bazanova, *Kniga o Vladimire Solov'eve*, 292–99.

Tschiževskij, Dmitrij. "Jacob Boehme in Russland." In *Aus zwei Welten: Beiträge zur Geschichte der slavisch-westlichen literarischen Beziehungen*, 197–219. Mouton: Gravenhage, 1956.

Turgenev, Ivan. *Fathers and Sons*. Translated by Michael R. Katz. New York: Norton, 1996.

Vagner, N. P. "Mediumizm." *Russkii Vestnik* (October 1875): 866–951.

Valliere, Paul. *Modern Russian Theology: Bukharev. Soloviev. Bulgakov: Orthodox Theology in a New Key*. Edinburgh: T&T Clark, 2000.

———."Vladimir Soloviev (1853–1900)." In *The Teachings of Modern Christianity on Law, Politics, and Human Nature*, edited by John Witte Jr. and Frank S. Alexander, 1:533–75. New York: Columbia University Press, 2006.

van den Bercken, Wil, Manon de Courten, and Evert van der Zweerde, eds. *Vladimir Solov'ëv: Reconciler and Polemicist*. Leuven, Belg., 2000.

van der Zweerde, Evert. "Obornost' als Gesellschafts Ideal bei Vladimir Solov'ev and Pavel Florenskij." In *Pavel Florenskij: Tradition und Moderne*, 225–46. Frankfurt am Main: Peter Lang, 2001.

Velichko, V. L. *Vladimir Solov'ev: Zhizn' i tvoreniia*. St. Petersburg: Knizhnyi Magazin A. F. Tsinzerlinga, 1902.

Versluis, Arthur, ed. *Wisdom's Book: The Sophia Anthology*. St. Paul, MN: Paragon House, 2000.

von Lilienfeld, Fairy. "Sophia: Die Weisheit Gottes, über die Visionen des Wladimir Solowjew als Grundlage Seine 'Sophiologie.'" *Una Sancta* 39 (1984): 113–29.

Wachtel, Michael. *Russian Symbolism and Literary Tradition*. Madison: University of Wisconsin Press, 1995.

Walicki, Andrzej. *A History of Russian Thought from the Enlightenment to Marxism*. Translated by H. Andrews-Rusiecka. Stanford: Stanford University Press, 1979.

———. *Legal Philosophies of Russian Liberalism*. Oxford: Oxford University, 1986.

———. *The Slavophile Controversy: History of a Conservative Utopia in Nineteenth-Century Russian Thought*. Oxford: Oxford University Press, 1975.

Ware, Timothy. *The Orthodox Church*. London: Penguin, 1997.

Weeks, Andrew. *Boehme: An Intellectual Biography of the Seventeenth-Century Philosopher and Mystic*. Albany: SUNY Press, 1991.

Westphalen, Timothy C. "The Ongoing Influence of V. S. Solov'ev on A. A. Blok: The Particular Case of *Belaja Lilija* and *Balagančik*." *Slavic and East European Journal* 36, no. 4 (1992): 435–51.

Wolfson, Harry A. *Philo: Foundations of Religious Philosophy in Judaism, Christianity, and Islam.* Cambridge: Harvard University Press, 1962 [c1947].

Zdenek, V. David. "The Influence of Jacob Boehme on Russian Religious Thought." *Slavic Review* 21 (1962): 42–64.

Zenkovsky, Serge, ed. *Medieval Russia's Epics, Chronicles, and Tales.* New York: Dutton, 1974.

Zenkovsky, Vasilii. *A History of Russian Philosophy.* Translated by George L. Kline. 2 vols. New York: Columbia University Press, 1953.

The Zohar. Translated by Harry Sperling, Maurice Simon, and Paul P. Levertoff. 2nd ed. 5 vols. London : Soncino Press, 1984.

Zohar: The Book of Enlightenment. Translated and with an introduction by Daniel Chanan Matt. New York: Paulist Press, 1983.

Zouboff, Peter P. *Vladimir Solovyev on Godmanhood (With a Translation of of Solovyev's Lectures on Godmanhood).* New York: International University Library, 1944.

Index

289

www.ingramcontent.com/pod-product-compliance
Ingram Content Group UK Ltd.
Pitfield, Milton Keynes, MK11 3LW, UK
UKHW041037130325
456188UK00001B/54